WIL   .L   C7
)707 8

ANCESTRAL ROOTS OF
SIXTY COLONISTS

ANCESTRAL ROOTS OF SIXTY COLONISTS

Who Came to New England between 1623 and 1650

The Lineage of Alfred the Great, Charlemagne, Malcolm of Scotland, Robert the Strong, and Some of Their Descendants

By
FREDERICK LEWIS WEIS

SIXTH EDITION

With Additions and Corrections by
WALTER LEE SHEPPARD, JR.

Assisted by David Faris

GENEALOGICAL PUBLISHING CO., INC.

Baltimore   *1988*

First Edition: Lancaster, Mass., 1950
Second Edition: Lancaster, Mass., 1951
Supplement to Ancestral Roots: Dublin, N.H., 1952
Additions and Corrections: Peterborough, N.H., 1956
Third Edition: Baltimore, 1964
Fourth Edition: Baltimore, 1969
Fifth Edition: Baltimore, 1976, 1979, 1982, 1985
Sixth Edition: Baltimore, 1988

TABLE OF CONTENTS

ANCESTRAL LINES

IN MEMORIAM

Frederick Lewis Weis, Th.D., F.A.S.G.

Frederick Lewis Weis died 11 April 1966, in Brattleboro, Vt., after a long illness. He was born 22 August 1895, in Cranston, R.I., the son of John Peter Carl and Georgina (Lewis) Weis. He is survived by his wife, the former Elizabeth Williams Stone, a son, and a daughter.

Dr. Weis attended Kimball Union Academy, Meriden, N.H., then moved to Hope Street High School and School of Design, Providence, R.I. He completed his secondary education at Wilmer and Chew's Preparatory School, Annapolis, Md., from which he was appointed to the United States Naval Academy. He graduated and was commissioned Ensign, U.S.N., 29 March 1917. He was assigned as Assistant Engineer Officer of the U.S.S. North Dakota and was promoted to Lieutenant (j.g.) on 1 July of the same year.

Dr. Weis left the Navy to attend the Meadville Theological School, from which he graduated B.D. in 1922, and was Cruft Fellow at the University of Strasbourg, France, 1922-24. He was ordained minister of the Third Religious Society of Dorchester, Mass., 9 November 1924, and served there until 1929. During his incumbency he received his S.T.M. from Meadville Theological School. He received the degree of Doctor of Theology from the University of Strasbourg in 1930 and was installed as the twelfth minister of the First Church of Christ (Unitarian) of Lancaster, Mass., from which office he retired 28 October 1951. After retirement he made his home in Dublin, N.H. In 1957 Dr. Weis was elected a Fellow of the American Society of Genealogists.

Dr. Weis was the founder of the Society of the Descendants of the Colonial Clergy in 1930. He was Historian General and Editor of Publications for that society for thirty-three years. Among their publications (of which he was also the author) are the useful Colonial Clergy of New England (1936), Colonial Clergy of Maryland, Delaware, and Georgia (1950), Colonial Clergy of Virginia, North Carolina, and South Carolina (1955) and Colonial Clergy of the Middle Colonies, New York, New Jersey, and Pennsylvania (1957).

Dr. Weis was a member of more than fifty societies, for many of which he did historical studies. Author of numerous genealogical articles, he is perhaps best known for his Ancestral Roots of Sixty Colonists and for his Magna Charta Sureties. He compiled many manuscript genealogies, noteworthy being his Phipps Genealogy (1929-38) and Genealogies of the Templeton Family (1930) (1,000 pages) at the Narragansett Historical Society. He was deeply interested in church history, and made many contributions to the study of colonial congregations and their membership.

The bulk of his manuscripts, historical and genealogical, have been placed in the Library of the American Antiquarian Society, Worcester, Mass. His printed works, and additional manuscripts (including second copies of many of the items at Worcester), are in the Library of the New England Historic Genealogical Society, Boston, Mass. Earlier works will often be found in local repositories.

Walter Lee Sheppard, Jr.

It is certainly paradoxical that Dr. Weis should be best known for his Ancestral Roots of Sixty Colonists, the Supplement to it, and his Magna Charta Sureties, 1215. His reputation as a genealogist rests on a firm foundation of colonial studies (unfortunately mostly in manuscript) and his four books on the colonial clergy. He turned to compiling pre-colonial lineages for publications in the late 1940s, after he had become ill and was less able to travel, and had to rely more and more heavily on material sent to him by correspondents whom he trusted — material that he did not or could not verify due to illness or unavailability of cited material.

The first edition of Ancestral Roots, in 1950, being his first effort in this type of compilation, contained many errors, and Dr. Weis produced the year following, a second edition embodying a vast number of corrections. In the next year he brought out his Supplement. Unfortunately, only fifty copies of the second edition were printed and the supply was quickly exhausted. The Magna Charta Sureties was published in 1955, and in the following year he published a sixteen page Additions and Corrections covering such material as he had collected up to this time on all three volumes. Unfortunately, some of these Additions and Corrections also contained errors, and many were without cited evidences. Cross citations in a few cases made corrections in Ancestral Roots by reference to Magna Charta, so that the reader had to have both books to correct one. A further set of corrections for the Magna Charta Sureties was issued in 1957.

When supplies of Dr. Weis' original editions were exhausted, the Genealogical Publishing Co. decided to reprint them. Dr. and Mrs. Weis asked me to see what I could do to bring together as many of the known corrections as possible, and to try to make the books more accurate. Unfortunately there was little time to do this, but I did what I could with corrections I had already noted and those sent to me by others with cited evidence which I could verify. Though some readers and reviewers have persisted in the belief that I was the editor of the third edition of Ancestral Roots, I had specifically disavowed responsibility for any of the material on which I had not myself worked. I did not see proofs of this reprinting prior to publication.

The 1964 edition (third for Ancestral Roots, second for the Supplement) was, in fact, merely a reprinting of the first edition, combined with the text of the Supplement, followed by the Errata page from the first edition, and then by the 1956 Additions and Corrections, just as these items were originally printed. The work includes a curious typographical error in the <u>Additions and Corrections,</u> where part of the last page was transferred in mid-sentence to the preceding page and grafted onto its text. My own typed corrections, having been received by the publisher after the book was in progress, were separately printed from a typed copy of my text, embodying a few typographical errors, and added to the copies as a slip-in. Two lines from the second edition (not included in the first), Nos. 141A and 144A, were thus omitted. Since 141A contained a serious error in the last generation that voided the line (which was caught in the 1956 <u>Additions and corrections</u>), the loss of this line was unimportant. However, Line 144A was an important addition, and was restored in later editions. In the fifth edition no textual changes were made by the publisher, and the corrections, when too extensive for footnotes, were assembled in the front of the volume. In this new edition of <u>Ancestral Roots</u> the text has been completely reset by my collaborator, David Faris, without whose splendid assistance this edition would not have been possible. All footnotes and corrections in earlier editions have been incorporated in the text, more recently discovered errors have been corrected, and many new lines added.

I want to make it absolutely clear to reviewer and public once more that I am not fulfilling the function of a true editor in this edition either. A true editor should verify all material offered. This I have not done, nor could I ever find time to do it. I have not checked the lines that I have not used. Where I have had occasion to use a line, I have verified those generations on which I worked, and in fact it is this work that has produced many of the changes in this edition. Some of the errors so corrected have been of long standing, and will be found in books long considered reliable, as well as in Wurts or Browning. Every one of my many correspondents has been asked to check anything he or she uses and to advise me of any errors found, <u>with cited evidence.</u> All these I have checked. I have especially to thank Douglas Richardson, David Humiston Kelley, John Insley Coddington, Milton Rubincam, John G. Hunt, Paul Prindle, Gary Boyd Roberts, the late George Andrews Moriarty and the late Walter Goodwin Davis for extensive comments. Those others who have furnished data are too numerous to mention individually, but all have my gratitude and when a new line has been included, if it is not one which I have myself prepared, I have identified the author. I know that there still remain errors, some perhaps typographical, such as transposed numbers or errors of copying, some due to the use of poor quality source material. I will maintain a corrected copy for the next edition and ask once more that if you find an error, please send the correction to me, <u>with cited reference,</u> for inclusion.

Lastly, all genealogists and the general public are warned that, although I consider this the best work of its kind in print, it is NOT a reference work and should NOT be cited (any more than any other similar work) as evidence on a lineage blank for membership in a hereditary society. Go to the <u>source</u> material for this kind of thing. To the degree that sources are cited in this text, it will help you to find the proper references.

Those interested in additional royal lines may wish to note the series of articles by me in the New England Historical and Genealogical Register on the illegitimate British royal children. The first article covering the period William I - Edward III appeared in volume 119, pages 94-102. Some corrections and additions to this appeared in volume 120, page 230, and in volume 121, pages 232-234. The second article, covering the period from Edward III through the end of the Stuart dynasty appeared in volume 121, pages 185-191. A third portion, covering the early Scots to James VI of Scotland and I of England, is in volume 122, p. 265. Some of the material here made available was missed or perhaps mis-identified in the compilation of a recent volume on the Royal Bastards, and I do not endorse all of the statements made in that book. The authors did not have the courtesy to acknowledge a large file of material I mailed to them.

Walter Lee Sheppard, Jr.
923 Old Manoa Road
Havertown, Pennsylvania 19083

1B
47A, 47B
56A, 56B
75A
98A
103A
105A
122A
132A, 132B, 132C
141A, 141B
152A
158A
163A
176A
177A, 177B
178A
234A
244A
246A, 246B, 246C, 246D, 246E, 246F

In addition, a number of lines have been extensively revised, and Line 179 for Griffith Bowen has been restored. Line 92 has been deleted since it duplicates gens. 10-15 in Line 187. Robert Abell, whose line was eliminated from an early edition, due to errors, has been restored in this one (Line 56A).

LINES OF IMMIGRANTS DISCUSSED IN THIS VOLUME

Gov. Thomas Dudley Line 40
Margaret Wyatt m. Mathew Allin Line 52
Robert Abell Line 56A
Bridget Yong m. George Wyllys Line 57
Rev. Charles Chauncey Line 69
Katharine Deighton m. (1) Samuel Hackburn, (2) Gov. Thomas
    Dudley Line 84
Rev. Samuel Whiting Line 85
Hon. Simon Lynde Line 99
Ellen Newton m. Edward Carleton Line 121D
Rosamund Lister m. Thomas Southworth Line 156
Alice Standish m. James Prescott Line 170
William Torrey Line 197
Agnes Mackworth m. Col. William Crowne Line 198
Elizabeth Coytemore m. Capt. William Tyng Line 199
Rev. George Burroughs Line 200
Rev. John Oxenbridge Line 201
Joseph Bowles (or Bolles) Line 202
Rev. Thomas James Line 203
Sir Ferdinando Gorges (d.s.p.) Line 209
Capt. Thomas Bradbury Line 210
John Josselyn Line 211
Oliver Mainwaring Line 217
Olive Welby m. Dea. Henry Farwell Line 223
Sarah Fiennes (d.s.p.) m. Maj. Gen. John Humphrey Line 225
Arbella Fiennes (d.s.p.) m. Isaac Johnson Line 225
Rev. Samuel Myles Line 228
Penelope Pelham m. Richard Bellingham Line 229
Rev. John Davenport Line 230
Margaret Tyndal m. Gov. John Winthrop Line 232
Edward Rigby Line 233
John Drake Line 234
Wymond Bradbury Lines 246 and 246A
Agnes Harris m. (1) William Spencer, m. (2) William Edwards Line
    246E
Samuel Appleton Line 249
John Barclay Line 252
Thomas Newberry Line 253
Thomas Gordon Line 256
Col. Richard Lee Line 258
Mary Gye m. Rev. Peter Maverick Line 261

LINES DISPROVEN, UNPROVEN OR DOUBTFUL

Pardon Tillinghast Line 5
Edward Southworth Line 9
James Prescott Line 23
Alice Freeman   Line 29A   (Other lines are available for Alice
    Freeman)
John Prescott Line 34
John Washbourne Line 91
Alice Tomes Line 98

A NOTE CONCERNING THE NUMBERING OF GENERATIONS

At a score or more places in the lines of descent, the number of one or more generations may be missing — e.g., in Line 151 there is apparently no Generation 23. This is not an error — it is intentional. The first edition of ANCESTRAL ROOTS contained a supposed Generation 23 between 22 and 24. Later research has proved that Generation 24 is actually the child of Generation 22, and is so designated in this sixth edition.

When research has disclosed that a generation (or generations) has been omitted, the missing generation has been inserted, with a letter after the preceding number. In Line 52, for example, 35A and 35B are inserted between 35 and 36. A third variant occurs when there are two sets of descendants from one line. In Line 12, the duplication of Generations 39 and 40 shows separate New England and Virginia descendants. In such a case, two persons have the same generation number because they are brothers and/or sisters, or cousins.

This is admittedly a flaw in the otherwise orderly and ingenious system devised by Dr. Weis for recording line and generation. To correct it is not, however, simply a matter of renumbering the generations in this edition. The lines contain hundreds on hundreds of cross-references to other lines and generations, based on the original numeration. Even using computers, some of these could be missed and confusion introduced. Then, too, during the nearly twenty years between the first edition and this sixth edition, this book has no doubt been cited many times in other books, in articles, and in the lineage papers of hereditary societies. Had the numbering of generations been changed in this sixth edition, citations based on the original numbering system would have been rendered valueless and add to the problems of society genealogists. The Editor believes that the advantages of renumbering are outweighed by the disadvantages — so the numbering of generations remains uniform with that of previous editions.

In his early editions Dr. Weis commenced his lines in a number of cases with Dark Age kings from whom descents are now considered very questionable. Where proofs of such descents are thought to be inadequate to support earlier generations, those generations have been omitted, and the text of the revised line commences with the ancestor from whom the evidence is considered sufficient for each generation.

The generation numbers are valid as a means of cross-referencing and citing — but they are, in many instances, no longer an accurate indication of the number of generations from the first progenitor of a line.

W. L. S. Jr.

LIST OF REFERENCES

and their abbreviations

Most lines and generations in the body of the book contain one or more references to the source of the information. References are given in parentheses, usually at the end of the generation. Since the same references are cited frequently throughout the book, abbreviations are used in the citations to conserve space. The following list of references is arranged alphabetically by abbreviations. The reader, coming upon "Gardiner" as a citation, has only to turn to this list of references to find the identification of the cited work.

The original work sometimes had several different abbreviations for the same reference, and not all abbreviations were identified. I have tried to standardize these abbreviations but realize that there still may be variants in the text. For the omission of any abbreviation from the list, the Editor apologizes, and asks that you call it to his attention.

W.L.S., Jr.

Am. Antiq. Soc., Coll. = Collections of the American Antiquarian Society, Worcester, Mass.
Anselme (see Père Anselme, below).
Armorial = The Armorial, a journal published currently in the U.K.
ASC = The Anglo-Saxon Chronicle (numbers given refer to dates).
Banks = Baronia Anglica Concentrata (I) and, Baronies in Fee (II).
Bartrum = Peter Bartrum, Welsh Genealogies, two sets of volumes, the first "AD 300 to 1400", the second a supplementary set "1400-1500."
Baumgarten = N. de Baumgarten, "Généalogies et Mariages Occidentaux des Rurikides Russes, du Xe au XIIIe siècle," (Orientalia Christiana, vol. IX, No. 38, Rome).
Beard = Timothy Beard, Pedigrees of Some of the Emperor Charlemagne's Descendants, vol. 2 (see v. Redlich).
Bede = Ecclesiastical History of the English Nation.
Brandenburg = Dr. Erick Brandenburg, Die Nachkommen Karls des Grossen, 1935.
Brenner = S. Otto Brenner, Nachkommen Gorms des Alten (Kopenhagen, 1978).
Burke = Extinct and Dormant Baronetcies.
Burton = Wm. Burton, Descr. of Leicester.
CCN = Century Cyclopedia of Names (for handy reference only).
Chaume = The Abbé Chaume, author of numerous articles and books — usually also cited by title in the text.
Clay = John W. Clay, The Extinct and Dormant Peerages of the Northern Counties of England, London, 1913.
Cleaveland = Cleaveland, The Family of Courtenay.
CME = Cambridge Mediaeval History.
Coll. Topo. & Gen. = Collectanea Topographica et Genealogica.
Collins = A. Collins (Collins-Brydges edition), The Peerage of

England.

CP = G.E. Cokayne's (new revised) Complete Peerage, vols. I-XII pt. 2, 1910-1959.

Cross = A Shorter History of England and Greater Britain, 1920.

Curwen = J.F. Curwen, Curwens of Workington.

DA = Journal of the Devonshire Association of Art, Sciences, and Literature.

Devon & Cornwall N. & Q. = Devonshire and Cornwall Notes and Queries (see note by N&Q below).

DNB = Dictionary of National Biography (English) (also Dict. Natl. Biog.)

Dunbar = Archibald H. Dunbar, Scottish Kings, 2nd edition, 1906.

DWB = Dictionary of Welsh Biography (also Dict. Welsh Biog.)

Dwnn = Heraldic Visitations of Wales.

Earwaker = The Standish Family of Standish and Duxbury, county Lancaster, Charters and Deeds. Manchester, 1898. (An excellent collection, but needs checking with Mrs. Temple, Porteus, VCH Lanc., etc.)

EB = Encyclopedia Britannica (For occasional reference).

Eisenberg (Sometimes mis-written for Isenberg, see below).

English Chronicles, 1000-1300, see Anglo-Saxon Chronicle, Domesday Book, Gesta Stephani, Florence of Worcester, Henry of Huntingdon, Ingulf, Matthew of Westminster, Ordericus Vitalis, Roger of Hovenden, Roger of Wendover and William of Malmsbury. For Scots and Irish Chronicles, see Line 170.

Eng. Hist. Rev. = English Historical Review.

EYC = Clay, Charles Travis, Early Yorkshire Charters, 1952. (First three volumes by Farrer).

Falaise Roll = M. Jackson Crispin, Falaise Roll, London, 1938.

Farmer = Farmer's Genealogical Dictionary of New England.

Farrer = Farrer, Honours and Knights Fees.

Fisher = G.P. Fisher, Outline of Universal History, 1885.

Foster = Visitations of Yorkshire, 1584/5.

Gardiner = Samuel R. Gardiner, A Student's History of England, 1899, genealogical tables xxvii-xxxii, 216, 265, 286.

Garnier = Éd. Garnier, Tableaux Généalogiques des Souverains de la France et de ses Grand Feudataires.

(The) Gen.; Genealogist = The Genealogist (Marshall, Editor) (the original magazine of this name).

The Genealogist (Neil Thompson, editor), a modern periodical (not abbreviated).

(The) Gen. Mag. = The Genealogists' Magazine (pub. by Soc. of Genealogists, London, Eng.)

Harl. Soc. Pub. = Harleian Society Publications.

Hempstead's (Diary) = Joshua Hempstead, Diary of . . . 1711-1758 (New London, 1901).

(The) Her. & Gen. = The Herald & Genealogist (Journal).

Hist. Cols. of Staffs. = Historical Collections of Staffordshire (William Salt Society).

Hodgkin = Hodgkin's History of England Before the Norman Conquest.

Hutchinson = Hutchinson's History of Cumberland.

Isenberg = Prinz von Isenberg, Stamtafeln zur Geschichte der Europäischen Staaten (ed. 1976 & later editions).
Libby & Noyes = Davis, Libby & Noyes, Genealogical Dictionary of Maine and New Hampshire.
Maddison('s Wills) = A.R. Maddison, Lincolnshire Wills, 1500-1617, 2 vols. 1888-1891.
Marant = Morant (see below).
MC = Adams and Weis, Magna Charta Sureties 1215.
Med. & Hum. = Medievala et Humanistica (A journal of medieval studies published by the University of Colorado).
Mis. Gen. Her. = Miscellanea Genealogica et Heraldica.
Morant = History of Essex, 1768.
Moriarty = George Andrews Moriarty, "The Plantagenet Ancestry" ms at New Eng. Hist. Gen. Soc., Boston; xerox at Hist. Soc. of Penna., Phila. Pa. & at Library of LDS, Salt Lake City. (Note: An early microfilm at Harvard College Library is incomplete.)
Moriarty Notebooks = 19 vols. ms at New Eng. Hist. Gen. Soc., Boston.
Muskett = Suffolk Manorial Families.
N. & Q. = Notes & Queries (England). There are also several separate Notes and Queries for individual counties.
N.G.S.Q. = National Genealogical Society Quarterly (Washington, D.C.)
NEHGR = New England Historic Genealogical Register.
Nichols = J. Nichols, Hist. of Leicester.
Norfolk Arch. = Journal of the Norfolk Archaeological Society.
Noyes, Libby & Davis = Davis, Libby & Noyes, Genealogical Dictionary of Maine and New Hampshire.
NSE = New Standard Encyclopedia.
Old-CP = Former edition of Cokayne, Complete Peerage.
Ormerod = Ormerod's History of Cheshire (Helsby Edition).
Page = Augustine Page, Topographical and Genealogical History of Suffolk, Ipswich, 1847.
Parkin = Rev. Chas. Parkin, An Essay . . . History of Norfolk, etc. London, 1775, 6 volumes.
Père Anselme = Père Anselme, Histoire généalogique de la maison royale de France. (Microfilm in many libraries, incl. L.D.S.)
Proc. Mass. Soc. = Proceedings of the Massachusetts Historical Society.
Reg. Mag. Sig. Reg. Scot. = Registrum magni sigilli regum Scotorum (Register of the great seal of Scotland).
Ritson = Annals of the Caledonians, Picts and Scots of Strathclyde, Cumberland, Galloway and Murray, Edinburgh 1828, 2 volumes.
Rogers = W.B. Hamilton Rogers, Antient Sepulchral Effigies and Monumental and Memorial Sculptures of Devon, Exeter 1876.
Saillot = Saillot, Le Sang de Charlemagne.
Salisbury = E.M. Salisbury, Family Histories and Genealogies.
Saltonstall Genealogy = Richard A. Saltonstall, Ancestors and Descendants of Sir Richard Saltonstall of New England, 1897.
Sanders = Sanders, English Baronies, a Study of Their Origin and Descent, 1086-1327, 203 pp., 1960.
Searle = Wm. George Searle, Anglo-Saxon Bishops, Kings and Nobles.

Cambridge, England 1899.

Sheppard, Ancestry of Edward Carleton and Ellen Newton his Wife (microfilm, c/r 1978).

Shrop. Parish Rec. Soc. = Shropshire Parish Register Society (various publications).

SP = James Balfour Paul, Scots Peerage. 9 volumes, 1904-1914.

Surtees Soc. (the original magazine of this name) = Surtees Society (Durham publications).

Sussex = Journal of the Sussex Archaeological Society.

TAG = The American Genealogist.

Thatcher = Oliver J. Thatcher, A Short History of Mediaeval Europe, New York 1897.

Topo. and Geneal. = Collectanea Topographica et Genealogica.

Trans. Shrop. Arch. Soc. = Transactions of the Shropshire Archaeological Society.

Turton = Lt. Col. W. H. Turton, Plantagent Ancestry, 1928 (not very reliable).

de Vayjay = Szabolcs de Vayjay, Annales de Bourgogne (1964); Der Eintritt des Ungarischen Stammesbundes in die Europäische Geschichte (862-933 (1968).

VCH = Victoria County Histories (followed by the name of the county).

Vis., Visit. = Visitations (of the various counties).

Vivian = Lt. Col. Vivian, Visitations of Devon and Visitations of Cornwall.

v. Redlich = Pedigrees of Some of the Emperor Charlemagne's Descendants, Chicago, 1941, vol. 1 (contains no references. Some lines questionable.) (Subsequent volumes, other editors, also without references.)

(The) Wandesfords = H.B. McCall, The Wandesfords of Kirklington and Castle Camer, 1904.

Waters = Genealogical Gleanings in England, 1901. 2 volumes.

Wedgewood = Author of various biographical studies of Members of Parliament.

Weever = Ancient Funerall Monuments, etc, London, 1631.

Weis = Various volumes of The Colonial Clergy.

Whitaker = Thomas Dunham Whitaker, The History and Antiquities of the Deanery of Craven in the County of York, London, 1805.

Winkhaus = Eberhard Winkhaus, Ahnen zu Karl dem Grossen und Widukin 1950; and his Supplement 1953.

Wm. Salt Soc. = William Salt Society, Historical Collections of Staffordshire.

GENEALOGICAL TERMS

and their abbreviations

adm. = admitted
aft. = after
ante = before; by
b. = born
bap., bapt. bp. = baptized
bur. = buried
ca. = about (circa)
cit. = the work cited (citato)
Coll. = College
cr. = created (as a peer)
d. = died
d.s.p. = died without issue (sine prole)
d.s.p. legit. = died without legitimate issue
d.s.p.m. = died without male issue
d.v.p. = died during father's lifetime (vita patris)
dau. = daughter
disp. = dispensation
dtd. = dated
ff. = following; and following
fl. = flourished (only approximate date known) (or living)
frm. = freeman, a voter in a colony. The date following is the date
  he was admitted.
h. = heir (or heiress)
Ibid. = the same
I.p.m.; Inq.p.m. = An inquest held to determine the deceased's land
  holdings. (Inquisition post mortem, usually dated by "regnal
  year"; example: 3 Hen. 4; 3 Hen. IV = Third year of the reign of
  Henry IV. (Many old dates are given in this manner, particularly
  those of Inq.p.m.).
k. = killed
K.B. = Knight of the Bath
K.G. = Knight of the Garter
knt.; kt. = knight
K.T. = Knight of the Thistle (Scotland)
lic. = license
m. = married
m. (1); m. (2); m. (3) = married first; married second; third; etc.
M.P. = Member of Parliament
matric. = matriculated (entered and recorded at College or
  University)
Mich. = Michaelmas, the Feast of St. Michael (Many old dates are
  given as of a Saint's feast day, or days preceding or following it.)
n.i. = no issue
op. cit. = The work cited above (opere citato)
p.; pp. = page; pages

post = after
prob. = probably
pro. = probated
regnal year. This is the date most often used in medieval documents and refers to the number of the year of the reign of the monarch at the time the document was dated. See example under I.p.m.
Rot. = Roll; Rolls (rotalus) A term used for many types of early records.
s. = son
sett. = settled
yr. = younger

Note to the Reader

   Mr. Frederick W. Sawyer, 8 Sachem Drive, Glastonbury, Conn. 06033, a computer scientist, programmed his computer with all the lines in <u>Ancestral Roots</u>,fifth edition, and will bring it up-to-date with this edition as soon as it is in print. He has done the same with the <u>Magna Charta Sureties</u>, third edition, and when the fourth edition is in print will bring that up-to-date as well. He can supply to any one wishing it a print-out for the ancestry of any colonist identified in either book as a compilation of all related lines in both books.

SAXON AND ENGLISH

MONARCHS

Line 1

1. CERDIC, King of the West Saxons, 519-534, was a Saxon earldorman who founded a settlement on the coast of Hampshire, England, in 495, assumed the title of King of the West Saxons in 519, and became the ancestor of the English royal line. "A.D. 495. This year came two leaders into Britain, Cerdic and Cynric, his son, with five ships . . . . 519. This year Cerdic and Cynric undertook the government of the West Saxons; the same year they fought with the Britons at a place called Charford. From that day have reigned the children of the West Saxon kings. 530. They conquered the isle of Wight . . . 534. This year died Cerdic, the first king of the West Saxons. Cynric his son succeeded to the government, and reigned afterwards twenty-six winters." (ASC, text by Ingram, Everyman's edition. See the following dates: 495, 519, 530, 854; CCN 230). (See also Trelawney Dayrell Reed, The Rise of Wessex, chart p. 31, gens. 1-8. This also discusses Cerdic's parentage.)

3. CYNRIC, son of Cerdic, was king of the West Saxons, 534-560. "A.D. 552. This year Cynric fought with the Britons on the spot that is called Sarum, and put them to flight . . . 556. This year Cynric and Ceawlin fought . . . at Beranbury." (ASC 534, 538, 552, 560, 854).

4. CEAWLIN, son of Cynric, undertook the government of the West Saxons, 560, and reigned thirty winters. "In 560, Ethelbert came to the kingdom of Kent, and held it fifty-three winters. In his day the holy Pope Gregory sent us baptism. And Columba, the mass-priest, came to the Picts . . . 591. This year there was a great slaughter of Britons at Wanborough; Ceawlin was driven from his kingdom . . . 593. This year died Ceawlin." (ASC 560, 568, 591, 593, 854; CCN 227).

5. CUTHWINE, killed in battle 584, son of Ceawlin and father of Cutha or Cuthwulf, did not rule. "A.D. 577. This year Cuthwine and Ceawlin fought with the Britons, and slew three kings . . . and took from them three cities, Gloucester, Cirencester, and Bath." (ASC 577, 854). (See: The Rise of Wessex, Trelawney D. Reed, p. 31).

6. CUTHA, or Cuthwulf, son of Cuthwine and father of Ceolwald and the younger Cynegils, did not rule. (ASC 854).

7. CEOLWALD, did not rule. He visited Rome 688. King Cynegils, his brother, was baptized, 635, by Bishop Birinus at

1

Dorchester. (ASC 688, 854; Bede, Book III, Chapter VII).

8. CENRED, son of Ceolwald, and father of King Ina and Ingild, did not rule. (ASC 688, 854).

9. INGILD, d. 718, son of Cenred and father of Eoppa, did not rule. "A.D. 718. This year died Ingild, the brother of Ina." Ina reigned thirty-seven winters, fought at Wanborough, 715, and in 728, "went to Rome, and there gave up the ghost." "A.D. 688. Ina was the son of Cenred, Cenred of Ceolwald; Ceolwald was the brother of Cynegils; and both were the sons of Cuthwin, who was the son of Ceawlin; Ceawlin was the son of Cynric, and Cynric of Cerdic . . . 854. And Ethelwulf was the son of Egbert, Egbert of Eahlmund, Eahlmund of Eafa, Eafa of Eoppa, Eoppa of Ingild; Ingild was the brother of Ina, King of the West Saxons, who held that kingdom thirty-seven winters, and afterwards went to St. Peter, where he died. And they were the sons of Cenred, Cenred of Ceolwald, Ceolwald of Cutha, Cutha of Cuthwine, Cuthwine of Ceawlin, Ceawlin of Cynric, Cynric of (Creoda, Creoda of) Cerdic." (ASC 688, 715, 718, 722, 728, 854; Bede, Book V, Chapter VII, last paragraph).

10. EOPPA, son of Ingild, father of Eafa, did not rule. (ASC 854).

11. EAFA, son of Eoppa, did not rule. (ASC 854).

12. EAHLMUND, son of Eafa. "A.D. 784. At this time reigned Elmund King in Kent, the father of Egbert; and Egbert was the father of Athulf (Aethelwulf)." (ASC 784, 854).

13. EGBERT, b. 775, d. after 19 Nov. 838, son of Eahlmund, King of Kent. Egbert was King of Wessex, 802-827, and was the first king of all England, 827-836; m. Raedburh. The male line of kings descend from him to Edward the Confessor and the female line to the present time. (ASC 800, 823, 825, 827, 828, 836; NSE, X 209-210; Searle, 342-43). (See: Harold W. Smith, Saxon England, gens. 9-13. This ref. omits Cutha (1-6) in early portion of pedigree.)

14. AETHELWULF, King of England, 839-858, d. 13 Jan. 858; m. (1) Osburh, dau. of Oslac, the royal cup-bearer. (ASC 823, 836, 840, 853, 854).

15. ALFRED THE GREAT, King of England, 871-899, b. Wantage, Berkshire, 849; d. 26 Oct. 899; m. 868, Ealhswith (Alswitha), d. ca. 905, dau. of Earl Aethelred of Mercia and Eadburh. Alfred was one of the greatest men in history. He was crowned king at Winchester, 871; founded the British Navy, organized the militia, compiled a code of laws, built schools and monasteries, and invited scholars to live at his court. He was a good scholar and translated many books. (ASC 853, 871, 891, 894, 897, 901; DNB, I 153-162; Asser: Life of Alfred).

16. EDWARD, the Elder, King of England, 899-924; b. 875; d. 924; m. (3) 919, Eadgifu, d. 961, dau. of Sigehelm, Earl of Kent. (ASC 924, 925; DNB I 157; NSE X 193).

17. EDMUND, the Magnificent, King of England, 940-946; b. 920; d. 946; m. St. Alfgifu. (ASC 942, 946; Hodgkin; DNB xvi 401).

18. EDGAR, the Peaceful, King of England, 959-975; b. 943; d.

975; m. 965, Elfrida (or Ealfthryth), b. 945; d. 1000; dau. of Earl Ordgar. (ASC 965; NSE X 165-166; DNB xvi 365).

19. AETHELRED II, the Redeless, King of England, 979-1016; b. 968; d. 1016; m. (1) 985, Alfflaed, dau. of Thored. (CP IV, 504; IX, 704. Generations 13-31: Thatcher, 321; Gardiner, xxvii-xxix; DNB xviii 27).

20. EDMUND Ironside, King of England, 1016; b. 989; d. 30 Nov. 1016; m. Ealgyth. (CCN, 352; DNB xvi 403).

21. EDWARD, the Atheling, called "the Exile", b. 1016; d. 1057; m. Agatha (of Hungary). For her ancestry, see TAG, 54:231. But see also Frank Barlow, "The Feudal Kingdom of England" 16-17; Ritchie, "The Normans in Scotland" 389-392, and Szabolcs de Vajay, "Agatha, Mother of St. Margaret, Queen of Scotland," Duquesne Review, vol. 7, no. 2, spring 1962, 71-80, with tables. The parentage suggested in the last reference is the most probable.

22. MARGARET (St. Margaret of Scotland); b. 1045; d. 16 Nov. 1093; m. Dunfermline, 1068/9, **MALCOLM III CANMORE** (170-21), King of Scots, 1058-1093; b. 1031; d. 13 Nov. 1093. (CP V 736 chart, VII 641-642; SP I, 1; Dunbar, 25-34, 280-281; DNB xxxvi 132, xxxv 400).

23. MATILDA of Scotland; b. 1079; d. 1 May 1118; m. 11 Nov. 1100, **HENRY I** (121-25), Beauclerc, King of England, 1100-1135; b. 1070; d. 1 Dec. 1135. (He m. (2) 29 Jan. 1121, **ADELIZA OF LOUVAIN** (149-24), b. ca. 1103; d. 23 Apr. 1151 (s.p. by this marriage); she m. (2) 1138, William d'Aubigny, Earl of Arundel, d. 12 Oct. 1176). (CP I 233-235, IV 669 chart II, V 736, VII 737; SP I 102; CCN 494. Generations 13-23: Cross, xv; DNB xxxvii 52, xxxv 436).

24. MATILDA, b. 1104; d. 10 Sep. 1167; m. (2) ~~3 Apr. 1127,~~ *17 June 1128 ?* **GEOFFREY V "PLANTAGENET"** (118-25), Count of Anjou, Duke of Normandy; b. 24 Aug. 1113; d. 7 Sep. 1151. (She was the widow of Henry V, Emperor of Germany, who d.s.p. 22 May 1125). (CP V 736; SP I 1-2; CCN 494; DNB xxxvii 54).

25. HENRY II, King of England, 25 Oct. 1154-1189, called Curt Mantel; b. 5 Mar. 1132/3; d. 6 Jul. 1189; m. 18 May 1152, **ELEANOR OF AQUITAINE** (110-26), b. 1123; d. 3 or 31 Mar. or 1 Apr 1204. (She had m. (1) **LOUIS VII** (102-25), King of France). (CP V 736; SP I 1-2; CCN 494; DNB xxvi, 1; xvii, 175).

26. JOHN, Lackland, King of England, 1199-1216; b. 24 Dec. 1166 or 1167; d. 19 Oct. 1216; m. (2) 24 Aug. 1200, **ISABELLA OF ANGOULÊME** (117-27, 153-28); b. 1188; d. 31 May 1246. (CP V 736; CCN 547-548; DNB xxix, 402; xxix, 63).

27. HENRY III, King of England, 1216-1272; b. Winchester, 1 Oct. 1207; d. Westminster, 15 or 16 June 1272; m. 14 Jan. 1236/7, **ELEANOR OF PROVENCE** (111-30), b. 1217; d. Amesbury, 24 or 25 Jun. 1291. (CP V 736; CCN 356, 494; DNB xxvi, 12; xvii, 179).

28. EDWARD I, King of England, 1272-1307; b. Westminster, 16 or 17 June 1239; d. near Carlisle, 7 Jul. 1307; crowned 19 Aug. 1274; m. (1) 18 Oct. 1254, **ELEANOR OF CASTILE** (110-30), d. 1290; m. (2) 8 Sep. 1299, **MARGUERITE OF FRANCE** (155-30). (CP V 736; CCN 353; DNB xvii, 14; xvii, 178).

3

29. EDWARD II, King of England, 1307-1327; b. Caernarvon, Wales, 25 Apr. 1284; d. near Gloucester, 21 Sep. 1327; m. **ISABELLA OF FRANCE** (101-31). (CP V 736; CCN 353; DNB xviii, 38; xxix, 64).

30. EDWARD III, King of England, 1327-1377; b. Windsor, 13 Nov. 1312; d. Richmond, 21 Jun. 1377; m. York, 24 Jan. 1328, **PHILIPPA OF HAINAUT** (103-34); b. 1312; d. 15 Aug. 1369, dau. of Count William of Hainaut and Holland. (CP II 153, V 736; CCN 353: DNB xvii, 48; xiv, 164. Generations 23-30: Cross xv-xvi; Thatcher 324; CME).

31. JOHN OF GAUNT, b. Ghent, 1340; d. Leicester Castle, Feb. 1399; Duke of Lancaster; m. (1) 19 May 1359, Blanche, d. 31 Sep. 1369, dau. of Henry, Duke of Lancaster; son of **HENRY**, Earl of Lancaster (17-29); m. (2) Jun. 1371, Constance, d. Jun. 1394, eldest dau. and coh. Pedro I "The Cruel", King of Castile and Leon; m. (3) Jan. 1396/7, Catherine (Roet) Swynford, b. 1350; d. 10 May 1403; dau. of Sir Paon Roet, a Gascon, and widow of Sir Hugh Swynford. (CP V 320, 736 chart; VII 415; DNB xxix; 417, lv, 243; S. Armitage Smith: John of Gaunt, reprint 1964). Son by (3) wife:

32. JOHN BEAUFORT, Earl and Marquis of Somerset, b. ca. 1370; d. 16 Mar. 1409/10; m. before 28 Sep. 1397, **MARGARET DE HOLAND** (47-33), d. 30 Dec. 1439; she m. (2) Thomas Plantagenet, Duke of Clarence. (CP IV 416; VII 415; XII pt. 1 39-45; DNB Suppl. i, 158).

33. EDMUND BEAUFORT, Marquis of Dorset, Duke of Somerset, Lieut.-General of France, Normandy and Guienne; b. ca. 1406; slain at St. Albans, 22 May 1455; m. ca. 1435, **ELEANOR (BEAUCHAMP) ROS** (87-34), b. Eddgenoch, co. Warwick, 1407; d. 6 Mar. 1467/8; widow of Thomas, Lord Ros, and dau. of Richard Beauchamp, Earl of Warwick; she m. (3) Walter Rokesley, Esq. (CP II 131, 145; IV 417; DNB iv, 38).

34. ELEANOR BEAUFORT, d. 16 Aug. 1501, Countess of Wiltshire; m. (1) James Butler, b. ca. 1420; d. ca. 1461, Earl of Ormond and Wiltshire; m. (2) ca. 1465, Sir Robert Spencer, Knt., of Spencercombe, co. Devon, b. ca. 1435, living 1502. (CP IX 720).

35. MARGARET SPENCER, b. ca. 1472; m. ca. 1490, Thomas Cary of Chilton Foliot, Wiltshire, b. ca. 1460. (CP IX 720).

36. WILLIAM CARY, b. ca. 1495; d. 22 Jun. 1528; Gentleman of the Privy Chamber and Esquire of the Body of King Henry VIII; m. 31 Jan. 1520/1, **MARY BOLEYN** (22-37), sister of Queen Anne. (CP II 146; IV 159-160; TAG 18: 211-218).

37. MARY CARY, d. 15 Jan. 1568/9; Chief Lady of the Bedchamber to Queen Elizabeth; m. ca. 1539, Sir Francis Knollys, K.G., b. ca. 1514; d. 19 July 1596, of Rotherfield Greys, co. Oxford. (CP IV 160; Weever 554; NEHGR 33: 287-291).

38. ANNE KNOLLYS, living 30 Aug. 1608; m. 19 Nov. 1571, **SIR THOMAS WEST** (18-38), Lord Delaware. (CP IV 159-160; NEHGR 33: 287-291).

39. PENELOPE WEST, b. 9 Sep. 1582; d. ca. 1619; m. ca. 1599, Herbert Pelham, b. ca. 1580; d. Boston, co. Lincoln, 20 Jul. 1624; of

Line 1 (cont.)

Hastings, co. Sussex, and Boston, co. Lincoln (see 228-39). (CP IV 159-160; NEHGR 33: 287-291).

40. HERBERT PELHAM, Esquire, b. ca. 1600; d. 1674; emigrated to New England, 1639/40; 1st Treasurer of Harvard College, 1643; Commissioner of the United Colonies, 1645; m. (1) Jemima Waldegrave; m. (2) Elizabeth (Bosvile) Harlakenden. (NEHGR 33: 287-291). By (1) w. he was f. of Penelope who m. Gov. Winslow. By (2) w. he was f. of Edward Pelham of Rhode Island. (TAG 18:210).

41. PENELOPE PELHAM, dau. by (1), bapt. Bures, 1633; m. Gov. Josias Winslow, of Plymouth Colony. (Goodwin: Pilgrim Republic, 540-542. For generations 31-41, see Meredith B. Colket, Jr. in TAG 18: 211-218, 19: 197-202. Few early New England settlers may be traced so far down in the Complete Peerage).

Line 1A

31. JOHN OF GAUNT (1-31), Duke of Lancaster, b. 1340; d. 1399; m. (1) 19 May 1859, Blanche of Lancaster (his cousin), had (DNB xxix, 417; xxvi, 101).

32. HENRY IV, King of England, 1399-1413; b. Bolingbroke Castle, Lincs. 3 Apr. 1367; d. Westminster Palace, 20 Mar. 1412/3; m. Rochford, Essex, betw. 30 Jul. 1380 and 10 Feb. 1380/1, Mary de Bohun, dau. and coh. **HUMPHREY DE BOHUN** (97-33), Earl of Hereford, Essex, and Northampton. She b. 1368/9; d. Peterborough, Northants, 4 Jul. 1394. (CP VII 417; VI 473-477; DNB xxvi, 31).

33. HUMPHREY, Duke of Gloucester, b. 3 Oct. 1390; d.s.p. legit. Bury St. Edmunds, 23 Feb. 1446-7; m. (1) bef. 7 Mar. 1422/3, Jacqueline, Countess of Holland, Zealand and Hainault, dau. and h. William, Duke of Bavaria, annulled 9 Jan. 1427/8; m. (2) 1428, Eleanor, dau. Sir Reginald Cobham, who had been his mistress, died a prisoner at Peel Castle, Isle of Man, 1454. It is often suggested, but without proof, that Eleanor was mother before mar. of Humphrey's 2 illegit. chn.: Arthur and Antigone. No proof of their maternity. (CP V 730,736; DNB xxviii, 241).

34. ANTIGONE, b. bef. 1428; perh. to Eleanor Cobham, raised by her father, Humphrey, and m. by him, 3 Jan. 1434/5 to Sir Henry Grey, Earl of Tankerville (whose m. he had bought); b. ca. 1419; d. 13 Jan. 1449/50. (CP V 736 (n); VI 138-9, 699; Vis. Salop. 1623: 105, 295).

35. ELIZABETH GREY (dau. of Antigone and Sir Henry Grey), b. ca. 1440; d. Shropshire aft. 1501; m. (2) 1465, Sir Roger Kynaston, kt., b. ca. 1430; d. 1495/6. (CP VI 143, App. C 697; Vis. Salop. 105, 295, 459).

36. JANE KYNASTON, b. ca. 1470; m. Roger Thornes of Shelvock, Salop, bur. St. Mary's Shrewsbury. (Blakeway: Sheriffs of Shropshire 73-4; Trans. Shrop. Arch. Soc. 2 Ser. VI pt. II (1894) 211-213, 215, on Kynaston).

37. JOHN THORNES (s. & h.) of Shelvock, liv. 1535; m. Elizabeth Astley of Patishull, Staffs. (Trans. Shrop. Arch. Soc.

Line 1A (cont.)

op.cit. 330; Bakewell I 56; Vis. Salop. 459).

38. RICHARD THORNES (2nd s.) of Condover, Salop; m. a Margaret N.; or a Joan, dau. of Evan Lloyd Vychan of Abertenent. (Vis. Salop 460; Trans. Shrop. Arch. Soc. 4 Ser. III pt. II 303, Littletons of Munslow).

39. ALICE THORNES, b. ca. 1530; d. Rushbury, parish of Munslow, Salop, 21 Mar. 1596, will 5 Mar. 1596, pro. 12 Dec. 1597 Consis. of Hereford; m. ca. 1548, the Rev. John Littleton, vicar of Munslow (B.L. Oxford 1532), d. Munslow 30 Nov. 1560, will 12 Aug. 1560, pro. 10 Jun. 1562 PCC. (Vis. Salop 460; Vis Worcs. (1634) 64; Trans. Shrop. Arch. Soc. 4 Ser. III pt. II 302-333).

40. SIR EDWARD LITTLETON, kt., of Hinley, Salop., bapt. Munslow, 23 Mar. 1550; d. Llanfaire, co. Denbigh, 25 Sep. 1662, admin. 22 Nov. 1622 PCC; m. Ludlow, Salop., 9 Apr. 1588, Mary Walter, b. Ludlow, 1 Nov. 1565, bur. Ludlow, 23 Oct. 1633. (Trans. Shrop. op.cit., and pp. 263-276, Walters at Ludlow; Vis. Worcs. (1634) 64; Vis. Salop. (1623) 483; Shrop. Parish Rec. Soc. 15 (Reg. of Munslow) 8, 16, 60, 351).

41. NATHANIEL LITTLETON, b. Hopton Castle, Salop; bapt. 22 Dec. 1605; d. in Northampton, Va., Oct.-Dec. 1654; m. Northampton Co., Va., ca. 1638, Ann Southy, b. in Somerset, Eng., ca. 1620; d. Northampton Co., Va., will pro. 28 Oct. 1656. (Vis. Worcs. (1634) 64; Shrop. Parish Reg. (parish of Hopton Castle) 9; Deeds & Wills, # 7 and # 8, Northampton Co., Va. 22, etc.).

Line 1B

14. AETHELWULF (1-14), King of Wessex (England) 839-858, d. 13 Jan 858, m. (1) Osburh, dau. Oslac.

15. AETHELRED I, King of Wessex (England) 868-872, d. 872.

16. AETHELHELM, d. ca. 898, Ealdorman of Wiltshire, was devised Compton & Crondall by King Alfred the Great.

17. AETHELFRITH, d. ca. 927, Ealdorman, first holder of the bequest from King Alfred.

18. EADRIC, ca. 946-47, Ealdorman, held Ogburn & Washington by devise.

19. AETHELWERD "the historian", seen 965, d. ca. 998, thegn in Sussex 973, Ealdorman in Wessex 974.

20. AETHELMAER CILD, "the Great", d. ca. 1015, thegn in Sussex ca. 1007, Ealdorman in Devonshire 1005.

21. WULFNOTH CILD, d. 1015, thegn in Sussex ca. 1007; held Compton, revolted 1009.

22. GODWIN, d. 15 Apr. 1053, thegn in Sussex, Ealdorman of Wessex 1018; m. 1019/20 Githa, dau. Jarl Thorkill Sprakalaeg.

Note: Isenburg (1976) II Table 70, shows (without citing his authority) Jarl Thorkill (or Thurkill) Sprakalaeg as son of Styr-Bjorn (son of Olaf Bjornson 985, King of Sweden) by Thyra, d. 18 Sept. 1000, dau. of Harold VII "Bluetooth", King of Denmark. This line is followed by Moriarty. (Harold was son of Gorm the old, King of Denmark d. 936 and Thyra "Danebod".) However Brenner in his

Line 1B (cont.)

Nachkommen Gorms des Alten (1978) does not include Thorkill as a child of Thyra, and only gives a dau. Gunhild, and a son (by Thyra's 3rd husband) Harold Olavsson who d. aged 1yrs.

23. HAROLD II "Godwinson", b. ca. 1022, slain in Battle of Hastings 14 Oct. 1066, Ealdorman of East Anglia, succ. father 1053 Ealdorman of Wessex, King of England 1066 (succeeded Edward the Confessor); m. as (2) husb. Edith, dau. Elgar (Aelfgar), d. 1059, Earl of Mercia; widow of **GRIFFITH I** (176-2), Prince of North Wales. By Ealdgith (Edith) "Swansneck", his "handfast wife" (non Christian mar.) before he m. Edith of Mercia) he had with others

24. GYTHA of Wessex, m. ca. 1070 **VLADIMIR II** "Monomachus" (242-7) b. 1053, d. 19 May 1125; Grand Prince of Kiev (Moriarty).

Line 2

31. JOHN OF GAUNT (1-31), Duke of Lancaster, son of Edward III, King of England; m. (3) Catherine Swynford. (CP V 320 chart, VII 415).

32. JOAN BEAUFORT, d. Howden, 13 Nov. 1440; m. (1) bef. 30 Sep. 1390, **SIR ROBERT DE FERRERS** (62-34), of Willisham, d. bef. 29 Nov. 1396; m. (2) bef. 3 Feb. 1396/7, **RALPH DE NEVILLE** (207-34), K.G., cr. Earl of Westmoreland, 1397; b. bef. 1364; d. Raby, 21 Oct. 1425; will made 18 Oct. 1424, pro. 14 Nov. 1425-7 Oct. 1426, son of John, 3rd Lord Neville of Raby, and Maud de Percy. (CP V chart, IX 502 ii-iii chart, XII pt. 1 39-40).

33. MARY DE FERRERS, Lady of Oversley, b. bef. 1394; d. 25 Jan. 1457/8; m. **SIR RALPH NEVILLE** (10-34), d. 26 Feb. 1457/8. (CP II 232-233, V 320, VII 415-416).

34. JOHN NEVILLE, Esq., d. 17 Mar. 1481/2, of Althorpe, co. Lincoln, j.u. (Inq.p.m.) M.P. for Lincolnshire, 1444; Sheriff of Lincolnshire, 1439-1440, 1452-1453; m. (1) Elizabeth Newmarch, dau. of Robert Newmarch of Wormsley. (CP II 232-233, V 320, VII 415-416).

35. JANE NEVILLE, of Oversley and Wormsley; m. ca. 1458/60, Sir William Gascoigne of Gawthorpe, co. York; d. 1463/4. (Generations 34-36: Foster: Visitations of Yorkshire, 1584/5, 384-385).

36. MARGARET GASCOIGNE, m. Sir Christopher Ward, d. 31 Dec. 1521, of Givendale, Yorks. (Inq.p.m. 4 Feb. 1522/2; she was sister of Sir William Gascoigne, Knt. of Gawthorpe, who m. **MARGARET PERCY** (3-35), q.v. (CP IX 717).

37. ANNE WARD, m. 1500/1, **SIR RALPH NEVILLE** (204-40), of Thornton Bridge, co. York. (CP IX 501 ff. for Neville of Raby; John Burke: Hist. of the Commoners I 57).

38. KATHERINE NEVILL, b. ca. 1500; m. (1) 1515, **SIR WALTER STRICKLAND** (41-36), of Sizergh, co. Westmoreland, d. 9 Jan. 1527/8. (John Burke: Commoners, op.cit. Generations 33-38: G.A. Moriarty in TAG 17: 105-109).

39. WALTER STRICKLAND, Esq., of Sizergh, b. 5 Apr. 1516; d. 8 Apr. 1569; prob. twice m. (See NEHGR vol. 114, pp. 51-58; vol.

Line 2 (cont.)

115, p. 316; will dated 23 Jan. 1568/9, left Ђ 200 to his dau. Ellen).
40. ELLEN STRICKLAND, dau. by prob. 1st wife Agnes prob.
Hammerton, liv. 1622; m. by 1582, John Carleton of Beeford, co.
York, b. ca. 1550/5, buried 27 Jan. 1622/3, son of Thomas and Jennet
(Wilson) Carleton.
41. WALTER CARLETON, bapt. Beeford, 28 Dec. 1582; d.
Horsea, 4 Oct. 1623; m. 1607 Jane Gibbon, living 1639.
42. EDWARD CARLETON, bapt. Beeford, 20 Oct. 1610; sett.
Rowley, Mass., 1639; m. York, 3 Nov. 1636, **ELLEN NEWTON** (121D-
41), bapt. Hedon, 24 Feb. 1614, dau. of Launcelot and Mary (Lee
Newton). (For Strickland of Sizergh, see John Burke: History of the
Commoners I 55-58. Generations 38-42: Dr. Tracy Elliot Hazen in
NEHGR 93: 10 chart opp.; S.H. Lee Washington in NEHGR 96: 106-
107 chart; 314 chart opp.; v. Redlich 151; Sheppard "Ancestry of
Edward Carleton and Ellen Newton his wife" (c 1978, microfilm)).

Line 3

32. JOAN BEAUFORT (2-32), granddau. of King Edward III of
England; d. 13 Nov. 1440; m. (2) **RALPH DE NEVILLE** (207-34),
K.G. (CP V 320 chart, IX 502 ii-iii chart).
33. ELEANOR NEVILLE, d. 1463; m. **SIR HENRY PERCY**, K.G.
(19-33), b. 3 Feb. 1392/3; slain at St. Albans, 22 May 1455, Earl of
Northumberland, Warden of the Marches of Scotland. (CP X 464;
Collins IV 84-91).
34. SIR HENRY PERCY, Knt., b. 25 Jul 1421; slain at the battle
of Towton Field, 29 Mar. 1461, Earl of Northumberland; m. ca. 25
Jun. 1435, Eleanor Poynings, d. Feb. 1483/4, dau. of Richard
Poynings, Lord Poynings, son of Robert, Lord Poynings, d. 2 Oct.
1446. (CP IX 716-717, X 464; Collins IV 84, 92-97).
35. MARGARET PERCY, m. Sir William Gascoigne, Knt., of
Gawthorpe, co. York, son of Sir William Gascoigne and **JANE
NEVILLE** (2-35). (CP IX 717).
36. DOROTHY GASCOIGNE, m. Sir Ninian Markenfield.
37. ALICE MARKENFIELD, m. Robert Mauleverer.
38. DOROTHY MAULEVERER, m. John Kaye, of Woodsome, co.
York, Esq., 1585. (Generations 35-38: Saltonstall genealogy 84).
39. ROBERT KAYE, Esq., of Woodsome, 1612, J.P.; m. Anne
Flower, dau. of John Flower of Whitewell, co. Rutland. (Waters II
939-940).
40. GRACE KAYE, m. Sir Richard Saltonstall of Huntwick, one
of the patentees of Massachusetts and Connecticut; sett. Watertown, Mass., 1630, J.P. (Waters II 939-940, 969-970; NEHGR 95: 72).
41. MAJOR RICHARD SALTONSTALL, b. 1610; d. 1694; sett.
Watertown, Mass., 1630, Ipswich, Mass., 1635; m. **MURIEL GURDON**
(4-41), dau. Brampton Gurdon of Assington Hall, Sheriff of Norfolk,
1625-1629. (Waters II 939-940, 969-970; NEHGR 95: 72; Richard A.
Saltonstall: Ancestors and Descendants of Sir Richard Saltonstall of
New England, 1897, p. 84. Generations 35-41: see Foster: Visitations
of Yorkshire, 1584/5 and 1612, pp. 220, 320, 384-385, 570)).

30. EDWARD III (1-30), King of England, 1327-1377; m. **PHILIPPA OF HAINAUT** (103-34). (CP II 153).

31. THOMAS PLANTAGENET, K.G., "of Woodstock," b. co. Oxford, 7 Jan. 1354/5; d. ca. 1397, Duke of Gloucester; m. ca. 1376, **ALIANORE DE BOHUN** (97-34), d. 3 Oct. 1399, dau. of Humphrey IX de Bohun, K.G., d. 1372, and Joan, dau. of Richard Fitz Alan, 5th Earl of Arundel. (CP II 153).

32. ANNE, Countess of Buckingham; m. (3) bef. 1420, Sir William Bourchier, d. Troyes, 28 May 1420, Count of Eu. (CP II 153).

33. SIR JOHN BOURCHIER, K.G., d. May 1474; Knt. 19 May 1426; M.P., 1455-1472; K.G., ca. 23 Apr. 1459; Constable of Windsor Castle, 1461-1474, 1st Baron Berners; m. Margery Berners, d. 18 Dec. 1475, dau. of Sir Richard Berners and Philippa, dau. of Sir Edward Dalyngridge. (CP II 153).

34. SIR HUMPHREY BOURCHIER, slain at the battle of Barnet, 14 Apr. 1471; m. Elizabeth Tylney, d. 4 Apr. 1497, dau. of Sir Frederick Tylney of Ashwellthorpe, co. Norfolk. (CP II 153).

35. SIR JOHN BOURCHIER, K.B., d. Calais, ca. 19 Mar. 1532/3, K.B., 17 Jan. 1477/8; M.P., 1495-1529; Chancellor of the Exchequer, 1516-1527, 2nd Baron Berners; m. **KATHERINE HOWARD** (16-35), d. 12 Mar. 1535-7, dau. of Sir John Howard, K.G., Duke of Norfolk, and Margaret Wyfold, dau. of Sir John Chedworth. (CP II 153-154; Vivian: Visitations of Devon 106; CCN 175; Berry: Berkshire Pedigrees 55).

36. JANE (or **JOAN**) **BOURCHIER,** will made 8 Apr. 1560, pro. 9 Mar. 1561; d. 17 Feb. 1561/2; m. **SIR EDMUND KNYVET** (188-14), b. 1490; will dated 24 Jun. 1537, pro. 1546; d. Apr. 1539, of Ashwellthorpe, co. Norfolk, Esq. (CP II 155; Vivian, op cit., 106; Berry: Berkshire Pedigrees, 55).

37. JOHN KNYVET, Esq., of Plumstead, Norfolk, living 1543, but d. in his mother's lifetime; m. (settlement, 28 Feb. 1513), Agnes Harcourt, dau. of Sir John Harcourt of Stanton-Harcourt, Knt. (CP II 155; Berry: Berkshire Pedigrees, 55). His dau. was no. 39.

39. ABIGAIL KNYVET, m. Sir Martin Sedley, b. 1531, will made 12 May 1608, pro. 5 Mar. 1609, of Morley, co. Norfolk. (Waters II 969-970; NEHGR 95:72). See Beard: Pedigrees of Some of the Emperor Charlemagne's Descendants II (1974), p. xcviii & xcvix.

40. MURIEL SEDLEY, m. Brampton Gurdon, Esq., will dated 19 Oct. 1647, codicil 1 Feb. 1648, pro. 15 May 1650; d. 1649, of Assington Hall, Suffolk; Sheriff of Suffolk, 1625-1629; son of John and Amy (Brampton) Gurdon of Assington. (Waters II 956-957; NEHGR 95: 72).

41. MURIEL GURDON, m. June 1633, **MAJOR RICHARD SALTONSTALL,** Esq. (3-41), b. 1610; d. 1694, of Ipswich, Mass. (NEHGR 95: 72; Harleian ms. 4630 (p. 512); Waters II 956-957; v. Redlich 175; Saltonstall Genealogy 84. This is a long established pedigree).

30. EDWARD III (1-30), King of England; m. **PHILIPPA OF HAINAUT** (103-34). (CP II 153; DNB; CCN 614).

31. LIONEL OF ANTWERP, b. Antwerp, 29 Nov. 1338; d. Alba, Italy, 7 Oct. 1368, Earl of Ulster, Duke of Clarence; m. 1352, Elizabeth de Burgh, dau. of **WILLIAM DE BURGH** (94A-33), 4th Earl of Ulster, and Maud de Lancaster, dau. of **HENRY** (17-29), Earl of Lancaster. (CP VIII 444-445, IX 714; CCN 614).

32. PHILIPPA PLANTAGENET, b. 16 Aug. 1355; m. 1368, **EDMUND MORTIMER** (29-34), b. 1352, d. 27 Dec. 1381, 3rd Earl of March. (CP VIII 444-447, IX 714; Thatcher 324; Gardiner 286).

33. ELIZABETH MORTIMER, living 8 Oct. 1407; m. bef. 10 Dec. 1379, **SIR HENRY PERCY**, K.G. (19-32), "Harry Hotspur," killed at Shrewsbury, 14 Aug. 1403. (CP IX 714; CCN 794).

34. ELIZABETH PERCY, d. 26 Oct. 1437; m. 1403/12, **JOHN DE CLIFFORD** (26-34), d. Meaux, France, 13 Mar. 1421/3; M.P., 1411-1421; 7th Lord Clifford, Sheriff of Westmoreland. (CP III 293).

35. THOMAS DE CLIFFORD, b. 26 Mar. 1414; slain at St. Albans, 22 May 1455, 8th Lord Clifford, Sheriff of Westmoreland, M.P., 1436-1453; m. aft. Mar. 1424, Joan Dacre, dau. of Thomas Dacre, Lord Dacre of Gillesland, by Philippa, dau. of **RALPH DE NEVILLE** (207-34), K.G., Earl of Westmoreland and **MARGARET STAFFORD** (10-33). (CP III 293).

36. MATILDA CLIFFORD, m. **SIR EDMUND SUTTON**, Knt. (81-37), d. aft. 6 Jul. 1483, son of John Sutton, K.G., Lord Dudley. (CP IV 479-480; DNB 16: 107-109; George Adlard: The Sutton-Dudleys, etc., N.Y., 1862: Pedigree A: The Suttons; Pedigree C: The Dudleys of Yeanwith, Cumberland).

37. THOMAS SUTTON, d. aft. 19 May 1537; m. Grace Threlkeld, dau. of Lancelot Threlkeld, Esq., of Yanwith. (Adlard, op.cit., Pedigree C; Burke: Peerage (1923), p. 763). See Cumberland & Westmoreland A.A. Soc. 9: 290, 319; 8:422; NS 16: 168, 23.

38. RICHARD SUTTON, of Yanwith, took name of Dudley; m. Dorothy Sanford, dau. of Edward Sanford of Asham. (Pedigree C, as above).

39. ELIZABETH DUDLEY, m. John Tichborne of Cowden, Kent, son of Sir John Tichborne, Knt., Sheriff of Hampshire, 1488, 1496, and Margaret Martin, dau. of Richard Martin of Edenbridge, Kent. (CP IV 642. Generations 36-39: Pedigree C, as above; Burke (1923), p. 2180).

40. JOHN TICHBORNE, 2nd, of Cowden; m. Margaret Waller.

41. JOHN TICHBORNE, 3rd, of Cowden; m. Dorothy Challoner, dau. of Francis Challoner of Lindfield, Sussex. (CP IV 642; Visitation of London, 1633/4, II 298).

42. ROBERT TICHBORNE, of Farrington within London; m. Joan Banckes, dau. of Thomas Banckes, merchant and alderman of London. (CP IV 642; Waters I 653-654, 742. This shows that Elizabeth Tichborne was unmarried 20 May 1630 and therefore did not marry Pardon Tillinghast. Visitation of London, 1633/4, II 298).

43. ELIZABETH TICHBORNE, not mother of # 44. (See TAG vol. 37, p. 34-38).

Line 5 (cont.)

* * *

44. REV. PARDON TILLINGHAST, b. Seven Cliffs, Sussex, 1622; d. 29 Jan. 1718; sett. Providence, R.I., 1643; m. Sarah, dau. Rev. Benj. Browne of Ifield, Sussex. (Weis: Colonial Clergy of N.E., 204; Berry: Genealogies of Kent, 361; Berry: Genealogies of Hampshire, 28; Visitations of London, 1633/4, II 298: Boston Evening Transcript, Note 6544, 4 Jan. 1928; Burke: Peerage (1923), p. 1436). He was son of Pardon Tillinghast of Ifield who had a wife Sarah (TAG vol. 37: 34-38). Pardon the father was the son of the Rev. John Tillinghast (will 1628) by wife Alice, dau. of Gregory Pardon.

Line 6

28. EDWARD I (1-28), King of England, 1272-1307; m. **ELEANOR OF CASTILE** (110-30). (CP IV 469, X 118; CCN 356).
29. ELIZABETH PLANTAGENET, b. 7 Aug. 1282; d. 5 May 1316; m. (2) 14 Nov. 1302, **HUMPHREY DE BOHUN VIII** (97-31), b. 1276; d. 16 Mar. 1321/2, Earl of Hereford and Essex. (CP IV 135, IV 469, X 118).
30. MARGARET DE BOHUN, d. 1391; m. 1325, **HUGH DE COURTENAY** (51-32), d. 1377, Earl of Devon. (CP IV 335, IV 469).
31. SIR EDWARD COURTENAY, b. c. 1331/2, d.v.p. betw. 2 Feb. 1368 & 1 Apr. 1371, of Godlington; m. in or bef. 1346 Emmeline, d. 28 Feb. or 20 Mar. 1371, dau. of Sir John Dauney, Knt., and Sybil Treverbin. (CP IV 335).
32. SIR HUGH COURTENAY, d. 15 Mar. 1425, of Haccombe, Devon, Knight of the Shire of Devon, 1395; m. (2) Philippa, dau. of Sir Warin l'Arcedekene (died 1400) by his wife Elizabeth, dau. of Sir John Talbot of Richard's Castle, co. Hereford. (CP I 187-188; IV 335. Family of Courtenay (Cleaveland, 1735), p. 238-239).
33. JOAN COURTENAY, m. **SIR NICHOLAS CAREW** (28-37), d. 1446, Baron Carew and Molesford (Courtenay cit.). She m. (2) Sir Robert de Vere.
34. SIR THOMAS CAREW, Baron Carew of Ashwater; m. Joan Carminow.
35. SIR NICHOLAS CAREW, of Ottery-Mohun, d. 6 Dec. 1470, Baron Carew and Mulsford; m. Margaret Dinham, d. 13 Dec. 1470, dau. of **SIR JOHN DYNHAM** (214-35), d.1458, and Jane, dau. of Sir Richard Arches. Margaret was the sister of John, Lord Dinham of Nutwell, Lord Treasurer of England. Sir Nicholas and Margaret were buried in Westminster Abbey.
36. SIR EDMUND CAREW, Knt., of Mohuns Ottery, d. 24 Jun. 1513; m. Katherine, dau. of Sir William Huddlesfield, Knt., d. 22 Mar. 1499, Attorney General.
37. KATHERINE CAREW, m. **SIR PHILIP CHAMPERNOUN** (51-38), of Modbury, d. 1545. (Generations 28-37: Waters: Pedigree of Captain Francis Champernoun of York, Maine, 1665, in the Essex Institute Proceedings, 17: 16; Vivian: Visitations of Devon, 244-245, 134-135).

11

Line 6 (cont.)

38. SIR ARTHUR CHAMPERNOUN, of Dartington, Knt., will pro. 19 Apr. 1578; m. Mary Norris, dau. of Sir Henry Norris of Rycote.

39. GAWINE CHAMPERNOUN, of Dartington, Esq., will pro. 3 Apr. 1592; m. Gabrielle Roberta, dau. of the Count of Montgomery in France (?).

40. ARTHUR CHAMPERNOUN, of Dartington, Esq., living 1620; m. Dunsford, 17 Jun. 1598, Bridget Fulford, dau. of Sir Thomas Fulford, Knt.

41. CAPTAIN FRANCIS CHAMPERNOUN, of York, Maine, 1665; will made 11 Nov. 1686, pro. 28 Dec. 1687. (Generations 37-41; Vivian: Visitations of Devon, 160, 162-163, 379-380; Waters: Proceedings of the Essex Institute, 17: 16).

Line 7

29. ELIZABETH PLANTAGENET (6-29), dau. of King Edward I of England and Eleanor of Castile, m. **HUMPHREY DE BOHUN VIII** (97-31), Earl of Hereford and Essex. (CP IV 669, X 118).

30. ELEANOR DE BOHUN, d. 7 Oct. 1363; m. 1327, **JAMES BUTLER** (73-32), or le Boteler, b. 1305; d. 6 Jan. 1337/8; cr. Earl of Ormond, Oct. 1328, son of Edmund and Joan (Fitz Thomas) le Boteler. (CP X 116-119).

31. JAMES BUTLER, b. 4 Oct. 1331; d. 1382, 2nd Earl of Ormond; m. Anne Darcy, d. 24 Mar. 1389/90, dau. of Sir John Darcy of Knayth, prob. by Joan de Burgh, 4th dau. of Richard, Earl of Ulster. (CP X 119-121).

32. JAMES BUTLER, b. aft. 1361; d. Sep. 1405; 3rd Earl of Ormond; m. bef. 17 Jun. 1386, Anne Welles, dau. of Sir John de Welles, Baron Welles. (CP X 121-123).

33. JAMES BUTLER, b. ca. 1390; d. 23 Aug. 1452, 4th Earl of Ormond; m. (1) ca. 28 Aug. 1413, **JOAN DE BEAUCHAMP** (120-36), d. Aug. 1430. (CP X 123-126, XI 705).

34. ELIZABETH BUTLER, b. 1420; d. 8 Sep. 1473; m. bef. 1448, **SIR JOHN TALBOT**, K.G. (8-35), b. 1413; d. 10 Jul. 1460, 2nd Earl of Shrewsbury, Lord Treasurer of England. (CP XI 705, 731 chart).

35. SIR GILBERT TALBOT, K.G., 2nd son, b. 1452; d. 16 Aug. 1517, of Grafton, co. Worcester; m. (2), as her 3rd husband, Audrey Cotton, dau. of Sir William Cotton, of Landwade, co. Cambridge (identification discovered by Chas. Fitch-Northen). (CP XI 706 note a, 717,731).

36. SIR JOHN TALBOT, Knt., son by (2), b. 1485; d. 10 Sep. 1549, of Albrighton, Shropshire, and Grafton, co. Worcester, Sheriff of Shropshire, 1527, 1537, 1541; m. (1) **MARGARET TROUTBECK** (20-36), b. 1492, living 1521, dau. of Adam Troutbeck, Esq., of Mobberly, co. Chester, by Margaret, dau. of Sir John Boteler of Bewsey in Warrington, co. Lancaster. (CP XI 717, 731).

37. ANNE TALBOT, b. 1515; m. Thomas Needham, of Shavington, Shropshire, b. 1510, son of Sir Robert Needham and Agnes Mainwaring.

38. ROBERT NEEDHAM, b. 1535, of Shavington; m. Frances Ashton, dau. of Sir Edward Ashton, of Tixwell, Staffordshire.

39. DOROTHY NEEDHAM, b. 1570; d. after 1629; m. **SIR RICHARD CHETWODE** (150-42), b. ca. 1560; d. aft. 1631; knighted 1602; son of Richard Chetwode and Agnes de Wahull, of Warkworth.

40. GRACE CHETWODE, b. 1602; d. New London, Conn., 21 Apr. 1669; m. as (2) wife, Apr. 1635, the **REV. PETER BULKELEY**, B.D. (31-40), first minister at Concord, Mass. (Generations 34-36; Collins III 30-49; Generations 36-40: Frank Bulkeley Smith: The Chetwode Family of England, (1910), 1945, pp. 76 ff. with charts, corrected by Donald Lines Jacobus: Bulkeley Genealogy, 69-83; v. Redlich 138).

Line 8

28. EDWARD I (1-28), King of England; m. **ELEANOR OF CASTILE** (110-30). (CP X 118; CCN 356).

29. JOAN PLANTAGENET, b. Acre, 1272; d. 23 Apr. 1307; m. Westminster Abbey, ca. 30 Apr. 1290, **SIR GILBERT DE CLARE**, Knt. (63-30), 9th Earl of Clare, Earl of Hertford and Gloucester. (CP I 346, IV 269, 670 chart iii, V 702-710, 736).

30. ALIANORE DE CLARE, b. Oct. 1292; d. 30 Jun. 1337; m. in 1306, bef. 14 Jun., **SIR HUGH LE DESPENSER**, Knt. (74-32), Baron Despenser, hanged and quartered at Hereford, 24 Nov. 1326. (CP IV 267-271, cf. 269, 670 chart iii, V 736), m. (2) Sir William la Zouche de Mortimer).

31. ISABEL DESPENSER, m. 9 Feb. 1320/1, **SIR RICHARD FITZ ALAN** (60-32), d. 1376. (CP I 243-244).

32. ISABEL FITZ ALAN, d. 1361; m. John le Strange (son of John le Strange, 2nd Baron, son of **FULK LE STRANGE** (29A-30), 1st Baron Strange of Blackmere), b. 1322; d. 12 May 1361, 4th Baron Strange of Blackmere. (CP I 244 note b; XII pt. 1 344; Banks I 421-422).

33. ANKARET LE STRANGE, b. 1361; d. 1413; m. bef. 1383, **RICHARD TALBOT** (14-32), b. ca. 1361; d. 8 or 9 Sep. 1396, aged ca. 35, Baron Talbot de Blackmere; M.P., 1384. (CP XI 161-7; Banks I 422, 427-428; Hamon le Strange: Le Strange Records, 289-321).

34. SIR JOHN TALBOT, K.G., b. 1384; d. 17 Jul. 1453, cr. 1st Earl of Shrewsbury, 1442, Lord Lieutenant of Ireland; m. bef. 12 Mar. 1406/7, Maude de Neville, b. 1392; d. 1423, Baroness Furnivall, dau. of Sir Thomas Neville, Baron Furnivall, and Joan, dau. of William, Baron Furnivall. (CP XI 698-704, 731 chart; Banks I 428).

35. SIR JOHN TALBOT, K.G., b. 1413; d. 10 July. 1460, 2nd Earl of Shrewsbury, Lord Treasurer of England; m. bef. Mar. 1444/5, **ELIZABETH BUTLER** (7-34), b. 1420; d. 8 Sep. 1473. (CP I 242-244, IV 267-272, XI 704-705, 731 chart).

29. JOAN PLANTAGENET (8-29), dau. of Edward I, King of England, and Eleanor of Castile, m. 1290, **SIR GILBERT DE CLARE**, Knt. (63-30). (CP I 346, IV 269, 670 chart III, V 702-710, 736).

30. MARGARET DE CLARE, b. ca. 1292; d. 13 Apr. 1342; m. (1) 1 Nov. 1307, Piers de Gaveston, Earl of Cornwall, executed 19 Jun. 1312; m. (2) Windsor, 28 Apr. 1317, Hugh de Audley, d. 10 Nov. 1347, Lord Audley, 8th Earl of Gloucester, 16 Mar. 1336/7; Ambassador to France, 1341; son of Hugh de Audley, Lord Audley, and **ISOLDE** (207-31), dau. of Edmund de Mortimer of Wigmore, but not by Margaret de Fiennes (NEHGR 116: 16-7; CP I 346, III 434, V 736, XI 101-102; Weaver, op.cit. 323). See also (207-31).

31. MARGARET DE AUDLEY, age 18 yrs. bef. 16 Edward III (1343), only dau. and heir; d. 7 Sep. 1349; m. bef. 6 Jul. 1336, **SIR RALPH DE STAFFORD**, K.G. (55-32), d. Tunbridge Castle, 31 Aug. 1372, M.P. 1337-1349, Baron of Tunbridge, Steward of the Royal Household, 1337, Seneschal of Aquitaine, 1345, fought at Crecy, cr. Earl of Stafford, 5 Mar. 1350/1, K.G., 23 Apr. 1349, son of Edmund de Stafford and **MARGARET BASSET** (55-31). (CP V 736, XI 101, XII pt. 1 174-177; Banks I 408-411; DNB 53: 458).

32. BEATRICE STAFFORD, widow of Maurice, Earl of Desmond; m. 1358, **THOMAS DE ROS** (89-32), d. 8 Jun. 1384, of Helmsley; M.P., 1362-1384. (CP V 736, XI 100-101; Banks I 378).

33. SIR WILLIAM DE ROS, K.G., d. Belvoir, 1 Sep. 1414, of Belvoir, 1400, M.P. 1394-1413; Treasurer of England, 1403-1404; K.G., 1403; m. 1394, **MARGARET FITZ ALAN DE ARUNDEL** (21-33), d. 3 Jul. 1438. (CP I 341; XI 101-103; Banks I 378. Generations 32-33: Robert Thornton: The Antiquities of Nottinghamshire, London, 1677, p. 115; John Nichols: History of Leicestershire, II Part I 27 ff).

34. MARGARET DE ROS, living 1423; m. ca. 1415, **JAMES TUCHET** (27-36), Lord Audley, b. ca. 1398; d. 23 Sep. 1459; M.P. 1421-1455. (CP I 341, XI 102-103; Banks I 100-102).

35. ANNE TUCHET DE AUDLEY, m. **SIR THOMAS DUTTON OF DUTTON** (32-35), d. 23 Sep. 1459, son of Sir John Dutton and Margaret Savage. (VCH Lanc. VI 305).

36. ISABEL DUTTON, m. Sir Christopher de Southworth, Knt., b. 1443; d. 1487, Lord of Samlesbury; knighted in Scotland, 1482. (VCH Lanc. VI 305. According to George Ormerod: History of the County Palatine and Duchy of Chester, London, 1819, pp. 662, 712, and Christopher Townley: Abstract of Inquisitions and Post Mortems from mss. at Townley (Chetham Society)—Sir Christopher de Southworth m. Isabel, dau. of Sir Thomas Dutton of Dutton, co. Chester, by wife, Ann, dau. of James, Lord Audley; and Sir Thomas Dutton was son of John Dutton, Esq. by wife Margaret Savage, dau. of Sir John Savage, of Clifton).

37. SIR JOHN DE SOUTHWORTH, Knt., b. 1478; d. 1517/9, Lord of Samlesbury, Sheriff of the co. of Lancaster; knighted 12 Feb. 1503/4; m. Helen de Langton, dau. of Sir Richard de Langton, d. 1500, Baron of Newton and Lord of Walton-le-Dale, by wife Isabel Gerard. (VCH Lanc. VI 305.).

38. SIR THOMAS SOUTHWORTH, Knt., of Samlesbury, b. 1497; d. 13 Jan. 1546; fought at Flodden Field, 9 Sep. 1513; High Sheriff of Lancashire, 1542; enlarged Samlesbury Hall, 1542-1545; m. (2) ca. 9 Aug. 1518, **MARGERY BOTELER** (46-38), dau. of Sir Thomas Boteler of Bewsey. (VCH Lanc. VI 306).

39. SIR JOHN SOUTHWORTH, Knt., b. 1526; d. 3 Nov. 1595, of Samlesbury Hall, Lancashire; knighted 1547; High Sheriff of Lancashire, 1562; M.P., 1566; commended for valor in Scottish wars, 1557; owned vast estates but was land poor, imprisoned for harboring Catholic priests; m. St. Leonard's, Middleton, 23 Jul. 1547, Mary (Asheton) Gouland, of Offerton, co. Derby, dau. of Sir Richard Asheton of Middleton, Lancashire, Knt. (VCH Lanc. VI 306; his will (published in James Croston: History of the Ancient Hall of Samlesbury) mentions Thomas, eldest son, and John, eldest son and heir of Thomas.

40. THOMAS SOUTHWORTH, eldest son and heir, b. ca. 1548; d. 30 Nov. 1616; m. between 1563 and 1571, **ROSAMOND LISTER** (156-41), dau. of William Lister, Esq., of Medhope and Thornton, co. York, d. 1582, by wife Bridget Pigot, of Midhope. (James Stowe: Survey of London, 1633). The will of Sir William Lister, probated in 1582, desires that he "be buried according to the Church of England." The will mentions the testator's son-in-law, Thomas Southworth, as the son of Sir John Southworth. With Thomas Southworth, his son-in-law, the testator left annuities for his four children, including Sir Matthew Lister, physician to King Charles I. Thomas Southworth had become a Protestant by 1584, for which reason his father, Sir John, a moderate Catholic, threatened to disinherit him. (Letter of Sir Francis Walsingham, 1584, in Peck: Desiderata Curiosa, 1779). The son was living in London in 1584; both father and son had returned to Samlesbury in 1594. (Generations 36-41; VCH Lanc. VI 305-306; Crosby: Visitations of Somersetshire, 102; Dr. Samuel G. Webber: Southworth Genealogy, Boston, 1905, 425-442, cf. 425-426).

41. EDWARD SOUTHWORTH, youngest son of Thomas and Rosamond (Lister) Southworth, b. London, 1590; living 1602, but d. bef. 1622. (The only support for the connection between generation 41 and 42 is in the coincidence of dates and names. Edward of Leyden may or may not be the same man as Edward of London. The line is inadequately supported at this point.)

* * *

Edward Southworth of Leyden was b. 1590; d. ca. 1621. (Letter of Robert Cushman to Edward Southworth at Heneage House, London, 17 Aug. 1620, in Bradford's History of Plimouth Plantation, Boston, 1901, page 86. Edward's wife was a widow in July 1623). He m. Leyden, Holland, 28 May 1613, Alice Carpenter, b. ca. 1590; d. Plymouth, Mass., 26 Mar. 1670, ae. ca. 80 yrs., dau. of Alexander Carpenter of Wrington, Somersetshire. She came to Plymouth, 1623; m. (2) Plymouth, 14 Aug. 1623, Gov. William Bradford. The sons, Constant and Thomas, were brought up in the home of Governor

Bradford. (Goodwin: Pilgrim Republic, 1920, 460-464; Col. Charles E. Banks: The English Ancestry and Homes of the Pilgrim Fathers. Best discussion in Boston Evening Transcript (I) 31 Aug. 1931; (II) 2 Sep. 1931).

42. ENS. CONSTANT SOUTHWORTH, b. Leyden, 1614; d. Duxbury, 10 Mar. 1678/9; m. Duxbury, 2 Nov. 1637, Elizabeth Collier.

42. CAPT. THOMAS SOUTHWORTH, b. Leyden, 1616; m. Sep. 1641, Elizabeth Raynor.

Line 10

31. MARGARET DE AUDLEY (9-31), m. ca. 1335, **SIR RALPH DE STAFFORD**, K.G. (55-32). (CP V 736, XI 100-101; Banks I 408-411; DNB 53: 458).

32. SIR HUGH STAFFORD, K.G., b. ca. 1342; d. 10 Oct. 1386, 2nd Earl of Stafford; M.P. 1371; m. bef. 1 Mar. 1350/1, Philippa de Beauchamp, d. bef. 6 Apr. 1386, dau. of **THOMAS DE BEAUCHAMP** (87-31), Earl of Warwick and **KATHERINE** (120-34), dau. of Roger de Mortimer, Earl of March. (Warwick Castle and its Earls, 828; CP XII, pt. 1 177-179).

33. MARGARET STAFFORD, d. 9 Jun. 1396; m. as his (1) wife, **SIR RALPH NEVILLE** (207-34), K.G., 1st Earl of Westmoreland. (CP IV 502a-502b, Neville Chart; Notes & Queries, 3rd Series, 9: 376; 152: 219; VCH Worcester).

34. SIR RALPH NEVILLE, 2nd son; m. **MARY FERRERS** (2-33). (CP V 320, chart, VII 415-416 note).

Line 11

29. JOAN PLANTAGENET (8-29), d. 1307, dau. of Edward I, King of England, and Eleanor of Castile; m. 1290, **SIR GILBERT DE CLARE**, Knt. (63-30), 9th Earl of Clare, Earl of Hertford and Gloucester. (CP I 346, IV 269, 670 chart III, V 346, 702-710, 736).

30. ELIZABETH DE CLARE, d. 4 Nov. 1360; m. as his (2) wife, **SIR THEOBALD DE VERDON** (70-32), d. 27 Jul. 1316, Lord of Weoberley, Baron, 1308, of Alton, co. Stafford. (CP IV 43-44, V 346; Old-CP VIII 25; Banks I 445).

31. ISABEL DE VERDON, b. Amesbury, Wilts., 21 Mar. 1317/8; d. 25 Jul. 1349; m. bef. 20 Feb. 1330/1, **HENRY FERRERS** (58-32), b. ca. 1294, d. Groby, co. Leicester, 15 Sep. 1343, 2nd Baron Ferrers of Groby. (CP V chart 332, 344-347; Old-CP VIII 25).

32. WILLIAM FERRERS, Knt., b. Newbold Verdon, co. Leicester, 28 Feb. 1332/3; d. 8 Jan. 1370/1, 3rd Baron Ferrers of Groby; knighted 6 May 1351; will pro. 19 Jul. 1372; m. (1) bef. 25 Apr. 1354, Margaret de Ufford, dau. of Robert de Ufford, Earl of Suffolk, and Margaret de Norwich, dau. of Sir Walter de Norwich. (See 87-32). (CP V chart 332, 348-351).

33. HENRY FERRERS, b. 16 Feb. 1355/6; d. 3 Feb. 1387/8, 4th Baron Ferrers of Groby; m. bef. 27 Apr. 1371, Joan, d. 30 May 1394,

Line 11 (cont.)

prob. dau. of Sir Thomas de Hoo and Isabel Seint Leger. (CP V chart 332, 351-353).

34. WILLIAM FERRERS, bapt. Luton, co. Bedford, 25 Apr. 1372; d. 18 May, 1445, 5th Baron Ferrers of Groby; m. (1) aft. 10 Oct. 1388, Philippa de Clifford, dau. of **SIR ROGER DE CLIFFORD** (26-32), Lord of Clifford, and Maud Beauchamp, dau. of **THOMAS** (87-31), Earl of Warwick, living 4 Jul. 1405; m. (2) Margaret, dau. John de Montague, Earl of Salisbury; m. (3) by 26 Oct. 1416, Elizabeth, dau. of Robert Standisshe, widow of John de Wrottesley and of William Botiller. (CP V chart 332, 354-357).

35. THOMAS FERRERS, Esq., (2nd son by (1)); d. 6 Jan. 1458/9; m. **ELIZABETH FREVILLE** (216-33), dau. of Sir Baldwin Freville, of Tamworth Castle, co. Warwick. (CP V chart 332, 357 note a).

36. SIR HENRY FERRERS, Knt., d. 28 Dec. 1500; m. Margaret Heckstall, dau. of Sir William Heckstall; their issue male still continued at Baddesy Clinton, co. Warwick, 1925. (CP V chart 332, 357 note a; Visitations of Warwick, 166).

37. ELIZABETH FERRERS, m. ca. 1508, James Clerke, gent., of Forde Hall, d. 20 Sep. 1553, son of John Clerke, of Ford, Kent. (Will of Sir Edward Ferrers dated 10 Jul. 1535, son of Sir Henry Ferrers and brother of Elizabeth (Ferrers) Clerke.) (CP V 357 note a; Visitations of Warwick and Kent).

38. GEORGE CLERKE, gent., b. 1510; d. 8 Mar. 1558; m. ca. 1533, Elizabeth Wilsford, dau. of Thomas Wilsford of Hartridge. (Will of Sir Edward Ferrers; Inq. p.m., 16 Oct. 1558).

39. JAMES CLERKE, gent., b. ca. 1540; d. 1614, of East Farleigh, Kent; will made 13 Jul. 1614; m. ca. 1566, Mary Saxby, dau. of Sir Edward Saxby, Baron of the Exchequer. (Visitations of Kent).

40. WILLIAM CLERKE, gent., of East Farleigh, Kent, and London; m. London, 10 Feb. 1598/9, Mary Weston, dau. of Sir Jerome Weston. (Parish Registers of East Farleigh and London).

41. JEREMY CLARKE, bapt. East Farleigh, Kent, 1 Dec. 1605; d. Newport, R.I., Nov. 1651; m. 1637, Frances (Latham) Dungan, dau. of Lewis Latham. (Generations 31 to 41; Justice: Jeremy Clarke, etc., 1922, pp. 34-35, corrected by CP; v. Redlich 154).

42. MARY CLARKE, m. Gov. John Cranston, of Rhode Island. See (220-42).

42. REV. JAMES CLARKE, b. Newport, R.I., 1649; ord. Newport, R.I., (2nd Bapt. Church), 1701; sett. Newport, 1700-1736; d. Newport, 1 Dec. 1736, ae. 87.

Line 12

30. MARGARET DE BOHUN (6-30), d. 1392, granddau. of Edward I, King of England, and Eleanor of Castile; m. 1325, **HUGH DE COURTENAY** (51-32), d. 1377, Earl of Devon. (CP IV 335).

31. ELIZABETH DE COURTENAY, d. 7 Aug. 1395; m. 1359, Sir Andrew Lutterell of Chilton, co. Devon. (Vivian 244, 537).

32. SIR HUGH LUTTERELL, of Dunster, co. Somerset, d. 24

17

Line 12 (cont.)

Mar. 1428; Privy Councillor to King Henry V; m. Catherine de Beaumont, d. 28 Aug. 1435, dau. of Sir John Beaumont, Knt. (Vivian 537).

33. ELIZABETH LUTTERELL, living 1439; m. (2) aft. 1423, John Stratton, Esq., of Lye Hall, Weston, co. Norfolk, living 1439. (Generations 30-33: Sir Henry Lyte: History of Dunster, Mohun and Lutterell; Bloomfield: History of Norfolk; Boston Evening Transcript, 19 Oct. 1926, 27 Feb. 1928, Note 4041; Ludlow-Brewster).

34. ELIZABETH STRATTON, living 1485; m. (1) Sir Thomas Backchurch; m. (2) John Andrews, Esq., of Bayleham, co. Suffolk. (Old-CP VIII 185; Banks I 466). By (2) she had

35. ELIZABETH ANDREWS, living 1485; m. Sir Thomas Windsor, d. 1485, of Stanwell, co. Middlesex. (CP XII, pt. 2, 792-794; Banks I 466).

36. SIR ANDREW WINDSOR, d. 1543, 1st Baron Windsor of Stanwell; m. **ELIZABETH BLOUNT** (59-39). (CP IX 337 note d; Old-CP VIII 185; Banks 1 466; Waters I 276; Berry: Buckinghamshire Pedigrees; Hoar: History of Wiltshire; Boston Evening Transcript, as above; v. Redlich 196-197; Colket in TAG 15: 129-143; CP XI 337 note a).

37. EDITH WINDSOR, m. George Ludlow, Esq., will pro. 4 Feb. 1580/1, of Hill Deverell, co. Wilts; Sheriff of Wiltshire, 1567; son of William and Jane (Moore) Ludlow. (Waters I 172-174, 275-276).

38. THOMAS LUDLOW, of Maiden Brailey, Dinton and Baycliffe, co. Wilts., buried at Dinton, 25 Nov. 1607, will pro. June 1608; m. Jane Pyle, dau. of Thomas Pyle. (Waters I 275-276).

39. ROGER LUDLOW, 3rd son, bapt. Dinton, 7 Mar. 1590; d. Dublin, Ireland, 1666; Balliol Coll., 1610; came to America 1630; Deputy-Governor of Mass., 1634, and of Conn.; m. Mary Cogan. (Waters I 275-276; Pedigree of Ludlow of Hill Deverell, 1884; v. Redlich 192, 197. Generations 35-39: Colket: The Royal Ancestry of the Ludlows, in TAG XV: 138-143; Seversmith: Ancestry of Roger Ludlow, all above generations).

40. SARAH LUDLOW, b. Fairfield, Conn., 1639; m. 1656, Rev. Nathaniel Brewster of Brookhaven, L.I. (Seversmith, cit. 2057).

39. GABRIEL LUDLOW, 2nd son (of #38), bapt. Dinton, 10 Feb. 1587; d. shortly after 1639; m. Phyllis whose will dated 12 Sep. 1657, pro. 18 Dec. 1657.

40. SARAH LUDLOW, b. ca. 1635; m. Col. John Carter of Virginia, and mother of Robert Carter, "King Carter of Corotoman". (Seversmith, cit. 2906-7).

Line 13

30. ELEANOR DE BOHUN (7-30), d. 7 Oct. 1363, granddau. of Edward I, King of England, and Eleanor of Castile; m. 1327, **JAMES BUTLER** (73-32), Earl of Ormond. (CP X 116-119).

31. PETRONILLA BUTLER, living 28 May 1365, dead 1368; m. as (1) wife by 8 Sept. 1352, **GILBERT TALBOT** (95-32), b. ca. 1332;

Line 13 (cont.)

d. 24 Apr. 1387, Lord Talbot, of Ecclesfield, co. Hereford; M.P. 1362. (CP IV 63,71, XII pt. 1, 614-617).

32. ELIZABETH TALBOT, m. Sir Henry de Grey, Lord Grey of Wilton. (CP IV 63-65, 71).

33. MARGARET DE GREY, d. 1 Jun. 1454; m. **JOHN DARCY** (88-35), b. ca. 1377; d. 9 Dec. 1411, 5th Baron Darcy of Knayth. (CP IV 63-65, 71).

34. JOHN DARCY, b. ca. 1400; d. 1458, 7th Baron Darcy; m. **JOAN GREYSTOKE** (62-36). (CP IV 71).

35. RICHARD DARCY, b. ca. 1424; d. bef. 1458; m. Eleanor Scrope, dau. of Sir John Scrope, Lord Scrope of Upsal, and Elizabeth Chaworth, dau. of Sir Thomas Chaworth of Wiverton, Notts. (CP IV 71).

36. SIR WILLIAM DARCY, b. 1443; d. 1488, 8th Baron Darcy; m. ca. 23 Jan. 1460/1, Eupheme Langton, dau. of John Langton of Farnley, co. York. (CP IV 71,73).

37. SIR THOMAS DARCY, K.G., b. ca. 1467; beheaded 30 Jun. 1537; cr. Baron, 1509; m. (1) Dowsabel Tempest, d. 1503/20, dau. of Sir Richard Tempest, of Giggleswick, co. York, and Mabel Strickland, dau. of **WALTER STRICKLAND** (41-33), of Sizergh. (CP IV 71).

38. SIR ARTHUR DARCY, of Brimham, co. York, b. ca. 1505; d. 3 Apr. 1561; m. Mary Carew, dau. of Sir Nicholas Carew of Beddington, co. Surrey. (CP IV 71).

39. SIR EDWARD DARCY, Knt., of Dartford, Kent, b. ca. 1543; d. 28 Oct. 1612; matric. Trinity Coll., Cambridge, 1561; M.P. 1584; knighted 1603; m. Elizabeth Astley, dau. of Thomas Astley, of Writtle, co. Essex. (TAG 21: 174).

40. ISABELLA DARCY, b. ca. 1600; d. London, 1669; will made May 1668, pro. 4 Aug. 1669, mentions "my dau. Mary Sherman"; m. (1) ca. 1619, John Launce, b. ca. 1597, of Penair, St. Clement's Parish, Cornwall, son of Robert and Susan (Tubb) Launce. (Waters II 1186-1187).

41. MARY LAUNCE, b. bef. 1625; d. Watertown, Mass., 9 Nov. 1710; m. ca. 1645, the Rev. John Sherman, ordained Watertown, 1647, d. Watertown, 8 Aug. 1685. (Generations 32-41: Given briefly and with slight errors in Your Family Tree, 1929, p. 184 which is not a reliable reference. This is a well known line, the paternity of Mary Launce being mentioned by Cotton Mather. The best account, by Donald L. Jacobus, may be seen in TAG 21: 169-177. Waters II 1186-1187; Weis: Colonial Clergy of N.E., p. 186).

Line 14

31. PETRONILLA BUTLER (13-31), great-granddau. of Edward I, King of England, and Eleanor of Castile; m. bef. 1316, **SIR GILBERT TALBOT** (95-32), Baron Talbot, d. 24 Apr. 1387. (CP XII pt. 1 345, 614-617).

32. SIR RICHARD TALBOT, b. ca. 1361; d. 7-9 Sep. 1396, Baron Talbot; m. bef. 1383, **ANKARET LE STRANGE** (8-33), b. 1361; d.

Line 14 (cont.)

1413, Baroness Strange. (CP XI 698; Old-CP VII 359-360).

33. MARY TALBOT, d. 13 Apr. 1433; m. Sir Thomas Greene, Knt., of Greene's Norton, co. Northampton; d. 14 Dec. 1417; Sheriff of Northamptonshire 1416.

34. SIR THOMAS GREENE, of Greene's Norton, b. Norton, 10 Feb. 1399/1400; d. 18 Jan. 1461-2; Sheriff of Northamptonshire 1454; m. (1) **PHILIPPA DE FERRERS** (61-35). (CP V 320 chart).

35. ELIZABETH GREENE, m. ca. 1440, William Raleigh, Esq., of Farnborough, Warwickshire, d. 1460. (Dugdale: Warwickshire, 382). See note at end of this pedigree.

36. SIR EDWARD RALEIGH, Knt., of Farnborough, b. ca. 1441; will pro. 20 Jun. 1509; Sheriff of Warwickshire and Leicestershire; m. 1467, Margaret Verney, dau. of Sir Ralph Verney, Lord Mayor of London. See (150-39). (Dugdale, op.cit. 382).

37. SIR EDWARD RALEIGH, Knt., of Farnborough, b. ca. 1470; d. ca. 1517; m. **ANNE CHAMBERLAYNE** (238-14), dau. of Richard Chamberlayne, of Sherburne, co. Oxford. (Dugdale 382-383).

38. BRIDGET RALEIGH, m. Sir John Cope, Knt., of Canons Abbey, co. Northampton; d. 22 Jan. 1558/9; Sheriff of Northamptonshire 1545; M.P. 1547; will 16 Aug. 1558. (VCH Warwick VI 115f.)

39. ELIZABETH COPE, m. John Dryden, Esq., of Canons Ashby, d. 3 Sep. 1584.

40. BRIDGET DRYDEN, b. ca. 1563; will made 12 Feb. 1644, adm. 2 Apr. 1645; m. ca. 1587, Rev. Francis Marbury, bapt. 27 Oct. 1555, d. ca. 1611, son of William and Agnes (Lenton) Marbury.

41. CATHERINE MARBURY, b. ca. 1610; d. Newport, R.I., 2 May 1687; m. Berkhampstead, Herts., 7 June 1632, Richard Scott, d. Providence, R.I., bef. Mar. 1681. (NEHGR 80: 12 chart).

41. ANNE MARBURY, bapt. 20 Jul. 1591; killed by the Indians, 1643; m. London, 9 Aug. 1612, William Hutchinson, bapt. Alford, Lincolnshire, 14 Aug. 1586; d. Boston, 1642, son of Edward Hutchinson. (Generations 31-41: v. Redlich 257-258; Meredith B. Colket, Jr.: Marbury Genealogy, 1936. Generations 39-41: White: Ancestry of John Barber White, 1913, pp. 151-152, 155-156; NEHGR 20: 283-284, 363-367; 98: chart opp. p. 18; see also Boston Evening Transcript, Note 5930, 28 Sep. 1927 and Note 1072, 6 Nov. 1935). Note: Questions have been raised regarding the paternity of Elizabeth Greene (gen. 35); At this time this matter has not been completely resolved.

Line 15

29. ELIZABETH PLANTAGENET (6-29), dau. of Edward I, King of England, and Eleanor of Castile; m. 1302, **HUMPHREY DE BOHUN VIII** (97-131), Earl of Hereford and Essex. (CP IV 669, X 118).

30. SIR WILLIAM DE BOHUN, K.G., b. 1310/1312; d. Sep. 1360; fought at Crécy; cr. Earl of Northampton, 16 Mar. 1336/7; m. (2) 1335/1338, **ELIZABETH DE BADLESMERE** (65-34). (CP I 245, 373

Line 15 (cont.)

note c, IV 669, IX 664-667).
    31. ELIZABETH DE BOHUN, d. 3 Apr. 1385; m. ca. 28 Sep. 1359, **RICHARD FITZ ALAN** (20-31, 60-33), b. 1346; beheaded 21 Sep. 1397, Earl of Arundel and Surrey. (CP I 244-245, IV 669).
    32. ELIZABETH FITZ ALAN, d. 8 Jul. 1425; m. (1) Sir William de Montagu; m. (2) Jul. 1384, Thomas de Mowbray, Duke of Norfolk, b. 22 Mar. 1365/6, d. Venice, 22 Sep. 1399; m. (3) bef. 19 Aug. 1401, Sir Robert Goushill, of Hoverington, Notts.; m. (4) bef. 3 Jul. 1414, Sir Gerard Usflete. (CP IX 604, XII pt. 1 604).
    33. ELIZABETH GOUSHILL, b. 1401/14; m. Sir Richard Wingfield of Letheringham. (CP IX 604 n; G.A. Moriarty in NEHGR 103: 95.
    34. ELIZABETH WINGFIELD, m. Sir William Brandon, Knt., fl. 1497. (DNB VI 218-22; NEHGR 102: 95).
    35. ELEANOR BRANDON, aunt of Charles Brandon, Duke of Suffolk; m. John Glemham of Glemham, co. Suffolk. (NEHGR 102: 95).
    36. ANNE GLEMHAM, m. Henry Pagrave, Esq., b. ca. 1470; d. 2 Oct. 1516, of Little Pagrave and Thruxton, Norfolk; son of John and Margaret (Yelverton) Pagrave. (Palgrave Memorials, 16; NEHGR 102: 95).
    37. THOMAS PAGRAVE, gent., b. 1505/10, of Thruxton; m. Alice Gunton, dau. of Robert Gunton of Thruxton. (NEHGR 102: 95).
    38. THE REVEREND EDWARD PALGRAVE, bapt. Thruxton, 21 Jan. 1540/1; d. Dec. 1623; Rector of Barnham Broom, 1567-1623; name of wife unknown. (Palgrave Memorials, 140; NEHGR 102: 96).
    39. DR. RICHARD PALGRAVE, b. ca. 1585; d. Oct. 1651; m. Anna, d. Roxbury, 17 Feb. 1669; physician at Wymondham, Norfolk, and Charlestown, Mass., 1630; frm. 18 May 1631. (NEHGR 102: 97).
    40. MARY PALGRAVE, m. ca. 1637, Roger Wellington of Watertown; ancestors of Roger Sherman, the Signer of the Declaration of Independence, 1776. (NEHGR 102: 97).
    40. SARAH PALGRAVE, m. ca. 1648, John Alcock (Harvard Coll., 1646), physician at Roxbury.
    40. ELIZABETH PALGRAVE, m. ca. 1651, Joshua Edwards, of Boston. (This line through John Glemham of Glemham to Edward I was given in the Boston Evening Transcript, 12 Feb. 1930, Note 9665; and Jan. 1928, Note 6455; TAG 25: 24-26).

Line 16

    28. EDWARD I (1-28), King of England, m. as his (2) wife, **MARGUERITE OF FRANCE** (155-30), dau. of Philip III, King of France. (CP V 736; CCN 353; Weever 775).
    29. THOMAS PLANTAGENET, "of Brotherton," b. 1 Jun. 1300; d. 1338, Earl of Norfolk; m. Alice Halys, dau. of Sir Roger de Hales. (CP XI 609; Weever 775).
    30. MARGARET PLANTAGENET, d. 24 Mar. 1398/9, Duchess of Norfolk; m. John de Segrave, Baron Segrave, d. 20 Mar. 1353. (CP XI 609-610; Weever 775).

Line 16 (cont.)

31. ELIZABETH DE SEGRAVE, b. 25 Oct. 1338; m. John de Mowbray, d. Thrace, 1368, 4th Baron Mowbray, crusader, son of John de Mowbray, 3rd Baron Mowbray, d. 1361, and **JOAN PLANTAGENET** (18-30), great-granddau. of Henry III, King of England. (CP XI 610; Weever 775).

32. SIR THOMAS MOWBRAY, K.G., b. 22 Mar. 1365/6; d. Venice, 22 Sep. 1399, Lord Mowbray, Segrave and Stourton; cr. Earl of Nottingham 1383, Earl Marshall of England 1384, Duke of Norfolk 1397; m. 1384, **ELIZABETH FITZ ALAN** (15-32). (CP I 253, IV 670, IX 601-604; Weever 775 for above gens.).

33. MARGARET DE MOWBRAY, m. ca. 1420, Sir Robert Howard, K.G., b. ca. 1383; d. 1436, of Stoke-by-Nayland, Suffolk. (CP I 253, IX 610-612).

34. SIR JOHN HOWARD, K.G., slain at Bosworth Field, 22 Aug. 1485; cr. Duke of Norfolk, 1483; m. (2) Margaret (Wyfold) Norreys. (CP I 253, IX 610-612).

35. KATHERINE HOWARD, d. 12 Mar. 1535-7 (half sister of Sir Thomas Howard, 2nd Duke of Norfolk); m. **SIR JOHN BOURCHIER,** K.B. (4-35), 2nd Lord Berners, d. 19 Mar. 1532; will made 3 Mar. 1532; translator of Froissart's Chronicles. (CP II 154; CCN 175; Berry: Berkshire Pedigrees 55).

Line 16A

30. MARGARET DE CLARE (9-30), b. ca. 1292; d. Apr. 1342; m. (1) 1 Nov. 1307, Piers de Gaveston, b. ca. 1284 (prob. son of Sir Ernaud de Gaveston by Clarmunda de Marsau et de Louvigny), cr. Earl of Cornwall, executed 19 Jun. 1312. She m. (2) 28 Apr. 1317, Hugh de Audley. (TAG 35: 100-106, 245; 37: 45-51; 40: 95-99, 253).

31. AMY DE GAVESTON, damsel of the Chamber to Queen Philippa, b. soon aft. 6 Jan. 1312; m. in or bef. 1334, John de Driby, son of Robert of Wokefield, Berks, d. aft. 30 Nov. 1357. (His desc. from Henry I shown in TAG 37: 50).

32. ALICE DE DRIBY, b. ca. 1340; d. 12 Oct. 1412; will as Alicia Basset de Bytham, Apr. 1412, pro. 26 Oct. 1412, Inq.p.m. 1413 #15; m. (1) Sir Ralph Basset, Lord Basset of Sapcote, d. 17 Jul. 1378, issue; m. (2) Sir Robert Tochet, no issue; m. (3) Sir Anketil Mallory, kt., of Kirkby Mallory, co. Leics., d. 26 Mar. 1393 (4 chn.). (TAG op.cit.) (Order of 1st two mars. uncertain.)

33. SIR WILLIAM MALLORY of Shawbury, 2nd son (by 3rd mar.). b. ca. 1385, d. 1445, prob. at Shelton, Beds., or at Papworth; m. (1) unknown wife (perh. a Papworth desc.); m. (2) Margaret, who may have been a relative of Giles de Erdington. (TAG op.cit.)

34. MARGARET MALLORY, b. ca. 1397; d. 1438 (Inq.p.m. 17 Hen. VI), dau. by unknown 1st wife; m. **ROBERT CORBET** (29B-33) of Moreton Corbet. (TAG op.cit.)

27. **HENRY III** (1-27), King of England, b. 1 Oct. 1207; d. Westminster, 16 Nov. 1272; m. Canterbury, Jan. 1236, **ELEANOR OF PROVENCE** (111-30), b. 1217, d. Amesbury, 25 Jun. 1291. (CP V 736).

28. **EDMUND PLANTAGENET,** "Crouchback," b. London, 16 Jan. 1244/5; d. Bayonne, 5 Jun. 1296; cr. Earl of Lancaster and Leicester, and High Steward of England, 26 Oct. 1265; M.P. 1276; m. (2) 1276, **BLANCHE OF ARTOIS** (45-30), d. Paris, 2 May 1302. (CP I 244).

29. **HENRY PLANTAGENET,** b. 1281, d. 22 Sep. 1345; cr. Earl of Lancaster, 10 May 1324; M.P. 1298/9; m. bef. 2 Mar. 1296/7 **MAUD DE CHAWORTH** (72-32), living 1345. (CP I 244, II 61, VII 156).

30. **ELEANOR PLANTAGENET,** d. at Arundel, 11 Jan. 1372; m. (1) bef. Jun. 1337, **JOHN DE BEAUMONT** (114-31), b. 1318, d. May 1342, Earl of Buchan, Lord Beaumont; knighted 2 May 1338; M.P. 1342; son of Henry, Lord Beaumont and **ALICE COMYN OF BUCHAN** (114A-29); m. (2) Ditton, 5 Feb. 1344/5, **RICHARD FITZ ALAN** (60-32), b. c. 1313, d. 1376, Earl of Arundel and Warenne. (CP I 243-244, II 60-61, IV 670).

31. **HENRY BEAUMONT,** Lord Beaumont, b. 1340, d. 17 Jun. 1369; m. as (1) husb., **MARGARET DE VERE** (79-32), d. 15 Jun. 1398, bur. Gray Friars with 3rd husb., dau. of John de Vere, 7th Earl of Oxford and Maud de Badlesmere; she m. (2) Sir Nicholas Lovain as his (2) wife (Gov. Thomas Dudley is a descendant of this marriage. See Line 79), and m. (3) 17 Jun. 1379, Sir John Devereux, Lord Devereux, d. 22 Feb. 1392/3. (CP II 60-61, IV 296-9; Gen.Mag. 15: 251-5, 284-92).

32. **JOHN BEAUMONT,** K.G., b. ca. 1361; d. Stirling, 9 Sep. 1396, Lord Beaumont; knighted 23 Apr. 1377; Warden of the West Marches towards Scotland, 1389, 1396, Admiral of the North Sea, Constable of Dover Castle and Lord Warden of the Cinque Ports, 1392; K.G., 1393; m. Catherine Everingham, d. 1426, dau. of Thomas Everingham, of Laxton, Nottinghamshire. (CP II 61).

33. **HENRY BEAUMONT,** K.B., b. ca. 1380; d. Jun. 1413, Lord Beaumont; cr. K.B. 1400; commissioner for peace in France 1410-1411; m. Elizabeth Willoughby, d. ca. 12 Nov. 1428, dau. of William, Lord Willoughby, and Lucy Strange, dau. of Roger, Lord Strange of Knokin. (CP II 61).

34. **SIR HENRY BEAUMONT,** b. 1411, d. bef. 1447/8; m. (2) Joan Heronville, dau. of Henry Heronville.

35. **SIR HENRY BEAUMONT,** Knt., of Wednesbury, d. 16 Nov. 1471, Sheriff of Staffordshire, 1471; m. **ELEANOR SUTTON** (221-37).

36. **CONSTANCE BEAUMONT,** b. ca. 1467; m. John Mitton (or Mytton), Sheriff of Staffordshire, M.P., son of **JOHN MYTTON,** Esq. (98-36), and Anne Swinnerton.

37. **JOYCE MITTON,** b. ca. 1487; m. by 1505/6, John Harpersfield of London.

Line 17 (cont.)

38. EDWARD HARPERSFIELD alias **MITTON**, Esq., of Weston-under-Lizard; m. 1530, Anne Skrimshire.

39. KATHERINE MITTON, m. Roger Marshall, merchant, of Shrewsbury, d. 4 Aug. 1612 (GS). Libby & Noyes I 340; NEHGR 101: 88-91).

40. ELIZABETH MARSHALL, d. bef. 1640; m. St. Chad's Shrewsbury, 29 Aug. 1618, Thomas Lewis, b. Shrewsbury, ca. 1590, emigrated to New England, lived at Saco, Maine by 1631, d. bef. 1640, son of Andrew and Mary (Herring) Lewis of Shrewsbury, Salop. Libby & Noyes I 430).

41. MARY LEWIS, bapt. 28 Jun. 1619; m. aft. 10 May 1638, the Rev. Richard Gibson, A.M., of Portsmouth, N.H. Libby & Noyes I 430, 259; Weis: Colonial Clergy of N.E., 91-92).

41. JUDITH LEWIS (sister of Mary above), bapt. 23 Oct. 1626; m. ca. 1646, James Gibbins of Saco. (Generations 34-38: Walter Goodwin Davis in TAG 19: 12-15. Generations 39-41: NEHGR 101: 16-23, 88-91. See also Walter Goodwin Davis: The Ancestry of Nicholas Davis (1956), 118-125, 137-188, includes many additional noble lines.)

Line 18

29. HENRY PLANTAGENET (17-29), m. 1298, **MAUD DE CHAWORTH** (72-32).

30. JOAN PLANTAGENET, m. John de Mowbray, 3rd Baron Mowbray, d. 1361, son of John de Mowbray, Knt., hanged at York, 1321; 2nd Baron Mowbray, Baron Gower and Brember, Governor of the City of York and of Scarborough Castle, Sheriff of York, son of Roger de Mowbray, 1st Baron Mowbray of Axholme, d. 1296, buried at Fountains Abbey, son of Roger de Mowbray, d. 1266, son of William de Mowbray, d. 1222, Baron of Axholme, Magna Charta Surety, 1215. (See also 16-31).

31. ALINORE MOWBRAY, m. as (3) wife, bef. 23 Jul. 1358, Roger la Warre, Baron de la Warre, b. 30 Nov. 1326, d. Gascony, 27 Aug. 1370, son of John la Warre, d. shortly bef. 24 Jun. 1331, and **MARGARET DE HOLAND** (47B-31), d. Aug. 1349, dau. of Sir Robert de Holand, first Lord Holand. John la Warre (d. 1331) was the son of John, Baron de la Warre, d. 9 May 1347, and **JOAN GRELLE** (99-31). (CP IV 144-147, VII 453-454, chart 452-453).

32. JOAN LA WARRE, d. 24 Apr. 1404; m. 1390, Sir Thomas West, 3rd Baron West of Oakhanger, Northampton, son of Sir Thomas West and Alice Fitz Herbert. (CP IV 152).

33. SIR REYNOLD DE WEST, Baron de la Warre, b. 7 Sep. 1395; d. 27 Aug. 1450; m. (1) bef. 17 Feb. 1428/9, Margaret Thorley, d. bef. 24 Nov. 1433, dau. of Robert and Anne (Lisle) Thorley. (CP IV 152-154).

34. SIR RICHARD WEST, 2nd Baron de la Warre, b. ca. 28 Oct. 1430; d. 10 Mar. 1475/6; m. bef. 10 Jun. 1451, Katherine Hungerford, d. 12 May 1493, dau. of Sir Robert Hungerford and Margaret Botreaux, dau. Sir William Botreaux, M.P. 1455-1472. (CP IV 154-155).

Line 18 (cont.)

35. SIR THOMAS WEST, K.G., 3rd Baron de la Warre, b. 1457, d. 11 Oct. 1525; m. ? (1) Elizabeth Bonville, gr.niece of William Lord Bonville ?, m. (2) Eleanor Copley, dau. of Sir Roger Copley and Ann Hoo, of Roughway, Sussex; knighted 18 Jan. 1477/8; M.P. 1482-1523; K.G. 11 May 1510. (CP IV 155-156, 159). Son by (2) -

36. SIR GEORGE WEST, of Warbelton, Sussex, d. 1538; m. Elizabeth Morton, dau. of Sir Robert Morton of Lechlade, co. Gloucester. (CP IV 159).

37. SIR WILLIAM WEST, Lord Delaware, b. ca. 1520, d. Wherwell, co. Northampton, 30 Dec. 1595; m. bef. 1555, Elizabeth Strange, dau. of Thomas Strange of Chesterton, co. Gloucester. (CP IV 158-159).

38. SIR THOMAS WEST, 2nd Lord Delaware, b. ca. 1556; d. 24 Mar. 1601/2; m. 19 Nov. 1571, **ANNE KNOLLYS** (1-38). He was M.P. 1571-1593; knighted 7 Dec. 1587. (CP IV 159-160; NEHGR 33: 286-291; Chester: Herbert Pelham, His Ancestors and Descendants. Generations 31-38: Baines: History of Lancashire, I 276-277; CP VII chart between pp. 452-453).

Line 19

29. HENRY PLANTAGENET (17-29), m. 1298, **MAUD DE CHAWORTH** (72-32).

30. MARY PLANTAGENET, b. 1320; ae. 14 yrs. at marriage; d. 1 Sep. 1362; m. Sep. 1334, **HENRY DE PERCY** (161-30), b. 1320, d. ca. 18 May 1368; fought at Crecy, 26 Aug. 1346. (CP I 244, X 462-463).

31. HENRY DE PERCY, K.G., b. 10 Nov. 1341, d. 19 Feb. 1407/8, 1st Earl Percy of Northumberland, 6 Jul. 1377, Lord Marshal of England; m. (1) 12 Jul. 1358, **MARGARET DE NEVILLE** (186-6), d. May 1372, widow of William de Ros of Helmsley. (CP IX 708-714, X 464).

32. SIR HENRY PERCY, K.G., "Harry Hotspur," slain at Shrewsbury, 1403; m. bef. 10 Dec. 1379, **ELIZABETH MORTIMER** (5-33). (CP IX 714, X 464).

33. SIR HENRY PERCY, K.G., b. 3 Feb. 1392/3, slain at St. Albans, 22 May 1455, Earl of Northumberland, Warden of the Marches of Scotland; m. **ELEANOR NEVILLE** (3-33), d. 1463. (CP X 464; Collins IV 84-91).

Line 20

30. ELEANOR PLANTAGENET (DE LANCASTER) (17-30), great-granddau. of King Henry III, d. 1372; m. Ditton, 5 Feb. 1344/5, **SIR RICHARD FITZ ALAN** (60-32), b. c. 1313, d. 24 Jan. 1375/6, Earl of Arundel and Warenne. (CP I 243-244, IV 670).

31. SIR RICHARD FITZ ALAN, K.G., b. 1346; beheaded, 1397, 10th Earl of Arundel and Surrey; m. **ELIZABETH DE BOHUN** (15-31), d. 1385, great-granddau. of Edward I, King of England, and Eleanor of Castile. (CP I 242-244, 253, IV 670 chart, IX 604).

Line 20 (cont.)

32. ELIZABETH FITZ ALAN, d. 1425; m. (3) as his 4th wife, Sir Robert Goushill, of Hoveringham, Notts. (CP I 253; IV 205; IX 604; Banks I 415; DNB 54: 75).

33. JOAN GOUSHILL, living 1460; m. **SIR THOMAS STANLEY,** K.G. (57-36), b. in or bef. 1405, d. 11 Feb 1458/9, Lord Stanley of Lathom and Knowsley; M.P. 1432; K.G. 1456; Lord Lieutenant of Ireland. (CP IV 205; Collins III 61: DNB 54: 75; VCH Lanc. I 345-349; CP XII pt. 1, pp. 250-251).

34. MARGARET STANLEY, m. (1) 1459, Sir William Troutbeck, Knt., b. ca. 1432, d. 1459, of Dunham-on-the-Hill, co. Chester; m. (2) 1460, **SIR JOHN BOTELER** (46-36), of Bewsey in Warrington, d. 26 Feb. 1463; m. (3) Lord Grey of Codnor. (CP IV 205; VCH Lanc. I 345-349).

35. ADAM TROUTBECK, d. bef. 1510, of Mobberly, co. Chester; m. Margaret Boteler, Warrington, co. Lanc.

36. MARGARET TROUTBECK, b. ca. 1492, d. aft. 1521; m. **SIR JOHN TALBOT** (7-36). (CP XI 717, 731 chart; Old-CP VII 147).

Line 21

30. ELEANOR DE LANCASTER (17-30), great-granddau. of King Henry III; m. **SIR RICHARD FITZ ALAN** (60-32). (CP I 243-244; IV 670).

31. SIR JOHN FITZ ALAN, Lord Arundel, d. 1379, Marshal of England, Lord Maltravers; M.P. 1377-1379; m. 17 Feb. 1358/9, **ELEANOR MALTRAVERS** (59-34), b. 1345, d. 10 Jan. 1404/5. (CP I 253, 259; VIII 585; XI 102-103).

32. SIR JOHN FITZ ALAN, of Arundel, b. 30 Nov. 1364, d. 14 Aug. 1390; m. bef. 1387, **ELIZABETH DESPENSER** (74-35). (CP I 253, 260; V 736; XI 102-103; Banks I 378).

33. MARGARET FITZ ALAN of Arundel, sister of Sir John (gen. 32) and dau. of Sir John (Gen. 31) and Eleanor, d. 1438; m. 1394, **SIR WILLIAM ROS,** K.G. (9-33), Lord Ros, d. 1414. (CP XI 102-103; Banks I 378).

Line 22

33. MARGARET MOWBRAY (16-33), descendant of **JOAN PLANTAGENET** (18-30), great-granddau. of King Henry III of England, and of **ELEANOR DE SEGRAVE** (16-31), great-granddau. of Edward I, King of England, and Eleanor of Castile; m. ca. 1420, Sir Robert Howard, K.G., b. ca. 1383, d. 1436, of Stoke-by-Nayland, Suffolk. (CP I 253; IX 610-612).

34. SIR JOHN HOWARD, K.G., slain at Bosworth Field, 22 Aug. 1485, Lord Howard; cr. Duke of Norfolk, 23 Jun. 1483, Earl Marshal; m. (1) 1440, Catherine Moleyns, d. Stoke-by-Nayland, 3 Nov. 1465, dau. of Sir William Moleyns of Stoke Poges, Bucks. (CP IX 610-612).

35. SIR THOMAS HOWARD, b. 1443, d. 21 May 1524; cr. Earl of Surrey, 28 Jun. 1483; cr. Earl Marshal, 10 Jul. 1510; Duke of Norfolk, 1 Feb. 1513/4; m. (1) 30 Apr. 1472, Elizabeth (Tilney)

Bourchier, d. 4 Apr. 1497, widow of Sir Humphrey Bourchier, and dau. of Sir Frederick Tylney, of Ashwellthorpe, co. Norfolk. (CP IX 612-615; Banks I 360).

36. ELIZABETH HOWARD, d. 3 Apr. 1537; m. by 1506, SIR THOMAS BOLEYN, K.G. (120-39), b. ca. 1477, d. 12 Mar. 1538/9, Earl of Wiltshire and Earl of Ormond. (CP II 146; X 137-140; XII pt. 2, 739; Banks I 360).

37. MARY BOLEYN (sister of Queen Anne, wife of King Henry VIII), d. 30 Jul. 1543; m. 31 Jan. 1520/1, WILLIAM CARY (1-36). (CP II 146; Banks I 360 pedigree; see also Meredith B. Colket, Jr., in TAG 18: 211-218, for full details).

Line 23

33. JOAN GOUSHILL (20-33), descendant of King Henry III and King Edward I; m. SIR THOMAS STANLEY, K.B. (57-36). (CP IV 205).

34. ELIZABETH STANLEY, sister of Thomas Stanley, first Earl of Derby; m. bef. 1432, Sir Richard Molyneux of Sefton, Lancashire, d. Blore Heath, 23 Sep. 1459, Chief Forester of the forests and parks of West Derbyshire. (VCH Lanc. III 69-70).

35. SIR THOMAS MOLYNEUX, Knt., eldest son, knight banneret; d. 12 Jul 1483; m. ca. 11 Jul 1463, ANNE DUTTON (27-38), d. 22 Oct. 1520, dau. of Sir Thomas Dutton of Dutton. (VCH Lanc. III 69-70).

36. SIR WILLIAM MOLYNEUX, lord of the manor of Sefton, 1483-1548, eldest son and heir, b. 1481, d. 1548; m. (1) Jane Rugge, only dau. and heir of Sir John Rugge of Shropshire. (VCH Lanc. III 69-70).

37. SIR RICHARD MOLYNEUX, Knt., of Sefton, lord of the manor of Sefton, 1548-1568; d. 3 Jan. 1568/9; Sheriff of Lancashire 1566-1568; m. (1) ELEANOR RADCLIFFE (36-39), dau. of Sir Alexander Radcliffe of Ordsall; they were the ancestors of Richard Molyneux, Viscount Molyneux of Maryborough. (Generations 33-37: VCH Lanc. III 69-70; Baines: History of Lancashire II, 390).

38. ALICE MOLYNEUX, d. 11 May 1581; m. James Prescott, gent. d. 1 Mar. 1583, eldest son of James Prescott and ALICE STANDISH (34-40); purchased the manors of Driby and Sutterby, Lincolnshire, 1579/80; transferred them to trustees. (Inq.p.m. James Prescott, gent., of Driby, 1583, No. 185 and Pedigree of James Prescott, gent., and Alice Molyneux, John Prescott, Esq., and Elizabeth Manby, James Prescott, gent., and Mary Copland, by the Rev. W.O. Massingberd, Rector of Ormsby with Driby, co. Lincoln, 21 Mar. 1901, in Frederick L. Weis: The Families of Standish of Standish and Prescott of Prescott of Standish Parish, Lancashire, England (typed ms.) 1948, 205 pp. (at the American Antiquarian Society, Worcester, Mass.) pp. 58-60, 65-67; White: Ancestry of John Barber White, Haverhill, 1913, p. 123; brass effigies in Driby church with inscription and arms of Prescott and Molyneux; F.L. Weis: The Descent of John Prescott, Founder of Lancaster, Massachusetts,

1645, From Alfred the Great, King of England, 870-901 Clinton, 1948, Part III p. 8).

39. JOHN PRESCOTT, Esq., of Driby, son and heir, 1583, b. ca. 1576; d. soon bef. 1617; m. Elizabeth Manby, dau. of Francis, Esq. and Anne Manby, of Elsham; she m. (2) Edward Willoughby, 3rd son of Lord Willoughby of Parham. "I, Anne Manby, of Driby, widow, to my dau. Willoughby, to Anne Prescott, my grandchild, to James Prescott, my grandchild . . . My daughter Willoughby oweth me ь, lent her in the time of her widowhood." Will made 12 Jan. 1609; pro. at Lincoln, 15 May 1612. (Maddison's Wills, 2nd Series, p. 64).

40. JAMES PRESCOTT, of Driby, gent., younger brother of Sir William Prescott, Knt.; mentioned in the will of his grandmother, 1609; m. Mary Copland, dau. of John Copland of Ross, co. Herts. He had a son James bp. at Driby in 1643.

* * *

41. JAMES PRESCOTT, d. Kingston, N.H., 23 Nov. 1728, ae. 85 yrs.; m. Mary Boulter, b. Exeter, N.H., 15 May 1648, d. Kingston, N.H., 4 Oct. 1735, ae. 87 yrs., dau. of Nathaniel and Grace (Swain) Boulter. He sett. Hampton, N.H., 1665, and Kingston, N.H., 1694, where he was the chairman of the first board of selectmen. Depositions place his birthdate as about 1648. See TAG 34: 180-181. James Prescott the colonist is neither proven nor disproven as the James bp at Driby in 1643. (Generations 37-41: Weis, op.cit., Part III, p. 8; Prescott Memorial, 1870, pp. 30-35, 225-232; Rev. John Holding (of Stotford, Baldock, Herts.): Pedigree of Prescott of Prescott, 1902 (in the Lancaster Collection, Lancaster Town Library, Lancaster, Mass.); Weis, typed ms. cited above, pp. 43-49, 53-54, 58-60, 64-67, 75-76, 82-83, 89; Noyes, Libby & Davis: Genealogical Dict. of Me. and N.H., II 568).

Line 24: Omitted. No longer acceptable.

Line 25 (Revised & expanded by Douglas Richardson. This corrects and replaces much of what has been printed in earlier editions.)

26. WILLIAM DE TRACY (222-26), b. aft. 1090, d. shortly aft. 1135, by unknown wife had

27. N.N. de TRACY (called Eva in Devon & Cornwall N&Q xix 194-201 but this is perhaps an error for her niece, Eva or Emma de Tracy, who mar. Warin de Bassingbourne), m. say 1165, Gervase de Courtenay who was probably closely related to **REGINALD DE COURTENAY** (138-25) as both families gave grants to Tor Abbey and Ford Abbey (the latter abbey having the Countenay family as its chief patron). Gervase de Courtenay and his wife had two identifiable children, Hugh de Courtenay (who had control of his uncle Sir William de Tracy's barony of Bradninch, Devon in the latter part of the 1190s) and William de Tracy (living 1198-1199). This 2nd son William de Tracy is perhaps identical with the William de Tracy

who was holding the manor of Bradford Tracy, (East) Spreweye and
Ivedon, Devon in 1242-3. Besides these two sons there may have
been a third son, Oliver (No. 28 below) but the evidence does not
prove or disprove it. (Book of Fees, pt. II, pp. 759 & 792; George
Oliver, Monasticon Dioecesis Exoniensis, pp. 183, 187, 338, 346, 347;
Devon & Cornwall N & Q xix 194-201; Calendar of Documents
Preserved in France, ed. Round, I: 194-195; Curia Regis Rolls, 12:
440, 13: 137-138, 247, 287, 364-385, 395).

28. OLIVER DE TRACY, possibly s. of the above couple,
perhaps identical with the Oliver de Tracy who witnessed a charter
dated about 1185-1191, granted by Hugh de Courtenay who is
mentioned above. In 1199 Oliver was granted the manor of
Bremridge, Devon, which he held of the honour of Barnstaple. In
1242-3 he was also holding the manor of Wollacombe (later called
Wollacombe Tracy), Devon which fee he held of the honour of
Bradninch, Devon. These two land holdings tend to suggest he was
either closely related to the Tracy family who held the honour of
Branstaple or else that he was closely related to the Tracy family
who held the honour of Bradninch. Circumstantial evidence would
lean toward the latter position as Oliver's descendants differenced
their Tracy coat of arms with a label of azure which label is a
remarkable feature of the Courtenays coat of arms. This heraldic
evidence such as it is would suggest that Oliver was likely a son of
Gervase de Courtenay and his wife (nee Tracy) above. (Devon &
Cornwall N & Q cit. xix 194-201; Calendar of Documents Preserved
in France, ed. Round, I: 194-195).

29. HENRY DE TRACY, held Wollacombe and Bremridge,
Devon in 1284. (Devon & Cornwall Notes & Queries cit.)

30. ISABELLA DE TRACY, dau. & event. h., born say 1275-80;
m. (1) Herbert Marcis (or le Mareys), m. (2) by 1303 Simon Roges or
Fitz Rogus of Porlock, held manor of Huntshaw, d. sh. bef. 22 July
1306 (Inq.p.m. Edw. I, IV 238-239), m. (3) Edmond Botiler (divorced);
m. (4) Sir John Stowford, living 1346, a noted judge. (Devon &
Cornwall N&Q cit.; Feudal Aids I: 418; Cal. Inq.p.m., Edw. I, IV: 238-
239; Pole's Collections towards a Description of Devon, pp. 420-421).

31. JOAN STOWFORD, dau. by (4), and event h. to Wollacombe
Tracy; m. Sir William Fitz Warin of Brightleigh, Devon, living 1363.
(Devon & Cornwall N & Q cit.; VCH Somerset III: 62-63 (manor of
Aller, Somerset, a Stowford property); Pole ibid.).

32. SIR JOHN FITZ WARIN (also known as John de Brightley), d.
1407, m. by 12 Nov. 1375 Agnes de Merton, b. 1 Dec. 1359, d. by 29
Nov. 1412, dau. & coh. of Sir Richard de Merton by his first wife,
Margaret. (VCH Somerset ibid.; Cal. Inq.p.m. Edw. III, XIII: 242-243,
XIV: 175-176; Register of Bishop Edmund Stafford, p. 187; Pole op.
cit., pp. 380, 420-421).

33. ISABEL (or Isabella) **DE BRIGHTLEY**, dau. & h., d. 21 Oct.
1466; m. (1) by 22 Nov. 1408, Robert Cornu, lord of Thornbury,
Devon, son of Walter and Constance; m. (2) aft. 1420, John Cobleigh
of Brightley in the parish of Chittlehampton, Devon. He m. (2)
Joanna (perh. a Pyre) who d. 1480 (Harleian MS 1538 fo. 154b

indicates that Isabel de Brightley had no issue by her marriage to Cobleigh but that she gave "all her inheritance of Brightly unto her husband and his heirs forever."). Isabel did have two sons by her marriage to Robert Cornu, namely Nicholas and William Cornu. At William Cornu's death in 1491, his heir was found to be his distant Cornu cousin John Speccot and no mention is made of any Cobleigh relations. In the time period 1486-1493 a chancery court case was filed which involved William Cornu's heirs John Speccot, Richard Pollard and William Willesford. Again, no Cobleigh is mentioned as being a party to this action. Therefore it would seem that Isabel did in fact have no issue by her Cobleigh marriage. That this is likely can be construed from Pole's statements that after Isabel's Cornu sons died without issue, her third share in the Merton estates passed on to her Stowell cousins. That such a transfer took place underscores that Isabel had issue only by her Cornu marriage. Although Isabel's memorial brass proves she married both Cornu and Cobleigh, Pole states that Cobleigh actually married Isabel's cousin, another Isabel de Brightley who was granddaughter or great-granddaughter of No. 31 above. If true, this could explain how only the Tracy, Stowford and Brightley lands came into the Cobleigh family and not the Merton lands. At the present time, there is no known corroborative evidence for this second Isabel de Brightley's existence except for the fact that the Brightley coat of arms was quartered by later Cobleigh descendants. The quartering would typically represent the marriage of a Cobleigh ancestor with a Brightly heiress; however, in this case, the Brightley arms might have been quartered on the basis of the Cobleighs being "representatives" of the Brightley Family due to the transfer of the Brightley estates into the Cobleigh family. In any case, this line would appear to break at this point until further research sheds more light on this family. If two Isabel de Brightley's did exist, it is obviously possible that both could have married John Cobleigh. If this is the case, it would appear that the second Isabel was John Cobleigh's first wife followed by her cousin, Isabel, widow of Cornu. (Pole, ibid., Register of Bishop Edmund Stafford; Devon N&Q I: 210-214; DA 34: 689-695; List of Early Chancery Proceedings Vol. III (Lists & Indexes no. XX), p. 103; Cal. Inq.p.m. Henry VII, I: 289-290).

* * *

34. JOHN COBLEIGH, perhaps a son by the second Isabel de Brightley mentioned above, b. say 1445, d. 1492 per the Inq.p.m. held on his estates; m. by 1479 Alice Cockworthy, dau. of John Cockworthy of Yarnscombe, Devon, Escheator of Devon, by his w. Thomasine, dau. Sir John Chichester. Alice almost certainly m. (2) John Fortescue of Spridleston in the parish of Brixton, Devon, d. 1537, by whom she had further issue. John Fortescue was uncle to Jane Fortescue below who m. Alice's son, John Cobleigh (No. 35). (Devon & Cornwall N&Q ibid., also XIII 42-44; Devonshire

Line 25 (cont.)

Association, ibid.; Thomas (Fortescue), Lord Clermont, History of the Family of Fortescue (1886); Vivian's Visitation of Devon, p. 353).

35. JOHN COBLEIGH, b. ca. 1479 (age 13 in 1492); m. (1) by 1502, **JANE FORTESCUE** (246F-37), dau. of William Fortescue of Pruteston or Preston in Ermington, Devon, d. 1 Feb. 1519/20 & wife Elizabeth, dau. & coh. Richard Champernoun of Inworthy, Cornwall (see Thomas Fortescue, History of the Family of Fortescue (1886) pp. 1-9.). Jane died by 12 May 1527, and he m. (2) Elizabeth Owpye, wid. He d. 24 Oct. 1540, Elizabeth surv., Inq.p.m. 33 Hen. VIII (1546) shows he held manors of Brightley, Stowford, Snape, Bremridge, Stowford Carder & Nymet St. George. (DA 34:619-692; Vivian, Visitations of Devon, pp. 353 & 357).

36. MARGARET COBLEIGH of Brightley, b. ca. 1502, d. 1547, Inq.p.m. 15 Oct. 1547, seized of the manors of Brightley, Stowford, Snape, Wollacombe Tracy, Bremridge, Nymet St. George; m. Sir Roger Giffard of Halsbury, son of Thomas of Halsbury, Inq.p.m. 1513. (DA cit. 34:692-693, 689, 679; Wm.Salt Soc. NS V 34, 32, 29).

37. JANE GIFFARD, d. 1596, will pro. 16 Apr. 1596; m. **AMYAS CHICHESTER** (52-41), b. 1527, d. 4 Jul. 1577. (Chichester: History of the Family of Chichester from 1086 to 1870, pp. 32, 77-80; Vivian: Visitations of Devon, 397, 400; Bolton: Ancestry of Margaret Wyatt, chart; NEHGR 51: 214).

Line 26

26. JOHN (1-26), King of England, 1199-1216. (CP V 736).

27. RICHARD FITZ ROY (natural son of King John), m. Rohese, d. 1264/5, dau. of Fulbert of Dover. (CP II 127).

28. ISABEL, d. 7 Jul. 1276; m. ca. 12 Jul. 1247, Maurice de Berkeley, b. 1218, d. 4 Apr. 1281, 6th Lord Berkeley. (CP II 127).

29. SIR THOMAS DE BERKELEY, d. 23 Jul. 1321; m. 1267, **JOAN DE FERRERS** (59-30), d. 19 Mar. 1309/10. (CP II 127-128).

30. SIR MAURICE DE BERKELEY, d. 1326, Lord Berkeley of Berkeley Castle; m. 1289, **EVA LA ZOUCHE** (39-30), d. 5 Dec. 1314. (CP II 128-129; III 291).

31. ISABEL BERKELEY, d. 1362; m. Robert de Clifford, son of **ROBERT** (82-32), b. 1305, d. 1344. (CP III 291).

32. ROGER DE CLIFFORD, b. 10 Jul. 1333, d. 13 Jul. 1389, Lord Clifford, Sheriff of Cumberland, Governor of Carlisle Castle, 1377; m. Maud de Beauchamp, d. 1402/3, dau. of **THOMAS DE BEAUCHAMP** (87-31), Earl of Warwick, K.G., and **KATHERINE DE MORTIMER** (120-34). (CP III 292).

33. THOMAS DE CLIFFORD, d. 18 Aug. 1391, Lord Clifford, Sheriff of Westmoreland, Governor of Carlisle Castle; m. **ELIZABETH DE ROS** (89-33), d. 1424 (CP III 292; V 736; Old-CP VI 401; Banks I 378).

34. JOHN DE CLIFFORD, K.G., d. 13 Mar. 1421/2, Lord Clifford; m. **ELIZABETH DE PERCY** (5-34), d. 26 Oct. 1437. (CP III 293).

26. JOHN (1-26), King of England, 1199-1216. (CP IX 276).

27. JOAN (natural dau. of King John); m. **LLEWELLYN AP IORWORTH** (176-7), the Great, 1173-1240, Prince of North Wales. (CP IX 276). No. 27 was not mother of No. 28.

*   *   *

28. GLADYS DHU, d. 1251, widow of Reynold de Braiose; m. 1230, **RALPH DE MORTIMER** of Wigmore (132C-29), d. 6 Aug. 1246 (CP IX 276). Gladys was not a dau. of Joan. She was child of Tangwystl, a mistress of Llewellyn.

29. ROGER DE MORTIMER, b. ca. 1231, d. Kingsland, bef. 30 Oct. 1282, 6th Baron Mortimer of Wigmore; m. 1247, **MAUD DE BRAIOSE** (67-29), d. bef. 23 Mar. 1300/1. (CP IX 276-281).

30. SIR EDMUND DE MORTIMER, b. 1261, d. 17 Jul. 1304, 7th Baron Mortimer of Wigmore; m. (2) ca. 1280, **MARGARET DE FIENES** (120-32), d. 7 Feb. 1333/4. (CP VIII 433; IX 281-283).

31. SIR ROGER DE MORTIMER, b. 25 Apr. 1287, d. 29 Nov. 1330, 8th Baron Mortimer of Wigmore; cr. Earl of March, Oct. 1328; m. bef. 6 Oct. 1306, **JOAN DE GENEVILLE** (71-32), b. 2 Feb. 1285/6, d. 19 Oct. 1356. (CP VIII 433-442; IX 284; Banks I 220-221; Turton 72).

32. JOAN DE MORTIMER, d. betw. 1337-1351, m. by 13 June 1330 as (1) wife **SIR JAMES DE AUDLEY**, K.G. (122-33), b. 1312/13, d. 1386, 2nd Lord Audley, m. (2) by Dec. 1351 Isabel, living 1366, said to be dau. of Roger le Strange, 5th Lord Strange of Knockyn. (CP I 339-40; XII pt. 2, 59; V 501); see also 71-33.

33. JOAN DE AUDLEY, b.c. 1332, m. (1) John Tuchet, b. 25 July 1327, dead 10 Jan 1361. She m. (2) by 31 Aug. 1381, Sir John Danbridgecourt. (CP cit.)

34. JOHN TUCHET, m. an unidentified wife. (CP I, 340; Banks I 100-101).

35. SIR JOHN TUCHET, b. 23 Apr. 1371, d. 19 Dec. 1408 (aged 38), Lord Audley, M.P. 1406-1408; m. Isabel, living Jun. 1405. (CP I 340-341; Banks I 100-102).

36. JAMES TUCHET, Lord Audley, b. ca. 1398, d. 23 Sep. 1459; M.P. 1421-1455; m. (1) ca. 1415, **MARGARET DE ROS** (9-34), living 1423. (CP I 341; XI 102-103; Banks I 100-102).

37. ANNE TUCHET, de Audley, d. 1503; m. **SIR THOMAS DUTTON** (32-35), of Dutton, d. 23 Sep. 1459. (VCH Lanc. VI 305).

38. ANNE DUTTON, d. 22 Oct. 1520; m. ca. 11 Jul. 1463, **SIR THOMAS MOLYNEUX** (23-35). (Ormerod: History of Cheshire, 662; VCH Lanc. III 69).

Line 28

29. ROGER DE MORTIMER (27-29), b. ca. 1231, d. Kingsland, 1282, 6th Baron Mortimer of Wigmore; m. 1247, **MAUD DE BRAIOSE** (67-29). (CP IX 276).

Line 28 (cont.)

30. ISABELLA MORTIMER, m. **JOHN FITZ ALAN** (149-29), b. 14 Sep. 1246, d. 18 Mar. 1271/2, Lord of Clun, Earl of Arundel. (CP I 240, 253; IV 670 chart II).

31. SIR RICHARD FITZ ALAN, b. 3 Feb. 1266/7, d. 9 Mar. 1301/2, Earl of Arundel, 1289; M.P. 1295; m. bef. 1285, Alasia de Saluzzo, d. 25 Sep. 1292, dau. of Thomas I, Marquis of Saluzzo in Piedmont, and Luisa de Cave, dau. of George, Marquis of Cave. (CP I 240-241, 253; IV 670).

32. SIR EDMUND FITZ ALAN, Knt., b. 1 May 1285, beheaded at Hereford, 17 Nov. 1326, 8th Earl of Arundel, knighted 22 May 1306; M.P. 1306; m. 1305, **ALICE DE WARENNE** (60-31, 83-30). (CP I 241-242, 253; IV 670).

33. RICHARD FITZ ALAN (60-32), d. 24 Jan. 1375/6, Earl of Arundel; m. (1) 9 Feb. 1320/1, **ISABEL DESPENSER** (8-31), m. (2) **ELEANOR PLANTAGENET** (17-30). (CP I 242-243).

34. SIR EDMUND FITZ ALAN, 2nd son (by (1)), Knt. 1352; living 1377; m. bef. Jul. 1349, Sibyl de Montacute, dau. of William de Montacute, d. 30 Jan. 1343/4, Earl of Salisbury, Earl Marshal of England, and Katharine, dau. of William, Lord Grandison. (CP I 244 note b).

35. ALICE FITZ ALAN, m. Sir Leonard Carew, b. 1342, d. 1370, son of Sir John Carew and Eleanor de Mohun. (CP I 244 note b).

36. SIR THOMAS CAREW, m. Elizabeth Bonville dau. Wm. Bonville, d. 1407/8 & Margaret d'Aumary.

37. SIR NICHOLAS CAREW, d. 1466, Baron Carew of Molesford; m. **JOAN COURTENAY** (6-33). (Generations 32-37: Waters: Pedigree of Francis Champernoun in Essex Institute Proceedings, 17: 16).

Line 29

32. EDMUND DE MORTIMER, d. 1331 of Wigmore (eldest son of **SIR ROGER DE MORTIMER** (27-31), 1st Earl of March, by Joan de Geneville) m. 27 June 1316 **ELIZABETH DE BADLESMERE** (65-34),d. 1356 (CP I 373 note c; VIII 442-3; IX 284-285; Banks I 112, 336).

33. SIR ROGER DE MORTIMER, K.G. (1349), b. Ludlow 11 Nov. 1328, d. 26 Feb. 1359/60, 2nd Earl of March, m. Philippa de Montacute, d. 5 Jan. 1381/2, dau. William de Montacute, Earl of Salisbury by Katharine Grandison (dau. William, Lord Grandison & Sibella de Tregoz). (CP I 373 note c, VIII 442-445; IX 285).

34. EDMUND DE MORTIMER, 3rd Earl of March, m. **PHILIPPA PLANTAGENET** (5-32), dau. of Lionel of Antwerp, Duke of Clarence, and granddau. of Edward III, King of England. (CP VIII 442-447; IX 714).

Line 29A

26. JOHN, King of England (1-26), b. Oxford, 24 Dec. 1167, d. Newark, 19 Oct. 1216, by an unknown mistress had (DNB; TAG 35: 29-32).

33

27. JOAN, Princess of Wales, b. well bef. 1200, d. 30 Mar. 1236 or Feb. 1237; m. 1206, **LLEWELLYN AP JORWERTH** (176-7), Prince of North Wales, b. 1173, d. Aberconway, 11 Apr. 1240; their dau. (DNB; J.E. Lloyd: History of Wales II, 587, 616, 693, 766; TAG op.cit.) (There has been some argument as to the identity of the mother of Margaret No. 28. However the editor has seen no evidence to convince him that she was not the Princess Joan.)

28. MARGARET m. (1) ca. 1219, John de Braose, (son of William, starved to death by King John 1210, who was eldest son of William de Braose (177-6)), dead by Jul. 1232 (issue); m. (2) aft. 1233, Walter Clifford, of Clifford's Castle, Herefordshire, d. 1263. They had (Lloyd op.cit.; TAG op.cit.)

29. MAUD DE CLIFFORD (child of 2nd m.), d. 1282-1285; m. (1) William Longespee III, Earl of Salisbury, d. 1257; m. (2) ca. 1257/8, Sir John Gifford, Lord Gifford of Brimsfield, b. ca. 1232, d. Boyton, Wilts., 29 May 1299. They had (CP XI 384; V 639-642; TAG op.cit.)

30. ELEANOR GIFFORD, dead 1324/5; m. Fulk le Strange, b. ca. 1267; dead 23 Jan. 1324/5, 1st Lord Strange of Blackmere. (CP XII pt. 1 341; TAG op.cit.) Fulk was the son of Robert le Strange of Wrockwarden, crusader, c. 1270; d. 1276 (4th son of John le Strange III and **LUCY TREGOZ** (255-30) by Eleanor de Whitchurch who m. (2) Bogo de Knevill, d. ca. 1304 (Le Strange Records 153, 170-175, 305).

31. ELIZABETH LE STRANGE, m. by Mar. 1323, Robert Corbet of Moreton Corbet, b. 1304, d. 1375. (TAG op.cit.) (See Line 29B).

32. JOAN CORBET, m. Sir Robert de Harley, the 1st (Inq.p.m. 1359). (Throckmorton Fam. in Eng. and the U.S. 33-48; A.E. Corbett: The Family of Corbett (1917) II: 47, 100-107.

* * *

(Connection with No. 33 disproved. See "The Genealogist" vol. I, pp. 27-39 (1980). Joan was dau. of another Sir Robert de Harley.

33. JOAN DE HARLEY, living 1341; m. by 1334, John de Besford, living 1341. (Misc. Gen. Her. 5 Ser. VI 295; Throckmorton op cit.; Corbett op.cit.)

34. ALEXANDER DE BESFORD, dead 1403; m. Beatrice (? Lech, or ? de Thorndon), d. 1404. (Misc. Gen. Her. op. cit. and pp. 226-227; Throckmorton op. cit.)

35. AGNES DE BESFORD, living 1428; m. ca. 1380, Thomas de Throckmorton, living 1411. (Misc. Gen. Her. cit. and p. 295; Throckmorton op. cit.)

36. SIR JOHN THROCKMORTON, M.P., d. 13 Apr. 1445; m. 1409, Eleanor Spinney, living 1466/7. (Misc. Gen. Her. cit. 225-227; Throckmorton op. cit.)

37. AGNES THROCKMORTON, m. Thomas Wynslow of Burton, co. Oxford, d. ca. 1463. (Misc. Gen. Her. cit. 226-227, 135, 138-139; Throckmorton op. cit.)

38. AGNES WYNSLOW, m. (1) 1460, **JOHN GIFFORD** (43-34) of Twyford, d. 1506. (Misc. Gen. Her. cit. 226-227, 129, 135;

Line 29A (cont.)

Throckmorton op. cit.; NEHGR 75: 133-143).

39. THOMAS GIFFORD of Twyford, d. 10 Oct. 1511; m. Joan Langston, d. 1535, dau. and h. of John Langston of Caversfield, co. Bucks. (Misc. Gen. Her. cit. 138-139, 129; NEHGR cit.)

40. AMY GIFFORD, b. ca. 1485-90; m. bef. 1511, Richard Samwell, son of John, of Edgecote, co. Northants, d. 3 May 1519. (Misc. Gen. Her. cit. 129; TAG 29: 215-218).

41. SUSANNA SAMWELL, m. ca. 1535, Peter Edwards, b. ca. 1490, d. ca. 1552. (TAG op.cit.).

42. EDWARD EDWARDS, gent. of Alwalton, b. ca. 1537, d. 1591/2, will dated 25 Dec. 1591; m. Ursula Coles, (dau. Richard Coles), bur. 2 Feb. 1606. (TAG op.cit. and 13: 1-8).

43. MARGARET EDWARDS, m. by 25 Dec. 1591, Henry Freeman of Cranford, b. 1560. (TAG 13: 1-8).

44. ALICE FREEMAN, d. New London, Conn., 11 Feb. 1664/5; m. (1) ca. 1615, John Thompson, gent., b. ca. 1580-90, d. Little Preston, parish of Preston Capes, Northamptonshire, Eng.; will dated 6 Nov. 1626, pro. 11 Apr. 1627. (The bapts. of children of Alice (Freeman) and John Thompson are recorded at Preston Capes.); m. (2) pres. at Roxbury, Mass., aft. 30 May 1644, Robert Parke, as his (2) wife.

Line 29B

31. ELIZABETH LE STRANGE (29A-31); m. by Mar. 1323, Robert Corbet, of Moreton Corbet, b. 1304, d. 1375. (TAG 35: 29-32).

32. ROGER CORBET of Moreton Corbet, d. ca. 1394; m. Margaret, d. 1395, dau. of Sir Giles de Erdington of Shrewsbury. (TAG op.cit.)

33. ROBERT CORBET of Moreton Corbet, Sheriff of Shropshire, 1419; d. 1440; m. **MARGARET MALLORY** (16A-34), dau. Sir William Mallory, kt. of Shawbury. (TAG op.cit.)

34. MARY CORBET, m. **ROBERT CHARLTON** (31-35) of Apley, b. by 1430; d. 1471. (TAG op.cit.)

Line 30

25. HENRY II (1-25), King of England, 1154-1189; b. 1133, d. 1189. (CP V 736; SP I 1-2).

26. WILLIAM LONGESPEE (natural son of Henry II by an unknown mistress, perh. Alix de Porhoët), b. prob. bef. 1173, d. 7 Mar. 1225/6, Earl of Salisbury; m. 1198, **ELA** (108-28), b. 1187-1191, d. 24 Aug. 1261, Countess of Salisbury. (CP XI 379-382, App. F 126; VCH Lanc. I 312; Dudley Pedigree, The Genealogists' Magazine vol. 14, p. 361-368).

* * *

Line 30 (cont.)

Though peerage articles, including CP V 472, have long identified Ida
No. 27 as a dau. of Gen. 26, it is clear that their dau. Ida actually m.
(1) Ralph de Somery (d.s.p.) and (2) bef. 1220 William Beauchamp of
Bedford (see 122A-29) (CP XII pt. 1, note g, which says this Ida liv.
10 Apr. 1262). Moriarty (ms. at NEHGS) suggested William
Longespee had two daus. Ida, or Idoine which may be correct. But
there appears almost a generation difference between the two Ida's,
so the chroniclers may have missed a generation and Ida No. 27 may
be the dau. of William's son **WILLIAM II** (122-29).

   27. **IDA LONGESPEE**, m. **WALTER FITZ ROBERT** (148-28), of
Woodham-Walter, Burnham, Roydon, Dunmow, Henham, Wimbish and
Tey, Essex; d. bef. 10 Apr. 1258. (CP V 472; XI 382; Dudley
Pedigree; Turton; D.L. Jacobus in Boston Evening Transcript (1 Feb.
1928), note 2257, Part XIII). (Walter fitz Robert and Ida had a son
Robert fitz Walter b. 1247.)

   28. **ELA**, m. William de Odingsells of Maxtoke, co. Warwick, d.
1294, son of William and Joan Odingsells. (CP VI 144-145; Banks II
108-109).

   29. **MARGARET DE ODINGSELLS**, m. Sir John de Grey of
Rotherfield, d. 17 Oct. 1311. (CP VI 144-145; Banks II 108-109).

   30. **SIR JOHN DE GREY**, K.G., of Rotherfield, d. 1 Sep. 1359,
1st Baron Grey of Rotherfield; K.G., 23 Apr. 1349; m. (1) bef. 27
Dec. 1317, Catharine, dau. and coh. Sir Brian Fitz Alan, Lord Fitz
Alan; m. (2) **AVICE** (219-31), dau. of John, Lord Marmion. (CP V
398; VI 145-147; Banks I 308; Dudley Pedigree).

   31. **MAUD DE GREY**, child by (2), m. (1) John de Botetourt,
d.s.p. 1369; m. (2) ca. 1374, **SIR THOMAS DE HARCOURT**, Knt. (50-
35). (Dudley Pedigree).

Line 31

   26. **WILLIAM LONGESPEE** (30-26), natural son of King Henry II
of England, d. 1226, Earl of Salisbury; m. 1198, **ELA** (108-28),
Countess of Salisbury. (CP XI 379-382; VCH Lanc. I 312; The Gen.
Mag. 14: 361-363).

   27. **STEPHEN LONGESPEE**, d. by 23 Jan. 1274/5, of Sutton, co.
Northampton; m. **EMMELINE DE RIDELISFORD** (33A-26), d. 1276,
widow of Hugh de Lacy. (CP X 16 note c; XI 382). (See 178-6).

   28. **ELA LONGESPEE**, m. **SIR ROGER LA ZOUCHE** (53-30), of
Ashby and Brockley, d. 1285, Baron Zouche of Ashby. (Old-CP VIII
222).

   29. **ALAN LA ZOUCHE**, b. 1267, d. 1313/4, Baron Zouche of
Ashby, 1299-1314, Governor of Rockingham Castle and Steward of
Rockingham Forest; said to have m. Eleanor de Segrave, dau. of Sir
Nicholas de Segrave. (CP VI 530; Old-CP VIII 222; SP 142; Nichols,
Hist. & Antiq. of the Co. of Leicester, III, ii; Baker, Hist. & Antiq.
of the Co. of Northampton, I, ii; Eng. Historical Review, 86:449-472.

   30. **ELENA LA ZOUCHE**, b. 1288; m. (2) ca. 1317, Alan de
Charlton, d. 3 Dec. 1360, of Apley, Shropshire.

   31. **ALAN DE CHARLTON**, b. ca. 1318/9, d. 3 May 1349; m.

Line 31 (cont.)

Margery Fitz Aer, b. 4 Apr. 1314, d. 1349.

32. THOMAS DE CHARLTON, of Appleby, co. Salop, b. 1345; d. 6 Oct. 1387.

33. ANNA DE CHARLTON, b. bef. 1380, d. by 1399; m. William de Knightley, son of Richard Knightley of Fawesley, co. Northampton.

34. THOMAS DE KNIGHTLEY DE CHARLTON, b. 30 Mar. 1394, d. 4 Jan. 1460; m. Elizabeth Francis, dau. of Sir Robert Francis of Foremark. (See TAG 35:62-63).

35. ROBERT CHARLTON, b. bef. 1430, d. 1471; m. **MARY CORBET** (29B-34), dau. of Robert Corbet of Morton, Shropshire.

36. RICHARD CHARLTON, b. 1450, d. 1522; m. Anne Mainwaring, dau. of William Mainwaring of Ightfield, Shropshire. (Generations 31-36: Visit. of Shropshire 1623, 100-101).

37. ANNE CHARLTON, b. ca. 1480; m. 1500, Randall Grosvenor, b. ca. 1480, d. 1559/60, of Bellaport, Shropshire.

38. ELIZABETH GROSVENOR, b. ca. 1515; m. Thomas Bulkeley, b. ca. 1515, d. 1591, of Woore, Shropshire.

39. REVEREND EDWARD BULKELEY, D.D. (245-40), b. ca. 1540, buried 5 Jan. 1620/1; m. Olive Irby, b. ca. 1547, buried 10 Mar. 1614/5.

40. REVEREND PETER BULKELEY, B.D., b. Odell, Bedfordshire, 31 Jan. 1582/3, d. Concord, Mass., 9 Mar. 1658/9; A.B., St. John's Coll., Camb., 1604/5, A.M., B.D.; Rector of Odell, succeeding his father, 1610-1635; Ord. Cambridge, Mass. (for Concord), Apr. 1637; sett. Concord, 1636-1659; m. (1) Goldington, Bedfordshire, 12 Apr. 1613, Jane Allen, d. Odell, 8 Dec. 1626; m. (2) Apr. 1635, **GRACE CHETWODE** (7-40). (Generations 30-40; Jacobus: Bulkeley Genealogy, 11-17, 22-25, 34-36; Misc. Gen. Her. I 95, 97-98; Frank Bulkeley Smith: The Chetwode Family of England, 76 ff. with charts; Weis: Colonial Clergy of N.E., 45-46, 103; v.Redlich 134).

40. MARTHA BULKELEY (sister of Peter), m. Abraham Mellowes.

40. FRANCIS BULKELEY (sister of Peter), m. Richard Welby.

41. OLIVE WELBY, m. Dea. Henry Farwell of Concord and Chelmsford.

40. ELIZABETH BULKELEY (sister of Peter), m. (1) Richard Whittingham; m. (2) Atherton Haugh, gent.

41. CAPTAIN JOHN WHITTINGHAM, m. Martha Hubbard; ancestors of Rev. Samuel Mather, D.D.

41. REV. SAMUEL HAUGH, minister at Reading, now Wakefield, Mass. (See also Line 203).

Line 32

29. ALAN LA ZOUCHE (31-29), said to have m. Eleanor de Segrave. (CP VI 530).

30. MAUD LA ZOUCHE, b. 1290, d. 31 May 1349; m. by 1309/10 Sir Robert de Holand of Upholland, co. Lancaster, b. ca. 1283, d. 7 Oct. 1328, buried at Preston, Lancashire, first Lord Holand; M.P.

1314-1321; son of Sir Robert de Holand and Elizabeth de Samlesbury. (CP VI 528-531; VCH Lanc. III 141; VI 303-304; English Historical Review 86: 449-472).

31. MAUD DE HOLAND, m. Sir Thomas de Swynnerton, d. 1381, of Swynnerton, co. Stafford, son of Roger de Swynnerton and Matilda. (CP VI 530-531 cf. 530 note i; Banks I 427; William Salt Soc. VII Part II p. 40, vol. (1914), p. 4; CP XII pt. 1 582). (Vis. Cheshire (1580) (Glover for Flower), Harl. Soc. Pub. 93, p. 203).

32. SIR ROBERT DE SWYNNERTON, Knt., d. ca. 1395, of Swynnerton, co. Stafford; m. Elizabeth Beke, dau. of Sir Nicholas Beke, Knt. (Banks I 427; v.Redlich 126, 130; Wm. Salt Soc. vol. (1914) pp. 2-5).

33. MAUD DE SWYNNERTON, only dau., b. ca. 1370; m. (3) Sir John Savage, of Clifton, Knt., d. 1 Aug. 1450. (Banks I 427; Wm. Salt cit.; TAG 26,21).

34. MARGARET SAVAGE, m. 1418, Sir John Dutton, d. 1445, son of Sir Piers Dutton of Dutton (TAG 26, 21).

35. SIR THOMAS DUTTON of Dutton, d. 23 Sep. 1459; m. **ANNE TUCHET DE AUDLEY** (9-35). (Generations 30-35; CP VI 528-531; Banks I 427; Old-CP VIII 222; SP III 142; George Ormerod: History . . . of Chester, 662, 712; VCH Lanc. III 141; VI 303-305; John Burke: History of the Commoners II, 602; v.Redlich 126, 130).

Line 32A Line dropped. The marriage of Randall Grosvenor and Margaret Savage, Gen. 35, can not be supported.

Line 33

34. MARGARET SAVAGE (32-34), a descendant of King Henry II; m. Sir John Dutton of Dutton.

35. MAUD DE DUTTON, m. Sir William Booth, Knt., of Dunham-Massie, co. Chester, Sheriff of Chester, fl. 1476.

36. SIR GEORGE BOOTH, of Dunham-Massie, d. 1483; m. **KATHARINE MONTFORT** (86-36).

37. SIR WILLIAM BOOTH, Knt., of Dunham-Massie, d. 9 Nov. 1519; m. (2) Ellen Montgomery, dau. of Sir John Montgomery, of Throwley, co. Stafford (Ancestry of John Barber White, 193, 200, corrected by v. Redlich 126-127, 130).

38. JANE BOOTH, m. (1) Hugh Dutton of Dutton; m. (2) Sir Thomas Holford, Esq., of Holford, co. Chester.

39. DOROTHY HOLFORD, m. John Bruen of Stapleford, Cheshire, d. 1587, son of John Bruen, Esq.

40. JOHN BRUEN, Esq., of Stapleford, b. 1560, d. 18 Jan. 1625/6; m. (2) aft. 1596, Anne Fox, dau. of John Fox.

41. OBADIAH BRUEN, bapt. Tarvin, 25 Dec. 1606, d. Newark, N.J., bef. 1690; sett. Marshfield, Mass., 1640, Gloucester, 1642, New London, Conn., 1651; m. Sarah, d. ca. 25 Mar. 1684.

42. MARY BRUEN, dau. of Obadiah and Sarah, d. Milford, Conn., 2 Sep. 1670; m. John Baldwin, senior. (Generations 34-41: Ancestry of John Barber White, 191-193, 200-204; v. Redlich 126-

Line 33 (cont.)

127; Boston Evening Transcript 16 Apr. 1928, article by Frank Bruen signed "Obadiah").

Line 33A

23. HENRY I, King of England (121-25), b. 1070, d. 1135, by **NEST** (178-2), dau. Rhys ap Tewdr, Prince of South Wales, father of (NEHGR 116: 278-279).

24. HENRY FITZ HENRY, of Narberth and Pebidiog, b. ca. 1105, d. 1157, by an unknown wife had, besides Meiler fitz Henry, Justiciar of Ireland, a dau. (NEHGR op.cit.; Orpen, Ireland under the Normans I, chart p. 18.)

25. AMABILIS FITZ HENRY, m. Walter de Ridelisford of Carriebenan, in Kildare, d. aft. 1226. They were the parents of (NEHGR op.cit.; Orpen, Ireland under the Normans I, chart p. 18, Chart. St. Mary's i.30.)

25A. WALTER DE RIDELISFORD, dead 12 Dec. 1244; m. Annora, had (NEHGR op.cit.)

26. EMMELINE DE RIDELISFORD, d. 1276; m. (1) Hugh de Lacy, d.s.p. 1242; m. (2) ca. 1243/4, **STEPHEN LONGESPEE** (31-27), Justiciar of Ireland, d. by 23 Jan. 1274/5, yr. son of **WILLIAM LONGESPEE**, Earl of Salisbury (30-26). (NEHGR op.cit.) (CP XI 302, footnote).

Line 34

19. AETHELRED II (1-19), the Redeless, King of England, 979-1016; m. (1) 985, Alfflaid, dau. of Thored. (CP IV 504; IX 704).

20. ALFGIFU (Elgiva), m. (3) Uchtred, Earl of Northumberland, murdered 1016, son of Waltheof, Earl. of Northumberland. (CP IV 504; IX 704; SP III 240-241).

21. EALDGYTH (Edith), m. **MALDRED** (172-20), slain in battle, 1045, Lord of Carlisle and Allendale (and brother of Duncan, King of Scots, 1034-1040), son of Crinan the Thane and Bethoc, dau. of Malcolm II, King of Scots. (CP IV 504; IX 704; SP III 239-241; Archibald H. Dunbar: Scottish Kings, 1005-1625, 2nd Ed., 1906, pp. 4-5).

22. GOSPATRIC I, b. ca. 1040, d. 1074/5, Earl of Northumberland, 1067-1072, 1st Earl of Dunbar, 1072-1075, Lord of Carlisle and Allendale, visited Rome, 1061; m. a sister of Edmund. (CP IV 504; IX 704; SP III 241-245; Surtees Soc., vol. 51; Dunbar 5).

23. GUNNILDA, m. Orm, son of Ketel, Baron Kendal; held the manor of Seaton, also the towns of Camberton, Craysother and Flemingsby. (SP III 245; Jackson; Curwen's of Workington Hall, 3).

24. GOSPATRIC, d. 1179, of High Ireby, Lord of Workington in Coupland; exchanged his lands with his cousin, William I de Lancaster (son of Gilbert, 4th Baron Kendal, son of Ketel, Baron Kendal, son of Eldred, Baron Kendal) for the lands of William de Lancaster at Workington in Coupland; m. Egeline, perh. dau. of Ranulf Engaine. (Hinde: Westmoreland Pipe Rolls, 24 Henry II, p.

167; NEHGR 96: 93; Pipe Roll, 24 Henry II).

25. THOMAS, son and h., d. soon aft. 13 Nov. 1200; m. Grace, who m. (2) bef. 1209/10, Roger de Beauchamp. (Register of St. Bees, 61-64, and charters numbers 35 to 37 and 61).

26. ADA, m. (1) William le Fleming, b. ca. 1150, d. 1203, of Aldingham, son of Michael le Fleming II, d. 1186, and Christian de Stainton, dau. of Gilbert, Lord of Stainton in Kendal, and prob. son of William I de Lancaster; she m. (2) William le Boteler, Lord of Warrington. (NEHGR 96:317-319).

27. SIR MICHAEL LE FLEMING III, b. 1197; m. Agatha, dau. of Henry Fitz Hervey, Lord of Ravensworth. (Generations 24-33: NEHGR 96: 93-94, 120, 307-320, cf. 318). (See 226-28).

28. WILLIAM LE FLEMING of Aldingham. (VCH Lanc. VIII 324 note 28).

29. ELEANOR (ALICIA) LE FLEMING, Lady of Aldingham; m. Sir Richard Cansfield, Knt., Lord of Cancefield and Farleton, co. Lancaster. (CP VI 314; VCH Lanc. VIII 324 note 29).

30. AGNES, Lady of Aldingham, d. 1293; m. Sir Robert de Haverington, of Harington, co. Cumberland, d. 1297. (CP VI 314).

31. SIR JOHN DE HARINGTON, Knt., b. ca. 1281, d. 2 Jul. 1347, of Aldingham, Cancefield and Farleton, knighted 22 May 1306, first Lord Harington, M.P. 1326-1347; m. Joan (prob. Joan Dacre). He held the manors of Aldingham, Thurnham and Ulverston in Lancashire, Witherslack and Hutton Roof in Westmoreland, and Austwick and Harington in Cumberland. (CP VI 314-315; VCH Lanc. VIII 202; Cal. Inq.p.m. vol. IX 30; Banks I 244).

32. SIR JOHN HARINGTON, d. 1359, of Farleton, Melling Parish, co. Lancaster (younger bro. of Sir Robert de Harington, Knt. CP VI 316); m. Katherine Banastre, dau. of Sir Adam Banastre, Knt., beheaded 1314, and Margaret de Holand, sister of Sir Robert de Holand of Upholland, Lancaster, and widow of Sir John Blackburn; in Sep. 1352, Henry, Duke of Lancaster, granted to John de Harington of Farleton a lease of the manor of Hornby. He also held the manors of Bolton-le-Moors, Chorley and Aighton; in 1358, he went to London in the King's service. (CP VI 314-315; VCH Lanc. VII 3, VIII 202).

33. SIR NICHOLAS HARINGTON of Farleton, b. 1345, living 1397; m. Isabel English, dau. of Sir William English, of co. Cumberland. (VCH Lanc. VIII 202).

34. SIR JAMES HARINGTON, Knt., of Blackrod, Justice of the Peace and soldier at Agincourt, 1415; m. Ellen Urswick, dau. of Thomas Urswick of Urswick, Esq. (VCH Lanc. III 424; V 300; Whitaker: Richmondshire II 251 for the Harington pedigree; Ancestry of John Barber White, 107-112).

35. SIR RICHARD HARINGTON of Blackrod and Westleigh, d. 1466/7; m. Elizabeth Bradshagh (or Bradshaw), b. 1402, of Blackrod in Westleigh, dau. of Sir William Bradshagh, d. 1415, and granddau. of the heiress of Sir John de Verdon, Knt., in 1437. (VCH Lanc. III 424; V 330; Inq.p.m. 1449 (29 Henry VI) of Margaret de Verdon, d. 1436/7, who m. (1) Sir Hugh Bradshagh (parents of Sir William Bradshagh), and she m. (2) Sir John Pilkington, knt. (see below); Sir

Line 34 (cont.)

Henry Chauncy: The Historical Antiquities of Hertfordshire, II 209-212; Old-CP VIII 26 gives the father of Elizabeth as Robert Bradshagh vice Sir William as above).

36. SIR WILLIAM HARINGTON, d. 12 Aug. 1488; m. 1442, Elizabeth Pilkington, dau. of Edmund Pilkington and Elizabeth Booth, dau. of Sir Thomas Booth, Knt., and granddau. of Sir John Pilkington, Knt. and his wife Margaret (Verdon) Bradshagh (Inq.p.m. 1449, as above), dau. of Sir John Verdon, Knt. Sir John de Verdon (or Verdun) of Brisingham, co. Norfolk, and Brixworth, co. Northampton, son of Thomas de Verdon of the same, was b. ca. 1300 (ae. 16 yrs on 24 Jun. 1316), and d. ca. 1346. By his first wife, Maud, he was father of Margaret (Verdon) (Bradshagh) Pilkington. Sir William Harington's sister Margaret married Sir Thomas Pilkington, slain 1437. (Old-CP VIII 26; VCH Lanc. III 242; V 300; Vis. of Lancashire, 1533, p. 89 note; Burke; Dict. of the Landed Gentry, 1847, II 1042-1043. For the Pilkington pedigree from the Escheat Rolls in the Tower, see Chauncy, op.cit., II 209-212).

37. SIR JAMES HARINGTON, b. 1448 (ae. 40 yrs. in 1488), d. 26 Jun. 1479, of Wolfage and Brixworth, co. Northampton, gen.; had license to build towers at Farleton; m. **ISABELLA RADCLIFFE** (35-36), d. 20 Jun. 1497, dau. of Sir Alexander Radcliffe of Ordsall, Knt. (VCH Lanc. III 424; VI 194; VIII 202; Inq.p.m., 14 Nov. 1498; Berry: Hertfordshire Families, 109-110; NEHGR 50: 31; Burke: Landed Gentry, 1847, II 1091; Ancestry of John Barber White, 111-112).

38. ALICE HARINGTON, b. ca. 1480, living 1537; m. ca. 16 Aug. 1498, **RALPH STANDISH** (170-35), of Standish, Esq., b. ca. 1479 (ae. 28 in 1507), d. 1538, eldest son and h. of Sir Alexander Standish of Standish, Knt., and Sibyl de Bold, dau. of Sir Henry Bold of Bold, Knt. (VCH Lanc. III 424; VI 194; VIII 202; Vis. of Lancashire, 1533; Inq.p.m., Sir James Harington, 14 Nov. 1498; Publications of the Chetham Society, vol. 98 (1876); J.P. Earwaker: The Standish Family of Standish and Duxbury, co. Lancaster, Charters and Deeds, Manchester, 1898, No. 182, p. 61; No. 218, p. 65; Frederick L. Weis: The Families of Standish of Standish and Prescott of Prescott of Standish Parish, Lancashire, England, 1948 (typed ms.), 203 pp. cf. pp. 43-49, at the American Antiquarian Soc., Worcester, Mass.)

39. ROGER STANDISH, Esq., of Standish, co. Lancaster, mentioned in Earwaker op.cit., No. 218, p. 65, dated 24 Mar. 1513/4, as third son of Ralph Standish of Standish, Esq. The Visitation of Berkshire, A.D. 1566, under "Standyshe of Wantage" gives the following: "Roger Standyshe of Standyshe, co. Lanc., Esq. had issue. — Rauffe, his eldest son and heir; and three daus., whereof one mar. __ Prescott, and another mar. to __ Barnes." (Genealogist, II 106; pedigrees of Standish of Standish and Prescott of Prescott in the Lancaster Collection, Lancaster Town Library, Lancaster, Mass., compiled from records, deeds and wills by the Rev. John Holding, of Stotford, Baldock, Herts, 1902).

40. ALICE STANDISH, buried at Standish, 1564; m. James Prescott of Standish, Shevington and Coppull, co. Lancaster, b. 1508, d. 1568, son of William and Alice Prescott. The Visitation of Berkshire, 1566, a contemporary record, explicitly states that she was the dau. of Roger Standish, Esq.

41. ROGER PRESCOTT, second son, of Shevington, d. Sep. 1594, will made 26 Sep. 1594; m. (1) an Elizabeth; m. (2) 23 Aug. 1568, Ellen Shaw of Standish. Will pro. at Chester, 1 Oct. 1594; to be buried in the parish church of Standish; wife Elene, son Ralph, nephew Alexander Wynnard, daus. Isabel, Ellen, and Anne.

42. RALPH PRESCOTT, of Shevington in Standish Parish, only son of Roger and Ellen (Shaw) Prescott; mentioned in his father's will and co-executor with his mother, 1594; b. ca. 1571/2, though the bapt. is not found on the Standish Parish register, d. 1608/9; m. Helen, living 1608. Will dated 7 Dec. 1608, pro. at Chester, 24 Jan. 1608/9, mentions legacies to wife Elene, three youngest daus. Elene, Alice and Cecillie, and (if it please his wife) he desired her to leave her share to his son John Prescott. Inventory: 12 Jan. 1608/9: ₤ 117-2-4.

* * *

The identification of John Prescott of Lancaster, Mass. with the son, John, of Ralph of Shevington is still challenged. See TAG 34:180 and elsewhere. While evidence is not conclusive, the alternatives are not conclusive either. This line requires further work.

43. JOHN PRESCOTT, founder of Lancaster, Mass., 1645, b. ca. 1604; made his own will, 1673, pro. 4 Apr. 1682, d. Lancaster, Mass., Dec. 1681; perh. the one who m. Halifax, Yorkshire, 11 Apr. 1629, Mary Platts, bapt. Sowerby Parish, Halifax, Yorkshire, 15 Mar. 1607; d. Lancaster, Mass., aft. 1678, dau. of Abraham and Martha (Riley) Gawkroger-Platts. The deposition of Mary Prescott of Lancaster dated 1678, when she was 66 yrs or thereabouts (NEHGR 95: 8, in Middlesex Co. files) identifies John Prescott of Lancaster, Mass., with Halifax, Yorkshire, where his children were bapt., while the will of his reputed father **RALPH** No. 42 does not identify him with the Prescott and Standish families of Standish Parish in Lancashire, Eng. (Prescott Memorial (1870), 32-40; Ancestry of John Barber White, 1913, 107-128, pedigrees of Fleming and Harington, 107-112, Standish and Prescott, 102-104, 122-128, are based upon the research of Mr. Holding, but the other pedigrees in this section of Ancestry of John Barber White are dubious or defective. For fullest details and authorities now available see: Weis: The Families of Standish of Standish and Prescott of Prescott of Standish Parish, Lancashire, England, ms., typed, 203 pp., 1948, cf. 43-49, 53-54, 58-60, 67-68, 78-79, 84-88. This work uses the 400 deeds, charters, inquisitions, marriage settlements, etc. of West, Earwaker, Mrs. Tempest, Porteus, the VCH Lanc. (8 vols.), Baines and the Rev. John Holding, and gives more than 500 of the ancestors of Roger Standish in charts, pp. 151-203.

33. SIR NICHOLAS HARINGTON (34-33), of Farleton, b. 1345, living 1397; m. Isabel English, dau. of Sir William English, of co. Cumberland. (VCH Lanc. VIII 202).

34. SIR WILLIAM HARINGTON, K.G., of Farleton and Chorley, d. 22 Feb. 1439/40; standard bearer at Agincourt, 1415; wounded at the siege of Rouen, 1419; m. **MARGARET NEVILLE** (247-31), b. bef. 1387. (CP V 204 note b; IX 490-491; Banks I 245; VCH Lanc. VIII 194, 202).

35. AGNES HARINGTON, d. 1490; m. Sir Alexander Radcliffe, or Ordsall, Knt., d. 1476, son of Sir John Radcliffe of Ordsall, Knt., and Clemency Standish, dau. of Hugh Standish, Esq., of Standish. (VCH Lanc. IV 211; Burke: Dict. of the Landed Gentry, 1847, II 1091; ibid., 1921, 1468-1469).

36. ISABELLA RADCLIFFE, d. 20 Jun. 1497; m. **SIR JAMES HARINGTON** (34-37), d. 26 Jun. 1479, of Wolfage and Brixworth. (VCH Lanc. VIII 202).

Line 36

35. AGNES HARINGTON (35-35), m. Sir Alexander Radcliffe of Ordsall. (VCH Lanc. IV 211).

36. WILLIAM RADCLIFFE, of Ordsall, Esq., d. 15 May 1498; m. 1443, Jane Trafford, dau. of Sir Edmund Trafford of Trafford, Knt. (VCH Lanc. IV 211).

37. JOHN RADCLIFFE, of Ordsall, d. 12 Apr. 1497; m. Elizabeth Brereton, dau. of Sir William Brereton, Knt. (VCH Lanc. IV 211).

38. SIR ALEXANDER RADCLIFFE, of Ordsall, Knt., high sheriff of Lancashire 1547; b. 1476, d. 5 Feb. 1548/9; m. Alice Booth, dau. of Sir John Booth of Barton, Knt. (VCH Lanc. IV 211).

39. ELEANOR RADCLIFFE, m. **SIR RICHARD MOLYNEUX** (23-37), of Sefton, Knt. (Baines: History of Lancashire II 370).

Line 37

25. THOMAS OF WORKINGTON (34-25), d. soon aft. 13 Nov. 1200, son of Gospatric, Lord of Workington in Cumberland; m. Grace. (Hutchinson: History of Cumberland, II, 143; Jackson; Curwens of Workington Hall, 1-21; Transactions of the Cumberland and Westmoreland Antiquarian and Archaeological Society. vol. 13, extra series).

26. PATRIC DE CULWEN of Workington (younger son), d. ca. 1212.

27. GILBERT CULWEN of Workington, 2nd son; m. Editha.

28. GILBERT CULWEN of Workington, d. 1329 (3 Edward III); m. Edith Harington, d. 1353. The arms of Harington also bear a fret, frette, the famous Harington Knot. Both the Haringtons and the Curwens are descended from Thomas of Workington (see 25 above), whence, perh., the similarity of the arms. (Boutell: Manuel of Heraldry, 1930, p. 30 and plate xxviii, opp.p. 236).

29. SIR GILBERT CULWEN, Knt., of Workington Hall, d. 1383 (7 Richard II), M.P. for the county of Cumberland, 1374-1377 (47-50 Edward III); had license to crenellate, 1379; m. (1) Avicia.

30. GILBERT CULWEN of Workington Hall, living 1403; m. Alice Lowther of Lowther.

31. WILLIAM CURWEN of Workington Hall, living 1403; m. (1) Ellen Brun; m. (2) Margaret Croft, dau. of Sir John Croft. About 1433 the spelling of Culwen was changed to Curwen. (VCH Cumberland II 218-219).

32. SIR CHRISTOPHER CURWEN, son by (2) wife, of Workington, d. 17 Jul. 1450; m. Elizabeth Huddleston of Millom. (VCH Cumb. II 218-219).

33. SIR THOMAS CURWEN of Workington Hall, d. 1470; m. Anne Lowther, dau. of Sir Robert Lowther of Lowther. (VCH Cumb. II 218-219).

34. SIR CHRISTOPHER CURWEN II of Workington Hall, d. 1499; m. Anne Pennington, dau. of Sir Roger Pennington. (VCH Cumb. II 218-219; John F. Curwen: Curwens of Workington, pedigrees v, viii, ix, x; Jackson: Curwens of Workington Hall, p. 21; Hutchinson).

35. MARGARET CURWEN (sister of Sir Thomas Curwen of Workington Hall who d. 1522); m. William Curwen of Camerton, fl. 1500, son of Thomas Curwen, "Black Tom". (Curwen pedigree viii).

36. THOMAS CURWEN, priest of Lowick, d. 1537 (had sons Thomas, Richard and John, and was bro. of Christopher Curwen of Camerton, who d. 1541). (Curwen pedigree viii).

37. THOMAS CURWEN of Sybertoft, Northamptonshire, will made 19 May 1557, pro. Jul. 1557, mentions son Henry Curwen. Also had daus. Margaret, Elizabeth, Ann, Sabyn and Eliza. (Curwen pedigree viii; Essex Institute Proc. 40: 299-304).

38. HENRY CURWEN of Sybertoft, d. 1592 (had son John Curwen, d. 1631; and Matthew Curwen, fl. 1627, who m. Margaret Shatchwell). (Curwen ped. viii; Essex Institute Proc. 40: 299-304).

39. JOHN CURWEN of Sibbertoft, Northamptonshire, d. 1 Jun. 1631; will made 14 May 1631, pro. 15 Jun. 1631. (Children: Thomas, b. 1608; George, b. 1610; Matthew; Elizabeth; Sarah; John, b. 1616. (Curwen pedigree viii; Essex Institute Proc. 40: 299-304).

40. CAPTAIN GEORGE CURWEN, b. Sibbertoft, Northamptonshire, 3 Nov. 1610, d. Salem, 1685; m. (1) 1636, Elizabeth Herbert, d. Salem, 15 Sep. 1668, dau. of the Hon. John Herbert, mayor of Northampton, Eng.; m. (2) 1669, Elizabeth Winslow, d. 1694, dau. of Edward Winslow. Arms: Argent, fretty, gules, a chief azure, with a crescent for cadency. (Curwen pedigrees v, viii, ix, x; J.G. Curwen: Castles and Fortified Towers of Cumberland; Essex Institute Proc. 17: 331-347, cf. 341, chart by Rev. George Curwen, 1698, made during his father's lifetime; Shipton: Sibley's Harvard Graduates V 37; Essex Institute Proc. 40: 299-304; Putnam's Historical Magazine, vol. VI 97-101. Generations 25-34: Jackson: Curwens of Workington Hall, pp. 1-21; Hutchinson: Hist. of Cumberland II 143; Generations 31-34: VCH Cumb. II 218-219).

22. GOSPATRIC I (34-22), b. ca. 1040, d. 1074/5, Earl of Northumberland, 1067-1072, 1st Earl of Dunbar, 1072-1075, Lord of Carlisle and Allendale; visited Rome 1061; m. a sister of Edmund. (CP IV 504; IX 704; SP III 241-245; Surtees Soc., vol. 51; Dunbar 5).

23. WALTHEOF, Lord of Allendale; m. Sigrid, living 1126. (SP III 243-245; CP IV 504).

24. GUNNILD OF DUNBAR, m. Uchtred, d. 1174, son of Fergus, Lord of Galloway, d. 12 May 1166, by Elizabeth, illeg. dau. of **HENRY I** (121-25). (SP III 245; IV 135-138).

25. ROLAND, Lord of Galloway, Constable of Scotland, 1189-1200; d. Dec. 1200; m. Elena de Morville, d. 11 Jun. 1217, dau. of Richard de Morville, Constable of Scotland. (SP IV 138-139).

26. ALAN, Lord of Galloway, named in the Magna Charta, Constable of Scotland, 1215-1234, d. 1234; m. (1) a dau. of Hugh de Lacy, Earl of Ulster (died 1243) by his first wife, Lesceline, dau. of Bertram de Verdun (Orpen, Ireland under the Normans III chart p. 286) or dau. or sister of Roger de Lacy of Pontefract (Trans. of the Dumfrieshire & Galloway Nat. Hist. Soc., v. 49: 49-55); m. (2) 1209, **MARGARET OF HUNTINGDON** (94-27). (CP IV 670 chart IV; SP IV 139-143).

27. HELEN OF GALLOWAY (dau. by first wife), m. **ROGER DE QUINCY** (53-28), d. 25 Apr. 1264, 2nd Earl of Winchester, 1235, Constable of Scotland. (Old-CP VIII 169-170; SP IV 142; Banks I 469; N&Q 3rd Series II 466 for Galloway).

28. ELENA DE QUINCY, d. ca. 20 Aug. 1296; m. Sir Alan la Zouche (see 39-29), d. 1260/70, Baron Zouche of Ashby la Zouche, co. Leicester; Constable of the Tower of London, eldest son and h. of **ROGER** (39-28); a descendant in the male line of the Counts of Porhoët in Brittany. (SP IV 142; Banks I 469; CP XII, pt. 2, 751-754, esp. note e, 932-934).

* * *

29. EUDO LA ZOUCHE (39-29) of Haryngworth, d. 1279, a younger bro. of **SIR ALAN LA ZOUCHE** (see 38-28 above); m. **MILICENT DE CANTELOU** (66-30), d. ca. 1299, dau. of William de Cantelou and Eva de Braiose. (CP I 22; XII pt. 2, 937-938).

* * *

30. ELEANOR or **ELLEN**, prob. dau. Milicent by 1st husb. John de Montault (see TAG 49: 4); m. **SIR JOHN DE HARCOURT**, Knt. (93-30), d. 1330.

31. SIR WILLIAM DE HARCOURT, Knt., of Stanton-Harcourt, d. 6 Jun. 1349; m. **JANE DE GREY** (50-34) of Codnor. (CP VI 126 note a). (Generations 27-30: Dudley Pedigree; Nichols: Leicestershire, IV Part II, 519a-520a for the pedigree of Harcourt; Banks I 122; Collins IV 240). Note: Josiah C. Wedgewood, in "Harcourt of Ellenhall" Wm. Salt Soc. N.S. 35 (1914) 195-196, says Jane sister, not dau. of John de Gray. CP agrees.

21. **ERMENGARD** (121-21), dau. of Geoffrey "Grisgonelle", Count of Anjou, m. Conan "le Tort", Count of Rennes, Duke of Brittany, ca. 970-990; killed 27 Jun. 992.

22. **GEOFFREY**, Duke of Brittany, d. 1008; m. Hawise, illeg. dau. of Richard I, Duke of Normandy (who was also father of Richard II of Normandy, who m. Judith, sister of Duke Geoffrey).

23. **ALAN III**, Duke of Brittany, d. 1040; m. ca. 1027, Berthe, d. 1084/5, dau. of **EUDES II** (136-21), Count of Blois, by his wife Ermengarde of Auvergne. (Saillot 36).

24. **HAWISE**, d. 1072; m. Hoël, Count of Cornouille, and jure uxoris Duke of Brittany 1066, d. 13 Apr. 1084.

25. **ALAN IV** "Fergent", d. 1119, Duke of Brittany; m. **ERMENGARD** (119-24), d. 1147, dau. Fulk IV, Count of Anjou.

26. **HAWISE**, m. Geoffrey, Vicomte de Porhoët, d. 1141, son of Eudon I and Anne de Leon. (Refs. to this point: Père Anselme III 50, 51; de la Borderie, Hist. de Bretagne, III 614; duPaz, Hist. Gén. de Plusiers Maison Illustré de Bretagne 20-21; P. Levot: Biographie Bretonne II 646; Brandenburg ix8, x9, x15, x16, x8, x14a; CP X chart 780, 786, 788-789; XII pt. 2 930-931).

27. **ALAN CEOCHE** or **LA COCHE**, otherwise **LA ZOUCHE**, d. 1190, in England by 1172, of North Molton, Devon, 1185; m. Alice, dau. and event. h. of Philip de Belmeis of Tong, Salop., and Ashley, Leics., by Maud, dau. and coh. of **WILLIAM LE MESCHIN** (132B-26). (CP XII pt. 2 930-931; Gen. n.s. 20: 223).

28. **ROGER LA ZOUCHE**, younger son, h. to bro. William 1199, Sheriff of Devon 1228-31, a witness to Henry III's confirmation of the Magna Charta, d. shortly bef. 14 May 1238; m. a Margaret, living 1220, and prob. 1232. (CP cit. 931-932).

29. **EUDO LA ZOUCHE**, younger bro. of **ALAN LA ZOUCHE** (see 38-28), of Haryngworth, d. 1279; m. **MILICENT DE CANTELOU** (66-30), d. ca. 1299, dau. of William de Cantelou and Eva de Braose and wid. of John de Mohaut. (CP I 22; XII pt. 2 937-938).

30. **EVA LA ZOUCHE**, d. 15 Dec. 1314; m. 1289, **SIR MAURICE DE BERKELEY** (26-30, 59-31), d. 1326, Lord Berkeley of Berkeley Castle. (Old-CP II 128-129; VIII 584).

31. **THOMAS DE BERKELEY**, d. 27 Oct. 1361, Lord Berkeley, Marshal of the English army in France 1340; Captain of the Scottish Marches 1342; m. (1) Jul. 1320, Margaret de Mortimer, d. 5 May 1337, dau. of **ROGER DE MORTIMER** (27-31) and **JOAN DE GENEVILLE** (71-32). (CP II 129-130).

32. **MAURICE DE BERKELEY**, d. 3 Jun. 1368, Lord Berkeley, wounded at the battle of Poitiers, 19 Sep. 1356; M.P. 1362-1368; m. (ae. 8), Aug. 1338, Elizabeth Despenser, d. 13 Jul. 1389, dau. of **HUGH LE DESPENSER** (74-32) and **ALIANORE DE CLARE** (8-30). (CP II 130).

33. **THOMAS DE BERKELEY**, b. 5 Jan. 1352/3, d. 13 Jul. 1417, Lord Berkeley; M.P. 1381-1415; served in the wars in France, Spain, Brittany and Scotland; m. (ae. 15), Nov. 1367, Margaret de Lisle, b. 1360, d. 20 Mar. 1391/2, only dau. of Warin de Lisle, Lord Lisle, by Margaret, dau. of Sir William Pipard.

Line 39 (cont.)

34. ELIZABETH DE BERKELEY, Countess of Warwick, m. (1) Sept. 1393 **RICHARD DE BEAUCHAMP** (87-33). (Generations 31-34: CP II 129-131 and 131 note c).

Line 40 (Gen. 31, Thomas de Multon, shown in earlier editions as father of Elizabeth, Gen. 32, was actually her brother).

22. GOSPATRIC I (34-22), Earl of Dunbar and Northumberland; m. a sister of Edmund. (CP IV 504; IX 704; SP III 241-245).

23. ATHELREDA, m. ca. 1094, **DUNCAN II** (171-22), King of Scots, her cousin. (CP VIII 247; SP I 2-3; III 245; Dunbar 282).

24. WILLIAM FITZ DUNCAN, m. Alice de Rumely, dau. of Robert de Rumely; Lord of Coupland and Skipton in Craven. (CP VIII 247-248; SP I 2-3; Dunbar 282; NEHGR 96: 93).

25. AMABEL, m. Reynold de Lucy, d. ca. 11 Jan. 1198/9. (CP VIII 247).

26. RICHARD DE LUCY, d. 1213, of Egremont, Lord of Coupland, co. Cumberland; m. 1200, Ada de Morville, living 1230, dau. of Hugh de Morville and Helwise de Stuteville; she m. (2) as (2) wife 1218, Thomas de Multon. (CP VIII 248-249; IX 397, 399-401; NEHGR 96: 93).

27. AMABEL DE LUCY, m. 1213, Lambert de Multon, m. (2) Ida, died bef. 16 Nov. 1246, son of Thomas de Multon by 1st wife, Sarah dau. & h. of Richard de Flete. (CP VIII 249; IX 397, 401-402; NEHGR 96: 93).

28. THOMAS DE MULTON, ae. 21 on 4 May 1246, d. sh. bef. 29 Apr 1294; m. (1) Ida. (CP IX 402-403).

29. SIR THOMAS DE MULTON, Knt., son & h. by (1), d. bef. 24 Jul. 1287; m. Jan 1274/5, Emoine le Boteler, dau. of Sir John le Boteler de Ireland. (CP IX 403).

30. THOMAS DE MULTON, Lord Multon, b. 21 Feb. 1276; d. 1321/2, bef. 8 Feb; m. 3 Jan. 1297, **ELEANOR DE BURGH** (75-32). (CP V 437; IX 403-404).

32. ELIZABETH DE MULTON, dau. of No. 30, ae 28 in 1334, m. (1) ca. 1327, Sir Robert de Harington, Knt., d. Ireland, 1334, of Aldingham, knighted 1331, son of **SIR JOHN DE HARINGTON** (34-31). (CP VI 316, IX 405; Banks I 244). She m. (2) Walter de Birmingham.

33. SIR JOHN HARINGTON, Lord Harington of Aldingham, b. ca. 1328, d. Gleaston Castle, 28 May 1363, M.P. 1347-1349; m. Joan, dau. of Walter de Birmingham. (CP VI 316).

34. SIR ROBERT HARINGTON, K.B., Lord Harington of Gleaston Castle, 28 Mar. 1356, d. Aldingham, 21 May 1406; m. (2) 1383, Isabel Loring, widow of Sir William Cogan of Huntsfield, d. 1382, dau. of Sir Nele Loring, K.G., 23 Apr. 1349, d. 1386. (CP VI 316-317).

35. ISABEL HARINGTON, of Hornby, co. Lancaster, m. **SIR JOHN STANLEY** (57-35), d. 1437. (CP IV 205).

47

22. GOSPATRIC I (34-22), Earl of Dunbar and Northumberland.
23. GOSPATRIC II, slain at the battle of the Standard, 23 Aug.
1138, Earl of Dunbar, Baron of Beanley; m. Sybil, dau.of Arkil Morel,
d. 1095. (SP III 246-249; CP IV 504-505).
24. EDGAR, living 1140; m. Alice de Greystoke, dau. of Ivo de
Greystoke and Agnes. (SP III 249).
25. AGNES OF DUNBAR, m. Anselm le Fleming of Furness, d.
1210/7, son of Michael le Fleming and Christian de Stainton. (See
also 34-26).
26. ELEANOR LE FLEMING, m. Ralph d'Eyncourt, of Sizergh,
co. Westmoreland, d. 1228/33.
27. SIR RALPH D'EYNCOURT of Sizergh, d. ca. 1251; m. Alice.
28. ELIZABETH D'EYNCOURT, d. 1272/4; m. 1239, Sir William
de Strickland, d. 1305/6, son of Sir Robert de Strickland of Great
Strickland.   Their dau. Joan de Strickland, m. 1292, Robert de
Washington of Carnforth in Wharton, so. Lanc., ancestors of Gen.
George Washington.
29. SIR WALTER DE STRICKLAND, of Sizergh, d. ca. 1342; m.
Eleanor de Goldington.
30. SIR THOMAS DE STRICKLAND, d. 1376; m. Cecily de
Welles, dau. of Sir Robert de Welles.
31. SIR WALTER DE STRICKLAND, d. 1407/8; m. Margaret de
Lathom.
32. SIR THOMAS DE STRICKLAND, d. 1455; m. Mabel de
Beethom.
33. WALTER STRICKLAND, Esq., d. 1467, knight of the Shire
of Westmoreland, 1442; m. Douce Croft, dau. of Nicholas de Croft.
34. SIR THOMAS STRICKLAND, d. 1497; m. Agnes Parr, dau. of
Sir Thomas Parr. (CP III 377; Clay 157; Topo. and Geneal. III 352-
360).
35. SIR WALTER STRICKLAND, K.B., d. 1506; m. Elizabeth
Pennington.
36. SIR WALTER STRICKLAND of Sizergh, d. 1528; m. (2)
KATHERINE NEVILLE (2-38).   (Generations 22-36: John Burke:
History of the Commoners I 55-58; S.H. Lee Washington in NEHGR
96, chart bet. pp. 106-107, chart opp. p. 314, 93: chart opp. p. 10 for
continuation.)

Line 42

23. GOSPATRIC II (41-23), d. 23 Aug. 1138, 2nd Earl of Dunbar,
Baron of Beanley; m. Sybil Morel. (SP III 246-249).
24. JULIANA OF DUNBAR, m. Ralph de Merlay, d. 1160, Lord
of Morpeth, son of William de Merlay. (SP III 249).
25. ROGER DE MERLAY, d. 1188; m. Alice de Stuteville, dau.
of Roger de Stuteville of Burton Agnes, d. 1202, Sheriff of
Northumberland, 1169-1183. (NEHGR 79: 372-378).
26. AGNES DE MERLAY, m. Richard Gobion, d. Gascony, bef.
29 Dec. 1230, son of Richard de Gobion and Beatrice de Lucelles.
(NEHGR 79:359-364).

27. HUGH GOBION, succeeded his father, 1230, d. 1275 (Inq.p.m.); m. Matilda. (NEHGR 79: 363-364).

28. JOAN GOBION, m. John de Morteyn, d. 1296, of Tilsworth and Marston, co. Bedford, son of John de Morteyn, d. ca. 1284, and Constance de Merston, d. ca. 1293. (NEHGR 79: 365-369).

29. SIR JOHN DE MORTEYN, d. 1346; m. Joan de Rothwell, dau. Richard de Rothwell. (Genealogist, n.s., vol. 38, pp. 194-203).

30. LUCY DE MORTEYN, living 8 Mar. 1361 (sister of Edmund de Morteyn, D.C.L., canon of York and parson of Merston); m. Sir John Giffard, of Twyford, Knt., b. 1301, d. 25 Jan. 1368/9, son of Sir John Giffard le Boef, of Twyford, Knt., and Alexandra de Gardinis. (NEHGR 75: 57-63, 79: 368, 81: 156-178).

31. SIR THOMAS GIFFARD, of Twyford, Knt., b. ca. 1345, d. 25 Sep. 1394; m. 1361, Elizabeth de Missenden, d. ca. 1367. (NEHGR 75: 132-133).

32. ROGER GIFFARD, of Twyford, Esq., b. ca. 1367, d. 14 Apr. 1409; m. ca. 1399, Elizabeth, d. bef. 1407. (NEHGR 75:133).

33. KATHARINE GIFFARD, b. ca. 1399; m. Sir Thomas Billing, Knt., Lord Chief Justice of England, d. 1481, son of John Billing of Rowell and Rushenden, co. Northampton. (NEHGR 75:133).

Line 43

32. ROGER GIFFARD (42-32), of Twyford, Esq.; m. (3) ca. 1407, Isabel Stretle.

33. THOMAS GIFFARD, of Twyford, 1408-1469; m. Eleanor Vaux.

34. JOHN GIFFORD, Esq., of Twyford, 1431-1506; m. **AGNES WINSLOW** (27A-38).

35. ROGER GIFFORD, Esq., of Middle Claydon, Buckinghamshire, 1463-1543; m. Mary Nanseglos.

36. NICHOLAS GIFFORD, of St. James, co. Northampton, 1506-1546; m. Agnes Master.

37. MARGARET GIFFORD, m. Hugh Sargent of Courteenhall, co. Northampton, 1530-1596.

38. ROGER SARGENT, 1560-1649, Mayor of Northampton; m. Ellen Makerness.

39. THE REVEREND WILLIAM SARGENT, bapt. Northampton, 20 Jun. 1602, d. Barnstable, Mass., 16 Dec. 1682; deacon and lay preacher at Malden, Mass. (F.L. Weis: Colonial Clergy of N.E., 182. Generations 32-39: NEHGR 75: 133-143; 79: 358-378).

Line 44

15. ALFRED THE GREAT (1-15), King of England; m. 868, Ealhswith.

16. ALFTHRYTH, d. 929; m. **BALDWIN II** (162-17), d. 918, Count of Flanders. (ASC; Ethelwerd: Chronicle, 1-2; William of Malmsbury, 121; L'Art de Verifier Les Dates; etc.) All descendants of lines 162 to 169 belong to the posterity of King Alfred the Great.

16. EDWARD the Elder (1-16), Saxon King of England; m. (2) Alfflaed.

17. EADGYTH (Edith), d. 26 Jan. 946; m. 929/30, **OTTO I**, the Great (147-19), b. 23 Nov. 912, d. 7 May 973, Holy Roman Emperor.

18. LUITGARDE (dau. of Otto and Edith), d. 953; m. 947, **CONRAD THE WISE** (192-20), d. 955, Duke of Lorraine.

19. OTTO, Duke of Carinthia, d. 1004; m. Judith, prob. dau. of Henry, Count of Verdun.

20. HENRY, Count of Spires, d. 997; m. Adelaide, dau. of Gerard of Lower Alsace. (Bruno of Carinthia, d. 18 Feb. 999, who became Pope Gregory V, 996-999, was his bro.) (CCN 495).

21. CONRAD II, the Salic, d. Utrecht, 4 Jun. 1039, King of Germany, 1024-1039; Emperor of the West, 1027-1039; m. (3) as her (3) husb. 1016/7, **GISELE** (157-21), b. 11 Nov 995; d. 14 Feb. 1042/3, dau. of Herman II, Duke of Swabia. (CCN 274, 495).

22. HENRY III, the Black, b. 28 Oct. 1017, d. Bodfeld, Hartz, 5 Oct. 1056, King of Germany 1039-1056, Emperor 1046-1056; m. (2) 21 Nov. 1043, Agnes, d. 14 Dec. 1077, dau. of **WILLIAM III** (110-23), Count of Poitou. (CCN 495).

23. HENRY IV, b. Goslar, 11 Nov. 1050, d. Liège, Belgium, 7 Aug. 1106, King of Germany 1056-1084, Emperor 1084-1106; m. (1) 1066, Bertha, dau. of Otto, Count of Maurienne, and Adelaide, prob. dau. of Ulric Manfred II, Count of Susa. (CCN 495); m. (2) 1089 Eupraxia, dau. **WSEVOLOD** (242-6), Grand Prince of Kiev (Brandenburg, XI 51b; XII 61a).

24. AGNES (dau. by (1) mar.), d. 1143, (m. (2) 1106 St. Leopold III (see 147-26), Markgraf of Austria, d. 15 Nov. 1136;) m. (1) 1080, Frederick I, b. ca. 1050, d. 1105, of Hohenstauffen, Duke of Alsace and Swabia, son of Frederick of Buren and Hildegarde.

25. FREDERICK II, son by (1) marriage, of Hohenstauffen, b. 1090, d. 6 Apr. 1147, Duke of Swabia; m. **JUDITH** (166-25), of Bavaria.

25. AGNES, dau. of (2) marriage (St. Leopold III), b. c. 1111, d. 25 Jan. 1157, m. 1125-1127 **WLADISLAW II** (147-26), King of Poland, d. 30 May 1159 (Brandenburg, XII 61a; XIII 119b.).

26. FREDERICK III, Barbarossa (son of Frederick no. 25) (Emperor of Germany 1152, as Frederick I), b. 1122, d. 10 Jun. 1190 on the 3rd Crusade and was bur. somewhere in the Holy Land, Duke of Alsace and Swabia; m. (2) 1156, Beatrix of Mâcon, d. 15 Nov. 1184/5, dau. of Renaud III, Count of Mâcon and Burgundy. (CCN 802).

27. PHILIP II, b. 1177/81, murdered at Bamberg by Otto of Wittelsbach, 21 Jun. 1208, Duke of Swabia, Margrave of Tuscany, Emperor of Germany, 1198; m. 1196, Irene Angelica, dau. of Isaac II Angelus, d. 1204, Eastern Roman Emperor, son of Andronicus Angelus (m. Euphrosyne Castamonita), son of Theodora Comnena (m. Constantinus Angelus), dau. of Alexis I, Comnenus, b. 1048, d. 1118, Emperor of the East, who m. 1080, Irene, dau. of Andronicus Ducas, by wife Maria, dau. of Trojan of Bulgaria, son of Samuel, d. 1014, King of Bulgaria. (CCN 802. Generations 21-27: Thatcher 322; G.P. Fisher, op.cit. 259).

Line 45 (cont.)

28. MARIE OF SWABIA (Mary of Hohenstauffen), d. c. 1240; m. (1) 1215, **HENRY II** (155-27), Duke of Brabant, d. 1 Feb. 1247/8. (CP VII 386).

29. MATILDA OF BRABANT, d. 29 Sep. 1288; m. (1) 1237, **ROBERT** (113-29), Count of Artois. (CP VII 386).

30. BLANCHE OF ARTOIS, d. 1302; m. (1) 1269, Henry I, d. 1274, King of Navarre; m. (2) 29 Oct. 1276, **EDMUND PLANTAGENET** (17-28), b. 16 Jan. 1244/5, d. Bayonne, 5 Jun. 1296, Earl of Lancaster and of Leicester. (CP VII 378-387; CCN 588).

31. JEANNE OF NAVARRE, d. 1305; m. 1284, **PHILIP IV** (101-30), d. 1314, King of France. (Generations 17-31: The Conradins by G.A. Moriarty in NEHGR 99: 243; 101: 41; Chaume: Les Origins de Duché de Burgoyne, I 542, 551-552; Thatcher 322; Voltaire: Ouvres (1829) 33: 384-388 — use with care — ; Boston Evening Transcript, 9 Nov. 1926, Note 2257, Part XV Brabant; Turton; TAG IX 113; Moriarty, The Plantagenet Ancestry).

Line 46

34. SIR WILLIAM HARINGTON, K.G. (35-34); m. **MARGARET NEVILLE** (247-31).

35. ISABEL HARINGTON, d. 1441; m. 1411, Sir John Boteler of Bewsey, Knt., b. Bewsey, 26 Feb. 1402/4; d. 12 Sep. 1430, Baron of Warrington, M.P. 1426.

36. SIR JOHN BOTELER, Knt., of Bewsey, b. 24 Aug. 1429, d. 26 Feb. 1463, Baron of Warrington, knighted 1447, Knight of the Shire 1449, M.P. 1449; m. 1460, **MARGARET STANLEY** (20-34), as his third wife. (Gen. 34-36: CP IV 205; VCH Lanc. VIII 194, 202).

37. THOMAS BOTELER, of Bewsey, Knt., b. 1461, d. 27 Apr. 1522, knighted 1485, J.P. 1486, Baron of Warrington; m. Margaret Delves, dau. of John Delves of Doddington, Knt.

38. MARGERY BOTELER, m. 1518, **SIR THOMAS SOUTHWORTH** (9-38). (Generations 36-38: VCH Lanc. I 345-349).

Line 47

30. MAUD LA ZOUCHE (32-30), m. by 1309/10 Sir Robert de Holand, first Lord Holand, of Upholland, co. Lancaster. (CP VI 530).

31. SIR THOMAS DE HOLAND, K.G., Earl of Kent, d. Dec. 1360; m. as her (2) husb. (after annulment of her (1) m. to Wm. de Montacute, Earl of Salisbury. She m. (3) Edward the Black Prince by whom she was mother of Richard II, King of England) **JOAN PLANTAGENET** (236-12), the "Fair Maid of Kent," d. 7 or 8 Aug. 1385, dau. of **EDMUND PLANTAGENET** of Woodstock (155-31) executed 19 Mar. 1329/30, son of **EDWARD I** (1-28) and **MARGUERITE OF FRANCE** (155-30). (CP VI 533; VII 150-154).

32. SIR THOMAS DE HOLAND, K.G., of Woodstock, d. 23 Apr. 1397, Earl of Kent; m. 1364, **ALICE FITZ ALAN** (78-33). (CP VI 533; VII 154-156).

33. MARGARET DE HOLAND, d. 30 Dec. 1439; m. **JOHN BEAUFORT** (1-32); m. (2) Thomas Plantagenet, Duke of Clarence. (CP XII pt. 1, 44; Clay 230).

Line 47A (Prepared by Douglas Richardson)

30. MAUD LA ZOUCHE (32-30, 47-30), m. by 1309/10 Sir Robert de Holand, b. ca. 1283 (Eng. Hist. Rev. 86: 449-472), first Lord Holand, of Upholland, co. Lancaster. (CP VI 528-531).

31. SIR ROBERT DE HOLAND, Lord Holand, s. and h., b. ca. 1312 (ae. 16 in 1328), d. 16 Mar. 1372/3, Halse or Hawes, Brackley, Northants, guardian of Garendon Abbey 1360, m. Elizabeth who died bef. his death. (CP VI 531).

32. ROBERT DE HOLAND, s. and h. apparent, d.v.p. 1372/3, m. in or by 1355 Joan (or Alice) when his father in that year settled on them by fine the manors of Nether Kellet, Wanborough and Denford. (CP VI 532).

33. MAUD DE HOLAND, b. ca. 1356 (ae. 17 in 1373), h. to her grandfather Lord Holand, d. 7 May 1423, m. **SIR JOHN LOVEL**, K.G. (215-32), Lord Lovel and Holand of Titmarsh, d. 10 Sep. 1408. (CP VI 532; VIII 219-221).

Line 47B (Prepared by Douglas Richardson)

30. MAUD LA ZOUCHE (32-30, 47-30, 47A-30), b. 1283 (Eng. Hist. Rev. 86: 449-472), d. 31 May 1349, m. by 1309/10 Sir Robert de Holand, first Lord Holand, of Upholland, co. Lancaster. (CP VI 528-530).

31. MARGARET DE HOLAND, d. 20 or 22 Aug. 1349, m. by 1326 John la Warre, d. shortly bef. 24 June 1331, son of Sir John la Warre, 2nd Baron la Warre by his wife, **JOAN DE GRELLE** (99-31). (CP IV 144-147; VII chart 452-453; Cal. Inq.p.m. 9: 239-240).

32. ROGER LA WARRE, Baron la Warre, b. 30 Nov. 1326, d. Gascony, 27 Aug. 1370, m. (3) bef. 23 July 1358 **ALINORE MOWBRAY** (18-31), dau. of John de Mowbray, 3rd Baron Mowbray by his wife, Joan Plantagenet. (CP IV 144-147).

GERMAN AND FRENCH

FAMILIES

Line 48

The lineage shown in the earlier editions is unproven. However the following is well supported. See NEHGR vol. 117, pp. 268-271.

12. LANTBERTUS (Lambert) II, adult ca. 690, dead 741.

13. RUTPERT I, Count in the Upper Rhine and Wormgau, seen 722-757; m. Williswint, dau. Count Adelhelm, wid. 764. (Note: Rutpert is often used interchangeably with Robert.)

14. TURINCBERTUS (Thuringbert), seen 767-770.

15. RUTPERT II, Count in the Upper Rhine and Wormgau, seen 770-807; m. (1) Theoderata, dead 789; m. (2) Isingard, seen 789.

16. RUTPERT III, son by (1), Count in Wormgau, seen 812-825, d. c. 834; m. as (2) husb. Wialdruth, said by de Vajay to be daughter of St. William d. 812, Count of Toulouse (see "Der Eintritt des Ungarischen Stammesbundes in die Europäische Geschichte (862-933)" (1968)) (Prof. Kelley doubts this identification.)

17. RUTPERT IV, Count in Wormgau, seen 836; of Anjou, Blois, Tours, Auxerre, Nevers; killed 15 Sep 866, called Robert the Strong; m. (1) _____ ; m. (2) ca. 864, **AELIS** (or **ADELAIDE**) (181-6) **OF TOURS & ALSACE**, b. ca. 819, d. ca. 866, wid. of Conrad I, Count of Aargau and Auxerre, d. 863, dau. of Hugh, Count of Tours by his wife Bava. He had chn by (2) wife: (1) Odo or Eudes, King of the Franks, and (2) **ROBERT I** (48-18) (53-18), Count of Paris 888, King of the Franks 922-3, father of Hugh Magnus (NEHGR 110: 290-91).

18. ROBERT I, born posthumously 866, d. 15 Jun. 923, Count of Poitiers, Count of Paris, Marquis of Neustria, King of the West Franks; m. (1) Aelis; m. (2) Beatrix, dau. of **HERBERT I** (50-17), Count of Vermandois.

19. HILDEBRANTE (or Liegarde), dau. by the first wife; m. **HERBERT II** (50-18, 136-18), d. 943, Count of Vermandois and Troyes.

20. ALIX DE VERMANDOIS, d. Bruges, 960; m. 934, **ARNOLD I** (162-18), the Old, d. 27 Mar. 964, Count of Flanders. (Generations 2-9 (in original editions, which are questionable and have been dropped): G.A. Moriarty: Chart of the Robertins in NEHGR 99: 130-131, corrected by chart in same 101: 112. Generations 9-17: Ibid. 99: 130-131; 101: chart 112. Generations 17-20: Crispin: Falaise Roll, 186-187; Turton; Thatcher 320; Isenburg, Book II, Table 10).

16. CHARLES II, the Bald (148-15), b. 828, d. 877, m. (2) 25 Nov. 870 Richaut, dau. Budwine, Count of Metz. (See Moriarty, <u>The Plantagenet Ancestry</u> which cites the Abbé Chaume and Depoin's <u>Thibaud le Tricheur</u>.)

17. ROTHAUT, b. ca. 870, m. Hugh, Count of Bourges.

18. RICHILDE, m. Theobald, d. 904, Viscount of Troyes.

19. THEOBALD I, Count of Blois, d. 978; m. **LUITGARDE DE VERMANDOIS** (136-19), d. 943, wid. of William I, of Normandy, and dau. of Herbert II de Vermandois. (Generations 16-19: G.A. Moriarty: <u>The Robertins</u> in <u>NEHGR</u> 99: 130-131; 101: 112 chart, corrected by Moriarty, <u>The Plantagenet Ancestry</u>, <u>cit.</u>; Brandenburg).

CHARLEMAGNE,

HOLY ROMAN EMPEROR

Line 50

9. **COUNT WARINUS** of uncertain parentage, d. 677 (bro. of St. Léger, d. 677, Bishop of Autun); m. Kunza, sister of Bazin, Bishop of Trèves.

10. **LEUTWINUS**, d. 713 (St. Liévin, Bishop of Trèves, 685–704). (The Abbé Chaume makes him the father of Rotrou No. 11 but cites no evidence.)

11. **ROTROU**, d. 724; m. **CHARLES MARTEL** (190-11), Mayor of the Palace in Austrasia; victor over the Saracens at Tours, 732.

12. **PEPIN THE SHORT**, b. 714, d. 768, Mayor of the Palace; first king of the Franks of the second race, 751-768; m. Bertha, d. 783, dau. of Count Canbert of Laon.

13. **CHARLEMAGNE**, b. 2 Apr. 747, d. Aix la Chapelle, 28 Jan. 813/4, King of France 768-814, crowned Holy Roman Emperor 25 Dec. 800; m. prob. (3) ca. 771, **HILDEGARDE** (182-5), b. 758, d. 30 Apr. 783, dau. of Count Geroud of Swabia. (For their descendants, see Lines 50 to 169 inclusive).

14. **PEPIN**, bapt. at Rome, 12 Apr. 781, by Pope Adrian I, d. Milan, 8 Jul. 810, King of Italy 781-810; consecrated King of Lombardy 15 Apr. 781. Apparently by a dau. of Duke Bernard, yr. bro. of Pepin the Short, he had Bernard a natural son. (NEHGR 109: 175-178).

15. **BERNARD**, natural son, b. 797, d. Milan, 17 Apr. 818; King of Italy 813-Dec. 817; m. Cunigunde, d. ca. 835.

16. **PEPIN**, b. 817/8, d. aft. 840, Count of Senlis, Peronne and St. Quentin.

17. **HERBERT I DE VERMANDOIS**, b. ca. 840, murdered ca. 902, Count of Vermandois, Seigneur of Senlis, Peronne and St. Quentin; m. Beatrice de Morvois (Isenberg, Saillot).

18. **HERBERT II**, b. 880-890, d. St. Quentin, ca. 943, Count of Vermandois and Troyes; m. **HILDEBRANTE** (or Liegarde) (48-19), dau. of Robert I, Duke of France, by his first wife, Aelis.

19. **ALBERT I**, the Pious, b. ca. 920, d. 987/8, Count de Vermandois; m. **GERBERGA OF LORRAINE** (140-19), dau. of Giselbert, Duke of Lorraine and Gerberga, dau. of **HENRY I**, "the Fowler" (141-18), of Saxony.

20. **HERBERT III**, b. ca. 955, d. ca. 1000, Count of Vermandois; m. as (2) husb. Ermengarde, dau. of Reinald, Count of Bar.

21. **OTHO** (Eudes or Otto), b. ca. 1000, d. 25 May 1045, Count de Vermandois; m. Parvie.

22. HERBERT IV, b. ca. 1032, d. ca. 1080, Count de Vermandois; m. Adela de Vexin, dau. of Raoul III the Great, Count of Valois and Vexin.

23. ADELAIDE DE VERMANDOIS, d. ca. 1120, Countess of Vermandois and Valois; m. (1) **HUGH MAGNUS** (53-23), d. 1101, Duke of France and Burgundy, Marquis of Orléans, Count of Amiens, Chaumont, Paris, Valois, and Vermandois; a leader of the 1st Crusade, m. (2) bef. 1103, c. 1102 Reinald, Count of Clermont d. 1162. (CP X 351).

24. ISABEL DE VERMANDOIS, d. 13 or 31 Feb. 1131, Countess of Leicester; m. (1) 1096, Sir Robert de Beaumont, b. ca. 1049, d. 5 Jun. 1118, Lord of Beaumont, Pont-Audemer and Brionne, Count of Meulan, cr. first Earl of Leicester, Companion of William the Conqueror at Hastings 1066, son of Roger de Beaumont and Adelise, dau. of Waleran, Count of Meulan; m. (2) William de Warenne (see 83-24), d. 11 May 1138, second Earl of Surrey, son of William de Warenne and Gundred. (CP IV 670 chart III; VII 520, 523-526, 737; X 351).

25. WALERAN DE BEAUMONT, b. 1104, d. 10 Apr. 1166, Count de Meulan, Earl of Worcester; m. ca. 1141, Agnes de Montfort, d. 15 Dec. 1181, dau. of Amauri de Montfort, Count of Évreux, and Agnes, niece of Stephen de Garlande. (CP VII 520, 708-717, 737-738).

26. SIR ROBERT DE BEAUMONT, d. 1207, Count de Meulan; m. 1165, Maud, dau. of **REGINALD FITZ-ROY** (121-26), Earl of Cornwall (base son of King Henry I of England), by Beatrix, dau. of William Fitz-Robert and granddau. of **ROBERT DE MORTAIN** (185-1). (CP VII 520, 739-740).

27. MAUD (Mabel) **DE BEAUMONT,** living 1 May 1204; m. William de Vernon, b. 1155, d. Sep. 1217, fifth Earl of Devon, son of Baldwin de Reviers and Adelise. (CP IV 317, 673; VII 520, 740 note i).

28. MARY DE VERNON, m. 1200 (1) Sir Peter de Prouz of Chagford, Devon; m. (2) **SIR ROBERT DE COURTENAY** (138-26), d. ca. 27 Jul. 1242 or 1243, Baron of Oakhampton. (CP IV 317, 335, 673; III 465 note c; X 125 note h; IV App. H 675). (See also Devon & Cornwall N&Q IV 229).

29. SIR JOHN DE COURTENAY, d. 3 May 1274, Baron of Oakhampton; m. Isabel de Vere, dau. of Hugh de Vere and **HAWISE DE QUINCY** (60-28). Hugh was son of **ROBERT DE VERE** (246-27) MC 1215, b. aft. 1164, d. bef. 25 Oct. 1221, 3rd Earl of Oxford, Lord Chamberlain of England, Magna Charta Surety, 1215, and his wife Isabel de Bolbec d. 2 or 3 Feb. 1245. (Hedley, Northumberland Fams. I 24-26; CP IV 317, 335, 675; X 210-213, 125 note h).

30. SIR HUGH DE COURTENAY, d. 20 Feb. 1291/2, Baron of Oakhampton; m. Eleanor le Despenser, d. 1 Oct. 1328, dau. Hugh le Despenser, Justiciar of England (see 72-31). (CP IV 335, 673; VI 124; Waters, in Essex Institute Proceedings, XVII 16: Vivian: Visitations of Devon, 243-244).

31. ELEANOR DE COURTENAY (sister of **SIR HUGH DE COURTENAY** (51-31), 9th Earl of Devon); m. **SIR HENRY DE GREY** (143-30), d. Sept. 1308, at Aylesford, Kent, Lord Grey of Codnor, co. Derby, Greys Thurrocks, Essex, Aylesford and Hoo, Kent. (CP IV 673; VI 124).

32. SIR RICHARD DE GREY of Codnor, b. 1281, d. 10 Mar. 1334/5; m. Joan, dau. of Sir Robert, Lord Fitz Payn and Isabella de Clifford. (CP VI 124-125). They were the parents of Jane No. 34.

(**33. SIR JOHN DE GREY**, Knt., d. Aylesford, Kent, 14 Dec. 1392, Lord Grey of Codnor; m. Eleanor. (CP VI 125-127).)

34. JANE DE GREY, almost certainly dau. of Richard No. 32, of Codnor (sister of Sir John, no. 33); m. **SIR WILLIAM DE HARCOURT**, Knt. (38-31), d. 6 Jun. 1349, of Stanton-Harcourt, co. Oxford. (CP VI 126 note a; Dudley Pedigree). (See Josiah C. Wedgewood, "Harcourt of Ellenhall", Wm. Salt Soc. n.s. v. 35, p. 195-196. He states Jane dau. of Richard (No. 32) not John (No. 33)).

35. SIR THOMAS DE HARCOURT, Knt., of Stanton-Harcourt, co. Oxford, Market Bosworth, co. Leicester, and Ellenhall, co. Stafford; d. ca. 12 Apr. 1417; knt. 1366; M.P. for co. of Oxford 1376; m. ca. 1374, **MAUD DE GREY** (30-31), dau. of **JOHN DE GREY** of Rotherfield (30-30) (and wid. of John Botetourt who d.s.p. 1369). (Wedgewood, cit. pp. 196-197).

36. SIR THOMAS DE HARCOURT, Knt., of Stanton-Harcourt, d. 1420; m. Jane Franceys, dau. of Sir Robert Franceys of Formark, co. Derby. (Wedgewood, cit., pp. 197-198).

37. SIR RICHARD HARCOURT, Knt., d. 1 Oct. 1486, of Wytham, Berkshire, will made 27 Apr. 1486, pro. 25 Oct. 1486; m. (1) bef. 16 Dec. 1445, **EDITH ST. CLAIR** (79-35), living 16 Sep. 1462, d. bef. 8 Nov. 1472, dau. of **THOMAS ST. CLAIRE** (79-34) of Wethersfield, Legham and Chalgrove, Suffolk. (CP V 397; VII 64-65; Wedgewood, cit. pp. 204-205).

38. ALICE HARCOURT, m. William Bessiles, of Bessiles-Leigh, Berkshire, d. 1515. Her will pro. 19 Jun. 1526. (Misc. Gen. Her. 5 ser. V 64-82; Wedgewood, cit., chart).

39. ELIZABETH BESSILES, m. Richard Fettiplace, of East Shelford, Berkshire, d. at Bessiles-Leigh, 1511. (idem 5 ser. II 186; V 64).

40. ANNE FETTIPLACE, b. Shelford Parva, 16 Jul. 1496, d. 16 Aug. 1568; m. Edward Purefoy, of Shalston, co. Buckingham, b. 13 Jan. 1494, d. 1558. (idem. 5 ser. II 186; Lipscombe, Hist. of Bucks III, 71).

41. MARY PUREFOY, of Yardley-Hastings, co. Northampton, sister of John Purefoy and mentioned in his will, 1579; m. Thomas Thorne, gent., of Yardley-Hastings, will made 29 Oct. 1588, pro. 9 May 1589 (Northampton Reg. of Wills, V 328-330). Thomas Thorne bequeaths "To the Children of Susan Dudley, my Daughter, widow. ₺ 10, to be equally divided." These children were (Gov.) Thomas Dudley, bapt. 12 Oct. 1576, and Mary Dudley, bapt. 16 Oct 1580.

42. SUSAN (or **SUSANNA**) **THORNE**, bapt. Yardley-Hastings, 5

Mar. 1559/60, living 29 Oct. 1588 (Parish Reg. at Yardley-Hastings, see NEHGR 68: 341-342); m. 8 June 1575 at Lidlington, co. Bedford Captain Roger Dudley, d. 1585. The will of John Purefoy, 1579, mentions Thomas Dudley. The arms of Thorne are: Sable, three fusills in fess, argent. (NEHGR 139:60).

    43. GOVERNOR THOMAS DUDLEY, bapt. Yardley-Hastings, co. Northampton, 12 Oct. 1576, bur. at Roxbury, Mass., 31 Jul. 1653, ae. 76 yrs.; m. (1) Hardingstone, near Northampton, 25 Apr. 1603, Dorothy Yorke, buried at Roxbury, 27 Dec. 1643, dau. of Edmund Yorke, of Cotton End, co. Northampton; m. (2) Roxbury, 14 Apr. 1644, **KATHERINE (DEIGHTON) HACKBURNE** (84-40). The Reverend Cotton Mather, D.D., of Boston, stated that Thomas Dudley was baptized at Yardley-Hastings. The will of Edmund Yorke was dated 18 Nov. 1614, and mentions his grandchildren Samuel and Anne Dudley, and appoints Thomas Dudley one of his overseers. (NEHGR 47: 120). Governor Dudley lived in Northampton as a young man; served under King Henry IV of France at the siege of Amiens; settled in Mass., 1630; Governor and Deputy-Governor of Mass., 1630-1653; a man of large and noble character. (Generations 34-43: Dudley Pedigree, Herald's College, 28 Jan. 1937, approved by A.T. Butler, Windsor Herald. Generations 9-13: G.A. Moriarty: Chart of the Robertins in NEHGR 99: 130-131, corrected by chart in 101: 112; see also references under line 48-13. Generations 13-24: D.L. Jacobus in Boston Evening Transcript, 12 Oct. 1927, Note 2257, Part IX, Note 5980, 28 Nov. 1927; Père Anselme; Brandenburg; v. Redlich I 120-121; CP I 22; IV 670, 672-674; V 736; VII 520, 737; X 351. Generations 24-27: CP IV 317; 670 chart III; VII 520, 708-737, 771; NEHGR 97: 342; Jackson: Falaise Roll, table IX; Waters: Pedigrees of Courtenay and Champernoun, in Essex Institute Proceedings, XVII 16: Generations 30-34: CP IV 676; VI 123-126; Dudley Pedigree; Collins IV 240-241; Stokes Records I 99-102. Generations 38-43: Visitations of Berks., I: Publications of the Harleian Soc., vol. 56 (Visitations of Bucks.) vol. 58, p. 199; Purefoy pedigree in Brit. Museum Harleian Mss. 1189, folios 18 and 19; Nichols: Hist. of Leicestershire, IV Part II pp. 519a-520a; Stokes Records I 93; Mary K. Talcott in NEHGR 66: 340-343; 47: 120; 49: 507; 56:189, 206; 97:342; Waters II 1087; Publications of the Dudley Family Association.

    44. REV. SAMUEL DUDLEY, bapt. All Saints, Northampton, Eng., 30 Nov. 1608; matric., Emmanuel College, Camb., 1626; came to N.E. 1630; minister at Exeter, N.H., 30 May 1650-1683; d. Exeter, 10 Feb. 1682/3. For his descendants, see Gen. Dict. of Me. & N.H., pp. 209-210.

    44. ANNE DUDLEY, b. Northants., ca. 1612; poetess; ancestress of many N.E. Clergymen; d. Andover, Mass., 16 Sep. 1672; m. 1628, Gov. Simon Bradstreet.

    44. MERCY DUDLEY, b. Eng., 1621; ancestress of sixteen colonial clergymen by name of Woodbridge and many bearing other names; d. Newbury, Mass., 1 Jul. 1691; m. 1639, Rev. John Woodbridge of Andover, Mass.

30. SIR HUGH DE COURTENAY (50-30), d. 28 Feb. 1291/2, Baron of Oakhampton; m. Eleanor (or Ailenor) le Despenser (see 72-31). (CP IV 335).

31. SIR HUGH DE COURTENAY, d. 23 Dec. 1340, 9th Earl of Devon; m. **AGNES DE ST. JOHN** (262-32), d. 1345. (CP IV 335).

32. HUGH DE COURTENAY, b. 12 Jul. 1303, d. 2 May 1377, Earl of Devon, K.G.; m. 11 Aug. 1325, **MARGARET DE BOHUN** (6-30), who d. 16 Dec. 1391.

33. SIR PHILIP COURTENAY, d. 29 Jul. 1406, of Powderham, Lord Lieutenant of Ireland, 1383; m. Anne, dau. of Sir Thomas Wake of Blysworth. (CP IV 335).

34. SIR JOHN COURTENAY, m. Joan Champernoun, dau. of Alexander Champernoun of Beer Ferrers and Joan, dau. of Martin Ferrers, and granddau. of Sir Richard Champernoun by his second wife, Alice, dau. of Thomas, Lord Astley. (CP IV 335).

35. SIR PHILIP COURTENAY, d. 16 Dec. 1463, of Powderham; m. Elizabeth Hungerford, d. 14 Dec. 1476, dau. of Sir Walter Hungerford, K.G., Lord Treasurer of England, and wife Catherine, dau. of Sir Thomas Peverell and Margaret Courtenay. (CP IV 335).

36. SIR PHILIP COURTENAY, of Molland, Sheriff of Devon, 1471; m. Elizabeth Hingeston.

37. MARGARET COURTENAY, m. Sir John Champernoun, d. 30 Apr. 1503, of Modbury. (CP IV 673; VI 124; Waters: Champernoun Pedigree in Essex Institute Proceedings, XVII 16. Generations 30-37: Vivian: Visitations of Devon, 162, 244, 246, 251).

38. SIR PHILIP CHAMPERNOUN, of Modbury, d. 2 Aug. 1545, will pro. 3 Feb. 1545/6; m. **KATHERINE CAREW** (6-37). (Vivian: Visitations of Devon, 160, 162-163, 379-380; Waters: Pedigree of Champernoun, in Essex Institute Proceedings 17: 16).

The earlier generations of Prouz, before No. 32, are not clear.

32. WILLIAM LE PROUZ, sheriff of Devon 1269, Inq.p.m. writ 21 Oct. 1270, held Gidley, Stodbury, Cumesheved, Hacche and Colton, Devon; m. (1) Alice, dau. William de Widworthy (living 1244) by 1st wife, unknown, and in her issue heir to her bro. Hugh d. 1292, prob. dead 1250; m. (2) ca. 1250, Alice, dau. and h. Sir Fulk de Ferrers (son of Gilbert), of Throwleigh by his wife Alice, dau. and event. h. Sir Hervey de Helion of Ashton.

33. SIR WILLIAM LE PROUZ, s. and h. by (1), b. ca. 1245 (ae. 25 in 1270), d. shortly bef. 26 Apr. 1316 when Inq.p.m. writ, bur. first at Holbeton, Devon, but under Bishop Grandisson's mandate of 19 Oct. 1329, his bones rebur. at Lustleigh, Devon in accordance with his will, held manors of Aveton Gifford, Gidleigh, Holbeton and Lustleigh, Devon, Conservator of Peace, Devon, 1308, Commissioner re. Statute of Winchester, 1310,; m. by 1275 Alice de Reigny, living 1318, dau. and eventual coh. of John de Reigny, adult by 1222, d. 1246, lord of Aisholt, Aley and Doniford, co. Somerset, Brixton

Reigney in Brixton, Devon, and Newton Reigny, co. Cumberland. With her three sisters, Alice was coh. in 1275 to her nephew Sir William de Reigny. (Knights of Edward I, 4: 103; Notes and Gleanings, Vol. 4, chart labelled Appendix B bef. p. 133; VCH Somerset 5: 152-153 (manor of Doniford, Soms.); Pole, Collections towards a History of the County of Devon, pp. 245-324; Cal. Inq.p.m. 1: 236; 2: 18, 94-95, 141-142, 177, 353).

34. ALICE PROUZ, b. ca. 1285/6, d. shortly bef. 15 Nov. 1335, held the manors of Aveton Gifford, Widworthy, Lustleigh, Holbeton, Gidleigh and Clist Widworthy; writ to partition her estates between her daus. 12 Mar. 1336; m. (1) ca. 1300, Sir Roger de Moels, Knt., died 1324, almost certainly son of Sir Roger Moels, Knt., died 1295, Keeper of Isle of Wight 1267 and Keeper of Forest of Braden 1292, by an unknown wife, and, if so, yr. bro. of Sir John de Moels, 1st Lord Moels, died 1310 (This Moels relationship has been questioned by Hugh Peskett, Devon, Eng.). During her widowhood Alice held mills at Diptford and Glas, Devon which mills were to revert on Alice's death to John de Moeles (apparently 4th Lord Moels), and to Margaret widow of Nicholas Moeles (2nd Lord Moels) and Reginald de Moels. Alice m. (2) ca. 1329 William de Moels by whom she had no issue. (CP IX 1-8; Knights of Edward I III 159-161; List of Inq. Ad Damnum part I 303; Notes and Gleanings IV 133-143, esp. chart App. B bef. p. 133).

35. JOAN DE MOELS, b. ca. 1306, inher. Widworthy, Devon; m. (1) John de Wotton, died bef. 1 Jan. 1335/6; m. (2) by 21 Sept. 1336 John de Northcote, Sheriff of Devon 1353, living 1356/7 (see Mark Hughes in Devon & Cornwall N&Q XXXV pp. 310-312, with refs.). She was living 13 Oct. 1343. (Notes and Gleanings IV 133-143; List of Sheriffs of England and Wales, List and Indexes IX 35).

35A. RICHARD WOTTON, m. Julian, perh. a dau. William le Prouz of Chagford, his cousin. She m. (2) Thomas Jewe.

35B. WILLIAM WOTTON, m. by 1374 Gundred, one of three daus. and coh. Thomas Wyger of Devon, and Christian his wife. (Notes and Gleanings IV 133-143; Somerset and Dorset Notes & Queries VII 49-55).

36. JOHN WOTTON, lord of Widworthy, Devon; m. by 8 Mar. 1408/9 Englesia (or Engaret), dau. of Walter Dymoke. (Notes and Gleanings IV 133-143).

37. ALICE WOTTON, m. by 1424 Sir John Chichester, Knt., lord of Raleigh in parish of Pilton, Devon, born 1386, d. 14 Dec. 1437, son John Chichester, died by 1399, by wife Thomasine, dau. and sole h. of John Raleigh, lord of Raleigh, Devon. (Sir Alex. P.B. Chichester: History of the Family of Chichester 13-25).

38. RICHARD CHICHESTER, Esq., b. 23 Feb. 1424, d. 25 Dec. 1498, bur. Pilton, Devon, Sheriff of Devon, 1363, 1468, 1474, held manors of Raleigh, Arlington, Rokysford, Widworthy and Sutton Sachefield, Devon; m. (1) Margaret Keynes, dau. of Sir Nicholas Keynes of Winkley. (Chichester: op. cit. 25-28; List of Sheriffs of England and Wales, List and Indexes IX 36; Cal. Inq.p.m. Henry VII II 82-84).

Line 52 (cont.)

39. NICHOLAS CHICHESTER, b. ca. 1452 (ae. 31 in 1483), d.v.p. 1498, m. Christina (or Christian) Pawlett, dau. of Sir William Pawlett of Sampford Peverel and widow of Henry Hall. (Chichester: op. cit. 26-27).

40. SIR JOHN CHICHESTER, of Raleigh in Pilton, co. Devon, b. ca. 1475 (ae. 24 1499), d. 22 Feb. 1537/8; m. (2) by 1527 Joan Brett, dau. of Robert Brett, Esq., Escheator of Devon, 1527. (Cal. Inq.p.m. Henry VII II 82-84; List of Early Chancery Proceedings VI 346 (John Chichester vs. Robert Trett & Joan Chichester); List of Escheators for England and Wales, List and Index Society 72: 38; NEHGR 51:214).

41. AMYAS CHICHESTER, b. ca. 1527, d. 4 Jul. 1577, ae 50, of Arlington, Devon; m. by 1545, **JANE GIFFARD** (25-37), dau. of Sir Roger Giffard of Brightleigh, in parish of Chittlehampton, Devon; her will was probated 16 Apr. 1596. (Generations 28-41: Crispin: Falaise Roll, Table IX; Vivian: Visitations of Devon, 1895, pp. 172-173, 179, 397, 400, 626, 823; v. Redlich 105-106; Chichester: op. cit., 32, 67-70, 77-80; Bolton: Ancestry of Margaret Wyatt, chart; NEHGR 51:214: See Wm. R. Drake: Notes of the Family of Chichester (London 1886) 324 et seq.)

42. FRANCES CHICHESTER, bur. Braunton, Devon 5 Apr. 1626, Braunton, Devon, m. by 19 Oct 1584, John Wyatt, gentleman, bapt. Braunton 11 Nov. 1557, bur. 29 Nov. 1598, Braunton, son of Philip and Joan (Paty) Wyatt of Braunton. (NEHGR 51: 214; Vivian: Devon 823; TAG 57: 115-119).

43. MARGARET WYATT, bapt. Braunton, Devon, 8 Mar. 1594/5, m. Braunton 2 Feb. 1626/7, Matthew Allyn (or Allen), bapt. Braunton, 17 Apr. 1605, d. Windsor, Conn., 1 Feb. 1670/1, son Richard and Margaret (Wyatt) Allyn of Braunton. They were the ancestors of President Grover Cleveland. (Vivian, Chichester and Bolton, as above; v. Redlich 106; Waters II 932, 1212-1213; TAG 57: 115-119). (Amended by Douglas Richardson).

Line 53

18. ROBERT I (48-18), b. posth. 866, d. Soissons 15 Jun. 923, Count of Poitiers, Marquis of Neustria and Orléans, Count of Paris, Duke of France, King of the West Franks; m. (2) Beatrix de Vermandois, d. aft. Mar. 931, dau. **HERBERT I** (50-17), Count of Vermandois by his wife Bertha de Morvois. (TAG 58: 164-5; Isenburg, Book II, Table 11; Saillot, Sang de Charlemagne, p. 5).

19. HUGH MAGNUS, b. ca. 895, d. Deurdan 16 Jun. 956, bur. St. Denis, Count of Paris, Orléans, Vexin and Le Mans, Duke of France, m. (3) at Mainz oder Ingelheim 938 **HEDWIG** (141-19), d. aft. 965, dau. of **HENRY I** (141-18), **THE FOWLER**, King of the Saxons. (Isenburg cit.)

20. HUGH CAPET, b. Winter 941, d. Les Juifs b Chartres 24 Oct. 996, bur. St. Denis, King of France 987-996, Count of Poitou, Count of Orléans, first of the Capetian Kings of France; m. summer 968 **ADELAIDE** (or Alice) **OF POITOU** (144A-20), b. ca. 950, d. 15

June 1006. (See Richard Barre, Lord Ashburton: Genealogical Memorial to the Royal House of France, London, 1825 — but use with care; Brandenburg; Isenburg cit.)

21. ROBERT II, the Pious, b. Orléans 27 Mar 972, d. Melun 20 Jul. 1031, bur. St. Denis, King of France, 1 Jan 996-1031, Count of Paris; m. (3) 998, Constance of Provence, b. ca. 986, d. Melun 25 Jul 1032, bur. St. Denis, dau. of William II, Count of Arles and Provence, by his wife, Adelaide (or Blanche), dau. of Fulk II, Count of Anjou. (Isenburg cit.)

22. HENRY I, b. 1008, d. Vitry-en-Brie 4 Aug. 1060, bur. St. Denis, King of France 1031-1060, Count of Paris; m. (3) 19 May 1051 ANNE OF KIEV (241-6), b. 1036, d. aft. 1075, bur. Abbaye Villiers b La-Ferté-Alais, dau. of Jaroslaus I, Grand Prince of Kiev, d. 1054, and Ingegard, dau. of Olaf II, King of Sweden. (CP X 351: CCN; N. de Baumgarten: Orientalia Christiana, Rome, 1927; Isenburg cit.)

23. HUGH MAGNUS, d. 1101, Duke of France, etc.; m. ADELAIDE DE VERMANDOIS (50-23), Countess of Vermandois. (CP X 351).

24. ISABEL DE VERMANDOIS (see 50-24 for details), d. 13 or 31 Feb. 1131; m. (1) 1096, Sir Robert de Beaumont, d. 5 Jun. 1118, Earl of Leicester. (CP VII 520, 523-526, 737; X 351).

25. SIR ROBERT DE BEAUMONT, b. 1104, d. 5 Apr. 1168, 2nd Earl of Leicester; knighted 1122; Justiciar of England, 1155-1168; m. aft. Nov. 1120, Amice de Montfort, dau. of Ralph de Gael de Montford, Seigneur de Gael & de Montfort in Brittany, son of Ralph de Gael, 1st Earl of Norfolk, Suffolk, and Cambridge, Lord of Gael and Montfort, in Brittany and Emma, dau. of William Fitz Osbern, a Companion of William the Conqueror at the Battle of Hastings, 1066, Earl of Hereford. (CP IV 672-673 chart, V 736; VII 520, 527-530; IX 568-574 and note n 574).

26. SIR ROBERT DE BEAUMONT, b. bef. 1135, d. Durazzo, Greece, 1190, 3rd Earl of Leicester, Crusader 1179; m. ca. 1155, Petronilla (or Pernell) de Grantmesnil, d. 1 Apr. 1212, dau. of Hugh de Grantmesnil, and great-granddau. of Hugh de Grantmesnil, a Companion of William the Conqueror at the Battle of Hastings, 1066. (CP IV 670 chart III; VII 520, 530-533; Old-CP VIII 168).

27. MARGARET DE BEAUMONT, d. prob. on 12 Jan. 1234/5 but shortly before 12 Feb. 1234/5; m. bef. 1173, Saher de Quincy, b. 1155, d. 3 Nov. 1219, Earl of Winchester, Magna Charta Surety, 1215, Crusader 1219 (son of Robert de Quincy, d. ca. 1198, Lord of Buckley and of Fawside, Crusader; m. Orabella, dau. of Ness; and grandson of MAUD DE ST. LIZ (148-25) by her 2nd husb., Saher de Quincy of Buckley and Daventy, q.v.) (See George Bellew, Esq., Somerset Herald, College of Arms, London, "The Family of de Quincy and Quincy" (typescript, vol. 2) at N.E.H.G. Society, Boston; also Lundie W. Barlow, "The Ancestry of Saher de Quincy, Earl of Winchester," NEHGR 112: 61 et seq. (CP VII 520; XII pt. 2 pp. 746-751; VCH Lancs. I 312; Sydney Painter: The House of Quincy 1136-1264, Med. et Hum. XI 3-9).

Line 53 (cont.)

28. ROGER DE QUINCY, d. 25 Apr. 1264, 2nd Earl of Winchester, Constable of Scotland; m. **HELEN OF GALLOWAY** (38-27), dau. of Alan, Lord of Galloway, Constable of Scotland, and a descendant of the English and Scottish Kings. (SP III 142; Old-CP VIII 169-170; Banks I 469).

29. ELENA DE QUINCY, d. ca. 20 Aug. 1296; m. **SIR ALAN LA ZOUCHE** (see 38-28), d. 1260/70, Baron Zouche of Ashby la Zouche, co. Leicester; Constable of the Tower of London; a descendant in the male line of the Counts of Porhoët in Brittany. (SP III 142; Old-CP VIII 222; Banks I 469).

30. SIR ROGER LA ZOUCHE, d. 1285, Baron Zouche of Ashby; m. **ELA LONGESPEE** (31-28), a great-granddau. of Henry II, King of England. (Old-CP VIII 222).

Line 54

28. ROBERT DE QUINCY, younger brother of **SAIRE DE QUINCY** (see 53-27), 1st Earl of Winchester (CP XII pt. 2, p. 748 note g and cited refs.), d. London, 1217, crusader; m. **HAWISE OF CHESTER** (125-29), b. 1180, d. 1242/3, Countess of Lincoln. (CP IV 670 chart IV; VII 677; VCH Lanc. I 306).

29. MARGARET DE QUINCY, d. bef. 30 Mar. 1266; m. (1) bef. 21 Jun. 1221, John de Lacy, b. 1192, d. 22 Jul. 1240, of Hatton, son of Roger de Lacy and Maud de Clare, cr. Earl of Lincoln, 1232, Constable of Chester, Magna Charta Surety 1215. (CP IV 670 chart IV; V 695, 736 chart; VII 677-680; VCH Lanc. I 306).

30. MAUD DE LACY, d. bef. 10 Mar. 1288/9; m. 25 Jan. 1237/8, **SIR RICHARD DE CLARE** (63-29), b. 4 Aug. 1222, d. 15 Jul. 1262, Earl of Clare, Hertford and Gloucester. (CP IV 670 chart IV; V 696-702, cf. 700, 736 chart; VII 677-680).

31. THOMAS DE CLARE, 2nd son, d. Ireland, 1287/8, Governor of London, Lord of Inchequin and Youghae; m. **JULIANE FITZ MAURICE** (178-7), dau. of Maurice Fitz-Maurice, Justiciar of Ireland. (CP VII 200; Banks I 112, 155). His dau. was Margaret, No. 33.

33. MARGARET DE CLARE, d. 1333; m. (1) 1289, Gilbert de Umfraville, son of Gilbert (See 224-30), Earl of Angus, dead s.p. 1303; m. (2) by 1308, Bartholomew de Badlesmere, hanged 1322, heiress to her nephew Thomas de Clare, son of Richard de Clare, 2nd son of Thomas and Juliane (Cal.Inq.p.m. VI #275, p. 159). She was therefore sister to Richard, 2nd son, and to Thomas, 1st son (see Goddard Orpen: Ireland Under the Normans; IV 94-6; Altschul: The Clares, pp. 195-196). (CP I 371-372 and 373 note c; X 223; Banks I 112; M. Altschul: The Clares, 187-197, and ped. fac. p. 332).

34. MARGERY DE BADLESMERE, b. 1306, d. 18 Oct. 1363; m. bef. 25 Nov. 1326 **WILLIAM DE ROS** (89-31), Baron Ros of Helmsley, d. 1343. (CP I 373 note c; VIII 633). (Cal.Inq.p.m. VI #275, p. 159).

35. ALICE DE ROS, d. bef. 4 Jul. 1344; m. **NICHOLAS DE MEINELL** (88-32), d. bef. 20 Nov. 1341, 1st Baron Meinell of Whorlton. (CP IV 60; VIII 632-634).

27. HAWISE DE PAYNELL, sister of Gervase Paynell; m. John de Somery. (CP X 320; Banks I 398). Their son was

27A. RALPH DE SOMERY (81-28) m. Margaret Marshall dau. of William the Marshall, Earl of Pembroke & **ISABEL DE CLARE** (66-27).

28. ROGER DE SOMERY, of Dudley, co. Warwick, d. by 26 Aug. 1273; m. (1) **NICHOLE D'AUBIGNY** (126-30) (CP II 1-2; VI 174; XII pt. 1, 112-113; DNB 3:385).

29. MARGARET DE SOMERY, d. aft. 18 June 1293, m. (1) Ralph Basset, Baron Basset of Drayton, slain at Evesham, 4 Aug. 1265; custos pacis for Shropshire and Staffordshire, 1264; M.P. 1264, son of Ralph Basset of Drayton, co. Stafford; m. (2) bef. 26 Jan. 1270/1, Ralph de Cromwell, d. bef. 18 Sep. 1289. (See 210-31). (CP I 237, 239; II 1-2; III 551; VI 174; Banks I 115; DNB 3:385).

30. RALPH BASSET, d. Drayton, 31 Dec. 1299, Lord Basset of Drayton, M.P. 1295-1299; m. Hawise. (CP II 2).

31. MARGARET BASSET, d. 17 Mar. 1336/7; m. by 1298, Edmund Stafford, b. 15 Jul. 1273, 1st Baron Stafford, M.P. 1300, d. by 12 Aug. 1308. (Banks I 115, 408-414; DNB 53: 456).

32. SIR RALPH DE STAFFORD, K.G., b. 24 Sep. 1301, d. 31 Aug. 1372; K.G. 23 Apr. 1349, 1st Earl of Stafford; m. (1) ca. 1326/7 Katharine, m. (2) bef. 6 Jul. 1336, **MARGARET DE AUDLEY** (9-31). (CP XI 100-101; XII pt. 1, pp. 173-177; TAG 9:213; Banks I 115, 408; DNB 53: 456-459; Weever 323).

33. MARGARET STAFFORD, 4th dau. by his 1st wife, m. as his 2nd wife, Sir John Stafford, Knt., of Bramshall, co. Stafford, son of Sir William Stafford of Bramshall.

34. RALPH DE STAFFORD, of Grafton, in the Parish of Bromsgrove, co. Worcester, d. 1 Mar. 1410 (Inq.p.m., 3 Jul. 1410); m. Maud de Hastings, bapt. 2 Feb. 1358/9, ae. 15 in 1374, dau. of John Hastings of Leamington House, co. Warwick. (TAG 9: 213).

35. SIR HUMPHREY STAFFORD, Knt. of Grafton, co. Warwick, b. 1384, ae. 26 in 1410, d. 20 Feb. 1419 (Inq.p.m., 8 Jun. 1419); m. Elizabeth Burdet, dau. of Sir John Burdet, Knt., of Huncote and Leire, co. Leicester, 1397-1400. (TAG 9: 213 (in TAG article given as Bindette, pos. error in reading original Inq.p.m.); Nichols, Leicestershire III 820).

36. SIR HUMPHREY STAFFORD, Knt., of Grafton, b. 1400, commissioner 1436, living 1467; m. **ELEANOR AYLESBURY** (187-10), dau. of Sir Thomas Aylesbury, Knt., of Blatherwyck. (TAG 9: 213).

37. ELIZABETH STAFFORD, m. **SIR RICHARD DE BEAUCHAMP** (84-34). (Generations 32-37: Genealogist, n.s. 31:173; Deighton pedigree certified by A.T. Butler, College of Arms, 11 Dec. 1928, in TAG 9:213). (Burdet ancestry, see Wm. Burton's Descr. of Leics., 2 ed, p. 129, Betham's Baronetage, 1801, p. 180-1) (Supplied by Laurence Eliot Bunker, Wellesley Hills, Mass.)

Line 56

27. MARGARET DE BEAUMONT (53-27); m. **SAIRE DE QUINCY** (53-27), Earl of Winchester, Magna Charta Surety 1215, d. 1219. (CP VII 520, 677; VCH Lanc. I 312). (Ancestry of Saire de Quincy, NEHGR 112: 61 et seq.; CP XII pt. 2, 745-751; Med. et Hum. XI pp. 3-9, reprinted in Painter's Feudalism and Liberty 231-239).

28. ORABELLA DE QUINCY, m. Sir Richard de Harcourt, d. 12 Henry III, son of William de Harcourt, Governor of Tamworth Castle, co. Warwick, 2 Henry III, and Alice Noel, dau. of Thomas Noel of Ellenhall, co. Stafford. (Collins IV 239: Wm.Salt Soc. n.s. vol. (1914) 189-193).

29. WILLIAM DE HARCOURT, m. (1) Alice la Zouche, dau. of **ALAN LA ZOUCHE** (53-29) (mother of Orabella Harcourt who follows); m. (2) **HILLARIA DE HASTINGS** (93-28), mother of **RICHARD DE HARCOURT** (93-29). (Collins IV 239; Dudley pedigree; Wm.Salt Soc. n.s. vol. (1914) 193-194).

30. ORABELLA DE HARCOURT, m. Henry de Pembrugge, d. bef. 25 Jan. 1279. (Wm.Salt Soc., cit.)

31. FULKE DE PEMBRUGGE, b. 1271, d. by 20 Feb. 1296, m. Isabel (living 17 Feb. 1297).

32. FULKE DE PEMBRUGGE, b. ca. 1291-2, d. by 21 Jan. 1325/6, m. Matilda (living 17 Mar. 1326).

33. MARGERY DE PEMBRUGGE, m. Sir Ralph Lingen, M.P. 1374, 1382.

* * *

Line breaks at this point. The mother of Isabel Lingen was not a Pembrugge. (Research by Col. Hansen, see The Genealogist, vol. 7).

34. ISABEL LINGEN, m. (1) her cousin, Fulke Pembrugge; m. (2) Sir John Ludlow; m. (3) Sir Thomas de Petyvine.

35. MARGERY LUDLOW, m. **SIR WILLIAM TRUSSELL** (150-35), Lord of Elmesthorpe. (Generations 27-35: Dr. Arthur Adams: The Elkington Family, Hartford, 1945, pp. 16-17, where full authorities are quoted; Collins IV 239 for Harcourt; v. Redlich xxvi and "Foreword" by Dr. Arthur Adams; Pembrugge pedigree in Nichols: Leicestershire IV Part I, p. 422).

Line 56A

31. FULKE DE PEMBRUGGE, b. 1271, d. by 20 Feb. 1296, m. Isabel (living 17 Feb. 1297).

32. FULKE DE PEMBRUGGE, b. ca. 1291-2, d. by 21 Jan. 1325/6, m. Matilda (living 17 Mar. 1326).

33. ROBERT DE PEMBRUGGE, living Michaelmas term, 1350, dead by 1 Aug. 1364, m. Juliana Zouche (living 1345).

34. JULIANA DE PEMBRUGGE, b. 1349 or before (ae. 60, 1409), heiress of her brother Fulk (d.s.p. 26 May 1409), m. (1) Sir Richard de Vernon of Haddon and Harlaston (d. 1376), Knt.

35. SIR RICHARD VERNON, Knt., d. 1400/1, m. Joanna (living 1402/3), daughter of Sir Rees ap Gruffydd, Knt.

36. SIR RICHARD VERNON, Knt., a minor 1402/3, Treasurer of Calais, Speaker of the House of Commons, d. 24 Aug. 1451, m. by 25 Nov. 1410 Benedicta, daughter of Sir John Ludlow of Hodnet and Stokesay, Knt., living 1427.

37. SIR WILLIAM VERNON, b. ca. 1421, d. 31 Jul. 1467, will PCC Godyn 9, m. Margaret, daughter of William and Joyce (Spernor alias Durvassal) Swinfen and heiress of Sir Robert Pype (d. 1490). (Margaret often, but wrongly, called Margaret Pype. See Genealogist Magazine 15:119-20 for an excellent Swinfen pedigree drawn from primary sources).

38. SIR HENRY VERNON, Knt., b. 1445, d. 13 Apr. 1515, will PCC 9 Holder, Sheriff, Governor of Arthur, Pr. of Wales, built Haddon Hall, m. 1467 to Anne Talbot (d. 17 May 1494), daughter of Sir John Talbot, K.G., 2nd Earl of Shrewsbury, etc., by **ELIZABETH BUTLER** (8-35, 7-34).

39. ELIZABETH VERNON, d. 29 Mar. 1563, m. **SIR ROBERT CORBET** (56B-39) of Moreton Corbet, Knt., b. ca. 1477, d. 11 Apr. 1513, Sheriff of Shropshire.

40. DOROTHY CORBET m. Sir Richard Mainwaring of Ightfield, Knt. b. ca. 1494, d. 30 Sep. 1558, Sheriff of Shropshire.

41. SIR ARTHUR MAINWARING of Ightfield, Knt., b. ca. 1520, d. 4 Sep. 1590, will PCC 49 Sainberbe, m. ca. 1540 to Margaret Mainwaring, daughter of Sir Randall Mainwaring of Over Peover, Knt. by Elizabeth Brereton.

42. MARY MAINWARING, b. ca. 1541, d. before 14 Jun. 1578, m. Combermere 6 Jan. 1559/60, as first wife, to Richard Cotton of Combermere, b. ca. 1539, d. Stoke 14 Jun. 1602.

43. FRANCES COTTON, b. ca. 1573, prob. dead by 16 Apr. 1646, m. George Abell of Hemington, Master of the Middle Temple, b. Stapenhill, co. Derby ca. 1561, bur. Lockington, co. Leicester 13 Sep. 1630, will PCC St. John 10.

44. ROBERT ABELL (2nd son), b. ca. 1605, d. Rehoboth, Mass. 20 Jun. 1663, m. Joanna. Early settler of Weymouth and Rehoboth, Mass. (Generations 31-38: G. Keith Thomson, "The Descent of the Manor (Aylestone, Leics.)" Transactions of the Leicester Archaeological Society 17:206-21 (1932-33); George Morris, Shropshire Genealogies (Ms. 2792, Local Studies Library, Shrewsbury, Salop. microfilm copy GSU, SLC) (31-34); 5:120, (35-38) 5:89-90; (34-39) G. Le Blanc Smith, Haddon: The Manor, The Hall, Its Lords and Traditions (London), 1906), pp. 15-21, 94-103; Generations 39-40: Corbet, The Family of Corbet, Its Life and Times (2 vols., London, 1918), 2:262-264; Generations 39-44: Neil D. Thompson, "Abell-Cotton-Mainwaring", The Genealogist 5:158-71 (1984). (Supplied by Neil Thompson).

Line 56B

34. SIR ROBERT DE FERRERS of Chartley (61-34), m.
MARGARET LE DESPENSER (70-36).
35. SIR EDMUND FERRERS of Chartley, ae. 26 1413, d. 17
Dec. 1435, m. Ellen, daughter of Thomas Roche of Castle Bromwich,
co. Worcs., d. 4 Nov. 1440 (she m. (2) as 1st wife, Sir Philip
Chetwynd. CP V 317-19).
36. SIR WILLIAM FERRERS of Chartley, ae. 23 1435, d. 9 Jun.
1450, m. Elizabeth, dau. of Hamon Bealknap of Seintlynge in St.
Mary Cray, co. Kent, etc., d. 28 May 1471. (CP V 320-21).
37. ANNE FERRERS, b. Nov. 1438, d. 9 Jan. 1468/9, first wife
of Sir Walter Devereux, Lord Ferrers, ae. 27 1459, killed at
Bosworth 22 Aug. 1485 and attainted. (CP V 321-25).
38. ELIZABETH DEVEREUX, d. 1541, m. (1) Sir Richard Corbet,
Knt., b. 1451, d. 6 Dec. 1493, son of Sir Roger Corbet of Moreton
Corbet, Knt., d. 1467, by Elizabeth Hopton, d. 22 Jun. 1498 (who m.
(2) John Tiptoft, Earl of Worcester, and (3) Sir William Stanley) and
grandson of **SIR ROBERT CORBET**, Sheriff of Shropshire (29B-33)
and **MARGARET MALLORY** (16A-34) (Corbet 2:243-58; CP XII, Pt.
2 842-46).
39. SIR ROBERT CORBET m. **ELIZABETH VERNON** (56-39A).
(Supplied by Neil Thompson).

Line 57

28. ROGER DE QUINCY (53-28), m. **HELEN OF GALLOWAY**
(38-27).
29. MARGARET DE QUINCY, d. ca. 12 Mar. 1280/1; m. ca.
1238, **WILLIAM DE FERRERS** (127-30), bur. 31 Mar. 1254, Earl of
Derby. (CP II 128; IV 197; V 340, charts, 320, 333; SP III 142).
30. ROBERT DE FERRERS, b. 1239, d. 1279, Earl of Derby; m.
26 Jun. 1269, **ALIANORE DE BOHUN** (68-30), d. 20 Feb. 1313/4.
(CP IV 198-202; V 320 chart and 333).
31. SIR JOHN FERRERS, b. Cardiff, 20 Jun. 1271, d. Gascony,
Aug. 1312, of Southoe and Keyston, first Baron Ferrers of Chartley;
m. bef. 1300, **HAWISE MUSCEGROS** (189-5), b. 21 Dec. 1276, d.
after June 1340, by Dec 1350, of Charlton. (See 61-31 for male line
continuation). (CP IV 205; V 305, 320-321, 333).
32. ALIANORE FERRERS, m. bef. 21 May 1329, Sir Thomas
Lathom of Lathom and Knowsley, Cheshire, b. 1300, d. 17 Sep. 1370,
son of Sir Robert de Lathom of Lathom and Katherine, dau. of
Thomas de Knowsley. (CP IV 205; V 305, 320-321, chart 320).
33. SIR THOMAS DE LATHOM, Knt., d. bef. 20 Mar. 1381/2; m.
Joan Venables of Kinderton. (CP IV 205).
34. ISABEL DE LATHOM, d. 26 Oct. 1414 (Inq.p.m.); m. ca.
1385, Sir John Stanley, K.G., b. 1350, d. Ardee, Ireland, 6 Jan.
1413/4, Lord Lieutenant of Ireland 1385, Constable of Rokesbergh,
Scotland; Constable of Windsor Castle, Steward of the King's
Household; K.G., 1413, son of Sir William Stanley, Lord of Stanley
and Hooton, and Alice, dau. of Hugh or Hamon Massey. (CP IV 205;
XII Pt. 1 247-249; Collins III 59; DNB 54:75-76; Weever 651).

35. SIR JOHN DE STANLEY, Knt., b. 1386 (ae. 28 in 1414), Knight of the Shire of Lancaster, 1415; Justice of Chester 1426-1427; Sheriff of Anglesey, Constable of Caernarvon Castle 1427; m. **ISABEL HARINGTON** (40-35). (CP IV 205: Collins III 61: DNB 54:76. Generations 32-35: Collectanea Topographica et Genealogica, London, 1841, III 1-21, article "Lathom").

36. SIR THOMAS STANLEY, K.G., of Lathom, b. 1406, d. 20 Feb. 1459, Lord Stanley of Lathom and Knowsley, M.P. 1432; K.G. 1456; Lord Lieutenant of Ireland; m. **JOAN GOUSHILL** (20-33), living 1460, dau. of Sir Robert Goushill of Hoveringham. (CP IV 205; Collins III 56; DNB 54:75; VCH Lanc. I 345-349).

* * *

Identity of wife of Sir John Savage uncertain. See note end of Gen. 43.

37. KATHARINE STANLEY, m. Sir John Savage, K.G., of Rocksavage, son of Sir John Savage, and Eleanor Brereton, b. ca. 1422, d. 22 Nov. 1495. (See note, end Gen. 43.)

38. SIR CHRISTOPHER SAVAGE, lord of manors of Aston Subedge, Camden, Burlington and Westington, co. Gloucs., d. 1513; m. Anne Stanley, dau. of Sir John Stanley of Elford, co. Warw., his cousin.

39. CHRISTOPHER SAVAGE, s. and h., d. 1546; m. Anne Lygon, dau. of **SIR RICHARD** and Margaret (Greville) **LYGON** (84-36) of Arle Court, Worcs.

40. BRIDGET SAVAGE, of Elmley, b. prob. ca. 1540, d. by May 1609; m. ca. 1557-60, Anthony Bonner, gent. of Camden, Burlington and Westington, d. 1580, son of Thomas and Joan (Skinner) Bonner.

41. MARY BONNER of Camden, b. ca. 1560, d. 5 Apr. 1617 at Stratford-on-Avon, co. Warw.; m. (1) by 1 Nov. 1579, William Yonge, gent., d. Dec. 1583, son of John and Mathilda (Bill) Yonge of Caynton and Tiberton, Salop; m. (2) 10 Jan. 158_, Thomas Combe, gent., of Stratford, will dtd 22 Dec. 1608, pro. 10 Feb. 1608/9.

42. BRIDGET YONG of Caynton and Stratford, b. 1580, bur. at Fenny Compton, co. Worcs. 11 Mar. 1629; m. Holy Trinity, Stratford, 2 Nov. 1609, George Wyllys, of manor of Fenny Compton, went to Hartford, Conn. 1638, Gov. of Conn. 1642, d. 9 Mar. 1645. All his children returned to or remained in England except

43. AMY WYLLYS, b. ca. 1625, to America with father, d. Springfield, Mass., 9 Jan. 1698/9; m. Hartford, 6 Nov. 1645, Maj. John Pynchon, b. ca. 1625, d. 17 Jan. 1702/3, son of William and Anne (Andrew) Pynchon. (Line from Gen. 36-43, see TAG 39:88-89; D.L. Jacobus, "Bulkeley Gen.", Currier-Briggs "English Wills of Colonial Families" 2-8, and ancestral fan.) Christopher Whitfield, "The Kinship of Thomas Combe III, Wm. Reynolds & William Shakespear" (1961) says "mother of Christopher Savage is unknown." (Chas. F.H. Evans, letter 20 Apr. 77).

29. MARGARET DE QUINCY (57-29), m. **WILLIAM DE FERRERS** (127-30). (CP V 333 top; SP VI 142).

30. SIR WILLIAM FERRERS, of Groby, b. ca. 1240, d. 24 Jan. 1298/9; m. (1) Anne (possibly dau. of Sir Hugh le Despenser). (CP V 332 chart, 340-342; SP III 139), m. (2) Eleanor Lovain.

31. SIR WILLIAM FERRERS, of Groby, b. Yoxale, co. Stafford, 30 Jan. 1271/2, d. 20 Mar. 1324/5; m. Ellen (possibly dau. of Sir John de Savage). (CP V chart 332, 343-344).

32. HENRY FERRERS, b. ca. 1294, d. Groby, co. Leicester, 15 Sep. 1343, 2nd Baron Ferrers of Groby; m. bef. 20 Feb. 1330/1, **ISABEL DE VERDON** (11-31). (CP V chart 332, 344-347; Old-CP VIII 25).

29. MARGARET DE QUINCY (57-29), m. **WILLIAM DE FERRERS** (127-30).

30. JOAN FERRERS, d. 19 Mar. 1309/10; m. 1267, **SIR THOMAS DE BERKELEY** (26-29), d. 23 Jul. 1321, great-grandson of King John of England. (CP II 128; IV 190-202).

31. SIR MAURICE DE BERKELEY, b. 1281, d. 31 May 1326, Lord Berkeley of Berkeley Castle; m. (1) 1289, neither being over 8 yrs. of age, **EVA LA ZOUCHE** (39-30), d. 5 Dec. 1314. (CP II 128-129; VIII 584).

32. MILICENT (ELA) DE BERKELEY, d. aft. 1322; m. (1) 1313, John Maltravers, b. ca. 1290, d. 1364, Lord Maltravers (or Maultravers), knighted 22 May 1306, son of Sir John Maltravers and Eleanor de Gorges. (CP VIII 581-585, cf. 584).

33. SIR JOHN MALTRAVERS, d. 22 Jan. 1348/9; m. Gwenthlin (or Welthiana), d. bef. Oct. 1375. (CP VIII 585; XI 102-103).

34. ELEANOR MALTRAVERS, b. 1345, d. 1405; m. **SIR JOHN FITZ ALAN** (21-31), of Arundel, d. 1379, Marshal of England. (CP VIII 586; XI 102-103).

35. JOAN FITZ ALAN of Arundel, d. 1 Sept 1404; m. (1) Sir William de Brien; m. (2) ca. 1401, Sir William de Echyngham of Echyngham, co. Sussex, d. 20 Mar 1412/13. (The Gen. n.s. XXI 244-246).

36. SIR THOMAS DE ECHNYGHAM of Echnygham, b. c. 1401, d. 15 Oct. 1444; m. 1415-1424 Margaret, living 1467, daughter of John Knyvet, Sr. and wife Joan of Norfolk, wid. of Sir Robert de Tye of Barsham dsp 1415. (The Gen. op. cit.)

37. SIR THOMAS DE ECHYNGHAM of Echyngham, b. ca. 1425, d. 20 Jan. 1482/3, bur. at Etchingham, Kent; m. Margaret West, dau. of **SIR REYNOLD DE WEST** (18-33), Baron de la Warre. (CP IV 152-154; IX 336-337; Old-CP VII 185: The Gen. op.cit.)

38. MARGARET DE ECHYNGHAM, liv. 11 July 1482 when pr. 2nd husband's will, d. Shoreditch, Mdsx.; m. (1) Sir William Blount, d. 14 Apr. 1471, Knight of the Shire of Derby, 1467, son of Sir Walter Blount, K.G., Baron Mountjoy, Treasurer of England, and Ellen, dau. of Sir John Byron of Clayton; m. (2) c. 1478 Sir John Elrington, Kt.,

Line 59 (cont.)

Treas. household of Edw. IV. (CP IX 336-337; Old-CP VIII 185; Banks
III 536; The Gen. op. cit.)
    39. ELIZABETH BLOUNT, m. **SIR ANDREWS WINDSOR,** K.B.
(12-36), d. 30 Mar. 1543, Baron of Stanwell, co. Middlesex, M.P.;
attended the "Cloth of Gold," 1520, son of Sir Thomas Windsor of
Stanwell and Elizabeth Andrews, dau. of John Andrews, Esq., of
Bayleham, co. Suffolk. (CP IX 337 note d; Old-CP VIII 185; Banks
466; Waters I 275-276).

Line 60

    27. MARGARET DE BEAUMONT (53-27), m. Saire (Saher) de
Quincy, Earl of Winchester, Magna Charta Surety, 1215. (CP IX
215).
    28. HAWISE DE QUINCY, m. aft. 11 Feb. 1222/3, Hugh de Vere,
b. ca. 1210, d. bef. 23 Dec. 1263, Earl of Oxford, Hereditary Master
Chamberlain of England, son of **ROBERT DE VERE** (246-27) (bapt.
1164, d. bef. 25 Oct. 1221, Earl of Oxford, Hereditary Master
Chamberlain of England, Magna Charta Surety, 1215), and Isabel de
Bolbec, d. 3 Feb. 1245, dau. of Hugh de Bolbec. (CP X 210-216).
    29. ROBERT DE VERE, d. 1240, d. bef. 7 Sep. 1296, 5th Earl of
Oxford, M.P. 1283, 1295-1296; m. by 22 Feb. 1252, Alice de Sanford,
d. bef. 9 Sept 1312, dau. of Gilbert de Sanford. (CP X 216-218).
    30. JOAN DE VERE, d. 1293; m. prob. 1285, **WILLIAM DE
WARENNE** (83-29), b. 1256, d. 1286, 7th Earl of Surrey. (CP I 242;
IV 670 chart; X 218 note b.)
    31. ALICE DE WARENNE, d. bef. 23 May 1338; m. 1305, **SIR
EDMUND FITZ ALAN** (28-32), b. 1 May 1285, beheaded at Hereford,
17 Nov. 1326, 8th Earl of Arundel. (CP I 241-242, 253; IV 670 chart).
    32. SIR RICHARD FITZ ALAN, b. ca. 1313, d. 24 Jan. 1375/6,
Earl of Arundel and Warenne; m. (1) 9 Feb. 1320/1, **ISABEL LE
DESPENSER** (8-31); m. (2) Ditton, 5 Feb. 1344/5, **ELEANOR DE
LANCASTER** (17-30), d. 1372. (CP I 242-244, 253; IV 670 chart; IX
604).
    33. SIR RICHARD FITZ ALAN, K.G., son of (2), b. 1346,
beheaded 1397, 10th Earl of Arundel & Surrey; m. **ELIZABETH DE
BOHUN** (15-31), d. 1385. (CP I 244-245, 253; IV 670 chart; IX 604).

Line 61

    31. SIR JOHN DE FERRERS (57-31), m. **HAWISE MUSCEGROS**
(189-5). (CP V 305-310).
    32. SIR ROBERT DE FERRERS, of Chartley, co. Somerset, b.
25 Mar. 1309, d. 28 Aug. 1350; m. (1) bef. Oct. 1330, Margaret; m.
(2) Joan de la Mote d. 29 June 1375, by whom he was father of
Robert of Wem. (CP V 310-312).
    33. SIR JOHN DE FERRERS, of Chartley, by (1), b. Southoe on
or ab. 10 Aug. 1333, slain at Najera, 3 Apr. 1367; m. as (2) husb.
Elizabeth de Stafford (who m. (3) as (1) wife Sir Reynold de Cobham,
Lord Cobham), d. 7 Aug. 1375, dau. of **RALPH DE STAFFORD** (55-

Line 61 (cont.)

32), Earl of Stafford, and **MARGARET DE AUDLEY** (9-31). (CP V 313).

    34. SIR ROBERT DE FERRERS, of Chartley, b. 31 Oct. 1357 or '59, d. 12 or 13 Mar. 1412/13; m. **MARGARET LE DESPENSER** (70-36), d. 3 Nov. 1415.

    35. PHILIPPA DE FERRERS, buried at Norton; m. **SIR THOMAS GREENE** (14-34). (Generations 31-35: CP V 320 chart).

Line 62

    32. SIR ROBERT DE FERRERS (61-32), of Chartley, d. 28 Aug. 1350; m. (2) Joan de la Mote, Lady of Willisham, d. London, 29 Jun. 1375. (CP V 320 chart).

    33. SIR ROBERT DE FERRERS, of Willisham, b. ca. 1350, d. ca. 31 Dec. 1380; m. ca. 27 Sep. 1369, **ELIZABETH LE BOTILLER** (77-34), of Wem and Oversley. (CP II 230-233; V 320 chart).

    34. SIR ROBERT DE FERRERS, b. 1373, d. bef. 29 Nov. 1396; m. **JOAN DE BEAUFORT** (2-32), d. Howden, 13 Nov. 1440, dau. of John of Gaunt, Duke of Lancaster. (CP V 320 chart).

    35. ELIZABETH DE FERRERS, Lady of Wem, b. bef. 1395, d. 1434, buried York; m. ca. 28 Oct. 1407, John de Greystoke, Baron of Greystoke, b. bef. 1389, d. 8 Aug. 1436, will 10 Jul. 1436, pro. 27 Aug.-17 Oct. 1436, son of Ralph de Greystoke and **KATHARINE CLIFFORD** (202-33). (CP V 320 chart).

    36. JOAN GREYSTOKE, m. **JOHN DARCY** (13-34), Baron Darcy. (CP IV 71: V 320 chart).

Line 63

    25. SIR ROBERT DE BEAUMONT II (53-25), b. 1104, d. 5 Apr. 1168, Earl of Leicester; m. Amice de Montfort. (CP V 736; VII 520).

    26. HAWISE DE BEAUMONT, d. 24 Apr. 1197; m. ca. 1150, **WILLIAM FITZ ROBERT** (124-27), d. 23 Nov. 1183, Lord of the manor of Glamorgan and of Cardiff Castle, 2nd Earl of Gloucester, son of Robert, Earl of Gloucester, d. 1147, and Mabel, dau. of Robert Fitz Hamon, and grandson of King Henry I of England. (CP V 687-688, 736; VII 520).

    27. AMICE, Countess of Gloucester, d. 1 Jan. 1224/5; m. **RICHARD DE CLARE**, d. ca. 28 Nov. 1217, 6th Earl of Clare, Hertford and Gloucester, Magna Charta Surety, 1215, son of **ROGER DE CLARE** (246B-26), Earl of Hertford, and Maud, dau. of James de St. Hilary. (CP V 736; VI 501-503).

    28. SIR GILBERT DE CLARE, b. ca. 1180, d. Penros, Brittany, 25 Oct. 1230, 7th Earl of Clare, Earl of Hertford and Gloucester, Magna Charta Surety, 1215; m. 9 Oct. 1217, Isabel Marshall, d. Berkhampstead, 17 Jan. 1239/40, dau. of William Marshall, Earl of Pembroke, and **ISABEL DE CLARE** (66-27); she m. (2) 30 Mar. 1231, Richard, Earl of Cornwall. (CP I 22; IV 670 chart iii; V 694-695, 736; X 364 and note e).

Line 63 (cont.)

29. SIR RICHARD DE CLARE, b. 4 Aug. 1222, d. 15 Jul. 1262, 8th Earl of Clare, Earl of Hertford and Gloucester; m. (2) ca. 25 Jan. 1237/8, **MAUD DE LACY** (54-30), Countess of Lincoln, d. bef. 10 Mar. 1288/9. (CP V 696-702, 736; Banks I 155).

30. SIR GILBERT DE CLARE, Knt., the Red, b. Christ Church, Hampshire, 2 Sep. 1243, d. Monmouth Castle, 7 Dec. 1299, 9th Earl of Clare, Earl of Hertford and Gloucester, knighted 14 May 1264; m. (1) 1253, **ALICE** (117-30), dau. of Hugh XI de Lusignan; m. (2) Westminster Abbey, ca. 30 Apr. 1290, **JOAN PLANTAGENET** (8-29), b. Acre, Holy Land, 1272, d. 23 Apr. 1307, dau. of Edward I of England and Eleanor of Castile. (CP V 702-710, 736. Generations 26-30: CP IV 670 chart III). (See also line 110-31).

Line 64

31. THOMAS DE CLARE (54-31), m. **JULIANE FITZ MAURICE** (178-7). (CP III 291).

32. MAUD DE CLARE, d. betw. 4 Mar. 1326/7 and 24 May 1327; m. (1) 13 Nov. 1295, **ROBERT DE CLIFFORD** (82-32), b. ca. 1 Apr. 1274, slain at Bannockburn, 24 Jun. 1314, Lord of Appleby, Westmoreland, Sheriff of Westmoreland, 1291, M.P. 1299-1313. They were the parents of Margaret de Clifford, No. 34. Maud de Clare m. (2) Robert de Welles, Lord Welles, d.s.p. 1320. (CP III 290-291; V 437; X 461-462; Banks I 155; Inq. p.m., 1315, No. 62).

34. MARGARET DE CLIFFORD (child of gen. 32), d. 8 Aug. 1382; m. **PIERS DE MAULEY** (156-30), d. 18 Jan. 1354/5. (Banks I 312).

Line 65

33. MARGARET DE CLARE (54-33), m. Bartholomew de Badlesmere.

34. ELIZABETH DE BADLESMERE, b. 1313, d. 1356; m. (1) **EDMUND DE MORTIMER** (27-32), d. 1331, of Wigmore; m. (2) 1338, **SIR WILLIAM DE BOHUN** (15-30), d. 1360, Earl of Northampton. (CP I 373 note c; Banks I 112, 336).

Line 66

24. ISABEL DE VERMANDOIS (50-24, 53-24), m. (1) Sir Robert de Beaumont, Earl of Leicester. (CP X 351).

25. ISABEL (or **ELIZABETH**) **DE BEAUMONT**, m. (1) **GILBERT DE CLARE** (184-4), d. 6 Jan. 1147/8, Earl of Pembroke, 1138, son of Gilbert Fitz Richard, 2nd Earl of Clare, and Adeliza. (CP IV 670 chart; V 736; VII 520; X 348-352, cf. 351).

26. RICHARD DE CLARE, "Strongbow," b. ca. 1130, d. ca. 20 Apr. 1176, 2nd Earl of Pembroke, Earl of Striguil, Justiciar of Ireland; m. at Waterford, Ireland ca. 26 Aug. 1171, **AOIFE** (or **EVE**) (175-7), living 1186, dau. of **DAIRMAIT MACMURCHADA** (175-6) (also called Dermot MacMurrough), King of Leinster in Ireland.

Line 66 (cont.)

"Haec jacet Ricarduo Strongbow, filius Gilberti, Comitis de Pembroke." GS in the Chapter House, Gloucester Cathedral. (CP I 22; IV 670 chart III; V 736; IX 590; X 352-357).

27. ISABEL DE CLARE, d. 1220; m. in London, Aug. 1189, Sir William Marshall, b. prob. 1146, d. 14 May 1219 at Caversham, bur. in the Temple Church, London, 3rd Earl of Pembroke, Marshal of England, Protector, Regent of the Kingdom, 1216-1219, son of John Marshall, by his 2nd wife, Sibyl, daughter of Walter de Salisbury, hereditary sheriff of Wilts & Constable of Salisbury Castle. (CP I 22; IV 670 chart; V 736; X 358-364).

28. EVE (or **EVA**) **MARSHALL,** d. bef. 1246; m. **WILLIAM DE BRAIOSE** (177-8), Braose or Briouze), d. 2 May 1230, 6th Baron de Braiose and a descendant of Griffith, King of Wales. (CP I 22; IV 670 chart III; IX 276; X 364 note e).

29. EVA DE BRAIOSE, d. 1255; m. bef. 15 Feb. 1247/8, William de Cantelou (Cantilou or Cantilupe), d. 25 Sep. 1254, Baron Abergavenny, son of William de Cantelou of Calne, Wilts. (CP I 22, Banks I 97, 149-150).

30. MILICENT DE CANTELOU, d. ca. 1299; **EUDO LA ZOUCHE** (38-29), d. 1279. (CP II 129. Generations 26-30: Dudley Pedigree).

Line 67

28. EVE (or **EVA**) **MARSHALL** (66-28), m. **WILLIAM DE BRAIOSE** (177-8).

29. MAUD DE BRAIOSE, d. bef. 23 Mar. 1300/1; m. 1247, **ROGER DE MORTIMER** (27-29), b. 1231, d. bef. 30 Oct. 1282, 6th Baron Mortimer of Wigmore. (CP I 240; IX 276).

Line 68

28. EVE (or **EVA**) **MARSHALL** (66-28), m. **WILLIAM DE BRAIOSE** (177-8).

29. ELEANOR DE BRAIOSE, m. **SIR HUMPHREY DE BOHUN VI** (97-29), d. 27 Aug. 1265, Earl of Hereford and Essex. (CP V 320 chart).

30. ALIANORE DE BOHUN, d. 20 Feb. 1313/4; m. 26 Jun. 1269, **ROBERT DE FERRERS** (57-30), d. 1279. (CP IV 198-202; V 320 chart).

Line 69

27. ISABEL DE CLARE (66-27), m. William Marshall, Earl of Pembroke. (CP X 364, and note a).

28. MAUD MARSHALL, d. 27 Mar. 1248; m. (1) 1207/12, Hugh Bigod, d. Feb. 1224/5, 3rd Earl of Norfolk, Feb. 1221, Magna Charta Surety, 1215, son of Roger Bigod, b. ca. 1150, d. bef. Aug. 1221, Baron le Bigod, Lord High Steward of England, 2nd Earl of Norfolk, 1189, Magna Charta Surety, 1215, and Ida; m. (2) 1225, **WILLIAM DE**

WARENNE (83-27). (CP IV 670 chart; IX 586-590; X 364; Turton 138; Weever 829; CCN).

29. SIR HUGH BIGOD, d. shortly bef. 7 May 1266, Chief Justice of England, 22 Jun. 1257-1260; m. bef. 5 Feb. 1243/4 Joan, d. shortly bef. 6 Apr. 1276, dau. of Nicholas de Stuteville of Liddel, Cumb. by wife Devorgilla, dau. **ROLAND OF GALLOWAY** (38-25), wid. of Hugh Wake (who she m. (1) bef. 29 Mar 1229), d. bef. 18 Dec. 1241 in the Holy Land (see 236-9). Their son, Roger Bigod was the 6th Earl of Norfolk. (CP IX 593, 590 note c, XII pt. 2, 298-299; DNB 5: 24-25; CCN).

30. SIR JOHN BIGOD, Knt., of Stockton, co. Norfolk, b. bef. 1266, ae. 40 yrs. in 1306; h. to his bro., Roger Bigod, Earl of Norfolk. (CP IX 590 note c, 596; DNB 5:21; Cal.Inq.p.m., IV 320; V 302). (See also 156-33).

31. SIR ROGER BIGOD, Knt., d. 1362, of Settrington, co. York. CP IX 590,596; Gerrish: Sir Henry Chauncy, Knight, pp. 4-5, which is in error in generations 31 and 32).

32. JOAN BIGOD, living 9 Sept. 1398, m. 1358, Sir William de Chauncy, Knt., lord of Skirpenbeck, co. York, 1399, and of Stepney, Middlesex, son of Sir Thomas de Chauncy, b. c. 1345 (GS in Weever 549; Inq.p.m., 9 Sep. 1398, in Cal.Inq.p.m. II 246; Gerrish, op.cit., pp. 4-5).

33. JOHN CHAUNCY, of Stepney, d. 22 Feb. 1444/5; m. Margaret Giffard, dau. of William Giffard of Samford, Essex, and Gedleston, Herts., sis. & h. of John, Inq.p.m. 2 Jan 1448/9. (GS, Weever 549).

34. JOHN CHAUNCY, Esq., d. 27 May 1479, will dtd. 15 May 1578, of Pishobury Manor, Sawbridgeworth; m. Anne Leventhorp, d. 2 Dec. 1477, dau. of John Leventhorp, Esq., d. 27 May 1433, of Shingley Hall, Sawbridgeworth, one of the executors of the will of King Henry V of England. (GS, Weever 549).

35. JOHN CHAUNCY, of Sawbridgeworth, ae. 27+ 5 Aug 1479, d. 8 Jun. 1510; m. Alice Boyce, dau. of Thomas Boyce.

36. JOHN CHAUNCY, lord of Netherhall in Gedelsom, also of Pishobury manor, d. 8 Jun. 1546, will dtd 30 Nov. 1543; m. Elizabeth Profitt, d. 10 Nov. 1531, dau. of John Proffit of Barcomb, Suffolk, and wid. of Richard Mansfield of co. Middlesex. He m. (2) Katharine, d. 30 Apr. 1535.

37. HENRY CHAUNCY (by (1), of New Place, lord of Giffords, d. 14 Apr. 1587, Inq.p.m. 5 Oct. 1587; m. Lucy, d. 25 Apr. 1566. He m. (2) lic. 27 Apr. 1574 Jane Salisbury, wid., liv. 1580, dead 1587.

38. GEORGE CHAUNCY, of Yardley-Bury, Hertfordshire, d. 1625-7, lord of Giffords etc., m. (1) Jane, dau. & h. John Cornwell, d. 1582; m. (2) aft. 1582, Anne, dau. of Edward Welsh, of Great Wymondley, Herts., and wid. of Edward Humberston.

39. THE REVEREND CHARLES CHAUNCY, B.D., bp. 5 Nov. 1592, d. Cambridge, Mass., 19 Feb. 1671/2; minister at Scituate and Plymouth, Mass. and second President of Harvard College, 1654-1672; m. 17 Mar. 1630, Catherine Eyre, bapt. 2 Nov. 1604, d. 23 Jun. 1667, dau. of Robert Eyre, of New Sarum, Wilts. (Generations 31-

Line 69 (cont.)

39: William Blyth Gerrish: Sir Henry Chauncy, Knt., 1907, pp. 4-8;
Sir Henry Chauncy: The Historical Antiquities of Hertfordshire,
London, 1700, pp. 57-60; William Chauncy Fowler: Chauncy
Memorial, in NEHGR X 259-262; Waters I 107-109; Weever 549;
Weis: Colonial Clergy of New England, 1934, p. 53; Visitation of
Hertfordshire, 1634, p. 39; Boston Evening Transcript, 13 Oct. 1933,
Note 6914, corrected as above). They were parents of the following
four clergymen.
    40. REV. ISAAC CHAUNCY, M.D., b. Ware, Eng., 23 Aug. 1632;
A.B., Harvard Coll., 1651, A.M., M.D.; sett. London, Eng. (Berry St.
Chh.); physician and clergyman; d. London, 28 Feb. 1712, ae. 80.
Issue.
    40. REV. BARNABAS CHAUNCY, A.M., b. Marston-St.
Laurence, Eng., 1637; A.B., Harvard Coll., 1657, A.M.; sett. Saco,
Me., 1665-1666; d. 1675.
    40. REV. NATHANIEL CHAUNCY, A.M., b. Plymouth, Mass.,
1639; A.B., H.C., 1661, A.M.; Tutor and Fellow, H.C., 1663-1666;
sett. Windsor, Conn., 1667-1680; sett. Hatfield, Mass., 1682-1685;
physician and minister; d. Hatfield, 4 Nov. 1685; m. 12 Nov. 1673
Abigail, dau. of Elder John Strong, issue.
    40. REV. ISRAEL CHAUNCY, A.M., b. Scituate, Mass., 1644;
A.B., H.C., 1661, A.M.; Founder and Trustee, Yale Coll.; ord.
Stratford, Conn., Dec. 1666-1703; chaplain, King Philip's War,
1675/6; chosen Pres. of Y.C., but declined; d. Stratford, 14 Mar.
1702/3, survived by wife Sarah.
    40. SARAH CHAUNCEY, b. 13, bp. 22 June 1631 at Ware, d.
Wethersfield, Conn. 3 June 1699, m. Concord, Mass., 6 Oct. 1659
Rev. Gershom Bulkely, b. Cambridge, Mass., Jan. 1635/6, d.
Glastonbury, Conn., 2 Dec. 1713, son of **REV. PETER BULKLEY** (31-
40). (Generations 32-40: See Misc. Gen. et Her. Ser. II, vol. I, p.
21,22,35; Generations 38-40: Weis: Colonial Clergy of N.E., 1934, p.
53; Note: John Chauncy No. 34 & John Chauncey No. 35 are
brother. No. 36 is son of No. 35. No. 35 is son of No. 33, not No. 34
(Plea Rolls Gen. n.s. 20: 90-91).

Line 70

    28. MAUD MARSHALL (69-28), m. 1207/1212 Hugh Bigod, Earl
of Norfolk.
    29. ISABEL BIGOD, m. (1) **GILBERT DE LACY** (177A-8), d.
1230, of Ewyas Lacy, co. Hereford, and of Trim and Weoberley, son
of Walter de Lacy, Lord of Meath, and Margaret dau. **WILLIAM DE
BRAOSE** (177-6) & Maud de St. Valery. (CP V 437; IX 589-590; XII
pt. II, 169, note d; Banks I 221).
    30. MARGARET DE LACY, d. 1256, Lady of Dulek; m. (1) ca.
1248, John de Verdun, d. 1274, son of Theobald le Boteler and
Rohese de Verdon. (Note: Maud, d. 27 Nov. 1283, dau. of Theobald
le Boteler and Rohese de Verdun, m. John Fitz Alan, Earl of Arundel
(149-28), q.v.) (CP I 239-240; Banks I 221, 445).

31. THEOBALD DE VERDON, d. Alton, co. Stafford, 24 Aug. 1309, M.P. 1289/90, Baron, 1308, Lord of Dulek; m. Margery (or Eleanor). (Old-CP VIII 24-52; Banks I 221, 445).

32. SIR THEOBALD DE VERDON, Knt., b. ca. 1280, d. Alton, 27 Jul. 1316, Lord of Weoberley, Baron, 1308, of Alton, co. Stafford, Knt., 1298, M.P. 1299-1314; m. (1) Wigmore, 29 Jul. 1302, Maud de Mortimer, dau. of **SIR EDMUND DE MORTIMER** (27-30) and **MARGARET DE FIENES** (120-32). (CP II 426; Old-CP VIII 25; Banks I 445). He m. (2) **ELIZABETH DE CLARE** (11-30).

33. ELIZABETH DE VERDON (by 1), d. 1360; m. bef. 11 Jun. 1320, Sir Bartholomew de Burghersh, d. 3 Aug. 1355, Lord Burghersh, son of Robert, Lord Burghersh, and Maud de Badlesmere, dau. of Guncelin de Badlesmere. (CP II 426-427; Old-CP VIII 25; Banks I 445).

34. BARTHOLOMEW DE BURGHERSH, K.G., d. 5 Apr. 1369, Lord Burghersh, fought at Crécy, 1346, original Knight of the Garter, 23 Apr. 1349; m. bef. 11 May 1335, Cicely de Weyland, dau. of Sir Richard de Weyland. (CP II 426-427; IV 269-277; V 736).

35. ELIZABETH DE BURGHERSH, b. 1342, d. ca. 26 Jul. 1409; m. bef. Dec. 1364, **SIR EDWARD DESPENSER**, K.G. (74-34), b. ca. 24 Mar. 1335/6, d. 11 Nov. 1375, Lord of Glamorgan. (CP II 427; IV 274-277; V 320, 736, charts).

36. MARGARET LE DESPENSER, m. **SIR ROBERT DE FERRERS** (61-34).

Line 71

29. ISABEL BIGOD (70-29), m. (1) **GILBERT DE LACY** (177A-8) of Trim. (CP V 437; IX 589-590, and note c p. 590).

30. MAUD DE LACY, d. 1299; m. Sir Geoffrey de Geneville, d. 1314, son of Simon de Joinville, Sénéchal of Champagne, Seigneur de Vaucouleurs in France. (CP V 628-631; Banks I 220-221).

31. SIR PIERS DE GENEVILLE, d. bef. 8 Jun. 1292, Baron de Geneville of Trim and Ludlow Castle; m. **JEANNE DE LUSIGNAN** (135-32), d. 1323. (CP I 339; V 632-634; Banks I 221).

32. JOAN DE GENEVILLE, b. 2 Feb. 1285/6, d. 19 Oct. 1356; m. bef. 6 Oct. 1306, **SIR ROGER DE MORTIMER** (27-31, 120-33), Earl of March. (CP I 339; V 634; Banks I 220-221).

33. JOAN DE MORTIMER, d. 1337/1351; m. bef. 13 Jun. 1330, as 1st wife, **SIR JAMES AUDLEY**, K.G. (122-33), 2nd Lord Audley, of Redcastle, Shropshire, b. Knesale, Notts., 8 Jan. 1312/3, d. 1 Apr. 1386, will dated 1385; fought at Poitiers, M.P. 1331-1386, son of Nicholas, 1st Lord Audley of Heleigh, and Joane, dau. of William Martin, Lord Martin (by Eleanor, dau. **SIR REYNOLD FITZ PIERS** (262-30), wid. of Henry de Lacy, Earl of Lincoln. (CP I 339-340; Banks I 100-102). Sir James Audley m. (2) by 1351, Isabel, living 1366, said to be dau. of Roger, 5th Lord Strange of Knockyn. Issue by both wives.

29. ISABEL BIGOD (70-29), wid. of Gilbert de Lacy of Ewyas Lacy; m. (2) aft. 1230, **SIR JOHN FITZ GEOFFREY** (246C-28), d. 23 Nov. 1258, of Shere, Farnbridge, etc., Justiciar of Ireland, 1245-1256, son of Geoffrey Fitz Piers, Earl of Essex, and **AVELINE DE CLARE** (246B-27). (CP V 433-434, 437).

30. MAUD FITZ JOHN, d. ca. 18 Apr. 1301; m. (2) bef. 1270, **WILLIAM DE BEAUCHAMP** (86-29), b. 1237, buried 22 Jun. 1298, 9th Earl of Warwick; she had m. (1) Gerard de Furnival, of Sheffield, co. York. (CP IV 265, 670 chart III; V 437, 439-441).

31. ISABEL DE BEAUCHAMP, d. 1306; m. (1) Sir Patrick de Chaworth, d. ca. 7 Jul. 1283, Lord of Kidwelley, Wales, son of Patrick de Chaworth; m. (2) 1286, Sir Hugh le Despenser, b. 1 Mar. 1260/1, hanged Oct. 1326, Earl of Winchester (son of Sir Hugh le Despenser, sum. 14 Dec. 1264 Lord Despenser, d. Aug. 1265 at Evesham, and Aline Basset, dau. of Philip Basset of Wycombe, Bucks who m. (2) Roger Bigod), by (2) Isabel was the parent of Ailenor (or Eleanor) who m. **HUGH DE COURTNEY** (51-30). (Sanders, 125).

32. MAUD DE CHAWORTH (by (1)), m. bef. 2 Mar. 1296/7 **HENRY PLANTAGENET** (17-29), b. 1281, d. 22 Sept. 1345, Earl of Lancaster. (CP I 244).

Line 73

29. ISABEL BIGOD (70-29); m. (2) **SIR JOHN FITZ GEOFFREY** (246C-28). (CP V 437).

30. JOAN FITZ JOHN, d. ca. 26 May 1303; m. ca. 1268, Theobald Butler (le Boteler), b. ca. 1242, d. 26 Sep. 1285, son of Theobald le Boteler, d. 1248, and Margery, dau. of Richard de Burgh. (CP II 449; V 437).

31. EDMUND BUTLER, d. London, 13 Sep. 1321, Justiciar and Governor of Ireland; m. 1302, **JOAN** (178A-8), dau. of John Fitz Thomas Fitz Gerald of Kildare. (CP II 449-450; III 60; V 437).

32. JAMES BUTLER, b. ca. 1305, d. 6 Jan. 1337/8, cr. Earl of Ormond; m. 1327, **ELEANOR DE BOHUN** (7-30). (CP V 437; X 116-119).

33. PETRONILLA BUTLER, liv. 28 May 1365, dead 1368, m. 8 Sept. 1352 **GILBERT TALBOT** (95-32), b. ca. 1332, M.P. 1362, d. 24 Apr. 1387, Lord Talbot. (See also 13-31). (CP XII pt. 1, 614-617).

Line 74

30. MAUD FITZ JOHN (72-30), m. (2) **WILLIAM DE BEAUCHAMP** (86-29). (CP IV 265, 670 chart III).

31. ISABEL DE BEAUCHAMP, d. 1306; m. (2) 1286, Sir Hugh le Despenser, d. 27 Oct. 1326, Earl of Winchester. (CP IV 262-265; V 433-434, 437).

32. SIR HUGH LE DESPENSER, hanged and quartered, 29 Nov. 1326, Baron Despenser; m. in 1306 bef. 14 Jun., **ALIANORE DE CLARE** (8-30), b. Oct. 1292, d. 30 Jun. 1337. (CP IV 267-271, cf. 269, 670 chart III; V 763).

Line 74 (cont.)

33. SIR EDWARD DESPENSER, d. 30 Sep. 1342; m. Groby, 20 Apr. 1335, Anne de Ferrers, d. 8 Aug. 1337, dau. of **WILLIAM FERRERS** (58-31). (CP IV 274-275, 670, chart III; V 343-344, 736).
34. SIR EDWARD DESPENSER, K.G., b. ca. 24 Mar. 1335/6, d. 11 Nov. 1375; m. 1364, **ELIZABETH DE BURGHERSH** (70-35), d. ca. 26 Jul. 1409. (CP II 425-427; IV 274-278, 670 chart III; V 736).
35. ELIZABETH DESPENSER, m. **SIR JOHN FITZ ALAN** (21-32), b. 30 Nov. 1364, d. 14 Aug. 1390. (CP I 253; V 736; Banks I 378).

Line 75

29. ISABEL BIGOD (70-29); m. (2) **SIR JOHN FITZ GEOFFREY** (246 C-28), Justiciar of Ireland. (CP V 437; IX 589-590).
30. AVELINA FITZ JOHN, d. ca. 20 May 1274; m. **WALTER DE BURGH** (177B-9), d. 28 Jul. 1271, 2nd Earl of Ulster. (CP V 437; XII pt. 2, 171-3).
31. RICHARD DE BURGH, d. Athassel, 29 Jul. 1326, 3rd Earl of Ulster; m. by 27 Feb 1280/1, Margaret, d. 1304, daughter perhaps of Arnoul III, Count of Guines (see 94A-31). (CP V 437; IX 403-404; XII pt. 2, 173-7; Gen. Mag. XX:335-340).
32. ELEANOR DE BURGH, m. 3 Jan. 1297, **THOMAS DE MULTON** (40-30), b. 21 Feb. 1276, d. 1321, Lord Multon. (CP V 437; IX 403-404).

Line 75A   (Prepared by Douglas Richardson)

30. AVELINA FITZ JOHN (75-30), d. ca. 20 May 1274, m. ca. 1257 **WALTER DE BURGH** (177B-9), b. ca. 1230, d. 28 July 1271, Earl of Ulster, son of Richard de Burgh, lord of Connaught (died 1242), by his wife, Egidia, dau. of Walter de Lacy (died 1241), lord of Meath. (Orpen: Ireland under the Normans, III, chart p. 286-287; IV, chart p. 159; CP XII, pt. II 171).
31. EGIDIA DE BURGH, m. James Steward, 5th High Steward of Scotland, b. ca. 1243, d. 1309, son of Alexander, High Steward of Scotland, by his wife, Jean, said to be daughter of James, Earl of Bute. (Orpen, op. cit., IV, chart p. 159; SP I: 13-14; Calendar of Documents Scotland II, no. 847).
32. WALTER STEWARD, 6th High Steward of Scotland, b. 1292, d. 9 Apr. 1326, m. (1) 1315, **MARJORIE BRUCE** (252-31), b. bef. 1297, died 2 Mar 1316, dau. of Robert de Bruce, Earl of Carrick, King of Scotland, by Isabel (also called Matilda), dau. of Donald, 6th Earl of Mar. (SP I 14-15; CP I 310-311).

Line 76

27. ISABEL DE CLARE (66-27), m. William Marshall, Earl of Pembroke. (CP I 22; X 364).
28. MAUD MARSHALL, d. 27 Mar. 1248; m. (2) **WILLIAM DE WARENNE** (83-27), d. 1240, Earl of Surrey. (CP IV 670; X 364 note e).

29. MAUD DE BRAIOSE (67-29), m. **ROGER DE MORTIMER** (27-29).

30. ISABELLA MORTIMER, m. **JOHN FITZ ALAN** (149-29).

31. RICHARD FITZ ALAN, Earl of Arundel; m. Alasia de Saluzzo. (CP I 240-241, 250).

32. MARGARET FITZ ALAN, m. as 1st wife, William le Botiller, of Wem and Oversley, b. 8 Sep. 1296, d. Dec. 1361, son of William le Botiller of Oversley, co. Warwick, and his (1) wife Beatrice. He m. (2) ca. 1354, **JOAN DE SUDELEY** (222-35). See Gen. Mag. 13: 173-174; CP II 230-233; Wm.Salt Soc. vol. (1945-6) pp. 40-43).

33. WILLIAM LE BOTILLER, Lord le Botiller of Wem and Oversley, b. bef. 1331, d. 14 Aug. 1369, M.P. 1368-1369; m. bef. Jul. 1343, Elizabeth, perh. Holand of Upholand. (CP II 230-235; V 320 chart; XII pt. 1, 417-418; Wm.Salt Soc. n.s. (1945-6) pp. 42-43). Note: Elizabeth was not dau. of Robert, Lord Holand as his daughter, Elizabeth, married by 1340 **SIR HENRY FITZ ROGER** (261-35). See refs cited under that line & generation.

34. ELIZABETH LE BOTILLER, of Wem and Oversley, b. bef. 1345, d. 19 Jun. 1411, will 6 Jan. 1410/11, pro. Jun. 1411; m. ca. 27 Sep. 1369, **SIR ROBERT DE FERRERS** (62-33). (CP II 230-235; V 320 chart; Wm.Salt Soc. cit.)

32. SIR RICHARD FITZ ALAN (60-32), m. **ELEANOR DE LANCASTER** (17-30). (CP XII pt. 1, 44; Muskett II 175).

33. ALICE FITZ ALAN, d. 17 Mar. 1415/6; m. 1364, **SIR THOMAS DE HOLAND,** K.G. (47-32). (CP VII 154-156; XII pt. 1, 44; Muskett II 175).

34. ELEANOR DE HOLAND (2nd dau. of the name, 5th child), m. 1399, Thomas de Montagu, K.G., d. ca. 3 Nov. 1428, Earl of Salisbury. (CP V 429; VII 156 note e; XI 394-395; XII pt. 2, 305 note a; Warwick Castle and Its Earls, I 144; II 829 chart).

35. ALICE DE MONTAGU, d. bef. Feb. 1462/3; m. in or bef. Feb. 1420/1, Sir Richard de Neville, K.G., beheaded at Pontefract, 31 Dec. 1460, Earl of Salisbury, son of **RALPH DE NEVILLE** (207-34), K.G., 1st Earl of Westmoreland, and **JOAN BEAUFORT** (2-32). (CP V 429; XI 395-398; Warwick Castle, etc., ibid.)

36. ALICE DE NEVILLE, living 22 Nov. 1503 (sister of Richard de Neville, Earl of Warwick and Earl of Salisbury, the "King Maker"); m. **HENRY FITZ HUGH** (219-35), Lord Fitz Hugh, d. 8 Jun. 1472, son of William Fitz Hugh and Margery de Willoughby. (CP V 427-429; X 309).

37. ELIZABETH FITZ HUGH, m. Sir William Parr, K.G., of Kendal, d. ca. 26 Feb. 1483/4. (CP V 428 note h; X 309; XI 398).

38. WILLIAM PARR, d. bef. 13 Dec. 1547, Baron Parr of Horton, co. Northampton (uncle to Queen Katherine Parr), Sheriff of Northamptonshire; m. bef. 1511, Mary Salisbury, d. 10 Jul. 1555, dau. of William Salisbury of Horton and Elizabeth Wylde. (CP X

309-311).

39. ELIZABETH PARR, m. as his 2nd wife, **SIR NICHOLAS WODHULL** (150-39), d. 5 May 1531. (TAG 21:72).

Line 79

29. ROBERT DE VERE (60-29), 5th Earl of Oxford; m. Alice de Sanford. (CP X 216-218).

30. ALFONSO DE VERE, of Great Hormean, Herts., d. ca. 20 Dec. 1329; m. Joan, prob. dau. of Sir Richard Foliot. (CP X 222, note a).

31. JOHN DE VERE, 7th Earl of Oxford, b. ca. 12 Mar. 1311/2, d. Rheims, Jan. 1359/60, Hereditary Chamberlain to the King of England; served in France and Spain; m. bef. 27 Mar. 1336, Margaret de Badlesmere, b. 1310, d. 24 May 1366, dau. Bartholomew de Badlesmere and **MARGARET DE CLARE** (54-33). (CP I 373; X 222-223).

32. MARGARET DE VERE, d. 15 Jun. 1398; m. (1) **HENRY DE BEAUMONT** (17-31), d. 17 Jun. 1369; m. (2) ca. 1370, Sir Nicholas de Lovaine, b. ca. 1325, d. 1376, (his first wife was Margaret, dau. of John de Bereford, wid. Sir John de Pulteney, d. ca. 1349); m. (3) Sir John de Devereux, Lord Devereux, d. 22 Feb. 1392/3. (CP I 373 note e; II 60-61; IV 296-299; X 224 note a; The Gen. Mag. vol. 15, pp. 251-255, 284-292).

33. MARGARET DE LOVAINE (dau. by (2) husb.), b. ca. 1372, d. 1408; m. bef. 1398, Sir Philip de Seyntclere (or St. Clair), d. 1408, leaving two minor chn. John and Thomas. (CP IV 299 footnote c; VCH Oxford V 284-285).

34. THOMAS ST. CLAIR, (yr. bro. and h. of John), d. 6 May 1434. Held Chalgrove, Oxon., and extensive property in Sussex and Suffolk; m. bef. 8 Feb. 1424 (fined for m. w/o a lic.) Margaret Hoo, dau. Sir William Hoo & Alice St. Omer (CP VI 567; Cal. Pat. Rolls 1424; Inq.p.m. 2 Hen VII on Thomas Hoo, nephew of Margaret) vol. 1, p. 93 no. 205; Genealogist n.s. 18 (1902) p. 101).

35. EDITH ST. CLAIR, b. ca. 1425, dau. and co-h. 1451; m. **SIR RICHARD HARCOURT** (50-37), sheriff of Oxford 1461, d. 1486.

Line 80

27. ISABEL DE CLARE (66-27), m. William Marshall, Earl of Pembroke.

28. JOAN MARSHALL, m. Warin de Munchensi, Lord of Swanscomb. (CP X 364 note a, 377-382).

29. JOAN DE MUNCHENSI, d. bef. 30 Sep. 1307; m. 13 Aug. 1247, **SIR WILLIAM DE VALENCE** (154-29), b. ca. 1225/6, d. bef. 18 May 1296, Lord of Valence, Montignac, Bellac, Rancon and Champagnac, knighted 13 Oct. 1247, crusader 6 Mar. 1250, 4th son of Hugh X, le Brun, Count de Lusignan, Count of la Marche and Angoulême, Lord of Lusignan, and **ISABELLA** (153-28), wid. of John, King of England. (CP X 364 note a, 377. Generations 27-29: CP IV 670 chart III).

27. JOHN DE SOMERY, m. Hawise (see 55-27), sister of Gervase Paynell and dau. of Ralph. (CP X 320).

28. RALPH DE SOMERY, Baron Dudley, held Dudley and Dinas Powis, d. 1211; m. Margaret, dau. William Marshall, Earl of Pembroke & **ISABEL DE CLARE** (66-27). (CP X 320).

29. ROGER DE SOMERY, d. on or bef. 26 Aug. 1273, Lord Dudley, held Dinas Powis; m. (1) **NICHOLE D'AUBIGNY** (126-30), m. (2) in or bef. 1254, Amabilia de Chaucombe, d. ca. 1278, dau. & coh. of Sir Robert de Chaucombe and widow of Sir Gilbert de Segrave. (CP X 320; XII pt. 1, 112-113; Segrave, The Segrave Family 1066 to 1935, pp. 13-16 which may or may not be correct in stating that this Gilbert d. 8 Oct—but year prob. not 1254 as shown here.)

30. ROGER DE SOMERY (by (2)), b. 24 Jun. 1255, ae. 18 in 1273, grandson of Ralph de Somery, d. 11 Oct. 1291, Baron Dudley, 1290, held Dinas Powis; m. Agnes, d. 23 Nov. 1308. (CP XII pt. 1, 114).

31. MARGARET DE SOMERY, b. 1290, d. 1384, Baroness Dudley; m. John de Sutton I, Lord of Dudley Castle, co. Stafford, Knt., 1326, living 1327, son of Richard de Sutton; she was sister and h. of John de Somery, b. 1278, d.s.p. 29 Dec. 1321. Baron Dudley, M.P. 1308-1321, d. ca. 1359. (CP XII pt. 1, 109-115 & p. 115 note g, 351-352; DNB 16: 107-109).

32. JOHN DE SUTTON II, d. 1359, seen 25 Feb. 1341/42, M.P. 25 Feb. 1341/2; m. Isabel de Cherleton, d. 1396, dau. of John de Cherleton, Lord of Powis. (CP IV 479 note e; Old-CP VII 190; DNB 16: 108). (MC-30-7).

33. JOHN DE SUTTON III, of Dudley Castle, b. 1338, living 1369; m. (1) 25 Dec. 1357, Katharine, b. ca. 1340, d. by 25 Dec. 1361, dau. of **RALPH DE STAFFORD** (55-32) and **MARGARET DE AUDLEY** (9-31); m. (2) aft. 1361, Margaret de Mortimer, dau. of Roger de Mortimer of Wigmore. (CP IV 479 note e; DNB 16: 107-109; Hist.Cols.of Staffs. XIII (1892) 38). (See also Elmendorf: Anc.of Gov. Thomas Dudley, p. 11. Marriage certificate shows she would be a minor for 4 years after marriage).

34. JOHN DE SUTTON IV, by (1), of Dudley Castle, b. 6 Dec. 1361, d. 1395/6, Inq.p.m. 1401; m. Jane, Inq.p.m. 1409. (CP IV 479 note e; DNB 16: 107-109). (Adlard says he m. (1) Alice prob. dau. of guardian Philip le Despenser. She d. 1392. He m. (2) Jane. Perh. Alice (1 wife) mother of John V).

35. JOHN DE SUTTON V, of Dudley Castle, b. 1379, d. 1407, Inq.p.m. 1407; m. Constance Blount, d. 1432, dau. of Sir Walter Blount of Barton. (CP IV 479; DNB 16: 107-109).

36. JOHN DE SUTTON VI, K.G., b. 25 Dec. 1400, bapt. at Barton-under-Needwood, co. Derby, d. 30 Sep. 1487, will 17 Aug. 1487, Baron Dudley, Lord Lieutenant of Ireland, 1428-1430, Constable of Clun Castle 1435, M.P. 1440-1487, Constable of Wigmore Castle 1459, K.G. bef. 1459, wounded at Bloreheath, 1459; m. aft. 1422, Elizabeth Berkeley, d. ca. 8 Dec. 1478, dau. of Sir John Berkeley of Beverstone, co. Gloucester, by his 1st wife, Elizabeth Betteshorne, dau. of Sir John Betteshorne. (CP IV 479-480; DNB 16:

Line 81 (cont.)

107-109; The Her. and Gen., vols. V and VI; Wm.Salt Soc., vol. IX).
John de Sutton VI was most probably an ancestor of Gov. Thomas
Dudley of Mass. (50-43), though the parentage of Captain Roger
Dudley, father of Gov. Dudley, is at present unknown.

37. SIR EDMUND SUTTON de Dudley, d. aft. 6 Jul. 1483, but
bef. 1487; m. (2) **MATILDA CLIFFORD** (5-36). (CP IV 480.
Generations 32-38: George Adlard: The Sutton-Dudleys of England
and New England. N.Y.C., 1862, Pedigree "A" The Suttons; Warwick
Castle and Its Earls, I, 224-227). (Generations 28-31: CP XII pt. 1,
109-115 note e; XII pt. 1, 351-352).

Line 82

29. ISABEL BIGOD (72-29), m. **SIR JOHN FITZ GEOFFREY**
(246C-28).

30. ISABEL FITZ JOHN, m. Robert de Vespont (or Vipont), d. 7
Jun. 1264, Lord of Westmoreland.

31. ISABEL DE VESPONT, d. 14 May 1292, Lady of Appleby and
Brougham; m. Roger de Clifford, drowned, 6 Nov. 1282.

32. ROBERT DE CLIFFORD, m. **MAUD DE CLARE** (64-32).
(Generations 29-32: CP V 437).

ISABEL DE VERMANDOIS

AND WILLIAM DE WARENNE

Line 83

24. ISABEL DE VERMANDOIS (50-24, 53-24), m. (2) 1118, William de Warenne, Earl of Surrey, d. 1138, son of William, d. 1088 & wife Gundred. (CP IV 670; VII 642; XII pt. 1, 492-495).

25. WILLIAM DE WARENNE, b. 1118, d. 1148, 3rd Earl of Surrey; m. **ELA TALVAS** (108-26), d. 1178. (CP IV 670).

26. ISABELLE DE WARENNE, Countess of Surrey, sole dau. and h., d. 13 Jul. 1199; m. (1) William of Blois, yr. son of King Stephen, n.i., m. (2) 1164, **HAMELIN PLANTAGENET** (123-26), d. 7 May 1202, Earl of Surrey, natural son of Geoffrey V Plantagenet. (CP IV 670).

27. WILLIAM DE WARENNE, d. 1240, Earl of Surrey; m. (2) 1225, **MAUD MARSHALL** (69-28, 76-28), d. 1248. (CP IV 670).

28. JOHN DE WARENNE, b. 1231, d. ca. Michaelmas 1304, Earl of Surrey; m. 1247, **ALICE (ALFAIS) DE LUSIGNAN** (153-29), d. 1291. (CP IV 670).

29. WILLIAM DE WARENNE, b. 1256, killed in a tournament at Croydon, 15 Dec. 1286; m. prob. 1285, **JOAN DE VERE** (60-30), d. 1293. (CP I 242; IV 670).

30. ALICE DE WARENNE, d. bef. 23 May 1338; m. 1306, **SIR EDMUND FITZ ALAN** (28-32), b. 1 May 1285; beheaded at Hereford, 17 Nov. 1326, 8th Earl of Arundel. (CP I 241-243, 253; IV 670).

Line 84

24. ISABEL DE VERMANDOIS (50-24, 53-24), m. William de Warenne, Earl of Surrey.

25. GUNDRED DE WARENNE, m. bef. 1130 (1) **ROGER DE NEWBURGH** (151-26), d. 1153, 2nd Earl of Warwick, crusader, son of Henry de Newburgh, d. 20 Jun. 1123, 1st Earl of Warwick, 1090. (Old-CP VIII 53-56).

26. WALERAN DE NEWBURGH, b. bef. 1153, d. 12 Dec. 1204, 4th Earl of Warwick; m. (2) Alice de Harcourt, dau. of Robert de Harcourt of Stanton-Harcourt, co. Oxford, (and his wife Isabel, living 1207/8, dau. of Richard de Camville of Stanton), and wid. of John de Limesi of Colley Weston, co. Northampton. (Old-CP VIII 53-56; Wm.Salt Soc. n.s. vol. 35 chart).

27. ALICE DE NEWBURGH, d. 1246-1263; m. William Mauduit, Baron Mauduit, d. Apr. 1257, of Handslope, Bucks. (Old-CP VIII 53-56).

28. ISABEL MAUDUIT, buried at the Nunnery of Cokehill; m. William de Beauchamp, 5th Baron Beauchamp of Elmley Castle, co.

Worcester, will dated 7 Jan. 1268/9. (CP II 44; Old-CP VIII 53-56. Generations 24-28: Warwick Castle and Its Earls, II 827-828; CP IV 670 chart III).

29. WALTER DE BEAUCHAMP, d. 1303, of Beauchamp's Court, in Alcester, co. Warwick, and Powyck, co. Worcester, Steward of the Household of King Edward I. (CP II 46 note f).

30. GILES DE BEAUCHAMP, of Beauchamp's Court, d. Oct. 1361; m. ca. 1329, **CATHERINE DE BURES** (189-6), dau. of Sir John de Bures. (CP II 46 note f; V 320 chart).

31. SIR JOHN DE BEAUCHAMP, d. 1378-1401; m. Elizabeth, d. 1411 (prob. dau. of Sir John St. John). (CP II 46 note f).

32. SIR WILLIAM DE BEAUCHAMP, of Powyck and Alcester, d. bef. 1431, Constable of the Castle of Gloucester, Sheriff of Worcestershire and Gloucestershire; m. bef. Mar. 1414/5, Catharine Ufflete, dau. of Sir Gerard de Ufflete. (CP II 46-47).

33. SIR JOHN DE BEAUCHAMP, K.G., d. bef. 19 Apr. 1475, cr. Baron Beauchamp of Powyck, 2 May 1447, Justice of South Wales, Lord Treasurer of England, 1450-1452; m. ca. 1434, Margaret Ferrers, sister of Richard Ferrers. (CP II 46-47).

34. SIR RICHARD DE BEAUCHAMP, K.B., b. 1435, d. 19 Jan. 1502-3, 2nd Baron Beauchamp of Powyck; m. 27 Jan. 1446/7, **ELIZABETH STAFFORD** (55-37), dau. of Sir Humphrey Stafford, Knt., of Grafton, co. Worcester. (CP II 47; Inq.p.m. 21 Nov. 1504).

35. ANNE DE BEAUCHAMP, b. 1462, d. 1535; m. Richard Lygon, Knt., of Arle Court, co. Gloucester. (CP II 47 note e; Visitation of Gloucester (1623), 204-206).

36. SIR RICHARD LYGON, Knt., of Arle Court, d. 1556, Sheriff of Worcester, 1547; m. Margaret Grevell, dau. of Sir William Grevell of Arle Court and Cheltenham, Judge of Common Pleas. (Visitation of Gloucester, 204-206).

37. HENRY LYGON, of Upton St. Leonard, co. Gloucester, d. ca. 1577, will dated 30 Jul. 1577, pro. 15 Aug. 1577; m. **ELIZABETH BERKELEY** (187-15), dau. of Sir John Berkeley. (Visitation of Gloucester (1623), 204-206).

38. ELIZABETH LYGON, m. Edward Basset of Uley, co. Gloucester, will dated 3 Jun. 1601, pro. 5 Nov. 1602. (Visitation of Gloucester (1623), 204-206).

39. JANE BASSET, d. 23 Apr. 1631; m. Dr. John Deighton, Gent., d. 16 May 1640, of St. Nicholas, Gloucester, will dated 30 Jan. 1639, pro. 21 May 1640. (Basset Genealogy, 245-246).

40. KATHERINE (DEIGHTON) HACKBURNE, bapt. Gloucester, England 16 Jan. 1614/5, d. 29 Aug. 1671, wid. of Samuel Hackburne; m. (2) Roxbury, Mass., 14 Apr. 1644, **GOVERNOR THOMAS DUDLEY** (50-43), d. 31 Jul. 1653; she was his second wife, the mother of Deborah Dudley, m. Jonathan Wade; Gov. Joseph Dudley, m. Rebecca Tyng; and Hon. Paul Dudley, m. Mary Leverett. Katherine (Deighton) (Hackburne) Dudley m. (3) the Reverend John Allin of Dedham, and had children by all three husbands.

41. GOVERNOR JOSEPH DUDLEY, A.M., (Harvard College, 1665), b. Roxbury, 23 Sep. 1647, buried Roxbury 8 Apr. 1720; m.

Line 84 (cont.)

1669, Rebecca Tyng, dau. of Maj.-Gen. Edward Tyng. He was Governor of Massachusetts, 1702-1715. (See Sibley; Harvard Graduates, II 166-188).

40. FRANCES DEIGHTON (sister of Katherine), bapt. St. Nicholas, Gloucester, 1 Mar. 1611; d. Taunton, Mass., Feb. 1705/6; m. Witcombe Magna, Gloucester, 11 Feb. 1632, Richard Williams, bapt. Wootton-under-Edge, 28 Jan. 1607, d. Taunton, Mass., Aug. 1693. (Waters I 551-552).

40. JANE DEIGHTON (sister of Katherine), bapt. St. Nicholas, 5 Apr. 1609, living in Boston, Mass., 1671; m. (1) St. Nicholas, 3 Jan. 1627, John Lugg, d. aft. 1644, came to N.E., 1638; m. (2) ca. 1650, Jonathan Negus, b. 1602, living 1678; children by both husbands. (TAG 9:221-222). (Generations 34-40: Certified by A.T. Butler, 11 Dec. 1928, of the College of Arms, London, cf. W.L. Holman in TAG 9:213-214. Generations 38-40: Waters I 551-552; NEHGR 45: 303, 96; 342-343; v. Redlich 158. See also Boston Evening Transcript, 9 Jul. 1938).

Line 85

30. GILES DE BEAUCHAMP (84-30), m. **CATHERINE DE BURES** (189-6).

31. ROGER DE BEAUCHAMP, d. 3 Jan. 1379/80, 1st Baron Beauchamp of Bletsoe, Chamberlain to the Household of King Edward III; M.P. 1364-1380; m. (1) bef. 1336/7, Sybil de Patshull, living 26 Oct. 1351, dau. of Sir John de Patshull (M.P. 1343) and Mabel de Grandison, dau. of Sir William de Grandison and Sybil de Tregoz. (CP II 44-45; Banks I 118-119; II 136-137).

32. ROGER DE BEAUCHAMP, who d. bef. his father. (CP II 45).

33. ROGER DE BEAUCHAMP, Knt., b. 1363, d. 3 May 1406, 2nd Baron Beauchamp of Bletsoe and Lydiard Tregoze; m. Joan Clopton, dau. of William Clopton. (CP II 45, Banks as above).

34. SIR JOHN DE BEAUCHAMP, Knt., 3rd Baron Beauchamp of Bletsoe, d. ca. 1412; m. (1) by Jan. 1405/6, Margaret Holand, dau. of Sir John Holand; m. (2) Esther Stourton, dau. of Sir John Stourton. (CP II 45).

35. MARGARET DE BEAUCHAMP, prob. but not certainly by (1), d. 1482; m. (1) Sir Oliver St. John, Knt., d. 1437, of Penmark, Gloucestershire. (CP II 45 note c, 206; XI 545; Banks as above; Gen. n.s. XVI 13).

36. SIR JOHN DE ST. JOHN, of Penmark, 1488; m. Alice Bradshagh, dau. of Sir Thomas Bradshagh of Haigh. (CP II 206; Collins V 104).

37. SIR JOHN DE ST. JOHN, K.B., of Bletsoe, co. Bedford, K.B., 1502; m. Sybil, dau. of Morgan ap Jenkyn ap Philip. (CP II 206; Collins V 104).

38. ALEXANDER ST. JOHN, Esq., of Thurley, co. Bedford; m. Jane Dalyson, dau. of George Dalyson of Cranesley, co. Northampton, and wid. of Thomas Lenthroppe of Shinglehall, Herts.

Line 85 (cont.)

(Collins V 104. Generations 35-38: The Visitation of the County of Huntingdon . . . 1613, Camden Society 1849, p. 2).

39. HENRY ST. JOHN, d. 1598, of Keysoe, co. Bedford; m. Jane Neale, d. 1618, sister of John Neale of Wollaston.

40. SIR OLIVER ST. JOHN, Gent., of Keysoe (Heishoe), co. Bedford, b. ca. 1575, d. Keysoe, 23 Mar. 1625/6, will made 13 Mar. 1625/6, pro. 1 May 1626; m. (1) 1597, **SARAH BULKELEY**, b. 1580, d. 1611, dau. of **REV. EDWARD BULKELEY**, D.D. (31-39) and Olive Irby; m. (2) at Goldington, co. Bedford, 16 Aug. 1611, Alice Haselden, half-sister of Jane Allen, first wife of the Rev. Peter Bulkeley. (Waters II 1420-1421).

41. ELIZABETH ST. JOHN, bapt. Bletsoe, co. Bedford, 12 Jan. 1604/5, d. Lynn, Mass., 3 Mar. 1676/7; m. Boston, England, 6 Aug. 1629, Rev. Samuel Whiting, A.M., b. Boston, Lincolnshire, 20 Nov. 1597, d. Lynn, Mass., 11 Dec. 1679, minister at Lynn, 1636-1679, son of the Hon. John Whiting, Mayor of Boston, Eng. (Generations 39-41: Bulkeley Genealogy, 17, 30-31; Waters II 1420-1421; Weis: Colonial Clergy of N.E., 223; NEHGR 14: 51-52; Harleian Soc., vol. 19, Visitations of Bedfordshire, 51-55).

42. REV. SAMUEL WHITING, Jr., A.M., b. Skirbeck, Lincolnshire, Eng., 25 Mar. 1633; A.B., Harvard Coll., 1653, A.M.; ord. Billerica, 11 Nov. 1663-1713, d. Billerica, 28 Feb. 1712/3, ae. 79.

42. REV. JOSEPH WHITING, A.M., b. Lynn, Mass., 6 Apr. 1641; A.B., H.C., 1661, A.M., Fellow, 1664-1665; ord. Lynn, 6 Oct. 1680-1682; sett. Southampton, L.I., N.Y., 1682-1723; d. Southampton, 7 Apr. 1723, ae. 82. (See TAG 34:15-17, supports this line).

Line 86

28. ISABEL MAUDUIT (84-28), m. William de Beauchamp, 5th Baron Beauchamp of Elmley Castle. (Old-CP VIII 54).

29. WILLIAM DE BEAUCHAMP, b. 1237, buried 22 Jun. 1298, 9th Earl of Warwick; m. bef. 1270, **MAUD FITZ JOHN** (72-30), d. 16 or 18 Apr. 1301, bur. 7 May 1301. (Generations 28-29: CP IV 670 chart III; V 437; Old-CP VIII 53-56; Warwick Castle and Its Earls, II 828).

30. GUY DE BEAUCHAMP, b. 1278, d. Warwick Castle, 10 Aug. 1315, 10th Earl of Warwick, knighted 25 Mar. 1296, will made 25 Jul. 1315; m. bef. 28 Feb. 1309/10, **ALICE DE TONY** (98-31), d. 1 Jan. 1324/5, dau. of Ralph de Tony, wid. of Thomas Leyburne. She m. (3) William Zouche, Lord Zouche of Mortimer. (CP XI 477; Old-CP VIII 56-57).

31. MAUD DE BEAUCHAMP, d. 1369; m. (1) Geoffrey de Say, d. 26 Jun. 1359, 2nd Baron Say, knight-banneret, Admiral of the Fleet. (CP XI 475-477).

32. IDONEA DE SAY, d. ca. 1384; m. Sir John Clinton, d. 6 Sep. 1398, 3rd Baron Clinton of Maxstoke, co. Warwick, son of John Clinton, 2nd Baron Clinton, b. ca. 1300, d. ca. 1335; m. by 24 Feb. 1328/9, Margaret Corbet, dau. Sir William Corbet of Chaddesley

Line 86 (cont.)

Corbet, Worcs. She was living 1343. (CP XI 478 note g; III 314). (John de Clinton, 2nd Baron Clinton was s. and h. of John de Clinton (s. and h. of Thomas de Clinton by Maud, dau. Sir Ralph Bracebridge of Kinsbury, co. Worcs.), b. ca. 1258, d. 1310; 1st Baron Clinton; m. ca. 1290, Ida, dau. Sir William de Odingsells of Maxstoke by ELA (30-28), dau. of **WALTER FITZ ROBERT** (148-28). She was 1st dau. b. ca. 1270, living 1321).

    33. MARGARET DE CLINTON, m. Sir Baldwin de Montfort, of Coleshill Manor, co. Warwick. (See TAG, Jan. 1950; Topo. and Geneal. I, 359-360; VCH Warwick IV 50-51).

    34. SIR WILLIAM DE MONTFORT, of Coleshill Manor; m. Margaret.

    35. ROBERT MONTFORT, Esq., of Bescote, co. Stafford, and Monkspath, co. Warwick. (Ancient Deeds V, 163, #A 11549; VCH Warwick IV 50-51).

    36. KATHARINE MONTFORT, m. **SIR GEORGE BOOTH** (33-36), d. 1483, of Dunham-Massie, co. Chester. (Warwick Castle and Its Earls, II 828; Ancestry of John Barber White, 200, corrected by v. Redlich 121-122; Ormerod (Helsby) I, 524).

Line 87

    30. GUY DE BEAUCHAMP (86-30), m. **ALICE DE TONY** (98-31). (CP II 50).

    31. THOMAS BEAUCHAMP, b. Warwick Castle, 1313, d. Calais, 16 Nov. 1369, K.G., 23 Apr. 1349, will made 6 Sep. 1369; m. 1337, **KATHARINE DE MORTIMER** (120-34), will made 4 Aug. 1369. (CP II 50).

    32. THOMAS BEAUCHAMP, b. ca. 1340, d. 8 Apr. 1401; K.G., ca. Jan. 1372/3, will made 1 Apr. 1400; m. bef. Apr. 1381, Margaret de Ferrers, d. 22 Jan. 1406/7, dau. of **WILLIAM DE FERRERS** (11-32). (Generations 30-34: CP XII pt. 2, pp. 370-382).

    33. RICHARD BEAUCHAMP, K.G., b. 28 Jan. 1381/2, d. Rouen, 30 Apr. 1439, 12th Earl of Warwick and Albemarle; m. (1) Sep. 1393, **ELIZABETH BERKELEY** (39-34), b. ca. 1386, d. 29 Dec. 1422, only dau. of Thomas Berkeley and Margaret, dau. of Warine, Lord L'Isle. (CP II 131 note c); m. (2) Isabel, dau. and event. heiress of Thomas le Despenser, Earl of Gloucester, wid. of Richard Beauchamp, Earl of Worcester. (CP IV 282).

    34. ELEANOR BEAUCHAMP, dau. by (1), d. 1467, wid. of Thomas, Lord Ros; m. (2) ca. 1435, **EDMUND BEAUFORT** (1-33), Duke of Somerset; m. (3) Walter Rokesley, Esq. (CP II 131 note c, 145; IV 417. Generations 30-34: CP XII pt. 2, 370-382; Warwick Castle and Its Earls, II 828-829).

Line 88

    24. ISABEL DE VERMANDOIS (50-24), m. William de Warenne.

    25. GUNDRED DE WARENNE, Countess of Warwick, wid. of Roger de Newburgh; m. (2) William de Lancaster I, d. 1170, 5th

Baron Kendal of Workington in Coupland, son of Gilbert, 4th Baron Kendal; he inherited an extensive fief held of the Honour of Coupland, served as castellan of William Fitz Duncan's castle of Egremont in 1138, and was Governor of the Castle of Lancaster. (CP VII 371-373; VCH Lanc. 357-366).

26. **WILLIAM DE LANCASTER II**, d. 1184, 6th Baron Kendal; m. Helwise de Stouteville, dau. of Robert de Stouteville of Lazenby, co. Cumberland, and Helwise, niece of Geoffrey Murdac; she m. (2) William de Greystoke. (VCH Lanc. I 357-366; NEHGR 79: 373-378; 96: 103-104).

27. **HELWISE DE LANCASTER**, only child, Baroness Kendal, living Sep. 1226; m. bef. 20 Jul. 1189, Gilbert Fitz Roger Fitz Reinfrid, Lord of Kendal, 1189, who had m. (1) ca. 1156, Rohaise, dau. of William de Rumare, and wid. of Gilbert de Gaunt, who d. 1156. Gilbert was Steward to Henry II, in France 1180-1189, and later to Richard I; was justice of the King's Court 1185, Sheriff of Lancaster 1205-1216, and of York 1209-1212, and d. bef. 13 Jun. 1220. His father, Roger Fitz Reinfrid, was witness to the King's will, Judge 1176, 1198, Sheriff of Sussex 1176, and of Berks 1186-1187. (CP V 269; VII 371; VCH Lanc. I 357-366).

28. **HELWISE DE LANCASTER**, m. **PETER DE BRUS** (136-26), d. bef. 1247, Crusader, Lord of Skelton. (CP V 269; VCH Lanc. I 357-366).

29. **LUCY DE BRUS**, m. Sir Marmaduke de Thwenge, Lord of Kilton Castle in Cleveland, and Daneby, Yorkshire, M.P. 1294. (CP V 269 note b; VII 373; Banks I 432; NEHGR 96:120).

30. **SIR ROBERT DE THWENGE**, of Kilton Castle in Cleveland, d.s.p.m. legit. (CP VII 373, 467-8, note c 467; XII pt. 1 738-739 notes h & i 739; Banks I 432).

31. **LUCY DE THWENGE**, (dau. & h. of Robert de Thwenge, by uncertain mother), b. Kilton Castle, 24 Mar. 1278/9, d. 8 Jan. 1346/7, m. bef. 20 Apr. 1295, William, Lord Latimer, from whom sought divorce on grounds of consanguinity, also claimed cruelty & fear for her life; had a son by Nicholas de Meinill, b. 6 Dec. 1274, 2nd Lord Meinill of Whorlton, son of Nicholas de Meinill and Christina. (CP VII 467-468, note d 467; VIII 568, 619-635, cf. 632-634).

32. **SIR NICHOLAS DE MEINILL** (natural son of Nicholas de Meinill and Lucy de Thwenge above), d. bef. 20 Nov. 1341, 1st Baron Meinill of Whorlton of the second creation; m. **ALICE DE ROS** (54-35), d. bef. 4 Jul. 1344. (CP IV 60; VIII 632-634).

33. **ELIZABETH DE MEINILL**, b. Whorlton, 15 Oct. 1331, d. 9 Jul. 1368, Baroness Meinill of Whorlton; m. (1) as his second wife, ca. 7 Jan. 1344/5, Sir John Darcy, 2nd Baron Darcy of Knayth, b. 1317, slain at Cresy, 5 Mar. 1355/6, son of Sir John Darcy, Baron of Knayth, co. Lincoln, and Emmeline Heron, dau. of Walter Heron of Hedlestone, Northumberland, and Alice, dau. of Sir Nicholas de Hastings of Allerton, co. York and Gissing, co. Norfolk; m. (2) bef. 18 Nov. 1356, **SIR PIERS DE MAULEY** (156-31), b. 1330, d. 20 Mar. 1382/3, Lord Mauley of Mulgrave Castle. (Sir John Darcy had m. (1)

Line 88 (cont.)

bef. 8 Jul. 1332, Alianore, dau. of Sir Robert de Holand, first Lord Holand, and Maud, dau. of **SIR ALAN LA ZOUCHE** (32-30) of Ashby, co. Leicester, Lord Zouche). (CP IV 58-61, 71; VIII 567-568, 632-634).

34. SIR PHILIP DARCY, b. 21 May 1352, d. 24 Apr. 1399, Baron Darcy of Knayth; m. Elizabeth Gray, d. 11 Aug. 1412, dau. of Sir Thomas Gray of Heton and Margaret de Presfen. (CP IV 61-63, 71).

35. JOHN DARCY, b. ca. 1377, d. 9 Dec. 1411, 5th Baron Darcy; m. **MARGARET DE GREY** (13-33), d. 1 Jun. 1454. (CP IV 63-65, 71).

Line 89

24. ISABEL DE VERMANDOIS (50-24), m. William de Warenne.

25. ADA DE WARENNE, d. 1178; m. 1139, **HENRY OF HUNTINGDON** (170-23), b. 1114, d. 12 Jun. 1152, son of David I, King of Scots, and Maud of Northumberland. (CP IV 670 chart iv; VII 642; SP I 4).

26. WILLIAM THE LION, King of Scots, 9 Dec. 1165-1214, b. 1143, d. Stirling, 4 Dec. 1214. (CP IV 670 chart iv; VII 644-645; Old-CP VI 400; SP I 4; Gardiner 216).

27. ISABEL (natural dau. of William the Lion by a dau. of Richard Avernal); m. (2) Haddington, 1191, Robert de Ros, d. bef. 23 Dec. 1226, of Helmsley in Holderness, co. York, Magna Charta Surety, 1215, Knight Templar, son of Everard de Ros and Roese Trusbutt, and grandson of Robert de Ros and Sibyl de Valognes. (CP XI 90-93; SP I 4; Banks I 377; DNB 49: 216-219).

28. SIR WILLIAM DE ROS (see also 170-26), d. ca. 1264, of Helmsley, M.P. 1235/6; m. **LUCY FITZ PIERS** (237-7), dau. of **PETER FITZ HERBERT** (262-29) of Brecknock, Wales. (CP XI 93-94).

29. SIR ROBERT DE ROS, d. 17 May 1285, of Helmsley and Belvoir, co. Leicester, M.P. 1261, 1265; m. bef. 17 May 1246, Isabel d'Aubigny, d. 15 Jun. 1301, of Belvoir Castle, dau. of William d'Aubigny of Belvoir and Isabel, and granddau. of **WILLIAM d'AUBIGNY** (149-26), d. 1236, Lord of Belvoir Castle, Magna Charta Surety, 1215. (CP XI 95-96; Banks I 377).

30. WILLIAM DE ROS, b. ca. 1255, d. bet. May and Aug. 1316, 1st Lord Ros of Helmsley, M.P. 1295-1316, great-grandson and h. of Isabel, dau. of William the Lion, King of Scots, and a competitor for the crown of Scotland 1291; m. 1287, Maud de Vaux, dau. of John de Vaux of Freston, co. Lincoln, and Walton in Norfolk, son of Sir Oliver de Vaux. (CP XI 96-97; SP I 4).

31. WILLIAM DE ROS, d. 3 Feb. 1342/3, 2nd Lord Ros of Helmesley, M.P. 1317-1340, served in Scotland 1316-1335, Sheriff of Yorkshire 1326; m. bef. 25 Nov. 1326, **MARGERY DE BADLESMERE** (54-34), b. 1306, d. 18 Oct. 1363. (CP VIII 632-634; XI 98-99; DNB 49: 216-219).

·32. THOMAS DE ROS, Knt., b. Stoke Albany, Northamptonshire, 13 Jan. 1336/7, d. Uffington, Lincolnshire, 8 Jun. 1384, 4th Lord Ros

Line 89 (cont.)

of Helmsley, M.P. 1362-1384, served in France 1369-1371, Warden of Scotland 1367, Knt. banneret 1372; m. ca. 1 Jan. 1358/9, **BEATRICE STAFFORD** (9-32). (CP V 736; XI 100-101. Generations 25-32: CP XI 90-101; Old-CP VI 400-401; Banks I 377-378; DNB 49: 216-219; Robert Thoroton: The Antiquities of Nottinghamshire, London, 1677, p. 115; John Nichols: History of Leicestershire, II Part 1 27 ff.; W.T. Lancaster: Early History of the Ripley and the Ingilby Family, 1918).

33. ELIZABETH DE ROS, d. 1424, m. **THOMAS DE CLIFFORD** (26-33).

Line 90 (dropped, duplicates line 170 gens. 26 & 27.)

Line 91

35. WILLIAM MYTTON, Esq. (98-35), Lord of Weston in Staffordshire, living 1485; m. Margaret Corbet, dau. of Thomas Corbet of Lee. (Wm.Salt Soc. I 367; Visitation of Shropshire in Publications of the Harleian Soc. (1889) 29: II 360).

36. JOAN MITTON, m. (as his first wife), John Washborn, b. ca. 1451, d. 6 May 1517, bur. at Wickenford Church, co. Worcester; Commissioner of the Peace, 1496/7, 1513-1515; will dated 3 May 1517, son of Norman Washburn and his wife Elizabeth Knivton, dau. of Henry Knivton of Derbyshire, and grandson of John Washborne, commissioner for peace for co. Worcester, 1405, knight of the shire, 1404, escheator, and his second wife, Margery Poher, dau. of John le Poher of Wickenford, and a descendant of Sir Roger de Washborn, fl. 1239, of Little Compton and Ashbourne. (Ada C. Haight: The Richard Washburn Family, Corning, N.Y., 1937, pp. 1-8). There is no proof that John Washburn No. 37 was the son of John Washburn and Joan Mitton. (See TAG 36: 63).

* * *

37. JOHN WASHBORN, perh. the son of No. 36, sett. at Bengeworth near Little Washbourne, will dated 27 Dec. 1546; bur. 8 Jan. 1548; m. Emma, will made 1 May 1547; buried 13 May 1547.

38. JOHN WASHBOURNE, 2nd son of No. 37, d. intestate, 1593; bur. 13 Oct. 1593 at Bengeworth; m. (2) 8 May 1561, Joan Whitehead, bur. 23 Apr. 1567.

39. JOHN WASHBOURNE, bapt. 1 Aug. 1566, at Bengeworth; one of the twelve principal Burgesses, 1605; will made 4 Aug. 1624, inventory 11 Dec. 1624, pro. 29 Feb. 1624/5; m. 6 Jul. 1596, Martha Stevens, d. 1625/6, will 29 Sep. 1625, pro. 9 May 1626.

40. JOHN WASHBOURNE, eldest son, bapt. Bengeworth, 2 Jul. 1597; Duxbury, Mass., 1631-1643; d. at Bridgewater, Mass.; m. 23 Nov. 1618, Margery More, dau. of Robert and Ellen (Taylor) More. (Generations 36-40: Ada C. Haight: The Richard Washburn Family, pp. 1-8; Burke: Landed Gentry, 1939, p. 2959).

Line 92 Line deleted. Duplicates gens. 10-15 of Line 187.

Line 93

24. ISABEL DE VERMANDOIS (50-24), m. William de Warenne.
25. ADA DE WARENNE, d. 1178; m. 1139, **HENRY DE HUNTINGDON** (170-23), b. 1114, d. 12 Jun. 1152, Earl of Huntingdon and Northumberland. (CP IV 670 chart IV; V 736; VII 642; SP I 4).
26. DAVID OF HUNTINGDON, b. 1144, d. Yardley, 17 Jun. 1219, Earl of Huntingdon; m. 26 Aug. 1190, **MAUD OF CHESTER** (131-29), b. 1171, d. 1233, dau. of Hugh, Earl of Chester. (CP IV 670 chart IV; V 736; VII 646-647; SP I 4,7; Dunbar 65, 280-281).
27. ADA OF HUNTINGDON, m. Sir Henry de Hastings, d. 1250, son of William de Hastings and Margaret Bigod, and grandson of **ROGER BIGOD,** Magna Charta Surety, 1215. (CP IV 670 chart IV; V 736; VII 646-647; SP I 4: Dunbar 281; Dudley pedigree; Gardiner 216).
28. HILLARIA (or **ELEANOR) DE HASTINGS,** m. as (2) wife **SIR WILLIAM DE HARCOURT** (56-29), of Stanton-Harcourt, co. Oxford, and Naylston, co. Leicester, son of Sir Richard Harcourt of Stanton-Harcourt, d. 1278. (Collins-Brydges IV 434).
29. RICHARD DE HARCOURT, of Stanton-Harcourt, d. 1293; m. Margaret Beke (Inq.p.m. on her brother Walter's estate, 1333), dau. of John Beke, d. ca. 1303/4, Lord of Eresby, co. Lincoln, son of Walter Beke, Lord of Eresby, and Eve, niece of Walter de Grey, Archbishop of York. (Collins-Brydges IV 434-5).
30. SIR JOHN DE HARCOURT, Knt., of Stanton-Harcourt, co. Oxford, and Bosworth, co. Leicester, d. 1330, knighted 1306; m. **ELLEN LA ZOUCHE** (38-30). (Generations 27-30: Dudley pedigree; Banks I 122; Nichols: Leicestershire, IV Part II pp. 519a-520a for the Harcourt pedigree; Collins-Brydges IV 434-6; Wm.Salt Soc. Vol. 1914, 187-204).

Line 94

26. DAVID OF HUNTINGDON (93-26), m. **MAUD OF CHESTER** (131-29).
27. MARGARET OF HUNTINGDON, m. 1209, **ALAN** (38-26), Lord of Galloway, d. 1234, hereditary Constable of Scotland. (CP IV 670 chart IV; V 675; VII 646-647; SP I 4, 7; IV 142-143).
28. DEVORGILLA OF GALLOWAY, d. 28 Jan. 1289/90; m. 1233, John de Baliol, d. 1269, of Barnard Castle; they were the founders of Balliol College, Oxford. (CP IV 670 chart IV; V 675; VII 646-647; SP I 4, 7; IV 142-143; Gardiner 216).
29. CECILY DE BALIOL, d. bef. 1273; m. Sir John de Burgh, d. shortly bef. 3 Mar. 1279/80, feudal Baron Lanvallei of Walkern, son of John de Burgh, knt. 1229, b. 1210, d. 1275 (son of Hubert de Burgh, Earl of Kent by Beatrice, dau. William de Warenne of Wormgay) and Hawise de Lanvallei, d. 1249, and grandson of William de Lanvallei, d. 1217, Magna Charta Surety, 1215, of Great Bromley, co. Essex. Sir John and Cecily had 3 daus. cohs.: (1) Devorguilla, wife of **SIR ROBERT FITZ WALTER** (148-29); (2) Hawise, wife of **SIR ROBERT DE GRELLEY** (99-30); (3) Margery, a nun. (CP V 437).

Line 94A

31. RICHARD DE BURGH (75-31), 3rd Earl of Ulster, b. ca. 1259, d. 29 Jul. 1326; m. by 27 Feb. 1280/1, Margaret d. 1304 (dau. perhaps of Arnold III, Count of Guines (d. 1283) (grandson of **WILLIAM DE FIENNES** (158A-27), and his wife Alice, sister of Marie de Coucy, wife of Alexander II, King of Scotland). (CP XII pt. 2, 173-177 & footnote k 176; Gen. Mag. XX: 335-340). (Earlier printings of this line show Richard de Burgh's wife as "said to be" a dau. of **SIR JOHN DE BURGH** (94-29). This is disproven by John C. Parsons in Gen. Mag. cit.)

32. JOHN DE BURGH, b. ca. 1290, d.v.p. 18 Jun. 1313; m. 30 Sep. 1308, Elizabeth, sister and coh. Gilbert de Clare, 7th Earl of Gloucester, dau. Gilbert, 6th Earl and **JOAN OF ACRE** (8-29). (See 63-30). She m. (2) 4 Feb. 1315/16 as (2) wife, Theobald de Verdun, Lord Verdun, d. 27 Jul. 1316; m. (3) by 3 May 1317, Roger Damory, Lord Damory, d. 13-14 Mar. 1321/2. She d. 4 Nov. 1360, ae. 65, leaving a will. (CP cit. 177-8).

33. WILLIAM DE BURGH, 4th Earl of Ulster, b. 17 Sep. 1312, murdered 6 Jun. 1333, ae. 20 at LeFord, Belfast; m. (Papal disp. 1 May 1327), Maud, dau. **HENRY**, Earl of Lancaster (17-29) by 1st wife **MAUD** (76-32), dau. Sir Patrick de Chaworth of Kidwelly. She m. (2) by 8 Aug. 1343, Sir Ralph de Ufford, Justiciar of Ireland, d. 9 Apr. 1346. She d. 5 May 1377. (CP op.cit. 178-179).

34. ELIZABETH DE BURGH, m. **LIONEL OF ANTWERP** (5-31), j.u. Earl of Ulster, b. 1338, Duke of Clarence.

Line 95

28. DEVORGILLA OF GALLOWAY (94-28), d. 1290; m. 1233, John de Baliol. (CP I 385, II 374 note c, IV 671 chart IV; SP I 4).

29. ALIANORA DE BALIOL, m. 1279/83, **SIR JOHN COMYN,** Black Comyn (121A-29), d. ca. 1303, Lord of Badenock. (SP I 507-508; IV 143: CP I 386 (d)).

30. JOHN COMYN, Red Comyn, d. 1306, Lord of Badenock; m. **JOAN DE VALENCE** (154-30), dau. of Sir William de Valence (or de Lusignan), Earl of Pembroke. (CP II 374 note c; Gardiner 216; SP I 508-509).

31. ELIZABETH COMYN, b. 1 Nov. 1299, d. 20 Nov. 1372; m. betw. 24 July 1326 & 23 Mar. 1326/7, Sir Richard Talbot, b. ca. 1305, d. 23 Oct. 1356, Lord Talbot. (CP XII pt. 1, 613-617; SP I 509).

32. GILBERT TALBOT, b. ca. 1332, d. 24 Apr. 1387, Lord Talbot, M.P. 1362; m. (1) bef. 8 Sept. 1352 **PETRONILLA BUTLER** (13-31, 73-33), dau. of James, Earl of Ormond, living 28 May 1365, said to have d. 1368. (CP cit.

Line 96

25. ADA DE WARENNE (93-25), m. **HENRY DE HUNTINGDON** (170-23).

26. MARGARET DE HUNTINGDON, m. (1) 1160, **CONAN IV** (119-27), d. 1171, Duke of Brittany, Earl of Richmond. (CP IV 669;

Line 96 (cont.)

SP I 4).
    27. CONSTANCE, Countess of Brittany, b. ca. 1162, d. 5 Sep. 1201; m. (3) 1199, Gui de Thouars, d. 1218, Count of Brittany, (2nd son of William, vicomte de Thouars & Aenor de Leusigne.) (CP X 794-795; Anselme III, 54-56). Anselme says Constance d. 21 Oct. 1221.
    28. ALIX DE THOUARS, d. 1221, Duchess of Brittany; m. **PIERRE DE DREUX** (135-29), d. 1240. (CP X 796 note).

Line 97

    26. MARGARET DE HUNTINGDON (96-26), m. (2) **HUMPHREY DE BOHUN, IV** (193-6), d. 1182. (CP IV 669; VI 457; SP I 4).
    27. HENRY DE BOHUN, b. 1176, d. on a Pilgrimage to the Holy Land, 1 Jun. 1220, Sheriff of Kent, 5th Earl of Hereford, 1200 Hereditary Constable of England; Magna Charta Surety, 1215; m. Maud Fitz Geoffrey de Mandeville, d. 27 Aug 1236, Countess of Essex, dau. of Geoffrey Fitz Piers (see also 246B-27), d. 1213, 4th Earl of Essex, and his (1) wife Beatrice de Say, dau. of William de Say. (CP IV 669 chart; V 116-117, 135, 437; VI 457-459).
    28. HUMPHREY DE BOHUN V, b. by 1208, d. 24 Sep. 1275, 2nd Earl of Hereford and Earl of Essex, Constable of England, Sheriff of Kent; m. (1) **MAUD D'EU** (or de Lusignan) (123-29), d. 14 Aug. 1241. (CP IV 669; V 135; VI 459-462; XII pt. 1, 768-777. See also Maclean: Deanery of Trigg Minor).
    29. HUMPHREY DE BOHUN VI, d.v.p. 27 Oct. 1265; m. by 15 Feb. 1247/8 (1) **ELEANOR DE BRAIOISE** (68-29). (CP IV 669; V 135; VI 462-463).
    30. HUMPHREY DE BOHUN VII, b. ca. 1249, d. Pleshey, 31 Dec. 1298, Earl of Hereford and Essex, Constable of England; m. 1275, **MAUD DE FIENNES**, dau. of **INGELRAM DE FIENNES** (152-28). (CP IV 669; VI 463-466).
    31. HUMPHREY DE BOHUN VIII, b. ca. 1276, slain at Boroughbridge, 16 Mar. 1321/2, Earl of Hereford and Essex, Lord High Constable of England; m. 14 Nov. 1302, **ELIZABETH PLANTAGENET** (6-29), b. Aug. 1282, d. 5 May 1316, dau. of King Edward I. (CP IV 669; VI 467-470).
    32. SIR WILLIAM DE BOHUN, K.G. (15-30), created Earl of Northampton, m. **ELIZABETH DE BADLESMERE** (65-34). (CP II 155; IV 669).
    33. HUMPHREY DE BOHUN IX, K.G., d. 1372, Earl of Hereford, Essex and Northampton; m. Joan Fitz Alan, dau. of **RICHARD FITZ ALAN** (60-32), 5th Earl of Arundel, by his (2) wife Eleanor de Lancaster. (CP IV 669; VI 473-4).
    34. ALIANORE DE BOHUN (dau. by (2)), m. **THOMAS PLANTAGENET** (4-31), of "Woodstock" (son of King Edward III and Philippa of Hainaut), Duke of Gloucester. (CP II 155; IV 669).

25. CONSTANCE, bastard dau. of King **HENRY I** (121-25); m. Roscelin, d. aft. 1145, Viscount of Maine. (CP XI App. D 116).

26. RICHARD I, d. aft. 1194, Viscount of Maine, Seigneur of Beaumont-le-Vicomte, Fresnay and Ste.-Suzanne, m. N.N. de L'Aigle. (CP XII pt. 1, 768).

27. CONSTANCE DE BEAUMONT, living 1226, m. by 1190 **ROGER IV DE TOENI** (98A-27), also styled de Conches, Knt., b. ca. 1160, adult by 1189, d. prob. Jan. 1209, lord of Flamstead, Hertford, founded the nunnery of St. Giles in the Wood, near Flamstead, Herts. She brought her husband in free marriage the manor of South Tawton (otherwise Ailrichescot), Devon. (CP XII pt. 1, 765-769; Sanders, English Baronies, 117-118; The Beauchamp Cartulary Charters 1100-1268, pub. as Vol. 81 (n.s. vol. 43), Publications of the Pipe Roll Society, pp. xliii-xlvii).

28. RALPH VI DE TOENI, born prob. 1189 or 1190, d. at sea about Michaelmas 1239, lord of Flamstead, Hertford, Crusader 1239; m. (1) 1232/3, Petronilla (or Pernel) de Lacy, living 1288, dau. of Walter de Lacy d. 1241, lord of Meath, Ireland and of Weobley, Hereford, by **MARGARET** (or Margery) **DE BRAIOSE** (177A-7), dau. of **WILLIAM DE BRAIOSE** (177-6). Petronilla had the manors of Britford, Wilts and Yarkhill, Hereford in free marriage. (CP XII pt. 1, 769-771; Orpen, Ireland under the Normans, III, chart pp. 286-287; Sanders, English Baronies, 117-118; The Beauchamp Cartulary Charters, op. cit.).

29. ROGER V DE TOENI, b. Michaelmas 1235, d. bef. 12 May 1264, lord of Flamstead, Hertford; m. (1) Alice de Bohun, dau. of **HUMPHREY DE BOHUN** (97-28), 2nd Earl of Hereford and Essex, by his wife, **MAUD D'EU** (123-29) (Alice had as her maritagium the manors of Newton Toney and East Coulston, Wilts); m. (2) after 1255, Isabel, living 1264/5. (CP XII pt. 1, 771-772; Sanders, op. cit.; The Beauchamp Cartulary Charters op. cit.)

30. ROGER VII DE TOENI, son by (1), b. 1255, d. Gascony, bef. 29 Jul. 1295, lord of Flamstead, Hertford, m. by 1276 Mary, living 1283, prob. a Scotswoman. (CP XII pt. 1, 773; Sanders, op. cit.; The Beauchamp Cartulary Charters op. cit.)

31. ALICE DE TOENI, b. ca. 1283, bef. 8 Jan., d. about 8 Jan. 1324/5; m. (1) Thomas de Leyburn (d.s.p.m. & v.p. bef. 30 May 1307), m. (2) bef. 28 Feb. 1309/10, **GUY DE BEAUCHAMP** (86-30), Earl of Warwick; m. (3) (as (1) wife) bef. 25 Feb. 1316/7, Sir William la Zouche (formerly de Mortimer), yr. son of Robert de Mortimer (d. 7 Apr. 1287) of Richard's Castle, Hereford, by Joyce, bur. 13 Mar. 1289/90, dau. & h. of William La Zouche, d. by 3 Feb. 1271/2, of King's Nympton, Devon, yr. son of **ROGER LA ZOUCHE** (39-28) of Ashby. (CP XII pt. 1, 774 note i).

32. JOYCE LA ZOUCHE DE MORTIMER (dau. by (3)), living 4 May 1372; m. 31 May 1347, **JOHN BOTETOURT** (216-31), Lord Botetourt of Weobley Castle, b. 1318, d. 1385, M.P. 1342-1385. (CP II 234-235).

33. JOYCE DE BOTETOURT, b. 1367/8, d. 12 Aug. 1420; m. (1) Sir Baldwin Freville of Tamworth Castle, d. 1387/8; m. (2) 1388, Sir Adam de Peshall, son of Adam de Peshall and Joan de Eyton. (Inq.p.m. Sir Adam Peshall, 20 Dec. 1419, mentions wife Joyce, and dau. Margaret, wife of Richard Mitton; Wm.Salt Soc. XV 312; Mis.Gen.Her. n.s. III 273; History and Genealogy of the Pearsall Family in England and America II 572; Gen. Mag. 21, no. 6, 373-375.)

34. MARGARET DE PESHALL, d. 5 Aug. 1420; m. Sir Richard Mytton, Knt., d. bef. 26 Oct. 1419. (Wm.Salt Soc. I 367; Vis. of Shropshire 360).

35. WILLIAM MYTTON, Esq., living 1485; m. Margaret Corbet, dau. of Thomas Corbet of Lee. (Wm.Salt Soc. I 367; Vis. of Shropshire 360).

36. JOHN MYTTON, Esq., of Weston, d. Feb. 1500; m. (1) Anne Swinnerton, who was the mother of a Margaret; m. (2) Joan Middlemoore. (Visitations of Warwickshire, in Harleian Soc. XII 237-238).

* * *

37. MARGARET MYTTON, m. Robert Fulwood, of Clay Hall, Tamworth, co. Warwick. (Generations 33-37: Visitations of Shropshire, 1623, in Harleian Soc., 29: 360). The Fulwood pedigree calls Margaret the dau. of "John Mitton of Shrewsbury" rather than Weston. If so, this Margaret may not be the Margaret, dau. of John of Weston and his wife Ann Swinnerton. This must be clarified before the line can be accepted.

38. ROBERT FULWOOD, of Alna Parva, co. Warwick; m. 12 Oct. 1539 Maria Hunter, dau. of Thomas Hunter of Studley. (Visitations of Warwickshire in Harleian Soc. XII 237-238; Mis.Gen.Her. n.s. III 273).

39. ANNE FULWOOD, m. 20 May 1566, Richard Gunne, of Saintbury, co. Gloucester, son of Richard and Mary (Horne) Gunne. (Mis.Gen.Her. n.s. III 273). Anne was prob. his (2) wife, since bp. @ Saintbury 7 Apr. 1563 Anne dau. Richard Gonne. Ellen also prob. by earlier mar. If so this line also fails at this generation.

* * *

40. ELLEN GUNNE, m. (1) Joseph Phelps, will dated 26 Oct., pro. Dec. 1579, m. (2) ca. 1579, John Tomes of Long Marston, co. Gloucs, 25 May 1602. Law proceeding 1579 by John Tomes agst wife's step chn. shows she had at least 2 chn. by that year. (Ibid., III 273; NEHGR 80: 300, 446; 89: 289).

41. ALICE TOMES, d. Connecticut, ca. 1646; m. soon aft. 5 Jul. 1615, Governor Thomas Welles of Connecticut. (NEHGR 80: 299-305; see TAG 28: 164-167).

23. JUDITH OF LENS (130-25, 148-23), niece of William the Conqueror, living 1086, m. 1070 Waltheof II, beheaded Winchester, 31 May 1076, Earl of Huntingdon, Northampton and Northumberland, son of Sigurd, Earl of Northumberland, by his wife, Aelfled, daughter of Aldred of Bernicia. (CP VI: 638-640).

24. ALICE OF NORTHUMBERLAND, dau. and coh., alive 1126, m. 1103, Ralph IV de Toeni, also styled de Conches, adult by 1102, d. ca. 1126, buried Conches, France, lord of Flamstead, Hertford, son of Ralph III de Toeni (de Conches) by his wife, Isabel (or Elizabeth), dau. of Simon de Montfort, Seigneur of Montfort L'Amaury in France. (CP XII pt. 1, 760-762; The Beauchamp Cartulary Charters 1100-1268, pub. as Vol. 81 (n.s. vol. 43), Publications of the Pipe Roll Society, pp. xliii-xlvii).

25. ROGER III DE TOENI, also styled de Conches, b. ca. 1104, d. 1157-62, lord of Flamstead, Hertford, m. Ida of Hainaut, dau. of **BALDWIN III** (163-25), Count of Hainaut, by his wife, Yolande of Guelders. With Ida, Roger had in marriage from King Henry I, 20 librates of land out of the royal demesne at East Bergholt, Suffolk. (CP XII pt. 1, 762-764; Sanders, English Baronies 117-118; The Beauchamp Cartulary Charters, op. cit.)

26. RALPH V DE TOENI, also styled de Conches, d. 1162, lord of Flamstead, Hertford, m. Margaret, living 1185, dau. of **SIR ROBERT DE BEAUMONT** (53-25), 2nd Earl of Leicester, by his wife, Amice de Montfort. (CP XII pt. 1, 764-765; Sanders, op. cit.; The Beauchamp Cartulary Charters, op. cit.)

27. ROGER IV DE TOENI, also styled de Conches, b. ca. 1160, d. prob. Jan. 1209, lord of Flamstead, Hertford, m. by 1190 **CONSTANCE DE BEAUMONT** (98-27).

Line 99

29. CECILY DE BALIOL (94-29), m. Sir John de Burgh, of Walkern. (CP V 474, VI 107 (d); Sanders: English Baronies 92).

30. HAWISE DE BURGH, b. 1256, d. aft. 1282; m. Sir Robert de Grelle, of Manchester, b. 1252, d. 15 Feb. 1282, son of Robert de Grelle, grandson of Thomas de Grelle, great-grandson of Roger Lord Grelle with the Barons at Runnemede. (CP IV 142-143; VI 107 (d); VIII 450-458, chart 452-453; Baines: History of Lancashire, I 274-275).

31. JOAN DE GRELLE, d. 20 or 21 Mar. 1352/3; m. soon aft. 19 Nov. 1294, **JOHN LA WARRE** (255A-32), 2nd Baron de la Warre, d. 9 May 1347, famous soldier in Flanders 1297, Scotland 1298-1327, at Sluys 1340 and Crécy 25 Aug. 1346, son of Sir Roger la Warre and Clarice de Tregoz, dau. of Sir John de Tregoz of Eywas Harold, co. Hereford, and Mabel, dau. of Sir Fulk Fitz Warin. (CP IV 141-143; VIII 453-454, chart 452-453; Baines op. cit. I 277).

32. CATHARINE LA WARRE, d. 9 Aug. 1361; m. (2) 1328, Sir Warin le Latimer, Lord Latimer, b. ca. 1300, d. 13 Aug. 1349, son of Thomas, Lord Latimer, and Lora de Hastings, dau. of Henry de Hastings. (CP VII 451-454, chart 452-453).

33. ELIZABETH LE LATIMER, m. Thomas Griffin, through whom the title of Lord Latimer descended. (CP VIII 453-457 and chart).

34. RICHARD GRIFFIN, d. 1411; m. Anna Chamberlain, dau. of Richard Chamberlain. (CP VIII 456-457 and chart).

35. NICHOLAS GRIFFIN, d. 1436; m. Margaret Pilkington, dau. of Sir John Pilkington; she m. (2) Sir Thomas Saville. (CP VIII 457).

36. NICHOLAS GRIFFIN, Lord Latimer, b. Brixworth, 5 Jun. 1426, d. 6 Jun. 1482, Sheriff of Northamptonshire 1473; m. (1) Catharine Curzon, dau. of Richard Curzon. (CP VIII 457-458, chart 452-453).

37. CATHERINE GRIFFIN, m. as (3) wife Sir John Digby, of Eye Kettleby, co. Leicester, knighted at Bosworth Field, d. ca. 1533 (will made 1 Aug. 1529, codicil 19 May 1533), son of Everard Digby, Esq., Sheriff of Rutlandshire, 1485, 1486, 1499, M.P., (will made 17 Jan. 1508-9, pro. 12 Feb. 1508/9) and Jacquette Ellis, dau. of Sir John Ellis. (Visitation of Warwick, 1619, Harleian Soc. 12:167; Visitation of Leicestershire, Harl. Soc. 2:40: Nichol's Hist. of Antiq. of Leicestershire II, 51,201).

38. WILLIAM DIGBY of Kettleby and Luffenham, co. Leicester, Esq., living 1558; m. (1) Rose Prestwich, dau. of William Prestwich of Lubenham and his wife, dau. of Sir Thomas Poultney. (Nichol's op. cit.).

39. SIMON DIGBY, executed Mar. 1570, of Bedale, co. York; m. Anne Grey, dau. and h. of Reginald Grey of York, attainted 1569, executed 28 Mar. 1570. (Nichol's cit.; Stow: Annals).

40. EVERARD DIGBY, m. Katherine, dau. of Mr. Stockbridge de Vanderschaff Theuber de Newkirk. (Nichol's cit.; The Diaries of Benjamin Lynde and of Benjamin Lynde, Jr., Boston, 1880, cf. Introduction, iii-viii, and Pedigree of Lynde in the Appendix.

41. ELIZABETH DIGBY, b. ca. 1584, d. London, 1669; m. Hackney, 25 Oct. 1614, Enoch Lynde, shipping merchant, Netherlands, d. London, 23 Apr. 1636, will pro. 7 Oct. 1636, wid. Elizabeth executrix. (Nichol's cit.; Digby pedigree, Sherborne Castle).

42. HON. SIMON LYNDE, bp. London, Jun. 1624, d. Boston, 22 Nov. 1687; m. Boston, 22 Feb. 1652/3, Hannah Newgate. (Bible, Geneva version, 1597, of Simon Lynde of Boston, "given to Enoch Lynde (of London), the son of Nathan, by his grandmother Elizabeth". Salisbury's Family Histories, referred to in previous editions for generations 37-41 is not reliable.)

Line 100

25. ADA DE WARENNE (93-25), m. **HENRY DE HUNTINGDON** (170-23).

26. ADA DE HUNTINGDON, m. 1162, Florent III, d. 1190, Count of Holland, Earl of Ross.

27. WILLIAM I, d. 4 Feb. 1223/4, Count of Holland and Zealand; m. Adelaide, d. 1218, dau. of Otto I, d. 1207, Count of Guelders and Zutphen. (CP VII 642).

Line 100 (cont.)

28. FLORENT IV, Count of Holland, d. 1245; m. bef. Dec. 1224 Mechtild, dau. of **HENRY I** (155-26), Duke of Brabant by Mathilde, dau. Count Matthew of Boulogne.

29. ADELAIDE OF HOLLAND, d. ca. 1284; m. **JOHN I D'AVENES** (168-30), d. 1256, Count of Holland.

Line 101

18. ROBERT I (48-18), Duke of France, chosen king 922, d. 15 Jun. 923; m. (2) Beatrix de Vermandois, dau. of **HERBERT I** (50-17), Count of Vermandois.

19. HUGH MAGNUS, d. Jun. 956, Count of Paris; m. (3) **HEDWIG** (141-19), dau. of **HENRY I, THE FOWLER** (141-18), King of the Saxons.

20. HUGH CAPET, b. aft. 939, d. 24 Oct. 996, Count of Paris 956-996, King of France 987-996, first of the Capetian kings of France; m. **ADELAIDE OF POITOU** (144A-20).

21. ROBERT II, the Pious, b. Orleans, 970/1, d. Meulun, 20 Jul. 1031, King of France, 1 Jan. 988-1031; m. (1) bef. 988 **ROSELA** (or **SUSANNA**) (146-19) as (2) husb.; repudiated; m. (2) 995 Berthe; repudiated 998, d. 1001, wid. of Eudes, Count of Blois, dau. Conrad, King of Burgundy; (3) 998, Constance of Provence (variously styled of Arles and of Toulouse) d. 25 Jul 1032, dau. William, Count of Provence & Adelaide of Anjou (dau. Fulk II).

22. HENRY I, b. 1005/11, d. 4 Aug. 1060, King of France 1031-1060; m. 19 or 20 Jan. 1051, **ANNE OF KIEV** (241-6), d. aft. 1075.

23. PHILIP I, b. 1053, d. Meulan 29 Jul. 1108, bur. Abbaye St-Benoît-sur-Loire, King of France 1060-1108, Count of Paris; m. (1) 1072, Bertha of Holland, b. ca. 1055, d. Montreuil-sur-Mer early 1094, dau. of Florent I, Count of Holland. (Isenburg, Book II, Table 11) (1984).

24. LOUIS VI, the Fat, b. Autumn 1081, d. Chateau Béthizy b Paris 1 Aug. 1137, King of France 1108-1137, Crusader; m. (2) Paris ca. 1115, Adelaide of Savoy, b. ca. 1092, d. 18 Nov 1154, dau. of Humbert II, Count of Maurienne and Savoy. (Isenburg cit.)

25. LOUIS VII, the Young, b. 1120, d. Paris 18 Sep. 1180, bur. Notre-Dame-de-Barbeau b. Fontainebleau, King of France 25 Dec. 1137-1180; m. (1) Bordeaux 22/25 July 1137, **ELEANOR OF AQUITAINE** (110-26), divorced 1152, d. 1204 (she m. (2) Henry II of England); m. (2) Orléans 1153/4, Constance of Castile, d. 4 Oct 1160, bur. St. Denis, dau. of Alfonso VII, King of Castile and Leon; m. (3) 18 Oct. 1160, **ALIX OF CHAMPAGNE** (137-25), b. ca. 1140, d. Paris 4 Jun. 1206, bur. Abbaye de Potigny. (Isenburg cit.)

26. PHILIP II Augustus (son of Louis and Alix), b. Gonesse 22 Aug. 1165, d. Mantes 14 Jul. 1223, bur. St. Denis, King of France 1180-1223, Count of Artois; Crusader; m. (1) Bapaume 28 Apr. 1180, **ISABELLA OF HAINAUT** (163-28), b. Valenciennes Apr. 1170, d. Paris 15 Mar. 1190, bur. Notre-Dame, Countess of Artois. (Isenburg cit.)

Line 101 (cont.)

27. LOUIS VIII, the Lion, b. 1187, d. Montpensier, Auvergne, 8 Nov. 1226, King of France 1223-1226; m. 1200, **BLANCHE OF CASTILE** (113-28), d. 1253.

28. LOUIS IX, "Saint Louis," b. Poissy, 25 Apr. 1215, d. near Tunis, 25 Aug. 1270, King of France 1226, 1270, Crusader; m. Marguerite of Provence, d. 1285, dau. of **RAYMOND IV BERENGER** (111-29), Count of Provence. (See Joinville: Chronicle of the Crusade of St. Louis for an account of his life).

29. PHILIP III, the Bold, b. 1245, d. Perpignan, 1285, King of France 1270-1285; m. (1) 1262, **ISABELLA OF ARAGON** (105-30), d. 1271; m. (2) 1272, **MARIE OF BRABANT** (155-29), d. 1321.

30. PHILIP IV, the Fair, b. Fontainebleau, 1268, d. 29 Nov. 1314, King of France 1285-1314; m. 1284, **JEANNE OF NAVARRE** (45-31), b. 1272, d. 1305, dau. of Henry I, King of Navarre.

31. ISABELLA OF FRANCE, b. 1292, d. 22 Aug. 1358; m. 25 Jan. 1307/8, **EDWARD II** (1-29), d. 21 Sep. 1327, King of England. (Generations 13-31: Moriarty, The Plantagenet Ancestry; Turton; G.P. Fisher: Outline of Universal History, 1885, p. 287; Thatcher 320, 323; Gardiner xxxi).

Line 102

25. LOUIS VII (101-25), King of France; m. **ELEANOR OF AQUITAINE** (110-26). (CCN 112).

26. MARIE OF FRANCE, b. 1145, d. 11 Mar. 1198, m. 1164 Henry, Count of Champagne, d. Troyes, 17 Mar. 1181. (Isenburg, Book II, Table 11).

27. MARIE OF CHAMPAGNE, m. **BALDWIN VI** (168-28), Count of Hainaut and Flanders, a leader of the Fourth Crusade.

Line 103

23. PHILIP I (101-23), King of France, m. Bertha, dau. of Count Florent I of Holland.

24. CONSTANCE OF FRANCE, m. (2) **BOHEMOND I,** d. Canossa, Italy, 1111, Prince of Antioch, son of Robert Guiscard; a leader of the First Crusade; captured Antioch, 1098. (CCN 166).

25. BOHEMOND II, Prince of Antioch, b. 1107, d. 1131; m. Alix, dau. of **BALDWIN II** (103A-25), King of Jerusalem, d. 21 Aug. 1131. (CCN 112).

26. CONSTANCE OF ANTIOCH, m. (2) ca. 1152/3, Renaud de Châtillon, son of Henry I de Châtillon. (v.Redlich 267-268).

27. AGNES (or **ANNE**) **DE CHÂTILLON,** d. ca. 1184; m. ca. 1171, **BELA III** (242-10), b. 1148, d. 18 Apr. 1196, King of Hungary, son of Geza II, and a descendant of Harold II, King of England. (CCN 139).

28. ANDREW II, d. ca. 7 Mar. 1235, father of St. Elizabeth of Hungary, King of Hungary 1205-1235; m. (1) Gertrude of Meran, d. 1213/4, dau. of Berthold IV, Duke of Meran. (CCN 57).

29. BELA IV, d. ca. 1275, King of Hungary 1235-1270; m. Marie, dau. of the Emperor Theodore Lascaris I. (CCN 139).

30. STEPHEN V, d. 1 Aug. 1272, King of Hungary 1270-1272; m. Elizabeth, dau. of Kuthen, Prince of Kumans. (CCN 957).

31. MARIE OF HUNGARY, d. Mar. 1323; m. **CHARLES II** (104-29), d. ca. 6 May 1309, King of Naples.

32. MARGARET OF NAPLES, m. Charles, Count of Valois, d. 1325, youngest son of **PHILIP III** (101-29), King of France, and **ISABELLA OF ARAGON** (105-30).

33. JEANNE OF VALOIS, d. ca. 1352; m. ca. 1305, **WILLIAM III** (168-32), d. 1337, Count of Hainaut and Holland.

34. PHILIPPA OF HAINAUT, b. 24 June 1311 (The Gen. I no. 2, 138), d. ca. 15 Aug. 1369; m. 24 Jan. 1327/8, **EDWARD III** of England (1-30). (Generations 23-34; v.Redlich 267-268; TAG IX 15; Arminuis Vambery: The Story of Hungary, 1894, pp. 120-147, etc.)

Line 103A

23. MANASSES III, Count of Rethel 1048, d. 1056; m. Yevette, dau. Giselbert, Count of Roucy.

24. HUGH I, Count of Rethel 1086, d. 1118; m. Melisende, dau. Guitchard (or Bouchard) of Montlhéry, Count of Corbeil and his wife Adelaide of Crécy.

25. BALDWIN II, b. ca. 1058, d. 21 Aug. 1131, count of Rethel. On 1st Crusade 1098, Count of Edessa 1110, King of Jerusalem 1118, m. Malfia, dau. of Gabriel, d. 1103, Armenian gov. of Melitene on the upper Euphrates. Baldwin's daughter Melisende, married as his second wife **FULK** (118-24), Count of Anjou, King of Jerusalem, through which marriage the royal line continued. Baldwin's second daughter, Alix, through her Antioch marriage, became ancestress to many of the noble families of Outremer. (See Stephen Runciman's History of the Crusades which is in error regarding the parentage of Hugh, Count of Rethel).

26. ALIX, d. 1131, m. **BOHEMOND II,** b. 1107 (103-25) Prince of Antioch. (Moriarty, The Plantagenet Ancestry.)

Line 104

27. LOUIS VIII (101-27), King of France; m. **BLANCHE OF CASTILE** (113-28).

28. CHARLES I, b. 1220, d. 1285, Count of Anjou, King of Naples and Sicily; m. Beatrix of Provence, dau. of **RAYMOND IV BERENGER** (111-29) and **BEATRICE OF SAVOY** (133-27). (CCN 237).

29. CHARLES II, d. ca. 6 May 1309, King of Naples; m. **MARIE OF HUNGARY** (103-31). (Generations 27-29: Thatcher 323).

Line 105

28. ANDREW II (103-28), King of Hungary; m. (2) **YOLANDE DE COURTENAY** (163A-27). (Moriarty, The Plantagenet Ancestry.)
29. YOLANDE OF HUNGARY, m. **JAMES I** (105A-29), b. 1213, d. 1276, King of Aragon, son of Pedro of Aragon.
30. ISABELLA OF ARAGON, m. **PHILIP III** (101-29), King of France.

Line 105A

24. ALEXIUS COMNENUS, Basileus (Emp.) of the East, b. ca. 1048, d. 15 Aug. 1118; m. 1078 Irene Ducena, b. ca. 1065, dau. Protovestuary Andronicus Dukas by Mary, dau. Khan or Tzar Trajan, of the West Bulgars.
25. JOHN II COMNENUS, Basileus of the East, b. 1088, d. 8 Apr. 1143 in Cilicia; m. 1105 **PRISCA (IRENE)** (244A-8) of Hungary, b. ca. 1088, d. Bethinia 13 Aug. 1134.
26. MANUEL COMNENUS, Basileus of the East, b. 1122, d. 24 Sept. 1180; m. 25 Mar. 1161 Maria, b. ca. 1145, murdered 22 Aug. 1182, dau. Raymond (or Reynaud) de Châtillon of Poitou, Prince of Antioche and **CONSTANCE** (103-26).
27. EUDOXIA, b. ca. 1162, div. 1187, d. a nun; m. 1174 William VIII, Seigneur de Montpellier, b. ca. 1158, seen 1172, 1202, will dtd. Nov. 1202, d. at Rome 1218, bur. St. Peters.
28. MARIE, dau. & h. b. 1182, d. Rome 1218, bur. St. Peters; m. as (3) husb. 25 June 1208, Pedro II, King of Aragon, Count of Barcelona and Gevandur, b. 1176, killed in Battle of Muret fighting for the Albigensians 13 Sept. 1213.
29. JAMES, King of Aragon 1213, b. Montpellier 1 or 2 Feb. 1208, d. Valencia 25 July 1276; m. (2) 8 Sept. 1235 **YOLANDE** (105-29) dau. Andrew II, King of Hungary, b. ca. 1216, d. 1251. (Moriarty, The Plantagenet Ancestry charts 32, 86, 87, 137, 138, 140, 132, 131).

Line 106

20. HUGH CAPET (101-20), d. 24 Oct. 996, King of France; m. **ADELAIDE OF POITOU** (144A-20). (NEHGR 109: 179-182; Moriarty, The Plantagenet Ancestry.)
21. HEDWIG, m. Regnier IV, d. 1013, Count of Hainaut, son of **RÉGNIER III** (155-19), b. ca. 958, d. 973. They were parents of Régnier V and of Beatrix. (Moriarty, cit.)
22. RÉGNIER V, d. ca. 1039, Count of Hainault 1013; m. ca. 1015 Mathilde, d. ca. 1039, dau. Herman, Count of Verdun. (Brandenburg IX 97 & X 119). They were the parents of Herman, Count in Hainault whose wid. Richilde m. (2) **BALDWIN VI** (163-22), Count of Flanders.
22. BEATRIX OF HAINAUT, m. **EBLES I** (151-21), Count of Rheims and Roucy, Archbishop of Rheims. (Boston Evening Transcript, Feb. 1928, Note 2257, Part XV Brabant; Moriarty, cit.)

19. HUGH CAPET (101-20), d. 24 Oct. 996, King of France; m. **ADELAIDE OF POITOU** (144A-20).

20. ADELE OF FRANCE, d. ca. 1063; m. Renaud I, d. 29 May 1040, Count of Nevers 1000-1040.

21. WILLIAM I, Count of Nevers, b. ca. 1030, d. Nevers, aft. 1083; m. 1045, Ermengarde, dau. of Renaud, Count of Tonnerre.

22. RENAUD II, Count of Nevers and Auxerre, da. ca. 1089; m. Ida, dau. of Artald V, Count of Forez.

23. ERMENGARD DE NEVERS, m. Miles, Sire of Courtenay, d. 1127, son of Jocelin de Courtenay, 1065, and Isabel, dau. of Guy de Montlhéry.

24. RENAUD DE COURTENAY, of Sutton, Berks., 1161, d. ca. 1190; m. a dau. of Frederick (or Guy) du Donjon and Corbeil.

25. ELIZABETH DE COURTENAY, living 1205; m. **PETER OF FRANCE** (117-25), d. bef. 1183. (Generations 21-25; CP IV 37; Turton; Vivian: Visitations of Devon 243).

26. PETER, Count of Courtenay, Marquis of Namur, Emperor of Constantinople, b. ca. 1155, d. Epirus, bef. Jan. 1218; m. betw. 24 June & 1 July 1193 **YOLANDE OF FLANDERS** (163A-28) Countess and h. of Namur, b. ca. 1175, d. Constantinople Aug. 1219. (Moriarty, The Plantagenet Ancestry.)

Line 108

21. ROBERT II (101-21), King of France; m. (3) 998 Constance of Provence.

22. ROBERT THE OLD, b. ca. 1011, d. 1075/6, Duke of Burgundy; m. (1) Irmgard of Anjou, d.s.p.; m. (2) ca. 1033 Helie, d. 1109, dau. Dalmas I of Semur en Auxois by his wife Aremburge. (Saillot, Sang de Charlemagne 43, 71).

23. HENRY, d. 1070-1074, Duke of Burgundy; m. Sibylle (de Vajay, Annales de Bourgogne, vol. 32 (1960), pp. 158-161, shows Sibylle as dau. of Raymond Berenger I, d. 1035, Comte de Barcelone by (3) wife Guisle d'Ampurias. He thinks Raymond was a child of Raymond Borel III d. 1019, Comte de Barcelone by Ermesende, dau. Roger I de Carcassonne and Adelaide.)

24. EUDES I, Borel, d. Cilicia, 23 Mar. 1102/3, Duke of Burgundy; m. Maud of Burgundy, sister of William Testard, Count of Burgundy. (CP XI 697; XII pt. 1, 497: CCN 371).

25. ALICE (or ELA) OF BURGUNDY, d. 1194/5; m. (1) Bertrand, Count of Toulouse; m. (2) William III, Talvas, d. 30 Jun. 1171, Count of Alençon, son of Robert II (1035-1113), 3rd Earl of Salisbury, Count of Alençon, and Agnes, Countess of Ponthieu, dau. of Guy I, Count of Ponthieu, and a descendant of Hugh de Montgomery. (CP XI 697; XII pt. 1, 497).

26. ELA TALVAS, sd. to have d. 4 Oct. 1174; m. (1) **WILLIAM DE WARENNE** (83-25), b. 1118, d. 1148, 3rd Earl of Surrey; m. (2) in or bef. 1152 Patrick, Earl of Salisbury, slain 27 Mar. 1167/8 (7 Apr. 1168), son of Walter of Salisbury and Sybil de Chaworth. (CP IV 670 chart II; XI 377, 697; XII pt. 1, 496-7).

Line 108 (cont.)

27. WILLIAM FITZ PATRICK, b. ca. 1150, d. 17 Apr. 1196, Earl of Salisbury; m. ca. 1190, Eleanor de Vitré, dau. of Robert de Vitré and Emma de Dinan, dau. of Alan de Dinan. (CP XI 377-379; XII pt. 1, 497-8; VCH Lanc. I 312).

28. ELA, Countess of Salisbury, b. Amesbury, Wilts., 1187-1191, d. 24 Aug. 1261; m. 1198, **WILLIAM DE LONGESPEE** (30-26), Earl of Salisbury, b. 1176, d. 7 Mar. 1225/6, natural son of King Henry II of England. (VCH Lanc. I 312; CP V 472; XI 379-382; XII pt. 1, 497-8. Generations 21-28: D.L.J. in Boston Evening Transcript (1927) Note 2257, Part XIII; Turton: Dudley pedigree; The Genealogist XIV, 361-368).

Line 109

25. ALICE OF BURGUNDY (108-25), m. (2) William III Talvas.

26. GUY II, d. 1147, Count of Ponthieu; m. Ida. (CP XI 697).

27. JOHN I, d. 1191, Count of Ponthieu; m. (1) Matilda; m. (2) a dau. of Bernhard of St. Valerie; m. (3) by 1177, Beatrice of St. Pol, dau. of Anselme who d. 1164, Count of St. Pol, and **EUSTACHE DE CHAMPAGNE** (169A-27).

28. WILLIAM III (by (3)), b. 1179, d. 1221, Count of Ponthieu; m. 1195, **ALICE OF FRANCE** (137-26), dau. of **LOUIS VII** (101-25), King of France.

29. MARIE, d. 1250, Countess of Ponthieu; m. (1) 1208-1211, **SIMON DE DAMMARTIN** (144-27), d. 1239, Count of Aumale, 2nd son of Alberic II, Count of Dammartin, d. 1200, and Maud; m. (2) Mathieu de Montmorency, killed Feb. 1250.

30. JOAN DE DAMMARTIN, d. 1279; m. (2) 1237, **FERNANDO III,** the Saint (110-29), b. 1191, d. 1252, canonized by Pope Clement X in 1671, King of Castile 1217-1252, and of Leon 1230-1252. (CP II 59 note b; CCN 385; N&Q 4th Series, VII 437-438. Generations 25-30: The Gen. Mag. XV 53-63).

Line 110

22. ROBERT THE OLD (108-22), b. ca. 1011, d. 1075/6, Duke of Burgundy; m. (2) ca. 1033 Helie, d. 1109, dau. Dalmas I of Semur en Auxois by his wife Aremburge.

23. HILDEGARDE (or Aldegarde), d. aft. 1104; m. (3) 1068/9, William VI, b. ca. 1026, d. 25 Sep. 1086, Count of Poitou 1058-1086 (William III of Poitou, [9]William II of Poitou, [8]William I of Poitou, [7]Ebbles Mancer of Poitou, [6]Ranulf II of Poitou, [5]). (Garnier, table XXXIX).

24. WILLIAM VII of Poitou, b. ca. 22 Oct. 1071, d. 10 Feb. 1126/7, Count of Poitou 1086-1126, Duke of Aquitaine; m. (2) 1094, **MAUD OF TOULOUSE** (185-3), d. 28 Nov. 1117, dau. of William IV of Toulouse.

25. WILLIAM VIII of Poitou, b. 1099, d. 9 Apr. 1137, Count of Poitou 1126-1137, Duke of Aquitaine; m. (1) 1121, **ELEANOR DE CHASTELLERAULT** (183-4), d. aft. Mar. 1130, dau. of Almeric (or

Line 110 (cont.)

Aimery) I, Viscount of Chastellerault. (Sugar: Vie de Louis VI, 127; Chronique des églises d'Anjou, p. 432).
    26. ELEANOR OF AQUITAINE (and Poitou), b. 1123, d. 31 Mar. or 1 Apr. 1204; m. (1) **LOUIS VII** (101-25), King of France, divorced 1152; m. (2) 18 May 1152, **HENRY II** (1-25), b. 5 Mar. 1132/3, d. 6 Jul. 1189, King of England. (Brandenburg; Winkhaus).
    27. ELEANOR OF ENGLAND, b. 1161, d. 1214; m. 1169, **ALFONSO VIII** (113-27), b. 1155, d. 1214, King of Castile.
    28. BERENGARIA OF CASTILE, d. 1244; m. (2) **ALFONSO IX** (114-27), b. 1166, d. 1229, King of Leon. (CP II 59 note b; CCN 385).
    29. FERNANDO III, the Saint, b. 1191, d. 1252, King of Castile 1217, and of Leon 1230; m. (2) 1237, **JOAN DE DAMMARTIN** (109-30), d. 1279. (CP II 59 note b; CCN 385).
    30. ELEANOR OF CASTILE, d. Grantham, England, 28 Nov. 1290; m. 1254, **EDWARD I** (1-28), d. 1307, King of England. (CP II 59 note b; X 118; CCN 356).
    31. JOAN PLANTAGENET, b. 1272, d. 1307; m. (1) 1290, **SIR GILBERT DE CLARE** (63-30). (CP V 736. Generations 22-30: Turton; Watts: Christian Recovery of Spain, 307).

Line 111

    24. WILLIAM VII (110-24), b. ca. 22 Oct. 1071, d. 10 Feb. 1126/7, Duke of Aquitaine; m. (2) **MAUD OF TOULOUSE** (185-3).
    25. MAUD OF AQUITAINE, m. Ramiro II of Aragon, d. 1147. (CCN 38).
    26. PETRONILLA OF ARAGON, b. 1135, d. 1172; m. 1151, Raymond V, d. 1162, Count of Barcelona. (CCN 38).
    27. ALFONSO II, b. 1152, d. 1196, King of Aragon, 1163-1196; m. (2) 1175, **SANCHA OF CASTILE** (116-26), d. 1208. (CCN 38).
    28. ALFONSO, d. 1209, Count of Provence; m. 1193, Gersenda II of Sabran, dau. of Rainou, Count of Forcalquier.
    29. RAYMOND IV BERENGER, b. 1195, d. 19 Aug. 1245, Count of Provence and Forcalquier; m. ca. 5 Jun 1219, **BEATRICE OF SAVOY** (133-27), d. 1266. (See also Line 104-28. CP IV 321; Garnier says "m. Dec. 1220".)
    30. ELEANOR OF PROVENCE, d. Amesbury, 25 Jun. 1291; m. Canterbury, 14 Jan. 1236/7, **HENRY III** (1-27), b. 1 Oct. 1207, d. Westminster, 16 Nov. 1272, King of England. (CP IV 321; V 736. Generations 24-30: Turton).

Line 112

    23. HENRY (108-23), Duke of Burgundy; m. Sibylle of (? Barcelona).
    24. HENRY I, b. 1035, d. 1112, Count of Portugal; m. 1093, Theresa of Castile, d. 1130. (CP 38).
    25. ALFONSO I, of Portugal, b. 1109, d. 6 Dec. 1185, King of Portugal, 1128-1185; m. 1146, Maud of Savoy, d. 1157. (CCN 38).

Line 112 (cont.)

26. URRACA OF PORTUGAL, d. 1178; m. (1) 1160, FERNANDO II (114-26), d. 1188, King of Leon. (Turton).

Line 113

22. ROBERT THE OLD (108-22), Duke of Burgundy; m. Eleanor of Semur-en-Auxois.
23. CONSTANCE OF BURGUNDY, d. 1092; m. (1) Alfonso VI, b. 1030, d. 1109, King of Castile and Leon, son of Fernando the Great. (CCN 37).
24. URRACA OF CASTILE AND LEON, d. 1126; m. RAYMOND (132-25), d. 1107, of Burgundy.
25. ALFONSO VII, b. 1103, d. 1157, King of Castile and Leon; m. (2) 1124, Berenguela of Barcelona, d. 1131, dau. of Raymond IV, Count of Barcelona, and Dulce or Aldonza, dau. Gilbert, Vicomte de Carlat, heiress of Provence; m. (3) RICHILDE OF POLAND (147-27). (CCN 38; Moriarty, The Plantagenet Ancestry).
26. SANCHO III, d. 1158, King of Castile; m. Blanche of Navarre. (CCN 37; EB 25: 554).
27. ALFONSO VIII, the Good, b. 1155, d. 1214, King of Castile 1158-1214; m. 1169, ELEANOR OF ENGLAND (110-27), b. 1161, d. 1214. (CCN 37: EB 25: 554-555).
28. BLANCHE OF CASTILE, d. 1253; m. 1200, LOUIS VIII (101-27), b. 1187, d. 1226, King of France. (CP VII 386).
29. ROBERT, Count of Artois, b. 1216, d. 1250; m. 1237, MATILDA OF BRABANT (45-29). (CP VII 386. Generations 22-29: Turton).

Line 114

25. ALFONSO VII (113-25), m. (2) 1124 Berenguela of Barcelona. (CCN 385).
26. FERNANDO II, d. 1188, King of Leon, 1157-1188; m. (1) 1160, URRACA OF PORTUGAL (112-26), d. 1178. (CCN 37, 385).
27. ALFONSO IX, b. 1166, d. 1229, King of Leon 1188-1229; m. (2) BERENGARIA OF CASTILE (110-28), d. 1244. (CP II note b; CCN 37).
28. BERENGARIA OF LEON, m. as 3rd wife, John de Brienne, b. ca. 1168, d. 21 Mar. 1237, King of Jerusalem, 1210-1215, Emperor of Constantinople, Crusader. (CP II 59 note b; CCN 183). (See Moncrieff, in Burke's Peerage (1963) 202). John of Brienne was yr. son of Erard II, Count of Brienne, (who fought in the 3rd Crusade, being killed at Acre, 8 Feb. 1191) by Agnes de Montfaucon (m. 1166), dau. Richard II, Count of Montbéliard. He was b. ca. 1168, d. 21 Mar. 1237; m. (1) 15 Sep. 1210, Mary, dau. Conrad de Montferrat, by wife Isabel, dau. Aumary I, King of Jerusalem. He became King of Jerusalem by election of the Barons, in right of his wife, who died shortly leaving a daughter and heiress, in whose right he reigned; m. (2) 1214, Stephanie, dau. and h. Leo II, King of Armenia, who d.s.p. 1219. On mar. of his dau. Yolande, he returned to Europe; m. (3)

105

1223, Berengaria (d. 12 Apr. 1237), dau. of Alphonso IV, King of Castile and Leon. He was elected Latin Emperor of Constantinople 1228; died 1237.

29. LOUIS DE BRIENNE, d'Acre, Vicount of Beaumont in Maine; m. Agnes de Beaumont, dau. of Raoul, Vicount of Beaumont. (CP II 59 note b).

30. HENRY DE BEAUMONT, Knt., d. 10 Mar. 1339/40, knighted 1308, M.P. 1308/9-1332, Lord Beaumont, Earl of Buchan, Justiciar of Scotland 1338; m. ca. 1310, **ALICE COMYN** (114A-29), d. bef. 10 Aug. 1349, dau. of Alexander Comyn, Sheriff of Aberdeen. (CP II 59-60, 375-376).

31. JOHN DE BEAUMONT, Knt., b. ca. 1318, M.P. 1342/3; m. **ELEANOR PLANTAGENET** (17-30) See Line 17.

Line 114A

26. WILLIAM COMYN (121A-26), d. 1233; m. (2) Marjorie, Countess of Buchan. (CP II 375-376).

27. ALEXANDER COMYN, Earl of Buchan, d. 1290, bef. Apr. 6; m. **ELIZABETH (or ISABEL)** (224-29), 2nd dau. and coh. **ROGER DE QUINCY** (53-28), Earl of Winchester, by 1st wife **HELEN OF GALLOWAY** (38-27), eldest dau. and coh. Alan of Galloway, living 1282. (CP II 374-375).

28. ALEXANDER COMYN, yr. son, Sheriff of Aberdeen. (CP II 375-376, 60), m. Joan, sister of William le Latimer.

29. ALICE COMYN, eldest dau. and coh.; m. by 14 Jul. 1310, **HENRY DE BEAUMONT** (114-30), Lord Beaumont, sum. as Earl of Buchan, d. shortly bef. 10 Mar. 1340. (CP II 375-376, 59-60).

Line 115 Line cancelled. No descendants of Gen. 27.

Line 116

25. ALFONSO VII (113-25), b. 1103, d. 1157, King of Castile and Leon; m. (3) 1152, **RICHILDE OF POLAND** (147-27), d. bef. 1176.

26. SANCHA OF CASTILE, d. 1208; m. 1175, **ALFONSO II** (111-27), King of Aragon, b. 1152, d. 1196.

Line 117

24, LOUIS VI (101-24), b. 1077, d. 1137, King of France; m. (2) 1115, **ADELAIDE OF SAVOY** (135-26), d. 1154.

25. PETER OF FRANCE, b. ca. 1125, d. bef. 1183, Crusader 1147, was in England in 1178; m. **ELIZABETH DE COURTENAY** (107-25), living 1205.

26. ALICE DE COURTENAY, m. **AYMER "TAILLIFER" DE VALENCE** (153-27), d. 1218, Count of Angouleme.

27. ISABELLA OF ANGOULÊME, b. 1188, d. 3 or 4 June 1246; m. (1) 24 Aug. 1200, **JOHN** (1-26), b. 24 Dec. 1166, d. 19 Oct. 1216, King of England; m. (2) 10 May 1220, Hugh X de Lusignan, d.1246,

Line 117 (cont.)

ca. 6 June, Count of la Marche and of Angoulême, son of Hugh IX de Lusignan and Matilda, dau. of Wulgram III, Count of Angoulême and la Marche. (CP V 736; CCN 547-548).

28. HUGH XI de Lusignan, b. 1221, d. 1250 in Egypt, prob. at the battle of Mansurah, Count of Ponthieu, La Marche and Angoulême; m. **YOLANDE DE DREUX** (135-30). They were the parents of Alice, No. 30.

30. ALICE DE LUSIGNAN, m. 1253, **GILBERT DE CLARE** (63-30), b. 1243, d. 7 Dec. 1299, Earl of Gloucester. (CP V 702-710, 736. Generations 24-27: Turton; see Watson on the Lusignans, The Gen. n.s. 21: 78+).

Line 118

17. HERBERT I (50-17), Count de Vermandois; m. Beatrice de Morvois (Isenberg, Saillot).

18. HERBERT II, d. 943, Count de Vermandois and Troyes; m. **LIEGARDE** (48-19).

19. ROBERT, b. ca. 920, d. ca. 967/8, Count of Troyes and Meaux; m. (1) Adelaide, dau. of Giselbert, Count of Burgundy and Ermengarde of Burgundy.

20. ADELAIDE DE VERMANDOIS, b. 950, d. 975/8; m. (2) Geoffrey I, Grisgonelle, d. 21 Jul 987, Count of Anjou, son of Fulk II, the Good, Count of Anjou, and Gerberga (of the Gatinais ?).

21. FULK III, the Black, d. 21 Jun. 1040, Count of Anjou; m. (2) aft. 1000, Hildegarde, d. Jerusalem, 1 Apr. 1040.

22. ERMENGARDE OF ANJOU, d. 21 Mar. 1076; m. (2) ca. 1035, Aubri-Geoffrey, d. 1 Apr. 1046, Count of the Gatinais, 1034-1043, son of Geoffrey III, Count of the Gatinais and Beatrix of Mâcon.

23. FULK IV, "Rechin," b. 1043, d. 14 Apr. 1109, Count of Anjou; m. (5) 1090/1, Bertrade or Beatrice, dau. of Simon I, Seigneur of Montfort l'Amauri and Agnes d'Évreux (Richard 3, Robert 2, Richard 1 of Normandy). (CP XI App. D, 114). (See Line 121).

24. FULK V, the Young, b. 1092, d. at Jerusalem, 10 Nov. 1143, Count of Anjou, King of Jerusalem; m. (1) 1110, Erembourg, d. 1126, dau. of Hélias, Count of Maine; m. (2) 2 Jun. 1129, Melisende de Rethel, d. 11 Sep. 1161, eldest dau. of **BALDWIN II** (103A-25), King of Jerusalem, by whom he was father of Baldwin III, King of Jerusalem, b. 1130, d.s.p. 10 Feb. 1162, and Amalric I, King of Jerusalem, b. 1136, d. 11 Jul. 1174. (Generations 19-25: NEHGR 99: 34.)

25. GEOFFREY V PLANTAGENET, b. 24 Aug. 1113, d. 7 Sep. 1151, Count of Anjou, Duke of Normandy; m. 3 Apr. 1127, **MATILDA** (1-24), b. 1104, d. 10 Sep. 1167, dau. of Henry I, King of England. (CP V 736; SP I 1-2; CCN 494).

Line 119

23. FULK IV (118-23), b. 1043, d. 14 Apr. 1109, Count of Anjou; m. (1) Hildegarde de Baugency. (CP XI App. D, 114).

24. ERMENGARDE OF ANJOU, d. 1 Jun. 1147; m. (2) **ALAN IV** (39-25) Fergant, d. 1119, Duke of Brittany, son of Hoël, Duke of Brittany and Hawise, d. 1072, dau. of Alan III, Duke of Brittany, d. 1040, and Bertha, d. 1084, dau. of Eudes, Count of Blois & Chartres. Alan III was a grandson of Richard I, Duke of Normandy. (CP X 788-789; Chart of the Dukes of Brittany in CP X opp. p. 781).

25. CONAN III, d. 1148, Duke of Brittany; m. Maud, natural dau. of **HENRY I** (121-25), King of England. (CP X 790, XI App. D 114).

26. BERTHA OF BRITTANY, d. bef. 1167; m. **ALAN** (227-25), d. 15 Sep. 1146, Earl of Richmond, son of **STEPHEN** (214-24), d. 21 Apr. 1135/6, Count of Brittany, Lord of Richmond. (CP X 780, XI App. D 114).

27. CONAN IV, d. 20 Feb. 1171, Duke of Brittany, Earl of Richmond; m. 1160, **MARGARET OF HUNTINGDON** (96-26), dau. of Henry, Earl of Huntingdon. (CP X 791-793).

Line 120

28. BERENGARIA OF CASTILE (110-28), d. 1244; m. (2) **ALFONSO IX** (114-27), b. 1166, d. 1229, King of Leon.

29. BERENGARIA OF LEON (114-28), m. as 3rd wife **JEAN DE BRIENNE**, d. 1237, King of Jerusalem. (See 114-28).

30. JEAN DE BRIENNE, d. 1296, Grand Butler of France, 1258; m. (1) Mary, wid. Alexander II, King of Scotland, dau. of Enguerrand de Coucy (she d.s.p.); m. (2) 1251, Jeanne, Dame de Château du Loir, dau. Geoffrey IV, Vicomte de Châteaudun. (Anselme, VI 134, III 314).

31. BLANCHE DE BRIENNE, Lady of Loupeland; m. **WILLIAM DE FIENNES** (152-29). (CP VIII 433). (See Moncrieff, Burke's Peerage (1963) 202).

32. MARGARET DE FIENNES, m. ca. 1280, **SIR EDMUND DE MORTIMER** (27-30), b. 1261, d. 1304, Baron Mortimer of Wigmore. (CP VIII 433).

33. SIR ROGER DE MORTIMER, Earl of March; m. **JOAN DE GENEVILLE** (71-32). (CP VIII 441).

34. KATHERINE DE MORTIMER, d. 1371; m. **THOMAS BEAUCHAMP**, K.G. (87-31), d. 1369, Earl of Warwick.

35. WILLIAM BEAUCHAMP, d. 1411, Baron Abergavenny; m. Joan Fitz Alan, dau. of **RICHARD FITZ ALAN** (60-33) and **ELIZABETH DE BOHUN** (15-31). (CP X 125).

36. JOAN BEAUCHAMP, d. 1430; m. ca. 1413, **JAMES BUTLER** (7-33), b. ca. 1390, d. 1452, Earl of Ormond. (CP X 125).

37. THOMAS BUTLER, K.B., 7th Earl of Ormond, Baron Ormond de Rocheford, d. 3 Aug. 1515, K.B., 6 Jul 1483; m. (2) bef. Nov. 1496, Lora Berkeley, d. bef. 30 Dec. 1501, dau. of Sir Edward Berkeley of Beverton, co. Gloucester, by Christian Holt, dau. of Richard Holt of Coldrey, Hampshire. (CP X 131-133).

38. MARGARET BUTLER, dau. by unknown 1st wife, b. 1465 (ae. 20 in 1485), d. 1539, m. 1485, Sir William Boleyn. (CP X 133 note b).

39. SIR THOMAS BOLEYN, cr. Earl of Wiltshire; m.

Line 120 (cont.)

ELIZABETH HOWARD (22-36), dau. of Thomas Howard, Duke of Norfolk. (CP X 137-140).

Line 121

20. **ADELAIDE DE VERMANDOIS** (118-20), m. Geoffrey I Grisgonelle, Count of Anjou.
21. **ERMENGARDE OF ANJOU**, m. 980, Conan I, d. 992, Duke of Brittany.
22. **JUDITH OF BRITTANY**, b. 982, living 1026; m. ca. 1000-1008, Richard II, the Good, d. Aug. 1027, Duke of Normandy.
23. **ROBERT I**, d. 22 Jul. 1035, Duke of Normandy. (CP I 351-352).
24. **WILLIAM I**, the Conqueror (natural son of Robert by Herleve, dau. of Fulbert of Falaise, a tanner), b. Falaise, 1027, d. Rouen, 9 Sep. 1087, Duke of Normandy, King of England 1066-1087; m. 1053, **MAUD (or MATILDA) OF FLANDERS** (162-23), b. 1032, d. 3 Nov. 1083. (CCN 494).
25. **HENRY I**, Beauclerc, b. 1070, d. 1 Dec. 1135, King of England 1100-1135; m. 11 Nov. 1100, **MATILDA OF SCOTLAND** (1-23), b. 1079, d. 1 May 1118. (CP V 736, VII 737; SP I 1-2; CCN 494). He had issue by a number of mistresses.
26. **REGINALD FITZ ROY** (or Fitz Henry) **DE DUNSTANVILLE**, d. 1 Jul. 1175 (natural son of King Henry I and Sybil Corbet), Earl of Cornwall, Apr. 1141, Sheriff of Devon, 1173; m. Beatrice de Mortain, dau. of William Fitz Robert and granddau. of Robert de Mortain (185-1)). (CP III 429, VII 737, XI App. D 107-108; Ordericus Vitalis; TAG 29: 13-17, 31: 118; Powley: House of de la Pomerai).

Line 121A

23. **DONALD BANE**, son of Duncan I, King of Scots (170-20), King of Scots, 1093-1094, by an unnamed wife had (SP I 504).
24. **BETHOC**, m. Huctred of Tyndale, son of Waldef; they had
25. **HEXTILDA**, m. Richard Comyn of Northallerton and Badenoch (son of William, son of John, son of Robert); m. ca. 1145. He d. 1176-82, when wid. m. (2) Malcolm, Earl of Athol. (SP I 504-555).
26. **WILLIAM COMYN**, d. 1233, j.u. Earl of Buchan; m. (1) unknown; m. (2) by 1214, Marjorie, Countess of Buchan, dau. of Fergus, Earl of Buchan. (CP II 374-375, see Line 224-29, connection on cited pages). By 1st wife, son (SP I 505).
27. **RICHARD COMYN**, Lord of Badenoch, d. 1244-9, by unknown wife, son (SP I 506).
28. **SIR JOHN COMYN**, "The Red Comyn #1", seen 1242, d. aft. 1273; by wife Alicia who survived him, had (SP I 507).
29. **SIR JOHN COMYN**, "The Black Comyn," seen 1281, d. ca. 1303, claimant of the Crown of Scotland on the above cited descent from Donald Bane; m. **ALIANORA** (95-29), dau. John Baliol and **DEVORGILLA OF GALLOWAY** 95-28). (SP I 508).

26. ELIZABETH, dau. of **HENRY I**, King of England (121-25), by unknown mistress; m. Fergus, Lord of Galloway, seen 1136-47; d. Holyrood Abbey, 1161 or 1166. (SP IV 135-137). They had

27. UCHTRED, seen 1136, killed 22 Sep. 1174 at Loch Fergus by nephew Malcolm, son of Gilbert, his brother; m. **GUNHILD**, dau. of **WALDEVE** (38-24), Lord of Allendale, son of Gospatric, 2nd Earl of Dunbar. (Also called Waltheof).

Line 121C

26. ELIZABETH (121B-26), illeg. dau. **HENRY I**; m. Fergus of Galloway, had (SP IV 136).

27. GILBERT, seen 1174, d. 1 Jan. 1185; by unknown wife had (SP II 421-422).

28. DUNCAN, Lord of Carrick, prob. a minor 1185, cr. Earl of Carrick 1225-30, d. 13 Jun. 1252, m. Avelina, dau. Alan Fitz Walter, High Sheriff of Scotland, who may or may not be mother of his son. (SP II 422-423; CP III 55; Duncan Stewart: Hist. of Scotland 48).

29. NEIL, Earl of Carrick, d. 1256, Regent of Scotland, and Guardian of Alexander III, 1255; m. Isabella or Margaret, parents not surely identified. (SP IV 423-426; IX, 55; CP III 55).

30. MARJORIE (or Margaret) (one of four daus.), s.j. Countess of Carrick, d. by 27 Oct. 1292; m. (1) Adam de Kilconquhar, d. in the Holy Land 1271 or 1272; m. (2) 1273, **ROBERT BRUCE** (252-29), son of Robert of Annandale and Cleveland, j.u. Earl of Carrick, which title he resigned to his son Robert (later **ROBERT I** (252-30) of Scots), 27 Oct. 1292. Marjorie d. 1292, bef. 27 Oct. (SP II 426-427; CP III 55; Farrer: Early Yorkshire Charters II 14-15).

Line 121D

30. ELIZABETH COMYN (224-30), dead Nov. 1328, 3rd dau. of **ALEXANDER COMYN** (114A-27), Earl of Buchan by **ELIZABETH** (224-29), 3rd dau. and coh. of Roger de Quincy, Earl of Winchester; m. Gilbert de Umfreville, d. 1307, Earl of Angus, son of Gilbert de Umfreville, Baron of Prudhoe, etc. by 1st wife Mathilda, Countess of Angus. (CP I 147-148; Clay 224-225).

31. ROBERT DE UMFREVILLE (224-31), Earl of Angus, aged 30+ in 1307, d. 12 Apr. 1325; m. (1) Lucy, dau. of Philip Lord Kyme; m. (2) Eleanore, d. 31 Mar. 1368, who m. (2) Sir Roger Manduit. (Clay 224; CP I 149-150). By (2) he had

32. THOMAS DE UMFREVILLE, of Harbottle, and of Hessel, Yorks., d. 21 May 1387; had by Joan, dau. Adam de Rodham (Clay, op.cit.; CP I 151).

33. THOMAS DE UMFREVILLE, b. ca. 1361, M.P., Northumb. 1387-1388, d. 12 Feb. or 8 Mar. 1390/1; m. Agnes, d. 25 Oct. 1420, pos. dau. Thomas Grey of Heton. (Clay, op.cit.; CP, op.cit.)

34. MARGARET DE UMFREVILLE, b. 1390-7, d. 23 Jun. 1444; m. (1) William Lodington, d. 9 Jan. 1419/20; m. (2) by 26 Apr. 1423, John Constable of Halsham and Burton Constable, will 23 Nov. 1449,

Line 121D (cont.)

pro. 17 Jan. 1451. (Clay 225, 28; CP I 152-153).
35. SIR JOHN CONSTABLE of Halsham, nunc. will 20 Dec., pro. 18 Mar. 1477/8; m. Lora, dau. Henry, Lord Fitz Hugh. (Clay 28-29; CP I 153; NEHGR 111: 196-198).
36. ISABEL CONSTABLE, will dated 20 Jul., pro. 12 Dec. 1505; m. ca. 1482 as (2) wife, Stephen de Thorpe of Thorpe and Welwyk, b. ca. 1446; m. (1) 1466-71, Dyonis, dau. William Eland of Hull, d. test. 1503. (NEHGR 114: 224-225).
37. MARGARET THORPE, m. aft. 20 Jul. 1505, John Newton of Ryhill, Yorks, and Burstwick juxta Skeklyng, d. 9 Jun. 1515. (NEHGR 111: 198).
38. JOHN NEWTON, b. ca. 7 Nov. 1515, dead 1562/3; m. Margaret, dau. John Grimston and Elizabeth (Eure) of Aldbrough. She bur. 9 Jun. 1587. (NEHGR 94: 13-14, 111: 199). (For the Grimston-Eure anc., see NEHGR 111: 261-265).
39. JOHN NEWTON of Flinton, buried 2 Apr. 1587; m. Marie, who m. (2) 18 Jul. 1587, William Skipsey. (NEHGR 94: 14-15).
40. LAUNCELOT NEWTON of Hedon, b. ca. 1580, bur. Hedon, 30 Aug. 1622; m. at Barmeston, 3 Jan. 1610, Mary Lee, bur. 12 Mar. 1632 at Hedon. (NEHGR 94: 15, 17-18).
41. ELLEN NEWTON, b. 24 Feb. 1614; m. 3 Nov. 1636, at St. Martin Michelgate, York, **EDWARD CARLETON** (2-42), b. Hornsea, bp. Beeford, 20 Oct. 1610. (NEHGR cit.; "Ancestry of Edward Carleton and Ellen Newton his wife" Sheppard).

Line 122

28. ELA (108-28), Countess of Salisbury, m. **WILLIAM LONGESPEE** (30-26), natural son of Henry II, King of England. (CP XI 379-382; The Gen. Mag. XIV 361-367).
29. SIR WILLIAM DE LONGESPEE, slain in battle with the Saracens, 8 Feb. 1250; m. 1226, Idoine de Camville, dau. and h. of Richard de Camville by Eustacia, dau. of Gilbert Basset. (Inq.p.m. 1299; CP I 338, XI 382-383, App. F 126-127; VCH Lanc. I 312).
30. ELA LONGESPEE, m. 1244, James de Audley (or Aldithley), b. ca. 1220, d. ca. 11 Jun. 1276, of Heleigh, co. Stafford, Keeper of the Castle of Newcastle-under-Lynn, 30 Oct. 1250, Lord Marcher, Sheriff of Salop 1261-1262, and Staffordshire 1270-1271, Justiciar of Ireland. (CP I 338).
31. NICHOLAS AUDLEY, b. bef. 1285, d. 28 Aug. 1299 (Inq.p.m. 1299), Lord Audley; m. Catherine Giffard, b. 1272, living 1322, dau. of John Giffard, 1st Lord Giffard of Brimsfield, by Maud, dau. of Walter de Clifford and wid. of William Longespee (son of No. 29). (CP I 338-339; Banks I 100). (See 29A-29).
32. NICHOLAS AUDLEY, of Heleigh, co. Stafford, b. 11 Nov. 1289, d. Dec. 1316, ae. 27, 3rd Lord Audley, M.P. 1312-1316; m. 1312, Joan de Martin, d. 1319/22, wid. of Henry, Earl of Lincoln, only child of William Martin, Lord Martin, and Eleanor, dau. of Sir **REYNOLD FITZ PIERS** (262-30) and **JOAN DE VIVONNIA** (261-32). (CP I 339; Banks I 101).

Line 122 (cont.)

33. SIR JAMES AUDLEY, K.G., b. Knesale, Notts., 8 Jan. 1312/3, d. Apr. 1386; m. (1) bef. 13 Jun. 1330, **JOAN MORTIMER** (71-33), d. aft. 1337. (CP I 340, XI App. F 127; Banks I 100-103).

Line 122A (Prepared by Douglas Richardson)

28. ELA (108-28), Countess of Salisbury, m. **WILLIAM LONGESPEE** (30-26), natural son of Henry II, King of England. (CP XI 379-382).

29. IDA (or Idonea) **DE LONGESPEE**, living 1266/7, m. (1) as a child, Ralph de Somery, d. 1212, son and h. of Ralph de Somery by his wife, Margaret Marshall; m. (2) by 1220, as his (2) wife, William de Beauchamp, b. say 1185, d. 1260, held barony of Bedford, co. Bedford, Baron of the Exchequer, Sheriff of Bedford and Bucks, son of Simon de Beauchamp (dead by 1206/7) by his wife Isabella. (CP XI 110-111, 382; Publications of the Bedfordshire Historical Record Society I 10-16, esp. chart p. 25). Note: This Ida is not to be confused with **IDA DE LONGESPEE** (30-27) who m. Walter Fitz Robert. See discussion under Line 30, Gen. 26.

30. BEATRICE DE BEAUCHAMP, 3rd dau. and coh., d. ca. 1280/1, m. (1) by 1264, Sir Thomas Fitz Otto (or Fitz Otes) of Mendelsham, Suffolk, b. ca. 1231 (ae. 30 in 1261), d. by 28 Mar. 1274, holding lands in Hunts., Essex, Beds., Bucks., Glouc. and Worc.; m. (2) by 26 June 1278, Sir William de Montchensy of Edwardeston, Suffolk, d. sh. bef. 15 May 1302. (CP II 233-235; Publications of the Bedfordshire Historical Record Society II 233-235); Knights of Edward I, II 49-50; III 279-180).

31. MAUD (or Matilda) **FITZ OTHO**, living 28 May 1329, m. by June 1292 **JOHN DE BOTETOURTE** (216-29), d. 25 Nov. 1324, first Lord Botetourte, natural son of Edward I, King of England. (CP II 233-235; Publications of the Bedfordshire Historical Record Society I, chart p. 25).

Line 123

25. GEOFFREY V PLANTAGENET (118-25), b. 23 Aug. 1113, d. 7 Sep. 1151, Count of Anjou, Duke of Normandy, by unknown mistress had:

26. HAMELIN PLANTAGENET, d. 7 May 1202, Earl of Surrey; m. 1164 as her (2) husb. **ISABEL DE WARENNE** (83-26). (CP IV 670 chart II).

27. MAUD DE WARENNE, d. ca. 1212; m. (1) Henry (see 139-27), Count d'Eu, Lord of Hastings, d. 11 Mar. 1183; m. (2) Henry de Stouteville. (CP V 158-160).

28. ALICE D'EU, Countess of Eu, Lady of Hastings, d. 15 May 1246; m. ca. 1191, Raoul I de Lusignan, d. 1 May 1219, Count d'Eu, son of Hugh VIII, Sire de Lusignan and Bourgogne, and Dame de Fonenay, dau. of Geoffrey de Rancon, Seigneur de Taillebourg. (CP V 160-166).

29. MAUD D'EU (or de Lusignan), d. 14 Aug. 1241; m.

Line 123 (cont.)

HUMPHREY DE BOHUN V, (97-28), b. by 1208, d. 24 Sept. 1275, 2nd Earl of Hereford and Earl of Essex. (CP V 163 note d; IV 669).

Line 124

   25. HENRY I (121-25), b. 1070, d. 1 Dec. 1135, King of England. (CP IV 670 chart III; V 736; VII 677).
   26. ROBERT DE CAEN (natural son of Henry I), b. ca. 1090, d. Bristol, 31 Oct. 1147, called "the Consul," Earl of Gloucester, 1122-1147; m. Maud, dau. of Robert Fitz Hamon, Lord of Crelly in Calvados, Baron of Thoringni, and Sybil, dau. of Roger de Montgomery, Earl of Shrewsbury. (CP IV 670 chart iii; V 736; VII 677; XI 683-687 App. D 106).
   27. WILLIAM FITZ ROBERT, d. 1183, 2nd Earl of Gloucester; m. 1150, **HAWISE DE BEAUMONT** (63-26), d. 24 Apr. 1197. (CP IV 670 chart III; V 736; VII 520).

Line 125

   26. ROBERT DE CAEN (124-26), m. Maud, dau. of Robert Fitz Hamon.
   27. MAUD, d. 29 Jul. 1189; m. ca. 1141, **RANULPH DE GERNON** (132A-27), b. ca. 1100, d. 16 Dec. 1153, Vicomte d'Avranches, Earl of Chester, son of Ranulph le Meschin, Earl of Chester, and Lucy. (CP III 167; IV 670 chart IV; V 736; VII 677).
   28. HUGH OF KEVELIOC, b. 1147, Kevelioc, co. Monmouth, d. 1181, Leeke, co. Stafford, Earl of Chester, Vicomte d'Avranches in Normandy; m. 1169, Bertrade, dau. of Simon de Montfort, Count of Évreux. (CP III 167; V 670 chart IV).
   29. HAWISE OF CHESTER, b. 1180, d. 1241/3, Countess of Lincoln; m. **ROBERT DE QUINCY** (54-28). (CP III 167; IV 670 chart IV; VII 677; VCH Lanc. I 312).

Line 126

   28. HUGH OF KEVELIOC (125-28), Earl of Chester; m. 1169, Bertrade de Montfort. (CP II 167).
   29. MABEL OF CHESTER, m. **WILLIAM D'AUBIGNY** (149-26), d. Mar. 1220/1, Earl of Arundel. (CP I 233-238).
   30. NICHOLE D'AUBIGNY, m. as (1) wife **ROGER DE SOMERY** (55-28), of Dudley, co. Warwick. He m. (2) Amabil, wid. Gilbert de Segrave & dau. Robert de Chaucombe. (Generations 28-29: CP I 236-237; II 1-2, IV 670 chart IV; VI 174; DNB 3: 285).

Line 127

   28. HUGH OF KEVELIOC (125-28), Earl of Chester; m. Bertrade de Montfort. (CP II 167).
   29. AGNES OF CHESTER, d. 2 Nov. 1247; m. 1192, **WILLIAM DE FERRERS** (194-7), d. 22 Sep. 1247, 4th Earl of Derby. (CP IV

Line 127 (cont.)

192).

30. WILLIAM DE FERRERS, b. ca. 1193, buried 31 Mar. 1254, 5th Earl of Derby; m. (1) by 14 May 1219, Sibyl, 3rd dau. William Marshall, Earl of Pembroke, by **ISABEL DE CLARE** (66-27), d.s.p.m.; m. (2) ca. 1238, **MARGARET DE QUINCY** (57-29), d. shortly bef. 12 Mar. 1280/1. (Generations 28-30: CP IV 192-198, chart p. 199; V 320 chart; VII 677; SP III 142).

Line 128

21. ROBERT II (101-21), b. 970, d. 1031, King of France; m. 998, Constance of Provence. (Falaise Roll, 187-187).

22. ADELE OF FRANCE, d. 8 Jan. 1079; m. (2) 1028, **BALDWIN** V (162-22), Count of Flanders. (M. Jackson Crispin: Falaise Roll, London, 1938, pp. 186-187).

Line 129

24. FULK V (118-24), Count of Anjou and King of Jerusalem; m. Erembourg, dau. of Helias de Maine. (NEHGR 99:34).

25. SYBIL OF ANJOU, m. (2) 1131, **THIERRY** (164-25), d. 1166, Count of Flanders. (Note: Thierry was also known as Dietrich II Count of Alsace and Count of Flanders.)

Line 130

23. ROBERT I (121-23), d. 22 Jul. 1035, Duke of Normandy; left issue by his mistress, Herleve, dau. of Fulbert of Falaise. (CP I 351-352).

24. ADELAIDE, b. ca. 1030, d. bef. 1090, Countess of Aumale, sister of William the Conqueror; m. (1) Enguerrand II, Count of Ponthieu, slain at the siege of Arques, 1053, son of Hugh II, d. 20 Nov. 1052, Count of Ponthieu and Bertha of Aumale; m. (2) **LAMBERT** (148-22) of Boulogne, Count of Lens in Artois, slain at the battle of Lille, 1054; m. (3) **EUDES** (136-23), Count of Champagne (which he was deprived by his uncle Theobald bef. 1071), Earl of Holderness, imprisoned 1096. (CP I 350-352).

25. JUDITH OF LENS (see also 148-23), b. 1054, m. 1070, Waltheof II, beheaded Winchester 31 May 1076, Earl of Huntingdon, Northampton and Northumberland, son of Sigurd, Earl of Northumberland, and Aelflaed, dau. of Alfred of Bernicia. (CP I, 350-353; IV 670 chart IV; V 472, 736; VII 640-641). Though generally shown as child of (2) Lambert of Lens, there is a possibility that she was a child of the 1st mar. to Enguerrand II of Ponthieu. See discussion under Line 148, Gen. 22.

Line 131

28. HUGH OF KEVELIOC (125-28), Earl of Chester; m. Bertrade de Montfort. (CP IV 640 chart IV; VII 677; VCH Lanc. I 312).

Line 131 (cont.)

29. MAUD OF CHESTER, b. 1171, d. 1233; m. 26 Aug. 1190, DAVID (93-26), b. 1144, d. 17 Jun. 1219, Earl of Huntingdon. (CP IV 670 chart IV; V 736; VII 677; SP I 4).

Line 132

22. JUDITH OF BRITTANY (121-22), b. 982, living 1026; m. ca. 1000-1008, Richard II, Duke of Normandy.
23. ALICE or ADELAIDE OF NORMANDY, m. 1023, Raynald (or Renaud) I, Count of Burgundy, d. 1057.
24. WILLIAM I, d. 1087, "The Great", Count of Burgundy, Count of Mâcon; m. Stephanie of unknown parentage, but perh. of Barcelona, dau. Raymond II (Garnier xxviii; Moriarty, The Plantagenet Ancestry).
25. RAYMOND OF BURGUNDY, d. 1107; m. URRACA OF CASTILE AND LEON (113-24), d. 1126. (Turton; Moriarty, cit.)

Line 132A (Prepared by Douglas Richardson)

22. JUDITH OF BRITTANY (121-22, 132-22), founded abbey of Bernay, Normandy about 1026, m. ca. 1000-1008 Richard II "the Good", son of Richard I "the Fearless", d. 20 Nov. 996, by a "Danish wife" (in other words not a Christian marriage), died 28 Aug 1026, Duke of Normandy, 20 Nov. 996-1026. (Rt. Hon. Earl of Onslow, "The Dukes of Normandy and their Origin" (Hutchinson, 1945) (Rich I pp. 63-94, chart p. 176; Rich II pp. 95-112, chart p. 176); Ed. Garnier, "Tableaux Généalogues des Souverains de la France et de ses Grand Feudataires", Table xlviii; David C. Douglas, William the Conqueror, pp. 15, 29, 109, chart labelled Table I; Saillot, 36; Moriarty Notebooks).
23. RICHARD III, eldest son, died 6 Aug 1028, s.p. legit. (except for Nicholas, Abbot of St. Owen), Duke of Normandy 1026-1028, by an unknown mistress had: (Onslow, op. cit. pp. 113-114; Douglas, op. cit. pp. 92-93, chart labelled Table I; David Douglas, "The Rise of Normandy", published in Proceedings of the British Academy 1947, Vol. 33; Garnier, op. cit.)
24. ALICE OF NORMANDY, illegitimate daughter, m. Ranulph I, vicomte of the Bessin, fought at the Battle of Val-es-Dunes, 1047, son of Anschitil, living 1031, vicomte of the Bessin. (Douglas, William the Conqueror, pp. 92-93; Douglas, "The Rise of Normandy", pp. 127-128; Gallia Christiana, Vol. XI, Instrumenta, col. 70; Chronique de Robert de Torigni (ed. L. Delisle), Vol. 1, p. 34; Recueil des Actes des Ducs de Normandie (911-1066), ed. M. Faroux, no. 111).
25. RANULPH II, adult by 1066, living April 1089, vicomte of Bayeux in Normandy, m. Margaret (or Maud), dau. of Richard (le Goz), living 1084, vicomte d'Avranches, by his wife Emma (Emma has been alleged to be a half-sister of William the Conqueror. Professor Douglas labels this fictitious.) (Douglas, William the Conqueror, pp. 92-93; Douglas, "The Rise of Normandy", pp. 127-

128; CP III 166; XII pt. 1, App. K, 32-33).

26. RANULPH III le Meschin, also styled de Briquessart, d. ca. 1129, bur. St. Werburg's, Chester, lord of Cumberland, vicomte of Bayeux in Normandy, became Earl of Chester in 1120, following the death of his first cousin, Hugh d'Avranches, Earl of Chester; in 1124 he was Commander of the Royal Forces in Normandy; m. prob. ca. 1098 Lucy, living 1130, widow of Roger Fitz Gerold. (CP III 166; VII, App. J, 743-746; Douglas, William the Conqueror, pp. 92-93; Sanders, English Baronies, pp. 32-33; Douglas, "The Rise of Normandy", pp. 127-128).

27. RANULPH DE GERNON, b. ca. 1100, in Castle of Gernon in Normandy, d. 16 Dec. 1153, bur. St. Werburg's, Chester, Earl of Chester, Vicomte d'Avranches in Normandy, m. ca. 1141, **MAUD OF GLOUCESTER** (125-27), d. 29 July 1189, dau. of Robert, d. 1147, Earl of Gloucester. (CP III 166-167; Sanders, English Baronies, pp. 32-33).

Line 132B   (Prepared by Douglas Richardson)

25. RANULPH II (132A-25), vicomte of Bayeux in Normandy, living Apr. 1089, m. Margaret (or Maud), dau. of Richard (le Goz), vicomte d'Avranches. (David C. Douglas, William the Conqueror, pp. 92-93; CP III 166; David Douglas, "The Rise of Normandy", in Proceedings of British Academy (1947), 33: 127-128).

26. WILLIAM LE MESCHIN, lord of Skipton-in-Craven, co. Yorkshire, m. Cecily de Romilly, dau. and h. of Robert de Romilly. (CP IX 270-272; XII, pt. II, 930-931; Eyton, Antiquities of Shropshire, 2: 201-205).

27. MAUD (or **MATILDA**) **LA MESCHINE**, dau. and coh., inherited the manor of Molland, co. Devon previously held by her maternal grandfather, Robert de Romilly, m. (1) by 1139 Philip de Belmeis, adult by 1127, lord of Tong, co. Salop, and Ashby, co. Leicester, son of Walter de Belmeis; m. (2) Hugh de Mortimer, d. 1180/1, lord of Wigmore, co. Hereford. (CP IX 270-272; XII, pt. II, 930-931; Eyton, op. cit.; Farrer, Early Yorkshire Charters, 3: 470; Farrer, Honours and Knights' Fees, 3: 35).

28. ALICE DE BELMEIS, dau. by (1), m. **ALAN CEOCHE** or **LA COCHE**, otherwise **LA ZOUCHE** (39-27), adult by 1153, d. 1190, lord of North Molton, co. Devon, son of Geoffrey, vicomte of Porhoët, by Hawise, dau. of Alan Fergant, Duke of Brittany. (CP XII, pt. II, 930-931).

Line 132C   (Prepared by Douglas Richardson)

27. MAUD (or **MATILDA**) **LA MESCHINE** (132B-27), m. (1) by 1138/9 Philip de Belmeis, lord of Tong, co. Salop, and Ashby, co. Leicester; m. (2) Hugh de Mortimer, d. 1180/1, Lord Mortimer of Wigmore, co. Hereford, son of Hugh de Mortimer, d. 1148/50, Lord Mortimer of Wigmore. (CP IX 268-272).

28. ROGER DE MORTIMER, d. bef. 19 Aug. 1214, Lord

Mortimer of Wigmore, co. Hereford, m. Isabel, d. bef. 29 Apr. 1252, inherited Lechlade, co. Gloucester and Oakham, co. Rutland which her brother Henry lost at the time of the conquest of Normandy, dau. of Walkelin de Ferrières, seigneur of Ferrières-Saint-Hilaire and lord of Oakham, co. Rutland. (CP IV 191; IX 272-273).

29. RALPH DE MORTIMER, d. 6 Aug. 1246, bur. Wigmore, co. Hereford, Lord Mortimer of Wigmore, m. 1230 **GLADYS DHU** (27-28), d. 1251, widow of Reynold de Braiose and dau. of Llewellyn ap Iorworth, Prince of North Wales. (CP IX 275-276).

Line 133 (revised from 4th edition)

19. MATILDA OF FRANCE (157-19), (dau. of **LOUIS IV** (148-18), King of France and of Gerberga of Saxony), b. ca. 943, d. 981/992; m. ca. 964, Conrad I of Burgundy, "the Peaceful", d. 19 Oct. 993, King of Burgundy, son of Rudolph II, King of Burgundy, and Bertha of Swabia.

20. MATILDA OF BURGUNDY, m. a Count, name unknown.

21. BERTHA OF BURGUNDY, m. a Count of Geneva, name unknown.

22. GERALD I OF GENEVA, d. 1061/80, Count of Geneva, bef. 1034; m. (1) Gisele, dead in 1060; m. (2) Thietburga, wid. of Louis of Faucigny.

23. AIMON I OF GENEVA (by the 2nd wife), b. ca. 1050, d. ca. 1125/8, Count of Geneva, 1091; m. Ida of Glane, dau. of Peter, Count of Glane.

24. AMADEUS I OF GENEVA, b. 1100, d. 26 Jun. 1178, Count of Geneva, 1128-1178; m. (2) Matilda, d. by 2 Jul. 1137.

25. WILLIAM I OF GENEVA, b. 1130, d. 27 Jul. 1195, Count of Geneva, 1178-1195; m. ca. 1165, perh. (though doubtful) Beatrix de Faucigny, dau. of Aimon I of Faucigny and of Clementia.

26. MARGARET OF GENEVA, b. ca. 1180, d. Pierre Chatel, 8 Apr. 1257; m. May 1195, Thomas I of Savoy, b. 20 May 1177, d. 1 Mar. 1233, Count of Savoy, son of Humbert III of Savoy and Beatrix of Mâcon. (CP IX 805; Brandenburg, p. 10 #52, 59; p. 11 #65, 67; p. 50, #138, 216; p. 51 #396, 393; Winkhaus, pp. 85, 95).

27. BEATRIX OF SAVOY, d. 1266; m. 5 Jun. 1219, **RAYMOND IV BERENGER** (111-29), b. 1195, d. 19 Aug. 1245, Count of Provence and Forcalquier. (CP IV 321; Moriarty, The Plantagent Ancestry). (The present line has replaced the old line through the elder Counts of Savoy, that line now being considered unsound.)

Line 134 Omitted

Line 135

26. LOUIS VI (101-24), King of France; m. 1115, Adelaide of Savoy, d. 1154, dau. of Humbert II of Maurienne and Gisele of Burgundy.

27. ROBERT I, b. ca. 1123, d. 1188, Count of Dreux; m. (3)

Line 135 (cont.)

1152, Agnes de Vaudemont, d. bef. 1218, dau. Guy de Vaudemont.
28. ROBERT II, b. ca. 1154, d. 1218, Count of Dreux; m.
Yolande de Courci.
29. PIERRE DE DREUX, d. May 1250; m. (1) 1212 **ALIX DE
THOUARS** (96-28), d. 1221, Duchess of Brittany; m. (2) 1235
Marguerite de Montagu.
30. YOLANDE DE DREUX, b. 1218, d. 10 or 16 Oct. 1272, m.
Jan. 1235-6, **HUGH XI** (117-28), "le Brun" de Lusignan, b. 1220, d.
1260, Count of Ponthieu, la Marche and Angoulême. (Generations
29-30: see Garnier xxxi; Painter, "Feudalism & Liberty" 115, 116).
31. HUGH XII, de Lusignan, d. 1270, Count de la Marche and
Angouleme; m. 29 Jan. 1253/4 Joanne de Fougères, dau. & h. of
Raoul de Fougères. (CP V 632, 634).
32. JEANNE DE LUSIGNAN, d. betw. Aug. & 14 Sept. 1322; m.
(2) bef. 11 Oct. 1283 **SIR PIERS DE GENEVILLE** (71-31), d. bef. 8
Jun. 1292, Baron Geneville of Trim. She m. (1) Bernard Ezy I, Sire
d'Albert, d. soon after.) (CP V 632-634; Turton; Isenburg).

Line 136

18. HERBERT II (50-18), d. 943, Count of Vermandois and
Troyes; m. **HILDEBRANTE** (or Liegarde) (48-19), dau. of Robert I,
Duke of France, and his first wife Aelis.
19. LUITGARDE DE VERMANDOIS, d. 943; m. (2) **THEOBALD I**
(49-19), "le Tricheur", d. 978, Count of Blois. (Saillot, p. 45).
20. EUDES I, b. ca. 950, d. 12 Mar. 995/6, Count of Blois; m. ca.
983, **BERTHA** (159-20), b. ca. 964, d. aft. 1010, of Burgundy.
(Saillot, p. 45).
21. EUDES II, b. 990, d. 15 Nov. 1037, Count of Blois, 1004, and
of Champagne, 1019; m. (2) ca. 1010, Ermengarde of Auvergne, d. 10
Mar. 1040, dau. of Robert I, Count of Auvergne. (Saillot, p. 45).
22. STEPHEN II, b. ca. 1015, d. 1047, Count of Champagne; m.
Adela. (CP I 350-352).
23. EUDES, Count of Champagne & Aumale, Earl of Holderness;
m. 1054/60, **ADELAIDE** (130-24), b. bef. 1030, d. bef. 1090, Countess
of Aumale, sister of William the Conqueror. (CP I 350-353).
24. STEPHEN, b. ca. 1070, d. 1127, Count of Aumale, Earl of
Holderness, Crusader, 1096; m. Hawise de Mortimer, dau. of Ralph
de Mortimer of Wigmore and Milicent. (CP I 352-353).
25. AGNES, Countess of Aumale, m. (2) Adam II Brus d. 1200.
25A. PETER DE BRUS I, d. 12 Feb. 1222, Baron of Skelton and
Danby in Cleveland, Yorkshire; m. Joan. (CP V 269, VII 373).
26. PETER DE BRUS II, d. bef. 1247, Baron of Skelton,
Crusader; m. **HELWISE DE LANCASTER** (88-28). (CP V 269; Banks I
431-432; Farrer, EYC II 15, III 87).

Line 137

21. EUDES II (136-21), d. ca. 1010, Count of Blois; m. (2) ca.
1010, Ermengarde de Auvergne. (Saillot, p. 45).

22. THEOBALD III, d. 1089, Count of Blois and Champagne; m. (2) Alix de Crepi.

23. STEPHEN, Count of Blois, d. 1101, a leader of the First Crusade, 1096; m. ca. 1080, bef. 1085, **ADELA** (169-24), b. ca. 1062, d. 1137, dau. of William the Conqueror. (Robinson: Readings in European History, I 321-325; Moriarty, The Plantagent Ancestry).

24. THEOBALD IV, d. 1152, Count of Blois; m. 1126, Maud of Carinthia.

25. ALIX DE CHAMPAGNE, d. 24 Jun. 1206; m. as his third wife, 13 Nov. 1160, **LOUIS VII** (101-25), b. 1120, d. 18 Sep. 1180, King of France.

Line 138

23. ERMENGARDE DE NEVERS (107-23), m. Miles de Courtenay, d. 1127.

24. RENAUD (or Reginald) **DE COURTENAY**, of Sutton, Berks., 1161, lost his lands in France; m. a sister of Guy du Donjon. (CP IV 317).

25. REGINALD DE COURTENAY, Crusader, 1147, d. 27 Sep. 1194; m. (2) Hawise de Abrincis, d. 31 Jul. 1219, dau. of Sir Robert de Abrincis, hereditary Sheriff of Devon, Vicount of Devonshire, Baron of Oakhampton, Governor of the Castle of Exeter. (CP IV 317; Vivian 243).

26. SIR ROBERT DE COURTENAY, d. ca. 27 July 1242, of Oakhampton; m. **MARY DE VERNON** (50-28). (CP IV 317, 673).

Line 139

23. STEPHEN OF BLOIS (137-23), Count of Champagne, Brie, Blois, and Chartres, d. 1101, a leader of the First Crusade, 1096; m. ca. 1080, bef. 1085, **ADELA** (169-24), b. ca. 1062, d. 1137, dau. of William the Conqueror. (CP V 156).

24. WILLIAM OF CHAMPAGNE, elder brother of **STEPHEN** (169-25), King of England; m. Agnes, dau. of Gilon de Sully, Sire de Sully-sur-Loire. (CP V 156).

25. MARGARET DE CHAMPAGNE, d. 15 Dec. 1145; m. (3) Henry, Count of Eu, Lord of Hastings, son of William, Count of Eu, Lord of Hastings, and Beatrice de Builly, and great-great-grandson of Richard I, Duke of Normany. (CP V 155-156; for the Norman pedigrees, see Moriarty The Plantagenet Ancestry).

26. JOHN, Count of Eu, Lord of Hastings, d. 26 Jun. 1170, held 56 Knight's fees; m. Alice, d. 11 Sep. 1188, dau. of William d'Aubigny, Earl of Arundel, and **ADELIZA OF LOUVAIN** (149-24). (CP 156-158).

27. HENRY, d. Mar. 1183, Count of Eu, Lord of Hastings; m. **MAUD DE WARENNE** (123-27), d. ca. 1212. (CP V 158-160).

13. CHARLEMAGNE (50-13), m. **HILDEGARDE** (182-5).

14. LOUIS I, the Fair, b. Aug. 778, d. near Mainz, 20 Jun. 840, Emperor 814-840; m. (1) 794/5, Ermengarde, d. ca. 3 Oct. 818, dau. of Ingerman, Count of Hasbaye; m. (2) Feb. 819, Judith, d. 19 Apr. 843, dau. of Welf I, Duke of Bavaria. (CCN 623).

15. LOTHAIR I, b. 795, d. Pruem, Germany, 29 Sep. 855, King of Italy 817-855, Emperor 840-855; m. 15 Oct. 821, Ermengarde, d. 20 Mar. 851, dau. of Hugh II, Count of Tours. (Saillot, Sang de Charlemagne, p. 9; Brandenburg III 8a; see Line 240.)

16. ERMENGARDE of Lorraine, m. 846, Count **GISELBERT** (240-16).

17. RÉGNIER I, d. aft. 25 Oct. 915, bef. 19 Jan 916, Count of Hainaut; m. (2) Alberade of Mons; m. (1) **HERSENT** of France, dau. of **CHARLES II** (148-15). (1st mar. ref.: Abbé Chaume: Les Origines de duché de bourgogne I 549).

18. GISELBERT (stated by the Abbé Chaume to be son of Hersent), d. 939, Duke of Lorraine; m. **GERBERGA** (142-18), d. 5 May 984. (She m. (2) 939, **LOUIS IV,** d'Outre-Mer (148-18)).

19. GERBERGA of Lorraine, b. ca. 935, m. **ALBERT I** (50-19), the Pious, b. ca. 920, d. 987/88, Count de Vermandois.

20. HERBERT III, b. ca. 955, d. ca. 1000, Count de Vermandois; m. Ermengarde, dau. of Reinald, Count of Bar.

21. OTHO, b. ca. 1000, d. 25 May 1045, Count de Vermandois; m. Parvie.

22. HERBERT IV, b. ca. 1032, d. ca. 1080, Count de Vermandois; m. Adela de Vexin, dau. of Raoul III, the Great, Count of Valois, Vexin, etc.

23. ADELAIDE DE VERMANDOIS, d. ca. 1120, Countess de Vermandois and Valois; m. **HUGH MAGNUS** (53-23), d. 1101, Duke of France, etc. (CP X 351).

24. ISABEL DE VERMANDOIS (50-24, 53-24), d. 13 Feb. 1131, Countesss of Leicester; m. (1) 1096, Sir Robert de Beaumont, Earl of Leicester, b. ca. 1049, d. 5 Jun. 1118; m. (2) ca. 1118, William de Warenne, d. 1138, Earl of Surrey. (CP IV 670 chart III; VII 520, 523-526, 737; X 351. Generations 13-15: See Larousse: Histoire de France, I 79 chart; Voltaire: Oeuvres (1827), vol. 33, Annales de l'Empire II, Catalogue des Empereurs, 381-383, and for a great many of the lines covered in this section, see also Voltaire: Oeuvres, vol. 20, Essai sur les Moeurs, passim, but the details must be watched. Generations 13-16: Boston Evening Transcript, 9 Nov. 1927, Note 2257, by D.L.J. Part X Carolingians. Generations 16-19: Ibid. Part XV Brabant. Generations 19-24: Ibid. Part IX Vermandois; see also refs. at the end of Line 50; see also Moriarty, The Plantagenet Ancestry.)

16. LUDOLPH, b. ca. 816, d. 6 Sep. 864, Duke of Saxony 859; m. Oda.

17. OTTO, the Illustrious, b. ca. 836, d. 30 Nov. 912, Duke of

Line 141 (cont.)

Saxony; m. Hedwige, d. 24 Dec. 903 (correction supplied by Robt. Stimmel). (Charlemagne & His World (Heer) p. 226, shows Otto's wife as dau. (illeg.) of Arnulf, King of Germany, Emp. ca. 863-99 & Oda of Bavaria; Arnulf was son of Carloman, King of Bavaria (ca. 828-80) & Litwinde; Carloman was son of Louis II "the German", King of the East Franks (ca. 805-76) and Emma of Bavaria. Louis was son of **LOUIS I** "the Fair" (148-14) (See Brandenburg for Arnulf's ancestry; however, Brandenburg shows no such dau. for Arnulf. Isenburg shows Hedwig as dau. of Henrich d. 886, Markgraf of the Netherlands. Saillot says Otto's wife was Hedwig, dau. of Henri, Comte de la Marche. Moriarty says Hedwig d. 24 Dec. 903, does not identify parents).

18. HENRY I, the Fowler, b. 876, d. Memleben, 2 Jul. 936, Duke of Saxony, King of the Saxons 912-936; m. (2) Mechtilde, dau. of Count Dietrich of Ringelheim. (CCN 495).

19. HEDWIG OF SAXONY, m. **HUGH MAGNUS** (53-19, 101-19), d. Jun. 956, Count of Paris. (CCN 517).

20. HUGH CAPET, b. aft. 939, d. 24 Oct. 996, King of France 987-996, first of the Capetian kings of France; m. **ADELAIDE OF POITOU** (144A-20). (CCN 517).

21. ROBERT II, b. 970/1, d. 20 Jul. 1031, King of France; m. (2) 998, Constance, d. 1033, of Provence. (CCN 859).

22. HENRY I, b. 1005, d. Aug. 1061, King of France; m. 29 Jan. 1044, **ANNE OF KIEV** (241-6). (CP X 351).

23. HUGH MAGNUS, d. 1101, Duke of France and Burgundy, Marquis of Orléans, Count of Amiens, Chaumont, Paris, Valois and Vermandois; m. **ADELAIDE DE VERMANDOIS** (50-23, 140-23), Countess of Vermandois and Valois. (CP X 351).

24. ISABEL DE VERMANDOIS (50-24, 53-24), d. 13 Feb. 1131; m. (1) 1096, Sir Robert de Beaumont, b. ca. 1049, d. 5 Jun. 1118, Earl of Leicester; m. (2) ca. 1118, William de Warenne, d. 1138, Earl of Surrey. (CP X 351. Generations 13-24: Cambridge Medieval History; EB; Dudley pedigree; NEHGR 99: 243 chart; Boston Evening Transcript, 9 Nov. 1927, Note 2257, Part X Carolingians; Moriarty, The Plantagenet Ancestry.)

Line 141A (Supplied by David H. Kelley)

15. EUDOCIA INGERINA, b. ca. 840, d. 882/3, mistress of Michael III, Emp. of Byzantium 842-867; m. Basil I, Emp. of Byzantium 867-886 (founder of the "Macedonian" family), his sucessor. Uncertain whether Leo was son of Michael or of Basil.

16. LEO VI, b. 1 Sept. 866, d. 12 May 912, Emp. of Byzantium 886-912, m. (2) 898 Zoe Tzautzina, previously his mistress.

17. ANNA, b. 886/8, d. ca. 914; m. ca. 900 **LOUIS** (141B-18) "the Blind", b. ca. 880, d. 5 June 928, King of Provence and Italy, Emp. (Brandenburg).

18. CHARLES CONSTANTINE, b. ca. 900/1, d. ca. Jan. 962, Count of Vienne, m. Teutberg, d. ca. 960. (Brandenburg; C.W. Previté-Orton, "Charles Constantine of Vienne", English Historical

Line 141A (cont.)

Review 1914, voL 29, pp. 703-6).
19. CONSTANCE, d. 961-5, m. ca. 930 Boson II, Count of Provence, d. 965).
20. GUILLAUME II, b. 950, d. 993-4, Marquis of Provence 979-993.
21. CONSTANCE, b. ca. 986, d. 25 July 1032; m. 1001/2 **ROBERT II** (141-21) the Pious, King of France, b. 985, d. Aug. 1032. (See Lindsay Brooks, "The Byzantine Ancestry of H.R.H. Prince Charles, Prince of Wales", The Genealogist (1981) voL 2, pp. 3-51 and notes 11-13; 131; Christian Settipani, "des Capetiens à Ramses II . . . pourquois pas?" Heraldique et Généalogie Aug. 1985, voL 17, no. 3, pp. 263-268, generations 8 to 2 and references.)

Line 141B

15. LOTHAIR I (140-15), b. 795, d. 29 Sept. 855, King of Italy 817-855; Emperor of the West 840-855; m. 15 Oct. 821 Ermenarde d. 20 Mar. 851, dau. Hugh II Count of Tours (Brandenburg, Table 1).
16. LOUIS II, b. ca. 823, d. 12 Aug. 855, Emperor 855, m. bef. 5 Oct. 851 Engelberge, d. ca. 900. (Brandenburg cit.)
17. ERMENGARD, b. ca. 855, d. 897, bef. 2 Apr.; said to be mistress before 866 of "an Emperor of Byzantium", m. 876 Count Boso, King of Provence 879. (Brandenburg, cit.)
18. LOUIS the Blind, b. ca. 883, d. 5 June 928, King of Provence and Italy 900; Emperor of the West; m. **ANNA** (141A-17) dau. Leo VI, Emperor of Byzantium. (Brandenburg, cit.)

Line 142

17. HENRY I (141-18), the Fowler, b. 876, d. 2 July 936, King of the Saxons; m. (2) 909 Mechtilde of Ringelheim, b. ca. 890, d. 14 Mar 968, dau. Dietrich, Count of Saxon-Hamelant (Ringleheim).
18. GERBERGA OF SAXONY, b. 913/14, d. 5 May 984, m. 929 (1) **GISELBERT** (140-18), Duke of Lorraine, b. ca. 890, d. ca. 2 Oct. 934. She m. (2) 940 Louis IV d'Outre-Mer, King of France.
19. GERBERGA OF LORRAINE (140-19), b. ca. 935, m. **ALBERT I** (50-19), Count de Vermandois, b. ca. 920, d. 987/88 (Moriarty, The Plantagent Ancestry.)

Line 143

16. LOUIS II (148-16), "the Stammerer", King of the Franks and Emperor; m. (3) 868/70, Adelaide (or Aelis) of Paris, d. ca. 10 Nov. 901, prob. (not proven) dau. of Bego, Count of Paris (d. 861) (who was 4th in descent from Charlemagne) (Brandenburg), or dau. of Count Girard (Saillot, Sang de Charlemagne 201).
17. ERMENTRUDE OF FRANCE, b. 870; m. N. (Winkhaus 103).
18. CUNEGUNDE, b. ca. 890; m. (1) Wigeric, d. 919, Count in the Triergau, Count Palatine of Aachen; m. (2) ca. 920, Richwin, d. 923, Count of Verdun. (Saillot p. 21).

19. SIEGFRIED OF LUXEMBOURG, son by (2), b. ca. 922, Count of Luxembourg, d. 15 Aug. 998; m. ca. 950, Hedwig, d. 13 Dec. 992, perh. dau. of Count Eberhard, Count in the Nordgau.

20. FREDERICK I OF LUXEMBOURG, b. ca. 965, d. 1019, Count of Salm and Luxembourg; m. bef. 995, Irmentrude of Gleiberg, dau. of Herbert I, d. 992, Count in the Kinziggau, Count of Gleiberg by his wife, Irmentrude. (Herbert I was son of Udo, Count in the Wetterau by his wife a dau. of **HERBERT I**, Count of Vermandois (50-17). (Saillot 5,6,51; Brandenburg).

21. GISELE (or **GISLA**) **OF LUXEMBOURG**, living 1058, bur. Chapel of St. Lawrence, Ghent; m. Rudolph I of Aalst (or Alost) (also called Ralph of Gand or Ghent), living 1058, Lord of Aalst (or Alost) in Flanders, hereditary Advocate or Protector of St. Peter of Ghent 1036-1056. (Brandenburg 7; Winkhaus 19, 21, 117; Clay 83; Gen. Mag. IX: 1-7).

22. GILBERT DE GANT (Gaunt or Ghent), d. ca. 1095, bur. Bardney, probably arrived in England in 1066; was a commander in York, 1068, and was taken prisoner there by the Danes in 1069. He was a tenant-in-chief and one of the largest landholders in co. Lincoln in 1086, Folkingham being the head of his barony; m. Alice de Montfort, dau. of Count Hugh de Montfort-sur-Risle. (Gen. Mag. IX: 1-7; CP VII 672; Sanders, English Baronies, 114). Parents of Gen. 24. See note at end.

24. WALTER DE GAUNT (156-24), d. 1139, held barony of Folkingham, Lincoln, a commander in the battle of the Standard 1138, founder Bridlington Priory, York bef. 1113-14; m. by 1120 Maud (or Matilda) of Brittany, dau. of **STEPHEN I** (214-24), Count of Brittany. (CP VII 672; X 786-787, chart p. 780; XII pt. 1, 674; Sanders: English Baronies 114; Brandenburg 10, 11, 66; Milton Rubincam, in Gen. Mag. (London 1940), IX 1-7; Winkhaus 21; Monasticon VI 284-291).

25. AGNES DE GAUNT, m. William de Mohun, adult by 1131, d. in or bef. 1155, Earl of Somerset, held barony of Dunster, Somerset, son of Sir William de Mohun, d. aft. 1190, lord of Dunster, Somerset, Sheriff of Somerset, 1084, 1086, by his wife Adeliz. The proof of Agnes de Gaunt's identity is the manor of Whichford, co. Warwick, a Gaunt family property, which she received as her maritagium. Agnes and her husband William de Mohun later gave the church at Whichford to Bridlington Priory which priory was founded by Agnes' father, Walter de Gaunt. (CP IX 17-18 and note h; XII pt. 1, 37-39; VCH Warwick V: 205; Maxwell Lyte: A History of Dunster, Part I, pp. 5-9; Sanders: English Baronies p. 114).

26. WILLIAM DE MOHUN, seen 1142, died 1176, held barony of Dunster, Somerset; m. by 1160 Godeheut (or Godehold) de Toeni, dead by 1186, dau. of **ROGER III DE TOENI** (98A-25), lord of Flamstead, Hertford, by his wife, Ida of Hainault. Godeheut's maritagium, the manor of Brinkley, co. Cambridge, proves her identity as a Toeni. This manor came into possession of the Toeni family upon the marriage of Godeheut's grandmother, **ALICE OF NORTHUMBERLAND** (148A-24) with Roger IV de Toeni. (CP IX 18:

Line 143 (cont.)

Maxwell Lyte: A History of Dunster, Part I, pp. 9-11; Sanders, English Baronies, p. 114; VCH Cambridge VI: 136; Beauchamp Cartulary, pub. of the Pipe Roll Society, New Series, XLIII 206,207, 217, 218; Calendar of Documents preserved in France, I 174, 282-3).

26A. WILLIAM DE MOHUN, s. and h., minor 1176, adult by 1177, pilgrimage to Jerusalem, d. Oct. 1193, held barony of Dunster, Somerset, benefactor of Bruton Priory; m. Lucy, who is seen 1201 with seven knts. fees in Cambridge. (CP IX 19; Maxwell Lyte: A History of Dunster, Part I 11-15; Sanders: English Baronies, p. 114).

27. SIR REYNOLD DE MOHUN, adult by 1204, d. 1213, held barony of Dunster, Somerset; m. Alice, living 1233, 4th dau. and eventual coh. of Sir William de Briwere, d. 1226, lord of Horsley, Derby, by his wife Beatrice de Valle; she m. (2) by 1224, William Paynel of Bampton, Devon, d. 1228. (CP IX 19; Maxwell Lyte: A History of Dunster, Part I, pp. 15-17; Sanders: English Baronies, pp. 114, 122-123; Notebook of Tristram Risdon, p. 71).

28. SIR REYNOLD DE MOHUN, born say 1206, minor in 1213 and 1222, adult by 1227, d. Torre Mohun 20 Jan. 1257/8, bur. Newenham Abbey, held barony of Dunster, Somerset, Justice of Common Pleas, Chief Justice of the Forests South of Trent, Gov. of Saubey Castle; m. (1) by 1227 **HAWISE** (246B-28), dead 1243, dau. of Geoffrey Fitz Piers, Earl of Essex, by his (2) wife, Aveline de Clare (Hawise received as her maritagium the manor of Streatley, Berkshire from her half-brother, William de Mandeville, Earl of Essex); m. (2) in or bef. 1243 Isabel, d. 26 Nov. 1260, wid. of Gilbert Basset, dau. of **WILLIAM DE FERRERS**, Earl of Derby (127-30) by Sybil, dau. of **WILLIAM MARSHALL**, Earl of Pembroke (177-8). Sir Reynold's arms were, Gules, a maunch ermine. (CP IX 19-20; V 116-117, 433, footnote e, 437; Roll of Arms Henry III, ed. Tremlett & London, pp. 126-127; Sanders: English Baronies, p. 114; VCH Berkshire III 512 (manor of Streatley); Maxwell Lyte: A History of Dunster Part I 15-34).

29. LUCY DE MOHUN, dau. prob. by (1), m. Sir John de Grey of Codnor, d. bef. 5 Jan. 1271/2, son of Sir Richard de Grey and Lucy de Humez. (CP VI 123-135; IX 19; Maxwell-Lyte: A History of Dunster, Part I 32 considers Lucy as child of her father's first marriage).

30. SIR HENRY DE GREY, of Codnor, co. Derby, Grays Thurrocks, Essex, Aylesford and Hoo, Kent; m. **ELEANOR DE COURTENAY** (50-31). (CP VI 123-124, 128-129, 133, 135. For Generations 17-22: see Boston Evening Transcript, 9 Nov. 1927, Note 2257, Part XV Brabant).

Note: Generation 23 included in former editions, but questioned, has been omitted. From charter evidence cited in CP VII 672 & 674 it is clear that Gen. 22 is parental to Gen. 24.

Line 144

22. WILLIAM I (132-24), "the Great", d. 1087, Count of Burgundy; m. Stephanie. (de Vajay, in "Annales de Bourgogne" vol. 32 (1960) 258-261 identifies Stephanie (Eteinnette) as dau. Clémence de Foix & Albert de Longwy d. 1048, Duke of Lorraine. Clémence is identified as dau. Bernard I Roger, Comte de Foix d. 1035 & Garsinde de Bigorre; & Bernard as son of Roger I de Carcassonne & wife Adelaide. Moriarty (cit.) supplies pedigree charts for these families, but does not agree with de Vajay as to her identity. Prof. Kelley believes her parentage still unproven.)

23. ERMENTRUDE OF BURGUNDY, m. 1076, **THIERRY II** (167-23), Count of Bar-le-Duc, d. 1115, son of Louis, d. 1067, Count of Montbéliard, and Sophia, d. 1092, Countess of Bar-le-Duc.

24. RENAUD I, Count of Bar-le-Duc, d. 1150; m. Gisèle de Vaudemont, dau. of Gerard of Lorraine 1057-1108, Count of Vaudemont, and Edith of Egisheim, d. 1118, dau. of Gerard II, Count of Egisheim, d. 1038, and Petronilla of Verdun.

25. CLÉMENCE OF BAR-LE-DUC, m. Alberic I, d. 1183, Count of Dammartin, son of Hugh II, Count of Dammartin, and Rothride.

26. ALBERIC II, Count of Dammartin, d. 1200; m. Maud.

27. SIMON DE DAMMARTIN, d. 1239, Count of Aumale; m. as (1) husb. 1208-1211, **MARIE** (109-29), d. 1250, Countess of Ponthieu. She m. (2) Mathieu de Montmorenci, Seigneur d'Attichy, killed 1250. (Generations 15-22; Boston Evening Transcript, 9 Nov. 1927, Note 2257, Part X Carolingians; Generations 23-27: Ibid., 28 Jan. 1939, Note 3044, et. seq.; Turton; N&Q 4th series, VII 437-438; Moriarty, cit.; Gen. Mag. XV 53-63).

Line 144A

14. LOUIS I "the Fair" (140-14), Emperor 814-840; m. (1) Ermengarde. (NEHGR 109: 179-182).

15. NN (an hitherto unknown dau. of Louis I and Ermengarde); m. Count Gerard of Auvergne. (Prof. Leonce Auzias, in Revue Historique 173: 91-102; G. Andrews Moriarty, NEHGR 109: 179-182).

16. RANULF I, d. 866, Duke of Aquitaine, ca. 852-866; m. ca. 845, a dau. of Rorick, Count of Maine. (NEHGR cit. Brandenburg p. 63,66).

17. RANULF II, b. ca. 855, d. 5 Aug. 890, Count of Poitou 867-890; m. Irmgard, d. 935.

18. EBLES MANCER, bastard of Ranulf II, d. 932, Count of Poitou 890-892, 903; m. (1) 892 Eremburg; m. (2) 911, Emliane.

19. WILLIAM I OF POITOU by (2), b. ca. 925, d. 3 Apr. 963, Count of Poitou; m. 935, Gerloc (Adèle), d. ca. 14 Oct. 962, dau. of Rollo, Duke of Normandy. (Brandenburg p. 66).

20. ADELAIDE OF POITOU, b. 945, d. ca. 1004; m. bef. 969, **HUGH CAPET** (53-20, 101-20, 106-20, 141-20), d. 24 Oct. 996, King of France 987-996. (Brandenburg p. 67). (Moriarty, The Plantagenet Ancestry).

21. HEDWIG OF FRANCE, d. aft. 1013; m. **RÉGNIER IV** (106-21), b. ca. 950, d. 1013, Count of Hainaut.

Line 144A (cont.)

22. BEATRIX OF HAINAUT, m. (1) **EBLES I** (151-21), d. 11 May 1033, Count of Rheims and Roucy, Archbishop of Rheims; m. (2) Manasses Calva Asina. (See also Isenburg).

Line 145

15. LOTHAIR I (140-15), m. 821, Ermengarde of Tours. (CCN 623).

16. LOTHAIR II, the Saxon, b. 827, d. 8 Aug. 869, King of Lorraine; m. (2) 862, Waldrada, d. 868.

17. BERTHA, b. 863, d. 8 Mar. 925; m. (1) ca. 879, Theobald, Count of Arles.

18. BOSO, b. 885, d. 936, Count of Arles, Margrave of Tuscany, 913-936; m. Willa of Tuscany.

19. WILLA, m. 936, **BERENGARIUS II** (146-18), d. 966, King of Italy. (CCN 147. Generations 15-19: See Boston Evening Transcript, 9 Nov. 1927, Note 2257, Part X, Carolingians).

Line 146

13. CHARLEMAGNE (50-13), m. **HILDEGARDE** (182-5).

14. LOUIS I (140-14), the Fair; m. (2) Judith of Bavaria.

15. GISELE, b. 820, d. 1 Jul. 874; m. bef. 840, **EBERHARD** (191-16), d. ca. 864, Margrave of Friuli. (NEHGR 99: 243 chart).

16. BERENGAR I, b. 850, d. 7 Apr. 924, King of Italy, Jan. 888-924, Emperor Dec. 915-924; m. 899, Bertila of Spoleto, d. Dec. 915, dau. of Suppo, Margrave of Spoleto in Perugia, Italy. (CCN 147).

17. GISELE, d. 910; m. Adalbert, d. 923, Margrave of Ivrea in Turin, Italy.

18. BERENGAR II, d. 6 Aug. 966, Margrave of Ivrea, King of Italy 950-966; m. 936, **WILLA** (145-19).

19. ROSELA (or Susanna), d. 26 Jan. 1003; m. (1) 968, **ARNOLD II** (162-20), d. 30 Mar. 987, Count of Flanders; m. (2) 988 **ROBERT II** of France (101-21), repudiated. (Generations 15-19: Crispin: Falaise Roll, London, 1938, pp. 186-187).

Line 147

18. HENRY I, the Fowler (141-18), Duke of Saxony, King of the Saxons; m. Mechtilde of Ringelheim. (CCN 767).

19. OTTO I, the Great, b. 912, d. Memleben, 7 May 973, King of Germany 939-973, Emperor 962-973; m. (1) **EDITH** (45-17), d. 947, granddau. of Alfred the Great of England; m. (2) aft. 951, St. Adelaide of Lombardy, b. 931, d. Selz, Alsace, 16 Dec. 999, dau. of Rudolph II, King of Burgundy, and wid. of Lothair of Italy. (CCN 767).

20. OTTO II (son of Otto I and St. Adelaide), b. ca. 955, d. Rome, 7 Dec., 983, Emperor 973-983; m. (2) 14 Apr. 972, Theophana, b. ca. 956-60, d. 15 Jun. 991. (Moriarty mms. at NEHGS pp. 88-89, cites Benrath, "Wer war die Kaiserin Theophano" (1939), shows Theo-

Line 147 (cont.)

phana prob. dau. of Leo Phokas, son of Sophia Phokas by her husb. Constantin Skleros, brother of Marie, 1st wife of the Basileus John Tsimices).

21. MATILDA OF SAXONY, d. 1024; m. Edzo, d. 1034, Count of Lorraine.

22. RIXA, m. 1013, Miesco II, d. 1034, King of Poland.

23. CASIMIR I, d. 1058, King of Poland; m. 1038, Dobronega, dau. of **ST. VLADIMIR I** (241-4), Grand Prince of Kiev.

24. VLADISLAV I, b. ca. 1043, d. 4 June 1102, King of Poland; m. (1) ca. 1080, **JUDITH** (244-8), d. 1085, dau. of Wratislav II, King of Bohemia. (See 244-8).

25. BOLESLAS III, d. 1138, King of Poland; m. (1) ca. 1103, **ZBYSLAVA** (241-8), d. 1113, dau. of Sviatpolk II, Grand Prince of Kiev.

26. VLADISLAS II, d. 1159, King of Poland; m. ca. 1125/27, Agnes de Babenberg (Bamberg), d. 1157, dau. of St. Leopold III, Margrave of Austria.

27. RICHILDE, d. bef. 1176, of Poland; m. 1152, **ALFONSO VII** (113-25), b. 1103, d. 1157, King of Castile and Leon. (Generations 19-27: G.A. Moriarty in NEHGR 101: 39-40; Brandenburg; N. de Baumgarten: Orientalia Christiana, Rome, 1927).

Line 148

13. CHARLEMAGNE (50-13), m. **HILDEGARDE** (182-5).

14. LOUIS I (140-14), the Fair, b. 778, d. 20 Jun. 840; Emperor 814-840; m. (2) Judith of Bavaria.

15. CHARLES II, the Bald, b. Frankfort-am-Main, 13 Jun. 828, d. near Mt. Cenis in the Alps, 6 Oct. 877, King of the Franks 840-877, Emperor 25 Dec. 875-877; m. (1) 14 Dec. 842; Ermentrude, d. 6 Oct. 869, dau. of Odo, Count of Orléans, and Engeltrude. (CCN 236, 642).

16. LOUIS II, the Stammerer, b. 844, d. Compiègne, 10 Apr. 879, King of the Franks 877-879, Emperor 878-879; m. (2) ca. 868, Adelaide, d. aft. 901. (CCN 624).

17. CHARLES III, the Simple, b. 17 Sep. 879, d. Peronne, 7 Oct. 929, King of the Franks 893-922; m. (3) 918, Eadgifu (or Edgiva), d. 951, prob. granddau. of Alfred the Great of England. (CCN 236, 624).

18. LOUIS IV, d'Outre-Mer, b. ca. 919, d. 10 Sep. 954, King of the Franks 936-954; m. 939, **GERBERGA OF SAXONY** (142-18), d. 5 May 984, dau. of **HENRY I, THE FOWLER** (141-18), and wid. of Giselbert, Duke of Lorraine. (CCN 624. Generations 13-18: Thatcher 319-320).

19. CHARLES OF LORRAINE, b. 953, d. 994, Duke of Lower Lorraine; m. bef. 979 Adelheid, parentage unknown. (Generations 13-20: Brandenburg; Thatcher 319-320; Fisher 238; Moriarty; Winkhaus; Saillot, p. 192).

20. GERBERGA, b. ca. 975, d. aft. 1017; m. ca. 990, **LAMBERT I** (155-20), the Bearded, Count of Louvain. (CP I 352).

21. MAUD, m. Eustace I, d. 1049, Count of Boulogne. (CP I 352).
22. LAMBERT OF BOULOGNE, Count of Lens in Artois, slain at the battle of Lille, 1054; m. as (2) husb. **ADELAIDE** (130-24), b. 1030, d. bef. 1090, Countess of Aumale, sister of William I, the Conqueror. She m. (1) Engerrand of Ponthieu. (CP I 350-353, V 736). The line is in question at this point. Judith, no. 23, may have been the child of the 1st mar. See "The Carmen de Hastingae Poelio of Guy, Bishop of Amiens" (by Catharine Morton & Hope Muntz). (Oxford '72), p. 27. See also The Gen. Mag. vol. 19, p. 176 b; TAG 54: 231-2. In fact Adelaide may not even have been Lambert's wife.

* * *

23. JUDITH OF LENS (98A-23, 130-25), niece of William the Conqueror, b. 1054; m. 1070, Waltheof II, beheaded at Winchester, 31 May 1076, Earl of Huntingdon, Northampton and Northumberland, son of Sigurd, Earl of Northumberland, and Aelflaed, dau. of Aldred of Bernicia. (CP I 350-353; IV 670 chart IV; V 472, 736; VII 640-641).
24. MAUD OF HUNTINGDON, b. 1072 (ae. 18 yrs. in 1090), d. 1130/1, Countess of Huntingdon and Northumberland; m. (1) ca. 1090, Simon de St. Liz, d. 1111, Earl of Huntingdon and Northampton, Crusader, son of Ranulph the Rich, a Norman; m. (2) 1113, **DAVID I** (170-22), "the Saint", King of Scots. (CP IV 670 chart IV; V 472 note f; VII 640-642; SP I 1; Dunbar 59).
25. MAUD ST. LIZ, d. 1140; m. (1) Robert Fitz Richard, d. 1134, son of Richard Fitz Gilbert of Clare, and grandson of Gilbert, Count of Brienne in Normandy; m. (2) **SAHER DE QUINCY** (53-27). (CP IV 670 chart IV; V 472 note f; VI 641 note b).
26. WALTER FITZ ROBERT, d. 1198, Lord of Dunmow Castle; m. (1) Maud, Lady of Diss, Norfolk, dau. of Sir Richard de Lucy, Knt., Justiciar of England. (CP V 472 note f; Weever 336-337).
27. ROBERT FITZ WALTER, of Woodham, d. 9 Dec. 1235; Leader of the barons who revolted against King John in 1215 and obtained the Magna Charta; m. Rohese. (CP V 472 note f; Weever 632).
28. SIR WALTER FITZ ROBERT, d. bef. 10 Apr. 1258, of Woodham-Walter, Burnham, Roydon, Dunmow, Henham, Wimbish and Tey; m. **IDA LONGESPEE** (30-27). (Note discussion of her parentage in Line 30). (CP V 472-474. Generations 13-28: Dudley pedigree; Brandenberg; Boston Evening Transcript, 9 Nov. 1927, Note 2257, Part X Carolingians, Part XV Brabant).
29. SIR ROBERT FITZ WALTER, b. 1247, d. 18 Jan. 1325/6, 1st Lord Fitz Walter; m. (1) Devorguilla, d. 1284, dau. of Sir John de Burgh and **CECILY BALIOL** (99-29); m. (2) 1289, Alianore, dau. Sir Robert Ferrers of Chartley, Earl of Derby, by (2) wife Alianore de Bohun; m. (3) 1308, Alice, wid. Sir Warin de Lisle.

19. CHARLES OF LORRAINE (148-19), Duke of Lower Lorraine; m. bef. 979 Adelheid, parentage unknown.

20. ERMENGARDE OF LORRAINE, m. Albert I, d. 998/1011, Count of Namur, son of Robert I, Count of Lomme.

21. ALBERT II, Count of Namur; m. Regilinde of Lorraine, dau. of Gothelo I, Duke of Lower Lorraine.

22. ALBERT III, Count of Namur; m. ca. 1067 Ida of Saxony, dau. prob. of Bernard II, b. ca. 995, d. 1057 Duke of Saxony, and Elicia (m. ca. 1020), dau. Henrich, Markgraf von Schweinfurt. Parents of 22A. (CP I 235; Moriarty, The Plantagenet Ancestry).

22A. ADELAÏDE OF NAMUR, b. 1068, d. 1124, dau. of Albert III of Namur and Ida of Saxony; m. Otto II, Count of Chiny, d. 1124-31, son of Arnold II of Warcq and Alix de Rameru. (Brandenburg 52-56).

23. IDA DE CHINY AND DE NAMUR, b. ca. 1083, d. 1117/22; m. ca. 1100, **GODFREY I** (155-23), Duke of Lorraine, son of Henry II, Count of Lorraine. (CP I 235).

24. ADELIZA OF LOUVAIN, b. 1103, d. 23 Apr. 1151, ae. 48 yrs.; m. (1) 1120, **HENRY I** (121-25), King of England, s.p.; m. (2) 1138, William d'Aubigny, d. 12 Oct. 1176, Earl of Arundel, 1141-1176. (CP I 233-235; IV 670 chart I).

25. WILLIAM D'AUBIGNY, d. 24 Dec. 1193, Earl of Arundel and Sussex; Crusader; m. Maud, d. 1173, wid. of Roger de Clare, Earl of Hertford, and dau. of James de St. Hilaire du Harcourt, and Aveline. (CP I 236, IV 670 chart I).

26. WILLIAM D'AUBIGNY, d. Mar. 1220/1, Crusader, Earl of Arundel, named in the Magna Charta, 1215; m. **MABEL OF CHESTER** (126-29). (CP I 236-237; IV 670 chart I).

27. ISABEL D'AUBIGNY, m. John Fitz Alan, Lord of Clun and Oswestry, Salop. (CP I 237, 253; IV 670 chart I).

28. JOHN FITZ ALAN, Earl of Arundel, 1243, made his will Oct. 1267, d. bef. 10 Nov. 1267; m. Maud, d. 27 Nov. 1283, dau. of Theobald le Boteler and Rohese, dau. of Nicholas de Verdon of Alton, co. Stafford. (See 70-30). (CP I 239-240, 253; IV 670 chart I).

29. JOHN FITZ ALAN, b. 14 Sep. 1246, d. 18 Mar. 1271/2, Earl of Arundel; m. **ISABELLA MORTIMER** (28-30). (CP I 240, 253; IV 670 chart I. Generations 19-24: Brandenburg; Boston Evening Transcript, 9 Nov. 1927, Note 2257, Part X Carolingians, Feb. 1928, Part XV Brabant).

27. ROGER DE MOHAUT, of Elford, Staffs, dead 1230/1, (when his h. was Agnes de Orreby), yr. son of Robert de Mohaut, of Howarden, succ. ca. 1141, d. ca. 1162, hereditary seneschal of the co. of Chester; by Leucha, living 1162, perh. dau. of William Fitz Neel of Halton, Constable of Cheshire. (CP IX 10-11; X 168-170; Wm. Salt Soc. IV 24, 46; III 89). This Roger de Mohaut was misidentified in the early editions and in von Redlich. He did not marry Cecily de Aubigny. That Roger de Mohaut was his nephew.

28. LEUCA DE MOHAUT, m. 1227, Philip de Orreby, b. ca.

129

1190, d. by 1230, son of Sir Philip de Orreby, Knt., b. ca. 1160, d. ca. 1230, Justiciar of Chester 1208-1229, and Emma de Coventre, dau. of Walter de Coventre by 1st wife Margery. (CP X 169-170; Farrer: Honours & Knights Fees II, 100-101).

29. AGNES DE ORREBY, only dau.; m. Sir Walkelin de Arderne, Knt., seen 1235/6, d. ca. 1265, Justiciar of Chester. (CP X 170).

30. SIR PETER DE ARDERNE, Knt., of Alford, seen 1262/3, d. 1292; m. Margery. (Generations 27-30: Farrer: Honours & Knights Fees II 110-111, 271-273).

31. AGNES ARDERNE, m. Sir Warin Mainwaring, Knt., of Wormingham.

32. MATILDA DE MAINWARING, m. Sir William Trussell, Knt., Lord of Cubbleston and Wormingham.

33. SIR WARIN TRUSSELL, of Cubbleston; m. prob. a dau. of Sir John Stafford, Knt.

34. SIR LAWRENCE TRUSSELL, of Cubbleston; m. Maud, dau. of Thomas Charnells, Lord of Elmesthorp.

35. SIR WILLIAM TRUSSELL, Lord of Elmesthorp; m. **MARGERY LUDLOW** (56-35), dau. of Sir John Ludlow.

36. ISABEL TRUSSELL, m. Thomas Wodhull, of Warkworth, b. 1411, d. 8 Aug. 1441, son of Thomas Wodhull and Elizabeth, dau. of Sir John Chetwode of Warkworth.

37. JOHN WODHULL, of Warkworth, b. 1435, d. 12 Sep. 1490; m. Joan, dau. of Henry Etwell, LL.D., of London.

38. FULK WODHULL, of Warkworth and Thenford, b. 1459, d. 1508, Sheriff of Northamptonshire, 1500/1; m. Anne Newenham, dau. of William Newenham, of Thenford, co. Northampton.

39. SIR NICHOLAS WODHULL, of Warkworth, b. 1482, d. 5 May 1531, Sheriff of Northampton 1516, 1518; m. (1) 1508, Mary Raleigh, dau. of **SIR EDWARD RALEIGH**, Knt. (14-36), of Farnborough, co. Warwick; m. (2) **ELIZABETH PARR** (78-39), own cousin to Queen Katherine Parr. (TAG 21: 72).

40. ANTHONY WODHULL, of Warkworth (by the first wife), b. 1518, d. 4 Feb. 1542; m. Anne Smith, dau. of Sir John Smith, Baron of the Exchequer.

41. AGNES WODHULL, only dau., b. 1542, d. 1575/6; m. Sir Richard Chetwode, son of Roger Chetwode.

42. SIR RICHARD CHETWODE, m. **DOROTHY NEEDHAM** (7-39). (Generations 27-40: Dr. Arthur Adams: The Elkington Family, Hartford, 1945, pp. 16,18; Ormerod: History of Cheshire; Wodhull Pedigree in Mis. Gen. Her., 2nd series, I 69-75; F.B. Smith: The Chetwode Family in England, Worcester, 1945, p. 71 chart, corrected by D.L. Jacobus: The Bulkeley Genealogy, pp. 61-62. Richard Woodhull of Setauket, L.I., N.Y., may be of this family though his parentage is currently unknown. However such relationship if it exists can not be close. See TAG 21: 72). (Generations 27-29: note error in cited references).

18. GISELBERT (140-18), d. 939, Duke of Lorraine; m. **GERBERGA OF SAXONY** (142-18), d. 5 May 984.
19. ALBERADE OF LORRAINE, m. Renaud, d. 15 Mar. 973, Count of Rheims and Roucy. (He is called the 8th son of Herbert II, Count of Vermandois, but is not so given by Père Anselme; though Anselme does give Hugh, Archbishop of Rheims, as a son of Herbert II). (Saillot, cit.)
20. GISELBERT, Count of Roucy, buried at Rheims, 990. (Saillot, cit.)
21. EBLES I, d. 11 May 1033, Count of Rheims and Roucy, Archbishop of Rheims; m. **BEATRIX OF HAINAUT** (106-22). (Saillot, cit.)
22. ALIX DE ROUCY, d. 1062, m. Hildouin III, Count of Montdidier. (See Genealogist X 85, for Montdidier). Parents of No. 24. (Brandenburg, p. 78; Saillot, cit.)
24. BEATRIX DE MONTDIDIER, dau. of Alix de Roucy (No. 22); m. Geoffrey II, Count de Perche, d. 1100, son of Routrou I, Vicount of Châteaudun, and Adeline de Domfront. (CP XI App. D 112-113; Genealogist X 85: Brandenburg 78; Saillot, p. 93).
25. MARGARET DE PERCHE, elder dau., living 1156; m. bef. 1100, Henry de Newburgh, b. ca. 1046, d. 20 Jun. 1123, cr. 1st Earl of Warwick ca. 1090, son of Roger de Beaumont, Seigneur de Pont Audemar, and Avelina (or Adelise), dau. of Waleran, Count of Meulan, and brother of Sir Robert de Beaumont, 1st Earl of Leicester, who m. **ISABEL DE VERMANDOIS** (50-24).
26. ROGER DE NEWBURGH, d. 12 Jun. 1153, Earl of Warwick; m. bef. 1130, **GUNDRED DE WARENNE** (84-25). (Generations 18-26: Boston Evening Transcript, Note 2257, Part XV Brabant, Feb. 1928, also 14 Nov. 1936; Turton; Genealogist X 85; Warwick Castle and Its Earls II 827-829; CP IV 672-673; VIII 53-56; XII pt. 2, 361-2.)

26. ALBERIC II (144-26), Count of Dammartin, d. 1200; m. Maud. (Anselme VIII 401-402). Parents of Agnes and of Juliane.
27. AGNES DE DAMMARTIN, m. **WILLIAM DE FIENNES** (or **FIENES**) (158A-27), d. 1241. (Baker: Northampton II 273-274; Gen. Mag. XV 56, 63 note 23).
27. JULIANE DE DAMMARTIN m. Hughes V de Gournay d. 1238, parents of Juliane m. William Bardolph of Wormegay, Norfolk who were parents of Hugh Bardolph (see 257-31).
28. INGELRAM (or **ENGUERRAND**) **DE FIENNES** (or **FIENES**), Seigneur de Fienes; m. a dau. of Jacques, Seigneur of Condé, Bailleul and Moriammez in Hainault. (Anselme VI 167-169; CP VI 466).
29. SIR WILLIAM DE FIENNES (or **FIENES**), d. 1302; m. **BLANCHE DE BRIENNE** (120-31). (Inq.p.m. 30 Edward I 33; CP VIII 433. Generations 26-29: N&Q 4th series VII 437-438; Anselme 6: 167).

Line 152A

28. INGELRAM DE FIENNES (152-28).
29. MAUD DE FIENNES, m. **HUMPHREY DE BOHUN** (97-30).

Line 153

24. BEATRIX DE MONTDIDIER (151-24), m. Geoffrey II, Count de Perche.
24A. ROUTROU II, d. Apr. 1144, Count de Perche, son of Beatrix and Geoffrey II; m. (1) **MATILDA,** b. 1086, d. 25 Nov. 1120, natural dau. of King **HENRY I** of England (121-25). They were the parents of **MAUDE DE PERCHE** (153-25), b. 1105, d. 1143. (CP XI App. D 112; Brandenburg 79, #343).
25. MAUDE DE PERCHE, d. 1143; m. Raymond I, d. ca. 1122, Vicount of Turenne, son of Boso I, Vicount de Turenne.
26. MARGUERITE DE TURENNE, m. (3) William IV, d. 1178, Count of Angoulême, son of Wulgrim II, Count of Angoulême.
27. AYMER DE VALENCE or "Taillifer", d. 1218, Count of Angoulême; m. **ALICE DE COURTENAY** (117-26).
28. ISABELLA OF ANGOULÊME, b. 1188, d. 31 May 1246; m. (1) 1200, **JOHN** (1-26), King of England, d. 1216; m. (2) 1217, Hugh X de Lusignan (see 117-27). (CP X 377-382).
29. ALICE (ALFAIS) DE LUSIGNAN (by (2)), d. 9 Feb. 1255/6; m. 1247, **JOHN DE WARENNE** (83-28), Earl of Surrey. (CP IV 670 chart II; XII pt. 1, 449-508).
30. ELEANOR DE WARENNE, b. 1251; m. York, 8 Sep. 1268, **SIR HENRY DE PERCY,** Knt. (161-27), b. ca. 1235, d. 1271.

Line 154

28. ISABELLA OF ANGOULÊME (153-28), m. (2) 1217, Hugh X de Lusignan. (CP X 377-382).
29. SIR WILLIAM DE VALENCE (or de Lusignan), Knt., Earl of Pembroke, d. bef. 18 May 1296; m. 13 Aug. 1247, **JOAN DE MUNCHENSI** (80-29). (CP X 346 note a, 377-382).
30. JOAN DE VALENCE, m. **JOHN COMYN** (95-30), Lord of Badenoch. (CP X 381; SP I 508-509).

Line 155

17. REGNIER I (140-17, 240-17), d. aft. 25 Oct. 915, bef. 19 Jan. 916, Count of Hainaut; m. (1) Hersent, dau. **CHARLES II** (148-15) of France; m. (2) Alberade of Mons. By (1) he had
18. REGNIER II, d. 932, Count of Hainaut; m. Adelaide of Burgundy.
19. REGNIER III, d. 973, Count of Hainaut; m. Adele, dau. of Hugh II, Count of Dagsbourg. (Saillot 102).
20. LAMBERT I, the Bearded, d. 1015, Count of Louvain; m. **GERBERGA OF LORRAINE** (148-20). (CP I 335).
21. LAMBERT II, b. ca. 991, d. aft. 21 Sep. 1062, Count of Louvain; m. Oda, dau. of Gothelo I, d. 1044, Duke of Lower Lorraine.

22. HENRY II, of Brabant, b. ca. 1021, d. aft. 1077, Count of Lorraine and Louvain; m. Adelaide of Orlamunda, d. aft. 1086, dau. of Count Eberhard. (Brandenburg).

23. GODFREY I of Brabant, the Bearded, b. ca. 1060, d. 25 Jan. 1139/40, Count of Louvain, Duke of Lorraine; m. (1) ca. 1105, **IDA DE CHINY AND DE NAMUR** (149-23) d. 1117/22. (CP I 235).

24. GODFREY II, d. 1143, Count of Louvain; m. 1139, Luitgarde of Sultzbach, dau. of Berenger I, Count of Sultzbach.

25. GODFREY III, b. 1142, d. 1186, Count of Louvain; m. (1) 1155, Margaret von Limbourg, d. 1172/3, dau. of Henry II, Count of Limbourg, and Matilda, dau. of Adolph, Count of Saffenberg; m. (2) Imaine, dau. of Louis, Count of Loos.

26. HENRY I, d. 5 Sep. 1235, Duke of Brabant; m. (1) 1179, **MAUD OF FLANDERS** (165-27), dau. of Matthew of Alsace. (See also 100-28).

27. HENRY II, d. 1 Feb. 1247/8, Duke of Brabant, 1235-1248; m. (1) **MARIE OF SWABIA** (45-28), d. ca. 1240.

28. HENRY III, d. 1291, Duke of Brabant; m. Alix, d. 1273, dau. of Hugh IV, b. 1212, d. 1272, Duke of Burgundy, and Yolande de Dreux, d. 1255, both of Capetian descent. (Garnier xxvii).

29. MARIE OF BRABANT, d. 1321; m. (2) 1271, **PHILIP III** (101-29), b. 1245, d. 1285, King of France. (Weever 775).

30. MARGUERITE OF FRANCE, m. as his 2nd wife, **EDWARD I** (1-28), King of England. They were the parents of Thomas of Brotherton, Earl of Norfolk and Edmond of Woodstock, Earl of Kent. (CP V 736; CCN 353; Weever 775. Generations 19-30: Boston Evening Transcript, 1927, Note 2257, Part XV Brabant, Part XII Early Plantagenets).

31. THOMAS OF BROTHERTON, Earl of Norfolk, b. 1 Jun. 1300, d. Aug. 1338; m. (1) Alice, dau. Sir Roger Halys, Knt., of Harwich by whom he left an heiress **MARGARET** (16-30), Duchess of Norfolk for life; m. (1) John, 4th Lord Segrave; m. (2) Walter, Lord Mauny; issue by both. Thomas of Brotherton m. (2) Mary, dau. William Lord Ros, no surv. issue. (DNB lvi, 152).

31. EDMUND OF WOODSTOCK, Earl of Kent, b. 5 Aug. 1301, beheaded 19 Mar. 1330; m. 1327, **MARGARET** (236-11), wid. of John Comyn of Badenoch and dau. John, 1st Lord Wake, by whom he left a dau. **JOAN** (236-12) "Fair Maid of Kent," his event. heiress. (DNB xvi, 410).

Line 156

24. WALTER DE GAUNT (143-24), d. 1139; m. Maud, dau. of **STEPHEN** (214-24), Count of Brittany. (CP VII 672; IX 18).

25. ROBERT DE GAUNT, d. 1191, m. (1) by 1167, Alice, widow of Richard de Curcy, dau. & h. of William Paynel of Drax; m. (2) Gunnor, dau. & coh. of Ralph D'Aubigny. Gunnor m. (2) Nicholas de Stuteville. (CP VII 674-675).

26. SIR GILBERT DE GAUNT, son by (2), minor in 1191, adult by 1201, d. shortly bef. 22 Jan. 1241/2, Earl of Lincoln; m.

Line 156 (cont.)

unknown. (CP V 625; VII 674-675).
27. SIR GILBERT DE GAUNT of Folkingham, co. Lincoln, M.P. 1264, d. Folkingham, 5 Jan. 1273/4. (CP V 625-627; VIII 554-556).
28. NICHOLA DE GAUNT, d. 1284; m. ca. 1273, Sir Piers de Mauley, of Mulgrave Castle, b. 22 Jul 1249, d. 8 Sep. 1308, son of Sir Piers de Mauley and grandson of Sir Piers de Mauley and Isabel de Turnham. (CP V 625-627; VII 672-677; VIII 554-556; Banks I 220).
29. PIERS DE MAULEY, Lord Mauley of Mulgrave Castle, b. 10 Mar. 1280/1, bapt. 19 Mar. 1290/1, d. aft. 23 May 1348; m. bef. 1299, Eleanor de Furnival, dau. of Thomas, Lord Furnival. (CP VIII 554-567).
30. PIERS DE MAULEY, Lord Mauley of Mulgrave Castle, b. ca. 1300, d. 18 Jan. 1354/5; m. ca. 1322, **MARGARET DE CLIFFORD** (64-34), d. 8 Aug. 1382. (CP VIII 554-567; Banks I 312).
31. SIR PIERS DE MAULEY, Lord Mauley of Mulgrave Castle, b. 1330, d. 20 Mar. 1382/3; m. bef. 18 Nov. 1356, **ELIZABETH DE MEINILL** (88-33), Baroness Meinill of Whorlton, b. 15 Oct. 1331, d. 9 July 1368. (CP IV 60; VIII 567-568, 632-634).
32. PIERS DE MAULEY, Lord Mauley of Mulgrave Castle, d. 1377/8; m. ca. 1371, Margery de Sutton, d. 10 Oct. 1391, dau. of Sir Thomas de Sutton. (CP VIII 568-571).
33. CONSTANCE DE MAULEY, will dated 1 Jan. 1449/50; m. Sir John Bigod of Settrington, d. ca. 1425, son of Sir John Bigod, Knt., of Settrington, d. 1389, and grandson of **SIR ROGER BIGOD**, Knt. (69-31), of Settrington, d. 1362. (CP VIII 571; IX 593-596; John Burke: History of the Commoners I 673).
34. JOANNA BIGOD, m. Sir Walter de Calverley, als Scot, Knt., of Calverley, Yorkshire, son of Walter Calverley and Margery de Dineley, dau. of John de Dineley. (Foster: Visitations of Yorkshire, 1584/5, pp. 9, 548, cf. Calverley of Calverley; Burke: History of the Commoners I 673). Line breaks at this point. Walter No. 35 was son of Sir Walter No. 34, not by Joanna Bigod, but by his other wife.

* * *

35. WALTER CALVERLEY, als Scot, fl. 1429, d. 1466; m. Elizabeth, dau. of Sir Thomas Markenfield. (Foster cit.)
36. SIR WILLIAM CALVERLEY, als Scot, Knt., d. 1488; m. 1441, Agnes Tempest, dau. of Sir John Tempest, Knt., of Bracewell, Sheriff of Yorkshire 1440, 1459, and Alice Sherburne, dau. of Sir Robert Sherburne of Stoneyhurst, 1443. (Foster: Visit. Yorks., 1584/5, pp. 9, 548; Thomas Dunham Whitaker: The History and Antiquities of the Deanery of Craven in the County of York, London, 1805, chart p. 35: Lister of Gisburn-Park in Craven; also ibid., p. 95: Pedigree of Lister of Mydhope and Thornton).
37. JOAN CALVERLEY, m. 1467, Christopher Lister, of Medhope, Yorkshire, son and h. of Laurence Lister who m. a dau. of Richard Banester of Brokden. (Whitaker, op.cit., 35, 95).
38. WILLIAM LISTER, of Medhope, Esq., buried at Gisburn, 1537/9; m. Elizabeth Banester, dau. of Thurstan Banester of

Line 156 (cont.)

Swinden. (Whitaker 35, 95).
39. CHRISTOPHER LISTER, of Medhope, 1521, d. 1548; m. Eleanor Clayton, dau. of John Clayton, Esq., of Clayton, Lancashire. (Whitaker 35, 95; Foster: Visit. of Yorks., 1584/5, and 1612, p. 290; Lister of Medhope).
40. SIR WILLIAM LISTER, d. 1582, of Thornton and Medhope, will pro. 1582, mentions dau. and son-in-law Thomas Southworth, son of Sir John Southworth; m. Bridget Pigot, dau. of Bartholomew Pigot of Aston Rowen, co. Oxford, and wid. of Thomas Banister of Brokden. (Whitaker 35, 95; Foster: Visit. 1584/5, 290; James Stow; Survey of London, 1633).
41. ROSAMOND LISTER, m. **THOMAS SOUTHWORTH** (9-40), "son and heir of Sir John Southworth of Samlesbury, co. Lanc." (Whitaker 35, 95; Foster: Visitations of Yorkshire, 1584/5, 1612, p. 290; ms. 1571; Stow: Survey of London, 1633).

Line 157

18. LOUIS IV (148-18), d'Outre-Mer, b. 919, d. 10 Sep. 954, King of the Franks; m. 939, **GERBERGA OF SAXONY** (142-18), dau. of **HENRY I, THE FOWLER** (141-18), King of the Saxons.
19. MATILDA, m. aft. 964, Conrad, d. 19 Oct. 993, King of Burgundy, son of Rudolph II, King of Burgundy. (See 133-19).
20. GERBERGA OF BURGUNDY, b. 965, d. 1016; m. (2) 988, Hermann II, d. 4 May 1003, Duke of Swabia.
21. GISELE OF SWABIA, b. 11 Nov. 995, d. 14 Feb. 1042/3; m. (3) 1016, **CONRAD II** (45-21), the Salic, d. 4 Jun. 1039, Emperor of Germany. (CCN 274, 495).

Line 158

21. MAUD OF LOUVAIN (148-21), m. Eustace I, d. 1049, Count of Boulogne. (CP I 352).
22. EUSTACE II, Count of Boulogne, a companion of William I, the Conqueror, at the battle of Hastings, 1066, d. ca. 1080; m. (2) 1057 Ida, d. 13 Aug. 1113, dau. of Godfrey the Bearded, Duke of Upper and Lower Lorraine (d. 1069) by his wife Ida. (CCN 444; Brandenburg p. 11; Anthony Wagner: Pedigree and Progress chart p. 159).
23. EUSTACE III, Count of Boulogne, Crusader; m. 1102, Mary, d. 31 May 1116, dau. of **MALCOLM III CANMORE** (170-21) and **ST. MARGARET** (1-22).
24. MATILDA OF BOULOGNE, m. ca. 1123, **STEPHEN OF BLOIS** (169-25), King of England. (CCN 956-957).

Line 158A (This text supplied by Prof. David H. Kelley. Douglas Richardson offered a similar line that contains the same data.)

22. EUSTACE II, Count of Boulogne (158-22), d. ca. 1080, m. (2) 1057 Ida, d. 13 Aug. 1113, dau. of Godfrey the Bearded, Duke of

Upper and Lower Lorraine (d. 1069) by his wife Ida. (Brandenburg p. 11; Anthony Wagner: Pedigree and Progress chart p. 159).

23. **GODFREY** (or Geoffrey), Count of Boulogne, Duke of Lower Lorraine, prob. born earlier than the 1061 usually given, at Baisy (?), Brabant, d. Jerusalem 18 Jul. 1100; Domesday tenant 1086 at Carshalton, Surrey; a leader of the First Crusade, elected King of Jerusalem, but took the title Advocate of the Holy Sepulcher (as Godfrey I); succeeded by his next younger brother Baldwin, Count of Edessa, who became Baldwin I, King of Jerusalem, d. 2 Apr. 1118, surviving issue, if any, unknown.); m. Beatrice de Mandeville, daughter of Geoffrey de Mandeville and aunt of the first Earl of Essex. (Wagner, who considers him "prob. illeg." and not identical with the Advocate of the Holy Sepulcher, op. cit. and explanatory note p. 253).

Note: Although the Lotharingian name, Godofred, borne by the famous leader of the First Crusade, has been transcribed into modern English as 'Godfrey', this is etymologically incorrect. The name is, instead, the equivalent of the name which normally appears in contemporary French or Anglo-Norman documents in such forms as 'Goisfrid' and 'Gauzfrid', the prototypes of modern 'Geoffrey'. There is every reason to believe that bearers of the name might be as well aware of that as many a modern William knows that his name is the etymological equivalent of French Guillaume or Spanish Guillermo. J. Horace Round (1895, p. 256), citing Domesday references to property held by Goisfrid, son of Count Eustace in right of his wife, daughter of Geoffrey de Mandeville, says that "Dr. Liebermann asks whether Geoffrey's daughter was not thus 'the first wife, else unknown, of the future King of Jerusalem'." The reference is presumably to the linguistically sophisticated Anglo-Saxonist, Felix Liebermann, who would have known the equation. However, in an article published a year later, on Faramus, grandson of 'Goisfrid', Round makes no mention of this identification. He had come to recognize that 'Goisfrid' was the equivalent of later Geoffrey and had been informed by his friend, M.V.J. Vaillant, of Boulogne that "the sons of Eustace are known and that Geoffrey is not among them". What M. Vaillant should have written was that there was no Godfrey among them. However, Round accepted the testimony of his linguistically naive friend against that of Liebermann and therefore invented a non-existent bastard son, Geoffrey, of Eustace of Boulogne. The truth was later recognized by Joseph Armitage Robinson in his study of the Crispins, and by H.W.C. Davis (1913) who drew attention to the fact that "Godfrey" of Jerusalem married Beatrice, daughter of Geoffrey de Mandeville and aunt of the first Earl of Essex.

While the holdings of Geoffrey de Mandeville were not nearly as great as those of Eustace of Boulogne, he was a very substantial landholder in 11 counties and his daughter a suitable match for 'Godfrey' who had already inherited a great deal from his maternal uncle. That De Mandeville would have alienated property in order to give his daughter in marriage to a bastard son of Count Eustace, lacking any substantial prospects, is highly unlikely.

More recently, Johnson and Cronne, good historians but poor linguists, have used Round's article to "correct" Davis. The true identity of Geoffrey/Godfrey was recognized again by Miss Catherine Morton, who has been in touch with DHK and with Sir Anthony Wagner on this matter. Wagner (1975, p. 253, with an unfortunate misprint) mentions the "confusion" between 'Godfrey' and 'Geoffrey'. It was there assumed that the confusion was ancient and that Eustace's son, Godofred, was genuinely a Godfrey. It should be emphasized, however, that actually the confusion is entirely modern due to the use of 'Godfrey' to transcribe a name which is etymologically 'Geoffrey' (the Germans use "Gottfried" both for the leader of the first crusade and for Geoffrey Plantagenet, Count of Anjou—one may regard this either as desirable consistency or doubled error).

Wagner cites the views of Stephen Runciman, a historian of the crusades, pointing out that crusader sources make no suggestion of a wife for "Godfrey" and emphasizing his chastity. However, a wife and child left in England would not necessarily have been known to such sources, nor was there anything notable in a Crusader leaving a wife behind, though certainly noteworthy if he brought a wife with him. Runciman's further suggestion that 'Godfrey' might have made some sort of "morganatic" alliance must be rejected. The concept is completely foreign to the period, save, perhaps, among the Welsh and would, in any case, hardly apply to a marriage of 'Godfrey'/Geoffrey with Beatrice de Mandeville, of a family whose status was fully comparable to his own. It is extremely unlikely that 'maritagium', the term used for Goisfrid's marriage, would be applied to a union which was in any way irregular. Runciman is looking back from the days of 'Godfrey's' greatness, rather than realistically appraising the situation at the time of his marriage.

The child left by 'Godfrey' in England was William de Boulogne, bearer of one of the oldest English surnames, for William was neither Count of Boulogne nor from Boulogne. He should appear with some frequency in the English records, for his son, Faramus, held extensive estates in widely separated parts of England (Somerset, Surrey, Essex, Oxford, Buckinghamshire, Suffolk, probably Kent and Northumberland). William appears as a witness to a document of 1106 and in a couple of later documents. Perhaps he is a still-unrecognized William Fitz-Geoffrey of other documents.

The heir of Faramus was his daughter, Sybil, who married Enguerrand de Fiennes, whose heirs are the extant Fiennes family. However, Faramus had known brothers, Eustace and Simon who appear with him in a legal document referring to Bec. The Eustace de Boulogne of that document may well be the Eustace de Boulogne who appears in a document of 1145-7 with his brother, Baldwin de Boulogne, the king's chaplain, who could, therefore, be another brother of Faramus. Widicumbe and Ash, in Martock, which had been held by Count Eustace before the Norman conquest, passed to his heir, William, Count of Boulogne (son of King Stephen), who granted these properties to his cousin, Faramus de Boulogne, from which the overlordship passed to the Fiennes family. The sub-holders, however, were Boulognes and in 1227 the sub-holder was a second Faramus de Boulogne, son of Thomas. Presumably Thomas was a grandson or greatgrandson of a brother of the first Faramus.

In the later mediaeval period, 'de Boulogne' (de Bolonia, de Bononia) became 'Boleyn' and still later 'Bullen'. Admiral Sir Charles Bullen, a hero of Trafalgar, and his relatives probably have a male line descent from 'Godfrey'/Geoffrey, as may also the Somerset families of Ashe, Martock, Crewkerne, Widicumbe/Whitcomb; the Boulognes, alias Bamptons, of Oxford; the Bernes, of Kent; and perhaps the Rochesters and Lavers of Essex. An apparent female relationship connected the Boulognes of Somerset with the Beaumonts of Northumberland and the Boulognes and Widicumbs of Yorkshire may be of the family.

However, the name Boulogne also came into England much later with merchants from the Boullonnais and it is apparently from one such family that Queen Anne Boleyn derived. Much remains to be done before fully documented unbroken pedigrees can be established but 'Godfrey's' English wife and child can now be recognized.

24. WILLIAM DE BOULOGNE, adult by 1106, d. about 1130. (Wagner, op. cit.).

25. FARAMUS (or Pharamus) **DE BOULOGNE**, also called 'de Tingry', adult by 1130, in charge of Dover Castle and of the Honour of Peverel of Dover in 1157-8, held lands at Eaton, Bedford and Wendover, Bucks, d. ca. 1183/4, m. Matilda. (Wagner, op. cit.; Beddfordshire Hist. Rec. Soc. V 211-212; Gen. Mag. XX 335-340).

26. SIBYL, dau. and h. (she had two brothers, William and Thomas, apparently both died before her, s.p.), m. Enguerrand (Ingelram) de Fiennes, who succeeded to his father-in-law's share of Eaton, Bedford in 1183/4, d. 1189. (Wagner, op. cit. and charts p. 159 & 161; Bedfordshire Hist. Rec. Soc. V 212).

27. WILLIAM (or Guillaume) **DE FIENNES**, d. 1241, m. **AGNES DE DAMMARTIN** (152-27). Wagner op. cit.; Gen. Mag. XX 335-340).

Line 159

19. MATILDA OF FRANCE (157-19), m. aft. 964, Conrad, King of Burgundy. (See 133-19).

20. BERTHA OF BURGUNDY, m. (1) **EUDES I** (136-20), Count of Blois.

Line 160

22. HENRY II (155-22), of Brabant, Count of Louvain and Lorraine, d. 1077; m. Adelaide of Orlamunda.

23. IDA OF LOUVAIN, d. 1139; m. 1084, **BALDWIN II** (163-24), d. 1099, Count of Hainaut. (Boston Evening Transcript, 9 Nov. 1927, Note 2257, Part VI Flanders, Part XV Brabant).

Line 161

23. GODFREY I (155-23), d. 1140, Duke of Brabant, Count of Louvain; m. (2) ca. 1121, Clemence of Burgundy, dau. of **WILLIAM I** of Burgundy, Duke of Brabant (132-24). (CP I 235; X 445-448; Collins: Peerage, 3rd Ed., 1756, IV 23-26; Garnier, Table xxviii).

24. JOCELIN OF LOUVAIN (natural son of Godfrey I by an unknown mistress), d. bef. 1180, Baron Percy; m. aft. 1154, Agnes de Percy, b. 1134, d. bef. 13 Oct. 1204, dau. of William de Percy and Adeliza de Tunbridge. (CP X 445-448; Collins IV 25-26; See Knetsche: Das Haus Brabant).

25. SIR HENRY PERCY, Knt., d. 1198; m. Isabel, living 1230, dau. of Adam de Brus II, of Skelton in Cleveland (see 136-25); she m. (2) Sir Roger Maudit. (CP X 448-449; Collins IV 29-30).

26. WILLIAM DE PERCY, 6th Baron Percy, b. ca. 1193, d. ca. 28 Jul. 1245; m. (2) ca. 1233, Ellen de Baliol, d. bef. 22 Nov. 1281, dau. of Ingram de Baliol and his wife, dau. of Walter de Berkeley. (CP X 452-455).

27. SIR HENRY DE PERCY, Knt., b. ca. 1235, d. 29 Aug. 1272, 7th Baron Percy, knighted 1257; m. York, 8 Sep. 1268, **ELEANOR DE WARENNE** (153-30), b. 1251, living 1282. (CP X 455-456).

28. SIR HENRY PERCY, Knt., 9th Baron Percy, b. ca. 25 Mar. 1273, d. Oct. 1314, knighted 1296, M.P. 1299-1314, Baron of Alnwick, co. Northumberland, 1309; m. Eleanor Fitz Alan, d. 1328, dau. of **SIR RICHARD FITZ ALAN** (28-31) de Arundel. (CP X 456-459).

29. HENRY DE PERCY, K.G., b. 1299, d. 26 Feb. 1351/2, 2nd Lord Percy of Alnwick, M.P. 1322-1352, knighted 1323, Constable of Scarborough Castle, Warden of the Marches of Scotland; m. **IDOINE DE CLIFFORD** (205-33), d. 24 Aug. 1365, dau. of **ROBERT DE CLIFFORD** (82-32), 1st Lord Clifford. (CP X 459-464).

30. HENRY DE PERCY, b. 1320, d. ca. 18 May 1368, fought at Crecy, 26 Aug. 1346; m. (1) Sep. 1334, **MARY PLANTAGENET** (19-30). (CP I 244, X 462-463).

Line 162

16. JUDITH, b. ca. 846, dau. **CHARLES II**, the Bald (148-15), King of the Franks and Emperor, and Ermentrude; m. (3) 862, Baldwin I "Bras de Fer," d. 879, Count of Flanders. (CCN 112).

17. BALDWIN II, the Bald, b. ca. 865, d. 2 Jan. 918, Count of Flanders and Artois; m. 884, **ALFTHRYTH** (44-16), d. 7 Jun. 929, dau. of **ALFRED THE GREAT** of England (1-15). (CCN 112).

18. ARNOLD I, the Old, b. ca. 890, d. 27 Mar. 964, Count of Flanders and Artois; m. 934, **ALIX DE VERMANDOIS** (48-20), d. *L-48-20* Bruges, 960.

19. BALDWIN III, d. 1 Jan. 961/2, Count of Flanders; m. Matilda, d. 25 May 1008, dau. of Hermann Billung, Duke of Saxony, and Hildegarde of Westerbourg.

20. ARNOLD II, the Young, b. ca. 961/2, d. 30 Mar. 987, Count of Flanders; m. 968, **ROSELA** (146-19), d. 26 Jan. 1003. She m. (2)

Line 162 (cont.)

ROBERT II, King of France (101-21) as (1) wife, repudiated.

21. BALDWIN IV, the Bearded, b. 980, d. 30 May 1036, Count of Valenciennes, 1007, and Count of Flanders; m. (1) ca. 1012, Ogive (or Otgiva) of Luxembourg, b. ca. 995, d. 21 Feb. 1030, dau. of **FREDERICK I** (143-20), Count of Luxembourg, by his wife Ermentrude of Gleiberg. He m. (2) ca. 1031 N.N. dau. **RICHARD II** (121-22), Duke of Normandy. (Brandenburg p. 7).

22. BALDWIN V, de Lille, b. 1012, d. Lille, 1 Sep. 1067, Count of Flanders; m. 1028, **ADELE DE FRANCE** (128-22), d. 8 Jan. 1079. (CCN 112).

23. MAUD (or **MATILDA**) **OF FLANDERS**, b. 1032, d. 3 Nov. 1083; m. 1053, **WILLIAM I**, the Conqueror (121-24), Duke of Normandy, King of England. (Generations 13-23: Crispin: Falaise Roll, 1938, pp. 186-187; Boston Evening Transcript, 26 Sept. 1927, Note 2257, D.L.J., Part VI Flanders).

Line 163

22. BALDWIN V (162-22), de Lille, Count of Flanders; m. **ADELE DE FRANCE** (128-22).

23. BALDWIN VI, de Mons, b. ca. 1030, d. 10 Jul. 1070, Count of Flanders, and (as Baldwin I) Count of Hainaut; m. ca. 1055, Richilde, or uncertain parentage, d. 15 Mar. 1088, of Hainaut, wid. of Herman, Count of Hainaut. Richilde m. (3) shortly bef. 1071, William Fitz Osbern, Earl of Hereford. (CP VI 447-449; IX 18; Brandenburg, p. 84; Moriarty, The Plantagenet Ancestry).

24. BALDWIN II, d. 1099, Count of Hainaut; m. 1084, **IDA OF LOUVAIN** (160-23), d. 1139. (Refs. as cited.)

25. BALDWIN III, d. 1120, Count of Hainaut; m. Yolande of Guelders, dau. of Gerald I de Wassenberg, Count of Guelders. (Refs. as cited).

26. BALDWIN IV, d. 8 Nov. 1171, Count of Hainaut; m. Alix de Namur, d. 1195, dau. of Godfrey, d. 1139, Count of Namur, and Ermesinde, d. 1143, dau. of Conrad I, d. 1086, Count of Luxembourg. (Refs. as cited.)

27. BALDWIN V, b. 1150, d. 17 Dec. 1195, Count of Hainaut and Namur; m. 1169, as (2) husb. **MARGARITE OF LORRAINE** (164-26), heiress of Flanders, d. 17 Dec. 1195. (Refs. as cited.)

28. ISABELLA OF HAINAUT, d. 1190; m. 1180, **PHILIP II** (101-26), b. 22 Aug. 1165, d. 22 Aug. 1165, King of France. (Generations 22-28: Boston Evening Transcript, 1927, Note 2257, Part VI Flanders; and refs. as cited under Gen. 23).

Line 163 A

27. BALDWIN V (163-27), Count of Hainaut, VIII of Flanders, b. 1150, d. 17 Dec. 1195, m. Apr. 1169 as (2) husb. Margaret (or Margarite), dau. & h. of Dietrich (or Thierry) of Alsace, Count of Flanders, b. ca. 1150/50, d. 12 Nov. 1194.

28. YOLANDE OF FLANDERS, b. ca. 1175, d. Constantinople

Aug. 1219, heiress and Countess of Namur, m. 24 June/1 July 1193
PETER DE COURTENAY (107-26), Count of Courtenay 1183, of
Nevers 1184, etc., Marquis of Namur 1212, Emperor of
Constantinople 1217, b. 1155, d. Epirus bef. Jan. 1218.

    29. YOLANDE DE COURTENAY, d. 1233, m. 1215 as (2) wife·
ANDREW II (105-28), King of Hungary, b. 1176, d. 21 Sept. 1235.
(Moriarty, The Plantagenet Ancestry.)

Line 164

    22. BALDWIN V (162-22) de Lille; m. **ADELE DE FRANCE** (128-
22).

    23. ROBERT LE FRISON, b. ca. 1035, d. 3 Oct. 1093, Count of
Flanders, m. 1063 Gertrude of Saxony, widow of Florent I, Count of
Holland, daughter of Bernard II.

    24. GERTRUDE OF FLANDERS, b. ca. 1070, d. 1117, m. (2) ca.
1100 Thierry II, Duke of Lorraine, d. 23 Jan. 1115.

    25. THIERRY OF LORRAINE, d. 17 Jan 1168, Count of
Flanders; m. (2) 1131, **SIBYL OF ANJOU** (129-25).

    26. MARGARITE OF LORRAINE, and heiress of Flanders, b. ca.
1140/5, d. 15 Nov. 1194; m. (1) ca. 1160 Rudolph II, Count of
Vermandois, d. 17 Jun 1167, m. (2) 1169, **BALDWIN V** (163-27), d. 17
or 21 Dec. 1195, Count of Hainaut and Namur. (Note: Thierry (164-
24 & 25) were also known as Dietrich I & II, Count of Alsace &
Count of Flanders). (Brandenburg).

Line 165

    25. THIERRY OF LORRAINE (164-25), Count of Flanders; m.
(2) 1131, **SYBIL OF ANJOU** (129-25).

    26. MATTHEW OF ALSACE, m. **MARY OF BLOIS** (169-26), b.
1136, d. 1182, dau. of **STEPHEN** (169-25), King of England.

    27. MAUD OF FLANDERS, d. 1240; m. 1179, **HENRY I** (155-26),
d. 5 Sep. 1235, Duke of Brabant.

Line 166

    22. BALDWIN IV (162-21), de Lille; m. (3) ca. 1031 Judith, dau.
of Richard II (see 121-22), Duke of Normandy. (Brandenburg).

    23. JUDITH OF FLANDERS, d. 4 Mar. 1094; m. (1) Tostig, d. 25
Sep. 1066, Earl of Northumbria, son of Godwin, Earl of Essex; m. (2)
1071, Welf IV, Duke of Bavaria, d. 6 Nov. 1101. (Not dau. of Baldwin
V). (Brandenburg).

    24. HENRY I, b. 1074, d. 13 Dec. 1126, Duke of Bavaria; m. ca.
1100, **WULFHILDA** (243-8), d. 29 Dec. 1126, dau. of Magnus, Duke of
Saxony, and Sophia, dau. of **BELA I**, King of Hungary (243-6).

    25. JUDITH OF BAVARIA, b. 1100, d. 1130; m. **FREDERICK II**
(45-25) of Hohenstauffen, b. 1090, d. 6 Apr. 1147, Duke of Swabia.
(Generations 22-25: Turton; Brandenburg).

Line 167

20. GERBERGA OF BURGUNDY (157-20), m. Hermann II, Duke of Swabia.

21. MAUD OF SWABIA, m. Frederick II, Count of Bar and Duke of Upper Lorraine.

22. SOPHIA, Countess of Bar-le-Duc, d. ca. 1092; m. ca. 1027, Louis, Count of Montbéliard, d. ca. 1067.

23. THIERRY II, Count of Montbéliard and Bar-le-Duc; m. ca. 1076, **ERMENTRUDE OF BURGUNDY** (144-23). (Turton).

Line 168

27. BALDWIN V (163-27), d. 17 Dec. 1195, Count of Hainaut; m. ca. 1169, **MARGARITE** (164-26), of Flanders, d. 15 Nov. 1194.

28. BALDWIN VI, Count of Hainaut and Flanders, b. Valenciennes, July 1171, d. 11 June 1205 or 1206; a leader of the Fourth Crusade; Emperor of Constantinople; m. **MARIE OF CHAMPAGNE** (102-27).

29. MARGARET, d. ca. 1280, Countess of Hainaut and Flanders; m. (2) ca. 1212, Bouchard d'Avenes, Archdeacon of Laon and Canon of St. Pierre de Lille, d. ca. 1243/4.

30. JOHN I, d'Avenes, d. 1256, Count of Holland; m. **ADELAIDE OF HOLLAND** (100-29), d. ca. 1284.

31. JOHN II, d. 1304, Count of Hainaut; m. Philippa, dau. of Henry of Luxembourg.

32. WILLIAM III, d. 7 Jun. 1337, Count of Hainaut and Holland; m. ca. 1305, **JEANNE OF VALOIS** (103-33), d. 1352.

Line 169

23. MAUD OF FLANDERS (162-23), m. 1053, **WILLIAM I,** the Conqueror (121-24), Duke of Normandy, King of England. (CCN 494).

24. ADELA OF NORMANDY, b. 1062, d. 1137; m. ca. 1080, bef. 1085, **STEPHEN OF BLOIS** (137-23), Count of Blois; a leader of the First Crusade.

25. STEPHEN OF BLOIS, cr. King of England, 26 Dec. 1135, b. 1095/6, d. 25 Oct. 1154; m. ca. 1119-1120, **MATILDA OF BOULOGNE** (158-24), b. ca. 1105, d. Hedingham Castle, Kent, 3 May 1152, dau. of **EUSTACE III** (158-23), Count of Boulogne, and Mary, dau. of **MALCOLM III CANMORE** (170-21), King of Scots, and St. **MARGARET** (1-22), dau. of Edward, the Aethling. (CP VII 641-642; SP I 2; Weever 278; Dunbar 32; Thatcher 324).

26. MARY, b. 1136, d. 1182; m. **MATTHEW OF ALSACE** (165-26), son of Thierry, Count of Flanders, and Sybil, dau. of Fulk V, Count of Anjou.

Line 169A

25. STEPHEN, King of England (169-25), b. 1095/6, d. 25 Oct. 1154; m. ca. 1119, **MAUD** (or Mathilda) (158-24), dau. Eustace III, Count of Boulogne, b. ca. 1105, d. 1157.

26. **EUSTACE IV**, Count of Boulogne, 1150, son and h. apparent, b. ca. 1120, d.v.p. 10 Aug. 1153; m. ca. Feb. 1140, Constance, d. ca. 1180 s.p. dau. **LOUIS VI** (101-24), King of France. Eustace had by unknown mistress:

27. **EUSTACHIE** de Champagne, m. (1) Geoffrey de Mandeville, d.s.p., Earl of Essex, div.; m. (2) Anselme Candavaine, Count of Saint-Pol, d. 1164. She had three sons; Hugh, count of St. Pol, Engerrand; Guy).

28. **BEATRICE CANDAVAINE**, de Saint Pol, m. as 3rd wife, **JOHN I**, Count of Ponthieu, d. 1191 (109-27). (The Genealogists' Magazine, vol. 15, pp. 186-187).

EARLY KINGS

OF SCOTLAND AND IRELAND

Lines 170 and 175 revised by Prof. David H. Kelley, University of Calgary, Alberta.

Line 170 (Each succ. generation, child of proceeding)

1. ERCC, king of Dalriada, in northern Ireland, son of Eochaid Muinremur, King of Dalriada, d. 474. (Annals of the Four Masters). Several sons including Loarn and Fergus.

2. FERGUS, established an Irish kingdom of Dalriada in Argyle, now Scotland. Ruled (for three years ?) in succession to his brother, Loarn, at an uncertain date 498-501?). He has sometimes been confused with Ercc, a son of Loarn's daughter.

3. DOMONGART, apparently briefly King of Dalriada in Scotland, at an uncertain date for a short time following his father's death. According to LL, BB, etc., he m. Feldelm Foltchain, dau. of Brion, son of Eochaid Mugmedon. Brion was a half-brother of the famous Niall of the Nine Hostages. This marriage is in good agreement with the revised chronology of Carney (Studies in Irish Literature and History) for the fifth century, which puts the death of Niall at about 542 A.D., and the death of Patrick about 490 A.D.

4. GABRAN. He and his son are both called, in Welsh sources, "the treacherous". Welsh pedigrees make him a son of Dyfnwal hen, allegedly of the line of Ceretic Guletic, regarded by later Welsh writers as an important ruler in northern Britain. According to Welsh Sources, his wife was Lleian, dau. of Brychan, the ruler who gave his name to Brecknock.

5. AEDAN. Details of his life and those of his children and grandchildren are well attested in the near-contemporary life of St. Columba, by Adamnan. Died about 608 A.D., after ruling Dalriada in Scotland for about 37 years.

6. EOCHU BUIDE (sometimes Eochaid Buide), a younger son of Aedan, succeeded his father as his brothers had been killed, d. ca. 630. Also called King of the Picts.

7. DOMNALL BRECC, killed at the battle of Strathcarron, prob. about 642 A.D. He is apparently the last king of Dalriada known to early Welsh tradition.

8. DOMONGART, did not reign.

9. EOCHAID II, King of Dalriada, killed about 697 A.D. (aft. ruling three years?).

9A. EOCHAID III, King of Dalriada, about 721-733.

10. AED FIND, or "the White", King of Dalriada, d. 778, aft. ruling 30 years.

11. EOCHAID, the Poisonous, King of Dalriada, 781 ff.

Line 170 (cont.)

12. ALPIN, slain in Galloway, ca. 837.

13. CINAED. This is the famous Kenneth MacAlpin, King of the Picts and Scots, 843-d. 858. (For more details on generations 1-13, see also H. Pirie-Gordon "Succession of the Kingdom of Strathclyde" The Armorial vol. I pp. 35-40, 79-87, 143-148, 192-196; vol. II 9-14, 92-102 with cited authorities. This reference also provides the descent to Kenneth MacAlpin of the lines of the Kings of Strathclyde and of the Picts.)

14. CAUSANTIN (Constantine), King of Scots, 862, d. 877, slain in battle by the Norse.

15. DOMNALL, King of Scots, 889, killed 900.

16. MAEL-COLUIM (Malcolm), King of Scots, 943, killed by the men of Moray, 954.

17. CINAED (Kenneth), King of Scots, 971, killed 995 by his own men. (Berchan's Prophecy indicates that his wife was a Leinster woman.

18. MAEL-COLUIM (Malcolm II), King of Scots, 25 Mar. 1005-1034; fought a battle in 1008 at Carham with Uchtred (d. 1016), son of Waltheof, Earl of the Northumbrians, and overcame the Danes, 1017; published a code of laws; was murdered, 25 Nov. 1034. "1004. Malcolm the son of Kenneth, a most victorious king, reigned 30 years. 1034. Malcolm king of Scots died." (Ritson II 104-109; Dunbar I 280; Anglo-Saxon Chronicle; at this point the New Revised Complete Peerage (G.E. Cokayne, vols. I-XII pts. 1 & 2) and the Scots Peerage (Sir James Balfour Paul, 9 vols., 1904-1914) begin the list of Scots kings. CP IX 704; SP I 1; CP X, Ap. A, p. 9 shows Malcolm MacKenneth had 3 daus: Bethoc; Donada m. Sigurd II, Earl of Orkney; and (?) Anleta. See also Marjorie Anderson, Kings & Kingship in Early Scotland.

19. BETHOC (Beatrix), m. 1000, Crinan the Thane (also called Albanach or Grimus), b. 978, d. 1045, Lay Abbot of Dunkeld, Governor of the Scots Islands. "1045. A battle between the Scots themselves, where fell Crinan abbot of Duncaillen." (Dunbar 4, 28; Ritson II 116; CP IV 504; IX 704; SP I 1).

20. DUNCAN I MACCRINAN, King of Scots, 1034-1040; murdered by Macbeth near Elgin, 14 Aug. 1040; m. a dau. of Siward, Danish Earl of Northumbria. He besieged Durham, 1035. "1034. Duncan, the son of Crinan, abbot of Dunkeld, and Bethoc, daughter of Malcolm, the son of Kenneth, reigned six years." Now being on solid ground, with the backing of CP and SP, we leave Ritson's Annals of the Scots. The above unbroken succession of the kings of the Scots from Fergus to Malcolm II is thus soundly and convincingly authenticated. (Dunbar 12-13, 280; Ritson II 111-116; CP IV 504 note b; IX 704; SP I 1; III 240).

21. MALCOLM III CANMORE, King of Scots 1058-1093, b. 1031, crowned at Scone, 17 Mar. 1057/8; slain while besieging Alnwick Castle, 13 Nov. 1093; m. (1) 1059, Ingibiorg, dau. of Earl Finn Arnason, and wid. of Thorfill Sigurdson, Earl of Orkney; m. (2) Dunfermline, 1068/9, **MARGARET** (1-22), St. Margaret of Scotland, d. 16 Nov. 1093, dau. of Prince Edward the Exile and a descendant of

Alfred the Great, Clovis I, Cerdic, and perhaps Hengist, and ancestress of the royal line of England. (CP V 736; VII 641-642; SP I 1; Dunbar 25-34, 280-281. Generations 12-21: Lang, 1901, I 56-57. For the whole line above the following sources are given by Ritson. Generations 2-20; Cronica regum Scottorum; Nomina regum Scot. et Pict.; Annals of Tigernach (d. 1080, cf. Roderic O'Flaherty: Ogygia, published in Latin, 1685, in English, 1793, pp. 477-478); Duan, a Gaelic or Irish poem, ca. 1050. Generations 4-20: Annalles Ultonienses (Annals of Ulster), a faithful chronology of great antiquity but uncertain date. Generations 11-20: Cronica de Mailros (Chronicle of Melrose). Generations 12-22: William of Malmesbury (d. aft. 1142), 56; Anglo-Saxon Chronicle; Florence of Worcester (d. 1118). Generations 13-17: Cronica de origine antiquorum Pictorum et Scotorum, ends 994, written at the time of Kenneth II. The Chronicon elegiacum extends to generation 20. Generations 16-20: Historia de Dunelmensis ecclesia, pp. 156-178 (by Turgotus, d. 1115, or Simon of Durham, d. 1130); Chronicle of Innisfallen; Synchronisms of Flan of Bute (d. 1056); Scala Chronica, 1365).

> *dd. Edith*
> *Matilda*
> *m.*
> *King Henry I*

    22. DAVID I, the Saint, b. ca. 1080, d. Carlisle, 24 May 1154, King of Scots, 23 Apr. 1124-1153; m. 1113/4, **MAUD** (148-24), Countess of Huntingdon, d. 1130/1. (CP IV 670 chart iv; V 736; VII 640-642; SP I 3-4; Dunbar 58-70, 280-281).

    23. HENRY OF HUNTINGDON, b. 1114, d. 12 Jun. 1152, Earl of Northumberland and Huntingdon; m. 1139, **ADA DE WARENNE** (89-25), d. 1178. (CP VI 670 chart iv; V 736; VII 642; SP I 4; Dudley pedigree; Dunbar 64-65, 280-281).

    24. WILLIAM THE LION, King of Scots, 9 Dec. 1165-1214, b. 1143, d. Stirling, 4 Dec. 1214. (CP IV 670 chart iv; VII 644-645; SP I 4; Gardiner 216).

    25. ISABEL (natural dau. of William the Lion by a dau. of Richard Avenal); m. (2) Haddington, 1191, Robert de Ros, d. bef. 23 Dec. 1126, of Helmsley in Holderness, co. York, Magna Charta Surety, 1215, Knight Templar, grandson of Robert de Ros and Sibyl de Valognes. (CP XI 90-92; SP I 4; Banks I 377; DNB 45: 216-219).

    26. SIR WILLIAM DE ROS, d. ca. 1264, of Helmsley, M.P. 1235/6; m. **LUCY FITZ PIERS** (237-7), of Brecknock. (CP XI 93-94).

    27. SIR WILLIAM DE ROS, of Ingmanthorpe, 3rd son, served in Scotland, 1257-1258, and in Gascony, 1294, d. ca. 28 May 1310; m. 1268, Eustache, wid. of Sir Nicholas de Cauntelo, dau. and h. of Ralph Fitz Hugh, son of Hugh Fitz Ralph by Agnes, dau. and heiress of Ralph de Greasley. (CP XI 117-118).

    28. LUCY (or **LUCIA**) **DE ROS,** m. Sir Robert Plumpton of Plumpton, Knt., fl. 1307, d. 1325, of an ancient family settled in Yorkshire since the time of the Conquest, 1066. (CP XI 117-118; York Deeds, York Record Society, V 273, 306; W.T. Lancaster: Early History of the Ripley and the Ingilby Family, 1918; Foster: Visitations of Yorkshire, 1584/5 and 1612, Plumpton of Plumpton, p. 386).

    29. SIR WILLIAM DE PLUMPTON, of Plumpton, d. 1362; m. (1) ca. 1330, Alice, dau. Sir Henry Byaufix (mar. sett. 1322). Her property did not go to the Plumptons, but to a distant cousin, so Alice No. 30 was not her dau.; m. (2) by 1338, Christianna, wid. of Richard de Emildon, d. 1333. (Foster, op.cit., 386; VCH Lanc. I 345; IV 143; VII 4-5; ms. dated 1487).

30. ALICE DE PLUMPTON, dau. of 2nd wife, living 21 Mar. 1400; m. (1) 1352, Sir Richard Shireburne, Knt., of Aighton, d. 1361, son of Sir John Shireburne; m. (2) 1374, Sir John Boteler of Bewsey in Warrington, Lancashire, d. 1400, son of William le Boteler of Bewsey and Elizabeth de Havering, dau. of Nicholas de Havering. Sir John Boteler was M.P. 1366, 1372, 1376-1378, 1380, Knight of the Shire of Lancaster 1388, 1397-1398, Baron of Warrington 1380-1400; fought in Gascony 1369-1370, in Aquitaine 1372-1373. (VCH Lanc. I 345; IV 143; VII 4-5; Foster 386).

31. ALICE BOTELER, d. 27 Feb. 1441/2; m. John Gerard of Kingsley and Bryn, b. 1386, d. 6 Nov. 1431, lord of the manors of Kingsley and Bryn, 1416-1431, eldest son of Sir Thomas and Isabel Gerard of Bryn. (Inq.p.m. 10 Henry VI; VCH Lanc. IV 143; Gerard of Kingsley, see Ormerod (Helsby) II 96, 131-132).

32. CONSTANCE GERARD, b. 1402, living 1468; m. ca. 1421-3, Sir Alexander Standish of Standish, d. 1445, eldest son of Lawrence and Lora (Pilkington) Standish. (Marriage settlement between Lawrence de Standish and John Gerard of Bryn that Alexander his son shall marry Constance, dau. of the said John Gerard, in Earwaker: The Standish family of Standish . . . Charters and Deeds, Manchester, 1898, No. 111, p. 40; VCH Lanc. VI 194).

33. RALPH STANDISH, of Standish, Esq., eldest son, b. ca. 1424, living in 1468; m. Margaret Radcliffe, d. 1476, dau. of Richard Radcliffe of Chadderton. (Ralph de Standish and his wife participate in the division of the manor of Chadderton, formerly belonging to Sir John Radcliffe, Knt., dated 1454/5. Earwaker, op.cit., No. 139, p. 48; VCH Lanc. VI 194).

34. SIR ALEXANDER STANDISH of Standish, Knt., eldest son, b. 1452 (ae. 24 in 1476), d. 1507; m. Sibyl de Bold, living as wid., 1507, dau. of Sir Henry Bold of Bold. Sir Alexander was knighted for service at the battle of Hutton Field, Scotland, 1482. (Ralph de Standish contracts for the marriage of his son and h. Alexander de Standish with Sibyl, dau. of Henry Bold, Esq., of Bold. Apparently a child marriage. Earwaker, Nov. 135, p. 47; VCH Lanc. VI 194-195).

35. RALPH STANDISH, of Standish, eldest son, b. 1479 (ae. 28 in 1507), d. 1538; m. ca. 16 Aug. 1498, **ALICE HARINGTON** (34-38) (Marriage contract between Alice, dau. of Sir James Harington, Knt., and Ralph, son of Sir Alexander Standish, Knt., dated 16 Aug. 1498. Inq.p.m., Sir James Harington, 14 Nov. 1498; Earwaker, No. 182, p. 61; VCH Lanc. VI 194-195).

36. ROGER STANDISH, Esq. (34-39).

37. ALICE STANDISH (34-40), m. James Prescott.

Line 171

21. MALCOLM III CANMORE (170-21); m. (1) Ingibiorg.
22. DUNCAN II, b. 1060, d. 12 Nov. 1094, King of Scots 1093-1094; m. **ATHELREDA OF DUNBAR** (40-23), his cousin. (SP I 2-3).

Line 172

19. BETHOC (170-19), m. 1000, Crinan the Thane, b. 978, d. 1045, Lay Abbot of Dunkeld. (CP IV 504; IX 704).
20. MALDRED (brother of Duncan I, King of Scots, 1034-1040), slain in battle 1045, Lord of Carlisle and Allendale; m. **EALDGYTH** (Edith) (34-21), granddau. of **AETHELRED II** the Redeless (1-19), King of England. (CP IV 504; IX 704; SP III 240-241; Dunbar 4, 280).

Line 173 Cancelled.

Line 174 Cancelled.

Line 175

1. BRIAN of the Tributes (Borama, Boroimhe, Boru), King of the Dalcassians, then King of Munster (976-1002), and finally usurped the high kingship of Ireland (1002-1014). Killed at the battle of Clontarf, 1014 A.D., fighting a mixed force of Norse and Leinstermen. He had at least three wives, the mother of his son, Donnchad, being Gormflaith of Naas, dau. of Murchad, King of Leinster (d. 972). Gormflaith was the wid. of Anlaf (Olaf), King of Dublin (d. 981) and had been the wife of Mael-Sechnaill, King of Ireland. She d. 1030.
2. DONNCHAD, King of Munster, 1023. On pilgrimage to Rome 1064, and d. the same year.
3. DARBFORGAILL, m. Diarmait MacMael nam Bo, King of Hy Kinsale, who subsequently usurped the high kingship of Leinster. Held the overlordship of Ossory, Dublin and other local kingdoms. Died 23 Feb. 1072. Darbforgaill d. 1080.
4. MURCHAD, d. in Dublin, v.p., 8 Dec. 1070; m. Sadb, dau. of MacBricc.
5. DONNCHAD MACMURCHADA, King of Dublin, killed in battle against Domnall Ua Briain, 1115. Of his wives, Orlaith, was the mother of Diarmait.
6. DIARMAIT MACMURCHADA, b. 1100, King of Leinster 1135, d. 1 Jan. 1171. He had several wives, of whom Mor, dau. of Muirchertach Ua Tuathail (O'Toole) was the mother of his dau. Aoife. Mor d. 1164.
7. AOIFE (or **EVE**) **OF LEINSTER,** living 1186, m. ca. 1171, **RICHARD DE CLARE** (66-26), Earl of Pembroke, d. ca. 20 Apr. 1176. (CP X 352-357).

KINGS OF WALES

Line 176

1. LLEWELLYN AP SEISYLL, d. 1023, Prince of North Wales 980-1023; m. 994, Angharat, dau. of Maredudd ap Owain.

2. GRIFFITH I AP LLEWELLYN, slain 5 Aug. 1063, Prince of North Wales; m. as 1st wife ca. 1057, **EDITH** (or **ALDGYTH**) (176A-4) who m. (2) ca. 1064, Harold, Earl of East Anglia (**HAROLD II** (1B-23), King of England), dau. of Elgar (Aelfgar), Earl of Mercia 1057 (ASC 1035, 1051, 1053, 1055, 1057, 1058; CCN 444, 604), son of Leofwine, d. bef. 1032, Earl of Mercia (ASC 1017; CCN 604). (CP VI, 451-453; DNB 23:307; NGSQ 50: 76-77).

3. NESTA, b. ca. 1055/7, dau. of Griffith and Edith; m. perhaps, Trahaern of Arwystli, d. 1081, Prince of North Wales. This marriage is very doubtful. It is probable that Llywarch was son of another woman. See Line 177 for her proven descendants.

* * *

4. LLYWARCH, prob. son of Trahaern by another woman, d. ca. 1129; m. Dyddgu, of Builth.

5. GLADYS, m. **OWAIN I GWYNED** (239-6), d. 1170, Prince of North Wales.

6. IORWORTH, Prince of North Wales; m. Maret of Powys-Vadoc. (CP IX 276).

7. LLEWELLYN AP IORWORTH, the Great, 1173-1240, Prince of North Wales; m. **JOAN** (27-27), natural dau. of **JOHN** (1-26), King of England. (CP IX 276; ASC; Turton 76, 119, 120; Jacobus: Bulkeley Genealogy 87-88). He had a number of mistreses, one of which, Tangwystl, was the mother of **GWLADYS DHU** (27-28) who m. Ralph de Mortimer.

Line 176A

1. LEOFWINE, d. by 1032, ealdorman of the Hwiccas, 1017 Earl of Mercia. (See refs. 176-2).

2. LEOFRIC, d. Bromley, Staffs 31 Aug. 1057, founder of the church of Coventry, seen as thegn from 1005, "dux" from 1026, Earl of Mercia by 1032, m. prob. by 1030 (pos. as her (2) husb.) Godgifu (or Godiva) b. prob. ca. 1010, sister of Thorold of Buckingham, sheriff of Lincs. Godgifu's ancestry is uncertain, but she was evidently of an old, noble family. She is the "Lady Godiva" of legend. They had one known child. (See refs. 176-2).

3. AELFGAR, of age 1051, d. shortly after 1062, Earl of East Anglia 1053, Earl of Mercia 1057, banished 1058; m. Aelfgifu by whom 3 known sons: Eadwine, Morkere and Burchard whose issue is unknown; and a dau. Aldgyth.

4. **EDITH** (or **ALDGYTH**), seen at "Doomsday" 1086, death date unknown, m. (1) ca. 1057 **GRIFFITH AP LLEWELLYN** (176-2) slain 5 Aug. 1062; m. (2) prob. 1064 **HAROLD** (1B-23) Earl of Wessex, as Harold II, King of England. By Griffith she had a dau. Nesta (see 176-3 and 177-2). By Harold she had a son Harold, seen at Domesday 1086, later life unknown, and possibly King Harold's son Ulf. (NGSQ, vol. 50, pp. 74-78 and cited references).

Line 177

1. **GRIFFITH AP LLEWELLYN** (176-2), slain 5 Aug. 1063, Prince of North Wales, m. (1) ca. 1057 **EDITH** (or **ALDGYTH**) (176A-4). (CP I 22; VI 451-453; DNB 23:307; NGSQ 50: 74-78).

2. **NESTA**, b. ca. 1055/7; m. Osborn Fitz Richard, son of Richard fitz Scrob of Richard's Castle, d. ca. 1080. (CP I 22; VI 452-453; J.E. Lloyd: Hist. of Wales II 369, 395, 397 and note 135: DNB 23:307; NGSQ 50:76-77).

3. **NESTA**, m. Bernard de Neufmarché, d. 1093, Lord of Brecon, son of Geoffrey (son of Thurcytel) by Ada, dau. of Richard de Hugelville, and grandchild of Richard "the Good", by his dau. Papia. (CP I 22; VI 452-453).

4. **SIBYL DE NEUFMARCHÉ**, m. 1121 Miles Fitz Walter, of Gloucester, Constable, Earl of Hereford 1141, d. 24 Dec. 1143, son of Walter Fitz Roger. (CP I 21,22; VI 452-453).

5. **BERTHA**, m. ca. 1150, William de Braiose, of Brecknock, Abergavenney and Gowr, 1st Baron of Gwentland, son of Philip de Braiose of Brember in Sussex and Aenor, dau. & h. of Johel de Toteneis. (CP I 21-22; VI 452).

6. **WILLIAM DE BRAIOSE**, d. Corbeil, 9 Aug. 1211, 5th Baron de Braiose; m. Matilda de St. Valerie de Haia, d. 1210, murdered by King John who had her walled up alive in her castle walls with her young son William. (CP I 22).

7. **REGINALD DE BRAIOSE**, d. 1227/8; m. Gracia de Briwere, d. bef. 1215, dau. William de Briwere and Beatrice de Vaux. (CP I 22).

8. **WILLIAM DE BRAIOSE**, d. 2 May 1230, 6th Baron de Braiose; m. **EVE** (or **EVA**) **MARSHALL** (66-28), d. bef. 1246. (CP I 22; Dudley Pedigree).

Line 177A (Prepared by Douglas Richardson)

6. **WILLIAM DE BRAIOSE** (177-6), lord of Briouze, Bramber, Brecon, Over Gwent, etc., died Corbeil, near Paris, France, 9 Aug. 1211, Sheriff of Hereford 1192-9, m. Maud de St. Valery, starved to death by King John, 1210. (CP I 22).

7. **MARGERY** (or Margaret) **DE BRAIOSE**, d. 19 Nov. 1200, m. Walter de Lacy, b. ca. 1172, d. 1241, lord of Meath, Ireland and of Weobley, Hereford, son of Hugh de Lacy, d. 1186, by his wife Roheis de Monmouth. (Orpen: Ireland under the Normans III, chart pp. 286-

287; CP XII, pt. II, 169, footnote d).

8. GILBERT DE LACY, d. 1230, of Ewyas Harold, co. Hereford and of Trim and Weobley, m. **ISABEL BIGOD** (70-29, 71-29), dau. of Hugh Bigod, Earl of Norfolk by his wife, Maud Marshall. (CP V 437; IX 589-590; Orpen op.cit., III, chart pp. 286-287).

Line 177B (Prepared by Douglas Richardson)

7. MARGERY (or Margaret) **DE BRAOISE** (177A-7), d. 19 Nov. 1200, m. Walter de Lacy, b. ca. 1172, d. 1241, lord of Meath, Ireland, and of Weobley, Hereford, son of Hugh de Lacy, d. 1186, by his wife, Roheis de Monmouth. (Orpen: Ireland under the Normans, III, chart pp. 286-287; CP XII, pt. II, 169, footnote d).

8. EGIDIA DE LACY, m. Richard de Burgh, lord of Connaught, d. 1242, son of William de Burgh (died 1205), lord of Connaught, by his wife, a daughter of Donnell O'Brien, K.T. (Orpen op.cit. III, chart pp. 286-287; IV, chart p. 159; DNB III 328).

9. WALTER DE BURGH, b. ca. 1230, d. 28 July 1271, Earl of Ulster, m. ca. 1257, **AVELINA FITZ JOHN** (75-30, 75A-30), d. ca. 20 May 1274, dau. of Sir John Fitz Geoffrey, Justiciar of Ireland by his wife, Isabel Bigod. (Orpen, op.cit. IV, chart p. 159).

Line 178

1. RHYS AP TUDOR MAWR, Prince of South Wales (CP X 11). (See J.E. Lloyd: Hist. of Wales II 767 for his ancestry).

2. NEST, of Wales; m. Gerald of Windsor, d. bef. 1136, Constable of Pembroke Castle, 1092, son of Walter Fitz Other and Beatrice. (CP VII 200; X 10-11).

3. MAURICE FITZ GERALD, b. ca. 1100, of Windsor, Lord of Lanstephen, Wales, Steward of St. Davids (brother of David Fitz Gerald, Bishop of St. Davids), landed in Wexford, 1 Sep. 1176; m. Alice de Montgomery. (CP VII 200; X 11-12).

4. GERALD FITZ MAURICE, b. ca. 1150, d. bef. 15 Jan. 1203/4, 1st Baron of Offaly, was at the siege of Dublin, 1171; m. as her (1) husb. Eve de Bermingham, d. bef. Dec. 1226, dau. and h. of Robert de Bermingham. She brought Offaly to her first husband and his heirs. She m. (2) Geoffrey Fitz Robert, baron of Kells, and (3) Geoffrey de Marisco. (CP VII 200: X 12-14; Orpen: Ireland under the Normans IV chart p. 128).

5. MAURICE FITZ GERALD, Knt., b. 1190, d. Youghal, 1257, 2nd Baron Offaly, Knighted Jul. 1217, Lord of Lea, Justiciar of Ireland, Sep. 1232-1245, Commissioner of the Treasury and Councillor, 1250; m. Juliane. (CP VII 200: X 14-16).

6. MAURICE FITZ MAURICE FITZ GERALD, d. 1286, Lord of Offaly in Ireland, Justiciar; m. prob. 1266 Emmeline de Longespee, b. ca. 1250, d. 1291, dau. of **STEPHEN LONGESPEE** (31-27), and **EMMELINE DE RIDELISFORD.** (33A-26). (CP VII 200; X 16 note c).

7. JULIANA FITZ MAURICE, m. **THOMAS DE CLARE** (54-31). (CP VII 200; X 16, note c.)

Line 178A (Prepared by Douglas Richardson)

5. MAURICE FITZ GERALD, Knt. (178-5), b. 1190, d. 1257, 2nd Baron of Offaly, Justiciar of Ireland, m. Juliane. (CP VII 200; X 14-16).

6. THOMAS FITZ MAURICE FITZ GERALD, d. 1271, enfeoffed in Banada, co. Sligo by Maurice Fitz Maurice. (Orpen, Ireland under the Normans, IV: 128-129).

7. JOHN FITZ THOMAS FITZ GERALD, d. 12 Sep. 1316 at Laraghbryan near Maynooth, bur. Church of the Friars Minor at Kildare; 5th Baron of Offaly, 1st Earl of Kildare, m. Blanche, dau. of John Roche of Fermoy. (Orpen, op. cit.; CP VII 218-221).

8. JOAN, m. 1302 **EDMUND BUTLER** (73-31), d. 13 Sep. 1312 at London, Justiciar and Governor of Ireland. (CP II 449-450).

Line 179

Note: This line, as originally included in the 1st edition (1950), offered a 17 generation pedigree from Twdur (Tudor) Mawr, Prince (not king) of South Wales, down to Griffith Bowen, of Boston, 1638/9, copied from a pedigree certified by the York Herald in 1891 as a true copy of one filed at the Herald's Office, College of Arms, London. The only references added to the Herald's pedigree and used "to correct minor errors" in it, were Clark's Genealogies of Morgan and Glamorgan (1886), 193-211, and the pedigree of "Berry of Berrynarbor" in Vivian's Visitations of Devon, 74. Due to the absence of dates and the lack of cited contemporary evidence, the pedigree was dropped from later editions. However in Sept. 1979 Lt. Gen. Herman Nickerson, Jr., USMC Ret, published in NGSQ (vol. 67, pp. 163-165) a short discussion of the pedigree with cited references for each generation referring to better researched material, the bulk of which were to Welsh compilations and translations of early Welsh manuscripts. A footnote to the article advises the readers that full documentation has been filed in the Society's library where it may be consulted. The pedigree has therefore been reinstated in this edition, except that to conform to Gen. Nickerson's work the first seven generations have been changed to carry the pedigree back to the Norman earls of Gloucester instead of to Twdur, Prince of South Wales, as in the first edition. However, in the absence of dates, pedigrees kept by bards consisting of strings of names without biographical data on the majority of the generations are not the most convincing to the experienced genealogist.

1. MABEL, illegitimate dau. of "The Earl of Gloucester" living (infant) 1128, d. 23 Nov. 1183 (identified by Nickerson (NGSQ 67: 163-166) as ch. of **WILLIAM**, 2nd Earl of Gloucester (124-27) d. 1183, m. ca. 1158 **GRUFFUDD** ap Ifor Bach, d. 1211. (Patterson, ed., Earldom of Gloucester Charters, p. 115, states that Mabel (No. 1) was illegit. dau. of Robert, Earl of Gloucester (124-26), rather than his son William, citing Clark, Cartae et alia, I 149 n. Bartrum in his article, "The Ancestors of My Lord Herbert," National Library of Wales Journal, xvii, no. 3, Summer 1972, 237-248, shows Mabel as dau. of William as indicated by Peniarth MS 134, 137 & 225. Mabel's husband, Griffith ap Ivor Bach, held the lordship of Senghenydd of the honour of Glamorgan. Bartrum, Welsh Genealogies A.D. 300-1400, p. 209, chart Cydrich 2).

    2. RHYS Ap Gruffudd, had by an unknown wife (David Edward's "Rice Merrick m.s.", Bartrum ibid.)

    3. JOAN verch Rhys m. Sir Ralph Maelog. (Edwards cit.; Bartrum cit. and Maelog.)

    4. ANN m. **SIR GWRGI GRANT.** (Bartrum, op.cit., p. 439, chart Grant 1).

    5. JENKIN AP GWRGI, by unknown consort had (Bartrum, op.cit., chart Grant 2).

    6. GWILYM AP JENKIN, by unknown consort had (Bartrum, ibid.).

    7. ANN m. **HYWEL AP GRUFFUDD FAB.** (Bartrum, Glam. 241., chart p. 115 (Bleddyn ap Maenyrch 31).

    8. HYWEL FYCHAN AP HYWEL m. Catrin, dau. Ieuan Llwyd of Castell Odyn. (Bartrum, ibid.)

    9. GWILYM GAM AP HYWEL FYCHAN m. Gwenllian, dau. Gwilym ap Ieuan. (Bartrum 117,563).

    10. HYWEL MELYN AP GWILYM GAM of Ynys Derw, by an unknown consort (but said in the Herald pedigree to be Catharine, dau. Griffith Llewelyn Voythys.) (Bartrum, op.cit., p. 117, chart Gleddyn ap Maenrych 33; Bartrum says no. 10 m. Mabel ferch Gruffudd by whom he had No. 11).

    11. IEUAN GWYN AP HYWEL MELYN, m. Mabel, dau. of Wilcock Cradock). (Bartrum, ibid.)

    12. JENKIN m. Jonet (or in the Herald's pedigree, Joan, dau. of Thomas ap Gwilim Vachan.)

    13. OWAIN (Owen ap Jenkin) living 1566, m. Alice, dau. of John of Swansea.

    14. GRUFFUDD BOWEN of Slade, seen 1557 and 1566, m. Anne, dau. of Nicholas Berry, d. 1565, lord of Berrynarbor and Martinhoe, Devon, by his first wife, Elizabeth, dau. & sole h. of John Bowden of Bradwill, Devon. (Vivian, Visitations of Devon, p. 74).

    15. PHILIP BOWEN of Slade, m. Elsbeth, dau. Hopkin John Vaughan.

    16. FRANCIS BOWEN, renewed the lease on Slade, 10 Aug. 1591, m. Ellen, dau. Thomas Franklyn.

    17. GRIFFITH BOWEN, b. ca. 1600 prob. at Langwith, d. ca. 1675 m. 1627 Margaret dau. Henry Fleming. They emigrated to Boston 1638/9, returned to Wales ab. 1650 to Swanzey, then to London 1669. (See also Suffolk, Mass. deed, I 48).

GALLO-ROMANS AND ALSATIANS

Line 180

1. AFRANIUS SYAGRIUS, Gallo-Roman Consul, 381.

2. A daughter of Syagrius, m. Ferreolus.

3. TONANTIUS FERREOLUS, Praetorian Prefect of Gaul, 451, at Rome 469, 475; friend and relative of Sidonius Apollinaris.

4. TONANTIUS (brother of Ruricius, Bishop of Uzes, d. 506).

5. ANSBERTUS, the Gallo-Roman Senator (see 190-9); m. Blithilde whose ancestry is unproven. (Generations 1-5: David H. Kelley, in NEHGR 101: 112).

Line 181

1. ADALRIC (or Ethic), obtained the Duchy of Alsace 662, d. 20 Feb. 690, head of the Alsatian House of the Ethiconides, Duke of Alsace 662-690; m. Berswinde.

2. ADELBERT, Duke of Alsace, d. 720 (brother of St. Odile, patron saint of Alsace, d. 5 Dec. 720).

3. LUITFRIDE I, Duke of Alsace 720-750; d. ca. 750.

4. LUITFRIDE II, Count of Alsace, d. 780; m. Hiltrude.

5. HUGH III, Count of Alsace and Tours, d. ca. 839; m. Bava.

6. ADELAIDE, m. as his second wife, **ROBERT THE STRONG** (48-17, 49-17), Count of Paris, Anjou and Blois; ancestor of the Kings of France. (Generations 1-6: J.D. Schoepflin: L'Alsace Illustrée, 1851, III 566, corrected).

Line 182

1. GODEFROY, Duke of Alamannia, seen 679-708, dead 709.

2. HOUCHING (brother of Lentfroy, Duke of Alamannia, 726, of Thibaud, Duke of Alamannia 727-744, and of Oatillo, Count of Thurgau).

3. HNABI, Duke of Alamannia; count in the Linzgau in 709, 720, 724.

4. EMMA, seen 778, d. 798, m. Gerold, count in the Anglachau 779.

5. HILDEGARDE, b. 758, d. 30 Apr. 783; m. 771 the Emperor **CHARLEMAGNE** (50-13); parents of Pepin, King of Italy and of Louis I, the Fair, Emperor. Their descendants are given in Lines 50 to 169 inclusive.

Line 183

1. AIMERY IV, Vicount de Thouars, d. 1093, companion of William the Conqueror at the battle of Hastings, 1066, son of Geoffrey, Vicount de Thouars; m. Aurengarde de Mauleon.

2. ELEANOR DE THOUARS, m. 1075, Boso II, Vicount de Chastellerault, d. 1092, son of Hugh de Chastellerault and Gerberga de la Rochefoucauld.

3. AIMERY I, Vicount de Chastellerault, d. 1136; m. Dangerose.

4. ELEANOR DE CHASTELLERAULT, m. 1121, **WILLIAM VIII** or **X** (110-25), d. 9 Apr. 1137, Duke of Aquitaine, Count of Poitou.

Line 184

1. WALTER GIFFARD, d. 1084, Lord of Longueville, a companion of William the Conqueror at the battle of Hastings, 1066, son of Osbern de Bolbec, Lord of Longueville in Normandy 1028-1035, and Avelina, sister of the Duchess Gunnora; m. Agnes, dau. of Girard Flatel.

2. ROHESE GIFFARD, m. Richard Fitz Gilbert de Clare, d. bef. 1090.

3. GILBERT FITZ RICHARD, b. bef. 1066, d. 1114 or 1117, 2nd Earl of Clare; m. **ADELIZA (or ADELAIDE) DE CLERMONT** (246-24). (CP IX App. I 66).

4. GILBERT DE CLARE, d. 6 Jan. 1147/8, Earl of Pembroke, 1138; m. **ISABEL DE BEAUMONT** (66-25). (Generations 1-4: CP IV 670 chart III; Altschul, "A Baronial Family in Medieval England: The Clares, 1217-1314".)

Line 185

1. ROBERT DE MORTAIN, b. 1031, d. 1095, Earl of Cornwall, half bro. of William the Conqueror and a companion at the battle of Hastings, 1066; m. Maud de Montgomery, dau. of Roger de Montgomery, Earl of Shrewsbury. (CP XI 687).

2. EMMA DE MORTAIN, m. 1080, William IV, d. 1093, Count of Toulouse, son of Pons, Count of Toulouse, and Arlette.

3. MAUD OF TOULOUSE, m. 1094, **WILLIAM VII** (110-24), Count of Poitou, b. 22 Oct. 1071, d. 10 Feb. 1126/7.

Line 186

1. JOHN FITZ ROBERT, of Warkworth, co. Northumberland, d. 1240, Magna Charta Surety, 1215; m. (2) Ada de Baliol, d. 1251, sister of John de Baliol who m. **DEVORGILLA OF GALLOWAY** (94-28).

2. ROGER FITZ JOHN, d. 1249; m. Isabel.

3. ROBERT FITZ ROGER, d. 1247, d. 1310, Baron of Clavering; m. 1265, Margery de la Zouche, dau. Alan (see 38-28 and 39-29) (see Dodsworth ms. Bodleian Lib.; Hedley "Northumberland Fams." I 62; CP III 274-275).

4. EUPHEMIA DE CLAVERING, m. Randolph de Neville, d. 1331, 1st Baron Neville of Raby. (CP IX 502 ii-iii chart).

5. RALPH DE NEVILLE, b. 1291, d. 1367, 4th Baron Neville of Raby; m. **ALICE DE AUDLEY** (207-32), d. 1374/5, dau. of Hugh de Audley, Lord Audley, d. 1325, and Isolde de Mortimer. (Bulkeley Genealogy 77).

6. MARGARET DE NEVILLE, d. May 1372; m. (1) William de Ros of Helmsley; m. (2) **HENRY DE PERCY,** K.G. (19-31). (CP IX 708-714; X 464; IX 502 ii-iii chart).

Line 187

1. ROGER DE HUNTINGFIELD, Lord of East Bradenham, co. Norfolk; m. Alice de Senlis, d. 1204. (CP VI 671).

2. SIR WILLIAM DE HUNTINGFIELD, Magna Charta Surety, 1215, of Frampton, b. ca. 1165, d. on a crusade bef. 25 Jan. 1220/1, Keeper of Dover Castle 1203, Warden of the Cinque Ports, Sheriff of Norfolk and Suffolk 1210-1212, 1215 excommunicated by the Pope; m. by 1194, Isabel, d. 1207, dau. of William Fitz Roger of Gressinghall, Norfolk, and wid. of Osmond de Stuteville. (CP VI 671-672).

3. SIR ROGER DE HUNTINGFIELD, of Huntingfield, co. Suffolk, and Frampton, d. ca. 10 Jul. 1257; m. (2) 1236, Joan de Hobrugg, d. ca. 7 Sep. 1297, dau. of William de Hobrugg. (CP IV 673-674).

4. SIR WILLIAM DE HUNTINGFIELD, of Huntingfield, b. 24 Aug. 1237, d. bef. 2 Nov. 1290; m. (1) Emma de Grey, d. 1264, dau. of Sir John de Grey of Shirland, co. Derby, and Emma de Glanville, dau. of Geoffrey de Glanville. (CP VI 171, 674-675).

5. SIR ROGER DE HUNTINGFIELD, of Huntingfield and Frampton, summoned for military service 14 Jun. 1294, d. bef. 5 Dec. 1302; m. ca. 1277, Joyce d'Engaine, dau. of Sir John d'Engaine of Colne Engaine and Laxton, co. Northampton, and Joan de Greinville, dau. of Sir Gilbert de Greinville of Hatton. (CP VI 676-677).

6. JOAN DE HUNTINGFIELD, m. Sir Richard Basset, 1st Lord Basset of Weldon, Great Weldon, co. Northampton, b. ca. 1273, minor in 1291, taken prisoner at Bannockburn, d. bef. 18 Aug. 1314. (CP II 10,13).

6A. RALPH BASSET of Great Weldon, b. 27 Aug. 1300, custody of father's lands 1314 to Richard Grey of Codnor, of age 29 Mar 1322; m. Joan, sd. to be a Sturdon of Winterbourne, Gloucs. He d. shortly bef. 4 May 1341. She m. (2) Robert de Fourneux bef. 1346 when both living. Ralph & Joan were parents of No. 7.

7. JOAN BASSET, m. Thomas de Aylesbury of Aylesbury, d. bef. 1350. (CP II 13).

8. SIR JOHN AYLESBURY, of Milton Keynes, co. Buckingham, d. 1410; m. Isabel Strange, dau. of Eubolo le Strange of Knokyn. (Le Strange Records, Hamon le Strange, 1916, pp. 321, 337-8.)

9. SIR THOMAS AYLESBURY, of Milton Keynes, b. ca. 1369, d. 9 Sep. 1418; m. Katherine Pabenham, b. 1372, d. 17 Jun. 1436, dau. of Sir Lawrence de Pabenham of Pabenham, co. Buckingham, d. 10 Jun. 1399, and Elizabeth Engaine, dau. of Sir John d'Engaine, 2nd Lord Engaine. (CP V 80 chart).

10. ELEANOR AYLESBURY, m. **SIR HUMPHREY STAFFORD**, Knt. (55-36), of Grafton, co. Warwick, b. 1400, living 1467.

11. SIR HUMPHREY STAFFORD, Knt., of Grafton, co. Worcester, executed at Tyburn, 8 Jul. 1486; m. Catherine Fray, dau. of Sir John Fray, Chief Baron of the Exchequer. (CP II 136, lines 3 and 4: Genealogist, n.s. 31: 173).

12. ANNE STAFFORD, m. Sir William Berkeley, K.B., of Stoke-Gifford, Sheriff of Gloucester, 1485. (CP II 136, lines 3 and 4).

13. RICHARD BERKELEY, of Stoke-Gifford; m. Elizabeth Conningsby, dau. of Sir Humphrey Conningsby, Knt.

14. SIR JOHN BERKELEY, of Stoke-Gifford; m. Isabel Dennis, dau. of Sir William Dennis, Knt., and Anne Berkeley (MCS 66/10).

15. ELIZABETH BERKELEY, m. **HENRY LYGON** (84-37) . . . (Visitation of Gloucester 204-206. Generations 1-14: Boston Evening Transcript, 9 Jul. 1938; with continuation to Deighton (line 84).

Line 188

6. JOAN DE HUNTINGFIELD (187-6), m. Sir Richard Basset. (CP II 10-13).

7. RALPH BASSET, b. 27 Aug. 1300, d. bef. 4 May 1341, summoned for service against the Scots, 5 Apr. 1327; m. Joan. (CP II 10-13).

8. ALIANORE BASSET, m. Sir John Knyvet of Southwick, co. Northampton, Chief Justice of the King's Bench, Lord Chancellor of England, d. 1381. (Banks I 158; DNB; CP II 10-13).

9. SIR JOHN KNYVET, m. Joan, dau. John de Botetourt (see 216-29). (Banks I 158. Generations 6-9: CP II 10-13).

10. SIR JOHN KNYVET, m. Elizabeth Clifton, dau. of Constantine Clifton and Elizabeth Scales, dau. of Robert, Lord Scales.

11. SIR JOHN KNYVET, m. Alice Lynne, dau. of William Lynne. (Surtees Soc.Pub. 144: 10, 155).

12. SIR WILLIAM KNYVET, m. Alice de Grey, dau. of John de Grey (brother of Reynold de Grey, Lord Grey of Ruthyn). (Banks I 158).

13. SIR EDMUND KNYVET, d. in a sea fight, temp. Henry VIII; m. Eleanor Tyrrel, dau. of Sir William Tyrrel, Knt. (Banks I 158).

14. SIR EDMUND KNYVET, of Ashwellthorpe; m. **JOAN** (or

Line 188 (cont.)

Jane) **BOURCHIER** (4-36). (Generations 6-14: Banks I 158; Surtees Soc. 144; Banks: Dormant and Extinct Peerage (1837) IV and App. I 20; Meredith B. Colket, Jr., in TAG 14: 10-12; Berry: Berkshire Pedigrees 55).

Line 189

1. SIR WILLIAM MALET (234A-28), d. ca. 1216, held barony of Curry Malet, Somerset, Sheriff of Somerset and Dorset, Magna Charta Surety, 1215; m. Alice Basset, dau. of Thomas Basset.

2. HAWISE MALET, m. (1) Sir Hugh Poyntz, d. sh. bef. 4 Apr. 1220; m. (2) bef. 11 Feb. 1220/1, Sir Robert de Muscegros, of Charlton, co. Somerset, d. sh. bef. 29 Jan. 1253/4.

3. SIR JOHN DE MUSCEGROS, of Charlton, b. 10 Aug. 1232, d. 8 May 1275; m. Cecily, d. 10 Aug. 1301, dau. of Sir William Avenal. (CP V 308 and notes a. b, c, e).

4. SIR ROBERT DE MUSCEGROS, b. ca. 1252, d. 27 Dec. 1280; m. Agnes, living 9 May 1281, dau. of **WILLIAM DE FERRERS** (127-30) and **MARGARET DE QUINCY** (57-29), dau. of **ROGER DE QUINCY** (53-28). (Sir Christopher Hatton's Book of Seals in Northants Rec.Soc. 1950, No. 98, p. 64; CP cit.; Hatton, cit., appears to answer note c completely).

5. HAWISE DE MUSCEGROS, b. 21 Dec. 1276, d. aft. Jun. 1340; m. bef. 1300, **SIR JOHN FERRERS** (57-31), of Southoe and Keystone, b. Cardiff, 22 Jun. 1271, d. Gascony, Aug. 1312, 1st Baron Ferrers of Chartley; she m. (3) Sir John de Bures, d. Bodington, 22 Dec. 1350. (CP V 305-310).

6. CATHERINE DE BURES, b. bef. 1315, living Oct. 1355; m. bef. 21 May 1329, **SIR GILES DE BEAUCHAMP** (84-30). (Generations 106: CP V 320-321 chart).

RIPARIAN BRANCH

OF THE MEROVINGIAN HOUSE

Line 190

1. **CLOVIS THE RIPARIAN**, Frankish King of Cologne, living 420, kinsman of Clovis I.
2. **CHILDEBERT**, King of Cologne, living 450.
3. **SIGEBERT THE LAME**, King of Cologne; murdered 509, by his own son at the instigation of Clovis I, King of the Salic Franks, 481-511.
4. **CLODERIC** the Parricide, King of Cologne, murdered 509, by agents of his kinsman, Clovis I, King of the Salic Franks. The identity of his wife is uncertain.
5. **MUNDERIC**, of Vitry-en-Perthois, very young in 509, when his father was murdered; revolted against Thierry I, who killed him.
6. **ST. GONDOLFUS**, Bp. of Tongres, consecrated 599 (brother of Bodegeisel I). He was almost certainly father of Bodegeisel II (gen. 7), not Bodegeisel I as shown in earlier editions. (Correction by Prof. Kelley).
7. **BODEGEISEL II**, m. Oda, Suevian.
8. **SAINT ARNULF**, b. ca. 13 Aug. 582, d. 16 Aug. 640, Mayor of the Palace and tutor of Dagobert; Bishop of Metz 612; m. abt. 596, Dode (Clothilde) who became a nun at Trèves 612. (They were the parents of St. Clodulf, Bishop of Metz, ca. 650; d. 690).
9. **DUKE ANSGISE**, b. 602, d. 685, Mayor of the Palace to Siegbert, 632, son of Dagobert; m. bef. 639, St. Begga, d. 694, dau. of Pepin of Landen, Mayor of the Palace in Austrasia, d. 694, and his wife Itta, presumed dau. of Arnoldus, Bsp. of Metz, son, it is said, of **ANSBERTUS**, the Senator (180-5).
10. **PEPIN OF HERISTAL**, Mayor of the Palace in Austrasia, d. 714; by concubine, Aupais, he was father of Charles Martel.
11. **CHARLES MARTEL**, b. 689, d. 741, Mayor of the Palace in Austrasia; victor over the Saracens at Poitiers, 732; m. (1) Rotrou, d. 724, sister of a Wido, identified without proof by the Abbé Chaume as son of St. Liévin, Bishop of Trèves.
12. **PEPIN THE SHORT**, b. 714, d. 768, Mayor of the Palace; deposed the last of the Fainéant (Merovingian) kings and became himself the first king of the Franks of the second race, 751-768; m. Bertha, d. 783, dau. of Count Canbert of Laon.
13. **CHARLEMAGNE** (50-13), b. 2 Apr. 747, d. Aix la Chapelle, 28 Jan. 813/4, King of France 768-814, crowned Holy Roman Emperor, 25 Dec. 800; one of the great men in history; m. ca. 771, **HILDEGARDE** (182-5), b. ca. 758, d. 30 Apr. 783, dau. of Count Geroud of Swabia. (Generations 1-13: NEHGR 98: 304-306, and

Line 190 (cont.)

corrected in 101: 109-112 charts, etc.: Boston Evening Transcript, 23 Jan. 1936 and 20 May 1937, citing J. Depoin: Grandes Figures Monocales au Temps Mérovingiens, in Revue Mabillon, XI (1921), 245-258; XII (1922) 13-15, 105-118; Cambridge Mediaeval History; Turton; L'Abbé Chaume: Les Origins de Duché de Bourgogne I 530-551. Generations 8-13: D.L. Jacobus in Boston Evening Transcript, Note 2257, Part IX: Anselme; Thatcher table p. 318).

Line 191

11. CHARLES MARTEL (190-11), b. 689, d. 741-4, Mayor of the Palace; m. (2) Swanhilde, a Bavarian.

12. CARLOMAN, d. 754, Mayor of the Palace; prob. m. a dau. of Alard, brother of Garnier, ancestor of the Margraves of Spoleto.

13. ROTRUDE, m. Girard, Count of Paris 743-755.

14. BEGUE, d. 816, Count of Paris, Chamberlain of Louis of Aquitaine 776; m. (2) Aupals (Alpais), natural dau. of **CHARLEMAGNE** (50-13).

15. ENGELTRON (dau.), m. (1) Hunroch, Margrave of Friuli.

16. EBERHARD, d. 864, Margrave of Friuli; m. **GISELE** (146-15), d. 1 Jul. 874, dau. of the Emperor Louis I and Judith of Bavaria. (See Chaume: Les Origins de Duché de B., I 542, 551-552, etc., and Moriarty: The Conradins in NEHGR 99: 342 chart).

Line 192

15. ENGELTRON (191-15), m. (1) Hunroch, Margrave of Friuli.

16. A daughter (sister of Eberhard, Margrave of Friuli), m. Gebhard, Count of Logenahe 832-860.

17. EUDES, Count of Logenahe 861-879; m. (prob.) a dau. of Conrad I of Burgundy.

18. CONRAD THE OLD, d. 906, Count of Logenahe; m. Glismode of Worms, d. 924, dau. of Uta and Walahon, Count of Worms, granddau. of Meingaud, Count of Worms 862-881, and great-granddau. of Witichin, Count of Soissons 835-844.

19. WERNER, Count of Worms.

20. CONRAD THE WISE, d. 955, Duke of Lorraine and Franconia, killed in the battle of Lechfeld; m. 947, **LUITGARDE** (45-18), dau. of the Emperor Otto the Great, and Edith, dau. of Edward the Elder, of England, and granddau. of Alfred the Great, King of England. (Generations 15-20: Chaume: Les Origins de Duché de Bourgogne I 542, 551-552, etc.; G.A. Moriarty: The Conradins in NEHGR 99: 342, and chart).

ADDITIONAL LINES

Line 193

4. SIBYL DE NEUFMARCHÉ (177-4), m. 1121, Miles Fitz Walter, cr. Earl of Hereford 1143, d. 24 Dec 1143. (CP I 22: IV 669 chart).

5. MARGARET OF HEREFORD, d. 1146; m. Humphrey de Bohun III, Baron de Bohun, Lord of Hereford. (CP I 22).

6. HUMPHREY DE BOHUN IV, d. 1182, Baron de Bohun, Lord of Hereford, Constable of England; m. **MARGARET OF HUNTINGDON** (97-26). (Generations 4-6: CP I 22; IV 669 chart; VII 457).

Line 194

5. BERTHA OF HEREFORD (177-5), m. ca. 1150, William de Braiose.

6. SIBYL DE BRAIOSE, prob. living ca. 5 Feb. 1227/8; m. William de Ferrers, 3rd Earl of Derby, d. at Acre 1190, bef. 21 Oct., on a crusade. (CP IV 192-194, 771).

7. WILLIAM DE FERRERS, d. 22 Sep. 1247, 4th Earl of Derby; m. 1192, **AGNES OF CHESTER** (127-29), Lady of Chartley, d. 2 Nov. 1247. (CP IV 192-196, 771; V 320 chart).

Line 195

25. HENRY I (121-25), b. 1070, d. 1 Dec. 1135, King of England. (CP V 736; VII 737).

26. ROHESE, living 1175/6 (natural dau. of Henry I and Sibyl Corbet); m. 1146, Henry de la Pomerai, a great Devonshire baron, son and h. of Joscelin de la Pomerai, commander in Normandy 1136, d. 1167. (They left sons Henry and Joscelin. CP XI App. D, p. 119).

27. HENRY DE LA POMEROY, living 1193, of Berry Pomeroy; m. (1) Matilda. (CP XI App. D, p. 119; Powley: House of de la Pomerai).

28. HENRY DE LA POMEROY, d. 1207; m. Alice de Vere, d. 1206. (Powley, cit.)

29. HENRY DE LA POMEROY, d. 1220, Governor of Rougemont Castle, Exeter, 1211-1215, Sheriff of Devon 1215; m. Joan de Vautort. (Powley, cit.)

Line 196 Cancelled.

Line 197

28. ISABEL MAUDUIT (84-28), great-great-granddau. of William de Warenne and Isabel de Vermandois; m. William Beauchamp of

Elmley Castle.
    29. JOHN BEAUCHAMP, of Holt, co. Warcester, living 1297. (CP II 45; VCH Worc. III 403).
    30. RICHARD BEAUCHAMP, of Holt, d. 1325; m. Eustache. (Ibid.)
    31. SIR JOHN BEAUCHAMP, Knt., b. 1319, d. 12 May 1388, knighted 1385, Justice of North Wales; m. ca. 1370, Joan, b. 25 Mar. 1352, living 1384, dau. of Robert Fitzwith. (CP II 45-46; VCH Worc. III 403-404: VCH Warw. VI 46).
    32. SIR JOHN BEAUCHAMP, Lord Beauchamp of Kyderminster, d. Sep. 1420; m. Isabel Ferrers, a niece of the Countess of Warwick. (CP II 46 note d; VCH Worc. III 298; VCH Warw. VI 46).
    33. MARGARET BEAUCHAMP, b. 1400; m. (2) aft. 1422, Sir John de Wysham, living 1428. (CP II 46 note d; VCH Worc. III 298; VCH Warw. VI 47).
    34. ALICE WYSHAM, d. 1487; m. John de Guise of Apsley Guise and Holt, 1472. (VCH Worc. III 298, 404; VCH Warw. VI 47; Burke, 1938, pp. 1174-1175).
    35. JOHN GYSE (or Guise), Knt., of Apsley Gyse, Beds. and Elmore, Gloucs., d. 30 Sep. 1501, Inq.p.m. 17 Hen. VII no. 18., Papal disp. for m. 15 May 17 Apr. o.s.) 1484 to Anne Berkeley of Stoke Gifford, his wife who survived him. By her, father of No. 36. VCH Worc. III 404; Burke's Peerage (1938) 1174-1175; Trans. Bristol and Gloucs.Arch.Soc. III 57-58).
    36. JOHN GYSE, Esq. of Elmore, Gloucs., b. ca. 1485 (ae. 16+ at father's death), d. at Brockworth, Gloucs. 20 Dec. 1556, bur. Elmore, Inq.p.m. 3 and 4 Philip and Mary pt. 2, no. 73; m. ca. 1510 **TACY** (Tasy, Thomasine) **DE GREY** (207-39), bur. Elmore 15 Nov. 1558, dau. "Lord Grey de Wilton". Dec. 13, 31 Hen. VIII (1539) John Gyse and Tase, and their son Anselme and his wife Alice (prob. just m.) exchanged manors and lordships of "Asple Gyse, co. Beds., and Wyggyngton, co. Oxon" with the King for manor and lordship of Brockworth, etc. Deed recites that John Gyse had indentured 24 Feb. 10 Hen. VIII (1518-9) covenanting to convey to his young son Anselme on m. to Alice dau. James Clifford of Frampton-upon-Severne estates in Wyggyngton, and in further agreements same date both parents undertook to share equally the costs of "school learning, meat, drink, apparel" of Anselme until aged 17 and if Alice die, Anselme to have another Clifford dau. within 10 years of his age. Anselme d.s.p. 9 May 1563 (Inq.p.m. 5 Eliz No. 22) next heir his brother William aged 49+. (Bristol and Gloucs. cit. 59-61).
    37. WILLIAM GYSE, 2nd son but event. h., b. ca. 1514, d. 7 Sep. 1574 (Inq.p.m. 17 Eliz. No. 50), bur. Elmore 9 Sep. 1574, will dated 10 Mar. 1568-9, Gloucs.; m. Mary, dau. John Rotsy of Colmore, King's Norton, Worcs. by Margaret, dau. John Walsh of Sheldesley Walsh, co. Worc., bur. 24 Nov. 1558 at Elmore. (cit. 61-2, 70).
    38. JOHN GYSE of Elmore and Brockworth, s. and h., b. ca. 1540 (ae. 34+ at father's death), d. 24, bur. 26 Jan. 1587/8, will dated 1 Dec. 1577, pro. 12 Nov. 1588 (Inq.p.m. 30 Eliz. pt. 1, No. 131); m. Jane, dau. Richard Pauncefort of Hasefield (m. at Elmore 27 Jun.

Line 197 (cont.)

1564), she bur. 27 Jun. 1587. (cit. 62-63, 70: VCH Warw. V 148; VI 47; Oxford VI 9; VIII 255; see also for all Gyse generations, Harleian Soc. Pub. XXI (Gloucs. 1623) 72-73).

39. ELIZABETH GYSE, bp. Elmore, 1 Aug. 1576; m. at Kenn, co. Somerset, 7 Jul. 1604, Robert Haviland of Tewkesbury, Gloucs. (cit. 71; Harleian Soc.Pub. XXI 72-73, 78).

40. JANE HAVILAND, bapt. St. Werbergh's Church, Bristol, 2 Aug. 1612, d. bef. 1642; m. 27 Apr. 1629, Capt. William Torrey, bapt. 21 Dec. 1608, d. Weymouth, Mass., 10 Jun. 1690, son of Philip and Alice (Richards) Torrey, will made 15 May 1686, pro. at Boston, Jul. 1691, freeman, Weymouth, 1642, deputy, 1642-47, 1648, 1649, 1679-1683, member of the Anc. & Hon. Art. Co. (Bishops Register at Welles; Torrey Gen., I 13, 15-16; Waters I 498-499, 555-556).

41. WILLIAM TORREY, b. England, 1638, d. Weymouth, 11 Jan. 1717/8; m. ca. 1669, Deborah Greene, b. Warwick, R.I., 10 Aug. 1649, d. Weymouth, 8 Feb. 1728/9, dau. of Deputy-Governor John and Ann (Almy) Greene of R.I.; they had children including a son, **DEACON HAVILAND TORREY**, b. Weymouth, 1684, who left issue. (Blake-Torrey Gen., 68-76).

Line 198

36. MATILDA CLIFFORD (5-36), m. **SIR EDMUND SUTTON**, Knt. (81-37).

37. DOROTHY SUTTON, m. Richard Wrottesley, of Wrottesley, High Sheriff of Staffordshire, 1492, 1502, 1516. (George Adlard: Sutton Dudleys, N.Y., 1862, ped. A; Burke: Peerage, 1938, p. 2631).

38. ELEANOR WROTTESLEY, m. Richard Lee, Esq., of Langley, Salop.

39. DOROTHY LEE, m. (mar. settlement 27 Jul. 1566), Thomas Mackworth of Betton Grange, living 10 Jan. 1585, son of John and Elizabeth (Hosier) Mackworth.

40. RICHARD MACKWORTH, of Betton Grange; m. Dorothy Cranage, dau. of Laurence Cranage, gent. (Generations 38-40: Burke, 1938, p. 1640).

41. AGNES MACKWORTH (sister of Col. Humphrey Mackworth of Betton Grange, Governor of Shrewsbury); m. (1) Richard Watts, d. 1635; m. (2) bef. 1640, Col. William Crowne, gent., b. ca. 1617, d. Boston, Mass., will dated 24 Dec. 1682, pro. 28 Feb. 1682/3; appointed Rouge-Dragon, 14 Sep. 1638; Lt.-Col., 1650; at the coronation of Charles II, 23 Apr. 1661. Their son Henry Crowne left issue. (NEHGR 5:46, 249; 58: 406-410; Blore: Hist. of Rutland; Lipscombe: Hist. of Buckinghamshire).

Line 199

34. MARGARET STANLEY (20-34), m. (1) Sir William Troutbeck, Knt., b. ca. 1432, d. 1459, of Dunham-on-the-Hill, co. Chester; m. (2) 1460, Sir John Boteler, Knt., Lord of Warrington, d. 26 Feb. 1463; m. (3) a Lord Grey of Codnor, N.B. (CP I 205).

Line 199 (cont.)

35. JOAN TROUTBECK, m. (2) Sir William Griffith of Penryhn, co. Carnarvon, Chamberlain of North Wales (Dwnn II 167-168).

36. SIR WILLIAM GRIFFITH, of Penrhyn, living 1520; m. **JANE** (199A-36), dau. of Thomas Stradling of St. Donat's, co. Glamorgan. (Dwnn II 154-159).

37. DOROTHY GRIFFITH, m. William Williams, Esq., of Cochwillan, co. Carnarvon (son, according to Burke, of William Williams and Lowry, dau. of Henry Salusbury, Esq., of Llanrhaidadr, cf. Burke, Peerage (1847), p. 1046). (Ibid. 166).

38. JANE WILLIAMS, m. William Coytemore, co. Carnarvon. (Generations 34-38: Anthony R. Wagner, Esq., in Genealogist VIII 204; Lewis Dwnn: Heraldic Visitations of Wales, 1846, II 167-168).

39. ROWLAND COYTEMORE, grantee of the second charter of Virginia, 23 May 1607 (undoubtedly identical with the Rowland Coytemore mentioned in Dwnn, op.cit.), widower at Wapping, d. 1626, will pro. Canterbury, 24 Nov. 1626; m. (1) Whitechapel, co. Middlesex, 28 Mar. 1594-5, Dorothy Harris; m. (2) Harwich, co. Essex, 23 Dec. 1610, Katherine (Miles) Gray, d. Charlestown, Mass., 28 Nov. 1659, wid. of Thomas Gray, bapt. Harwich, 18 Aug. 1572, bur. Harwich, 7 May 1607, whom she had m. in 1592. (Waters I 160-171, 404; NEHGR 106: 15).

40. ELIZABETH COYTEMORE, b. ca. 1617 (child of 3rd wife; m. as (2) wife, Capt. William Tyng (brother of Col. Edward Tyng of Boston), b. ca. 1605, Treasurer of the Mass. Bay Colony 1640-1644, d. Braintree, Mass., 18 Jan. 1652/3. They were ancestors of President John Quincy Adams and many other distinguished New Englanders. (Waters I 160-171, 404; NEHGR 34: 253, 259; 106: 15; see TAG 32: 16-17; see also MC, Line 103).

Line 199A

33. JOAN BEAUFORT (234-32), m. Sir Edward Stradling.

34. SIR HENRY STRADLING, Knt., s. and h. of St. Donat's Castle, b. ca. 1423, ae. 30 in 1453, knighted at the Holy Sepulchre, Jerusalem, 1477, d. soon at Famagusta, Cyprus; m. Elizabeth, dau. Sir William ap Thomas of Raglan Castle, who d. 1446. (TAG 32: 11).

35. THOMAS STRADLING, of St. Donat's Castle, b. ca. 1454/5, d. 8 Sep. 1480 "being under the age of 26"; m. Janet Mathew, d. 1485, dau. of Thomas Mathew of Radyr, co. Glamorgan. She m. (2) Sir Rhys ap Thomas, K.G. (TAG 32: 11-12).

36. JANE STRADLING, b. ca. 1477-80, d. by 1520; m. as (1) wife, **SIR WILLIAM GRIFFITH,** Knt. (199-36), of Penrhyn Castle, co. Carnarvon, Chamberlain of North Wales, High Sheriff of Carnarvon 1493/4, banneret 1513; m. (2) Jane Puleston.

Line 200

30. MILICENT DE CANTELOU (66-30); m. **EUDO LA ZOUCHE** (38-29).

31. SIR WILLIAM LA ZOUCHE, 1st Lord Zouche of

Haryngworth; m. before 15 Feb. 1295/6 Maud, dau. of **JOHN**, 1st Lord Lovel (215-29).

32. MILICENT LA ZOUCHE, m. bef. 26 Mar. 1326, Sir William Deincourt of Blankney, co. Lincoln, Lord Deincourt, d. 2 Jun. 1364, son of John Deincourt. (CP IV 122, 290). Parents of No. 34.

34. MARGARET DEINCOURT, m. Sir Robert de Tibetot, Lord Tibetot, of Nettlestead, Suffolk. (CP IV 290). (See MC-30-9).

35. ELIZABETH DE TIBETOT, b. ca. 1371, d. bef. June 1424; m. (2) Sir Philip le Despenser, Knt., of Goxhill, Camoys Manor, b. ca. 1365, d. 20 Jun. 1424, Knt., ca. 1385. (CP IV 290).

36. MARGERY DESPENSER, d. ca. Apr. 1478; m. (2) 25 Jun. 1423, Sir Roger Wentworth, Knt., d. 24 Oct. 1445, of North Elmsall, co. York, son of John Wentworth. (CP IV 290).

37. HENRY WENTWORTH, of Cobham Hall, Wethersfield, co. Essex, d. 22 Mar. 1482/3; m. (1) Elizabeth Howard, dau. of Henry Howard, son of Sir John Howard. (Wentworth Genealogy (1878) I 27).

38. MARGERY WENTWORTH, bur. Bures, Suffolk, 7 May 1540; m. bef. 1483, Sir William Waldegrave, K.B., bur. Bures, 30 Jan. 1527/8.

39. GEORGE WALDEGRAVE, Esq., of Smallbridge; m. **ANNE** (257-39), dau. of Sir Robert Drury. (Musket II 345).

40. PHILLIS WALDEGRAVE (sister of Sir William Waldegrave); m. Thomas Higham, son of Sir John Higham of Higham, co. Suffolk.

41. BRIDGET HIGHAM, living 1595; m. (1) Thomas Burrough, Esq., bapt., Wickhambrook, co. Suffolk, d. 19 Jun. 1597, son of William Burrough, gent.; will made 12 May 1595, pro. 26 Jun. 1597; arms granted 1596.

42. REV. GEORGE BURROUGH, LL.B., bapt. Wickhambrook, 26 Oct. 1579, bur. Pettaugh, 24 Feb. 1653; LL.B., Trinity Hall, 1600; Rector of Pettaugh, 1604, and of Gosbeck, 1621; m. Frances, dau. of Nicholas Sparrow of Wickhambrook, and sister of Nicholas Sparrow of Gosbeck.

43. NATHANIEL BURROUGH, of Limehouse, co. Middlesex, living 1663, will dated 1681, pro. 23 Mar. 1682; m. (Rebecca), sister of John Style of Stepney, co. Middlesex, will made 26 Oct. 1685.

44. REV. GEORGE BURROUGHS, A.B., b. ca. 1650, executed for witchcraft, Salem, 19 Aug. 1692, ae. 42; Harvard College, A.B., 1670; minister at Portland, Me., 1674-1676, 1683-1690; ord. Danvers, Mass., 25 Nov. 1680. (Generations 34-44; J.J. Muskett: Suffolk Manorial Families, London, 1900, I 311-314; Weis: Colonial Clergy of N.E., Lancaster, 1936, p. 47; Waters I 737).

Line 201

37. ELIZABETH FITZ HUGH (78-37), m. (2) Nicholas Vaux, Lord Harrowden, d. 14 May 1523. (CP V 428; VI 398; X 309; Throckmorton Genealogy 106; Burke: Peerage, 1923, pp. 2176, 2223-2224).

38. KATHARINE VAUX, m. Sir Thomas Throckmorton, Knt., of Coughton, co. Warwick, d. 6 Aug. 1552, son of Robert and Elizabeth (Baynham) Throckmorton. (Throckmorton Gen., 105, 164-166; Burke,

2176). (DNB says Katharine Vaux was wife of George Throckmorton).

39. CLEMENT THROCKMORTON, of Haseley, co. Warwick, d. 14 Dec. 1573, M.P. 1541, 1562, 1572; m. Katherine Neville, dau. of Sir Edward Neville, of Aldington, Knt., and Eleanor, dau. of Lord Windsor. (Throckmorton Gen., 165; Burke, 2176).

40. KATHERINE THROCKMORTON, m. as third wife, Thomas Harby of Adston, Northants, son of William Harby of Ashby. (Throckmorton Gen., 166).

41. KATHERINE HARBY, m. Daniel Oxenbridge, "Dr. of Phisick," of Daventry, Northants, son of the Rev. John Oxenbridge, scholar and divine. (Throckmorton Gen., 166).

42. THE REVEREND JOHN OXENBRIDGE, A.M., b. Daventry, 30 Jan. 1608/9; matric. Emmanuel Coll., Cambridge, 1626; Magdelen Hall, Oxford, A.B., 1628, A.M., 1631; inst. First Chh. in Boston, Mass., 10 Apr. 1670; d. Boston, 28 Dec. 1674; m. (2) Frances Woodward, dau. of Rev. Hezekiah Woodward of Uxbridge, England. (Waters I 418-423, 442; Weis: Colonial Clergy of N.E., 155).

43. THEODORA OXENBRIDGE, b. 1658, d. Milton, Mass., 18 Nov. 1697; m. 21 Nov. 1677, Rev. Peter Thacher, A.M. (H.C., 1671). The various Oxenbridge Thachers (H.D., 1698, 1738, 1796 and 1901) were among their descendants. (Weis, op.cit., 155, 210, etc.)

Line 202

32. ROGER DE CLIFFORD (26-32), Lord Clifford, 13 Jul. 1389; m. Maud de Beauchamp, dau. of **THOMAS DE BEAUCHAMP** (87-31), and **KATHERINE DE MORTIMER** (120-34). (CP III 292).

33. KATHARINE CLIFFORD, m. Ralph de Greystoke, b. 18 Oct. 1353, d. Apr. 1418, Lord Greystoke. (CP VI 190-196).

34. MAUD DE GREYSTOKE, m. Eudo de Welles, eldest son of Sir John de Welles, Lord Welles, of Gainsby, and Eleanor de Mowbray, dau. of **ELIZABETH DE SEGRAVE** (16-31). (CP VI 196; v.Redlich 216; TAG 37: 114-115; 38: 180).

35. SIR LIONEL DE WELLES, K.G., d. Towton, 29 Mar. 1461, Baron Welles, Governor of Ireland 1438-1442; m. ca. 1426, Joan de Waterton, dau. of Robert de Waterton, co. York. (v.Redlich 216).

36. MARGARET DE WELLES, d. bef. 1504; m. Sir Thomas Dymoke, Knt., of Scrivelsby, co. Lincoln, son of Sir Philip Dymoke, b. ca. 1428, beheaded 12 Mar. 1470; ancestors of President George Washington. (v.Redlich 216; Harleian Soc.Pub., vol. 53 (Lincolnshire Pedigrees) 1204; Samuel Lodge, "Scrivelsby, Home of the Champions," 56; Burke: Landed Gentry, 1937, 372).

37. SIR LIONEL DYMOKE, Knt., d. 17 Aug. 1519; twice m. and by Joan, dau. of Richard Griffith, he had (Harl. Soc. 53: 1204; Lodge 56; Burke 372).

38. ANNE DYMOKE, m. John Goodrick, of Kirby, Lincolnshire. (Genealogist IV 31: Harl.Soc. (Linc. Pedigrees), vol. 51, p. 416; Early Chancery Proceedings, Bundle 444/43 which identifies her as Anne and her mother as Johanne).

39. LIONEL GOODRICK, m. prob. Winifred, dau. of Henry Sapcott, of Lincolnshire. (Authorities as for generation 38).

40. ANN GOODRICK, m. Benjamin Bolles of Osberton, Nottinghamshire. (Genealogist IV 31; Harl. Soc. 53: 1204; 51: 416; 4: 94; Nottinghamshire Visitations).

41. THOMAS BOLLES, of Osberton, 1614; m. Elizabeth Perkins, dau. of Thomas Perkins, of Fishlake, co. York. (Authorities as for generation 40; Charles Thornton Libby, Noyes & Davis: Genealogical Dictionary of Maine and New Hampshire, 101).

42. JOSEPH BOLLES (Bowles), bapt. at Worksop, 19 Feb. 1608; at Winter Harbor, Me., 1640, and Wells, d. 1678; m. Mary, prob. sister of Morgan Howell. (Waters I 606-607; Genealogy of Edward Small III 1289-1294; TAG 37: 114-115; 38: 120).

Line 203

39. REV. EDWARD BULKELEY, D.D. (31-39); m. Olive Irby.

40. DORCAS BULKELEY, m. Anthony Ingoldsby.

41. OLIVE INGOLDSBY, bapt. 1602; m. Rev. Thomas James, A.M., bapt. Boston, Lincolnshire, England, 5 Oct. 1595. A.B., Emmanuel Coll., Cambridge, 1614/5, A.M. 1618; ord. Charlestown, Mass., 2 Nov. 1632-1636; sett. New Haven, Conn., 1636-1642; d. Needham-Market, England, Feb. 1682/3, ae. 90 years.

42. REV. THOMAS JAMES, b. England, 1620/22; d. East Hampton, L.I., N.Y., 1696; first minister at Southampton, 1650-1696; m. Ruth Jones, b. ca. 1628, d. ca. 1668. (Bulkeley Gen; TAG XI 29 ff; Weis; Col. Clergy of N.E., 116).

Line 204

35. SIR RALPH DE EURE, d. 10 Mar. 1422, (son of John, b. ca. 1304, d. 1366/7 by (2) wife Margaret. He had m. (1) Agnes de Lisle.) Sheriff of Northumberland 1389-1397, Governor of the Castle of Newcastle, Constable of York Castle; m. (1) Isabel de Valence; m. by 1387 (2) **CATHERINE DE ATON** (206-35). (VCH Yorks N. Riding I, 383, 533).

36. CATHARINE EURE, child of (2), d. bef. 31 Aug. 1459; m. Sir Alexander Neville, of Thornton Bridge, d. 1457, will pro., York, 25 Jun. 1457.

37. WILLIAM NEVILLE, b. ca. 1425/6, Squire of Thornton Bridge.

38. WILLIAM NEVILLE, b. ca. 1450, d. 1484; m. (1) (under age), 1457, Joan Boynton; m. (2) Alice. By (1) parent of No. 40.

40. RALPH NEVILLE, s. and h. of No. 38 by (1), d. 1522, of Thornton Bridge; m. **ANNE WARD** (2-37). (New County History of Northumberland XII 494-495; Generations 33-36: Joseph Foster: Visitations of Yorks, etc. 607-617, cf. 608-611; Generations 36-40: "Neville of Thornton Bridge" in Genealogist, n.s. 33 p. 15 which has one too many Williams; TAG 17: 108; see ms. notes of G. Andrews Moriarty, at NEHGS, Boston).

32. ROBERT DE CLIFFORD (82-32), Lord Clifford; m. **MAUD DE CLARE** (64-32).

33. IDOINE DE CLIFFORD, d. 24 Aug 1365; **HENRY DE PERCY** (161-29), 2nd Lord Percy, d. ca. 26 Feb. 1351/2. (CP X 459-462).

34. MAUD PERCY (see 2-32), d. bef. 18 Feb. 1378/9; m. **JOHN DE NEVILLE,** K.G. (207-33). (CP IX 502-503).

Line 206

33. IDOINE DE CLIFFORD (205-33), m. **HENRY DE PERCY** (161-29).

34. ISABEL DE PERCY, m. Sir William de Aton, Knt., Lord Vesci, M.P. 1317-1320. (CP X 459-462).

35. CATHERINE DE ATON, m. **SIR RALPH DE EURE,** Knt. (204-35).

Line 207

30. SIR EDMUND DE MORTIMER (9-30, 27-30), 7th Baron Mortimer of Wigmore; was father, prob. by unknown 1st wife (NEHGR 116: 16-17).

31. ISOLDE DE MORTIMER, d. 1338; m. (1) Walter de Balun; m. (2) Hugh de Audley, Lord Audley, d. 1325, Ambassador to France, son of James de Audley and **ELA LONGESPEE** (122-30). (CP I, 347-348; IX 499-501. See p. 88).

32. ALICE DE AUDLEY, d. 12 Jan. 1374/5; m. (1) ca. 14 Jan. 1326/7, **RALPH DE NEVILLE** (186-5), b. ca. 1291, d. 5 Aug. 1367, Baron Neville of Raby. She m. (2) Ralph, 1st Lord of Greystoke. (CP IX 499-501; IV 190).

33. JOHN DE NEVILLE, K.G., Baron Neville of Raby (See 2-32), b. ca. 1331, d. Newcastle, 17 Oct. 1388, Knt. 1360, K.G. 1369; m. (1) **MAUD PERCY** (205-34), d. 1378/9. (CP IX 502-503).

34. RALPH DE NEVILLE, K.G., b. bef. 1364, d. Raby, 21 Oct. 1425, cr. 1st Earl of Westmoreland 1397; m. (1) **MARGARET STAFFORD** (10-33); m. (2) **JOAN BEAUFORT** (2-32, 3-32, 78-35), granddau. of King **EDWARD III** (1-30) and **PHILIPPA OF HAINAUT** (103-24). (CP IX 503; Edward Blore: The Monumental Remains of Noble and Eminent Persons, etc., London, 1826, section 21, p. 9).

35. ELEANOR NEVILLE (3-33) (by 2nd wife), m. **SIR HENRY PERCY,** K.G. (19-33).

36. KATHERINE PERCY, b. 28 May 1423; m. well bef. 1458/9, Edmund Grey of Ruthin, cr. Earl of Kent 1465, b. 26 Oct. 1416, d. 22 May 1490, son of Sir John Grey, K.C., d. 27 Aug. 1439 and (m. by 24 Feb. 1412/13) Constance, d. Nov. 1437, dau. of John de Holand (son of **SIR THOMAS DE HOLAND,** K.G. (47-31) and Joan Plantagenet, granddau. of King Edward I and Margaret of France) and his wife Elizabeth, dau. of **JOHN OF GAUNT** (1-31) (by wife Blanche of Lancaster), son of Edward III and Philippa of Hainaut. (CP VI 159, 180; VII 164; Weever 425).

37. ANNE GREY, m. ca. 1468 as 1st wife, John Grey, 8th Lord

Grey of Wilton, d. 3 Apr. 1499, who m. (2) Elizabeth, d. 15 Jan. 1514/5, wid. of Sir Thomas Cokesey, ae. 28+ in 1480, d.s.p. 6 Mar. 1497/8, and dau. of Thomas Vaughn. She m. (3) by 25 Nov. 1501, Sir Edward Stanley, afterwards Lord Mounteagle. John Grey was s. and h. of Sir Reynold Grey, 7th Lord Grey of Wilton, ae. 21+ in 1461, d. 22 Feb. 1493/4, by Thomasine or Tacine, living May 1461, illeg. dau. of **JOHN BEAUFORT** (1-32), Duke of Somerset, whom he m. by 6 Oct. 1447. (CP VI 180-181; VII 165 note e, 166 note f; XII pt. 1, p. 48 note a). "Gyse of Elmore" (Trans. Bristol & Gloucs. cit. III 59, 70) and 1623 Visitations of Gloucs. (Harleian Soc. Pub. XXI 72) show that **JOHN GYSE** of Elmore (197-36), b. 1485, d. 20 Dec. 1556; m. bef. 1518 (actually bef. 1512), Tase (Tace, Thomasine), dau. of "Lord Grey of Wilton". In some pedigrees it appears as "Lord Grey of Ruthin" though the former is that which is recorded by "the Heralds' College" (Bristol & Gloucs. cit. III 77). The father of **ANNE GREY** (No. 37) was a member of the family of Ruthin, which may be the source of the confusion. John Grey of Wilton was the proper age to be Tase's grandfather, and his mother bore the same name. Though there is no positive evidence seen identifying John and Anne as grandparents of Tase, wife of John Gyse, everything fits chronologically and the identification appears most probable.

38. EDMUND GREY, Lord Grey of Wilton, b. ca. 1469, d. 5 May 1511; m. bef. May 1505, Florence Hastings, living 5 May 1511, dau. of Sir Ralph and Anne Hastings. (CP VI 181-182; v.Redlich 199).

39. TACY GREY, dau. of Edmund Grey of Wilton, perh. by an earlier m., b. ca. 1490, buried at Elmore, co. Gloucester, 15 Nov. 1558; m. ca. 1510, **JOHN GYSE,** Esq. (197-36), b. ca. 1485, d. 20 Dec. 1556, bur. at Elmore, son of Sir John Gyse of Aspley Gyse and Agnes Berkeley of Stoke-Giffard. (Sir Robert Atkyns: . . . State of Gloucestershire. . . 1712, p. 325; Burke: Peerage and Baronetage, 1949, p. 899).

Line 208

29. SIR ROBERT DE ROS (89-29), d. 1285; m. Isabel d'Aubigny.

30. ISABEL DE ROS, m. (1) Walter de Faucomberge, d. 31 Dec. 1318.

31. JOHN DE FAUCOMBERGE, Lord Faucomberge, d. 18 Sep. 1349; m. Eve, prob. dau. of Ralph, Lord Bulmer. (CP V 270; XI 95-96).

32. JOAN DE FAUCOMBERGE, m. (2) 1376/7, Sir William Colville of Arncliffe, d. ca. 1380/1. (Brown: "Ingleby and Arncliffe" in Yorks. Arch. Journ. XVI 159-170, 211).

33. SIR JOHN DE COLVILLE, of Arncliffe and Dale, beheaded at Durham, 20 Aug. 1405, with his wife; m. Alice d'Arcy, dau. of John, Lord Darcy. (Y.A.J. cit.).

34. ISABEL DE COLVILLE, living 1442/3; m. (1) John Wandesford, of Kirklington, d. ca. 1400, son of John de Wandesford. (Y.A.J. cit. 217-219; H.B. McCall: The Wandesfords of Kirklington and Castle Camer (1904); The Ancestor X 98-99).

35. THOMAS WANDESFORD, merchant of London, Sheriff of London, 1443, Alderman of London, d. 13 Oct. 1448; m. Idonea. (The Ancestor cit.; The Wandesfords cit.; Bevan: Aldermen of London I 206, 336; II 7).

36. ALICE WANDESFORD, co-h.; m. William Mulso of Creatingham, co. Suffolk, d. 1495. (Rot. Parl. VI 493; Wedgewood: Hist. of Parliament, Biogs. 1439-1509, pp. 557, 618; Coppinger's Manors of Suffolk IV 243).

37. ANNE MULSO, m. Thomas Louthe, of Sawtry, co. Hunts., M.P., d. 1533. (Same as 208-36; Camden Soc. 77: 4 and App. 2).

38. EDMUND LOUTHE, d.v.p. (killed 1522); m. Edith Stukeley, dau. of John Stukeley of Stukeley, co. Hunts. (Authorities as above).

39. ANNE LOUTHE, d. 1577; m. Simon Throckmorton of Earsham, co. Suffolk, d. 10 Jul. 1527. (Authorities as above; Metcalf's Vis. Suffolk; NEHGR 98: 67-72, 111-123).

40. LIONEL THROCKMORTON, of South Elmham and Bungay, co. Suffolk, d. 1599; m. (2) 1560, Elizabeth Blennerhasset, dau. of John Blennerhasset of Barsham and his first wife, Elizabeth Cornwallis. (Metcalf, op.cit.; NEHGR 98: 67-72, 111-123).

41. BASSINGBOURNE THROCKMORTON, Esq., grocer, citizen, and Alderman of Norwich, b. 1564, d. 21 Sep. 1638; m. (1) 1591, Mary Hill, d. 1615, dau. of William Hill, gent. of Bury St. Edmunds, and his wife, Joan Annabel. (NEHGR 98: 67-72, 111-123).

42. JOHN THROCKMORTON, of Providence, R.I., bapt. 8 May 1601, d. 17 Mar. 1683/4-25 Apr. 1684; m. Rebecca. (This line was kindly furnished by Mr. G. Andrews Moriarty, Moriarty Notebook XIV 17-18. NEHGS).

Line 209

36. SIR RICHARD LYGON, Knt. (84-36), of Arle Court, d. 20 Mar. 1557; m. Margaret Greville. (Wm. D. Ligon, The Ligon Family, 1947, pp. 33-34, 37-38, 45-46; TAG 52: 176-7, 247).

37. WILLIAM LYGON, of Redgrove and Madresfield, b. 1518, d. 29 Sep. 1567, Sheriff of Worcestershire 1550, 1560; m. 1529, Eleanor, dau. of Sir William Dennis (or Denys), of Durham, co Gloucester, and his wife Anne, dau. of Maurice Berkeley. (Ibid., 45-46).

38. CICELY LYGON, of Madresfield, co. Worcester; m. 1559, Edward Gorges, Esq., of Wroxall, b. 1537, d. 29 Aug. 1568, son of Edmund, Esq., and Anne (Walsh) Gorges. (Ibid., 45-60, 101, 177-178).

39. SIR FERDINANDO GORGES, Knt., colonizer of Me., b. ca. 1565, d. Ashton Court near Bristol, England, 4/14 May 1647; m. (1) Westminster, 24 Feb. 1589/90, Anne Bell, bur. London, 6 Aug. 1620, dau. of Edward Bell and **MARGARET BARLEY** (210-40), of Writtle, co. Essex; m. (2) 21 Dec. 1621, Mary Fulford, dau. of Sir Thomas Fulford, and sister of Bridget Fulford, wife of **ARTHUR CHAMPERNOUN** (6-40), and thereby **CAPT. FRANCIS CHAMPERNOUN** (6-41) was nephew by m. of Sir Ferdinando Gorges; Katherine Dudley and Frances Williams were second cousins. (Ibid., 178; Noyes, Libbey and Davis: Gen. Dict. of Maine and N.H. , II 274).

Line 210

Note: This line, as published in earlier editions, contains many errors. Rather than simply dropping it, it is here republished showing the breaks and corrections in it for the benefit of those who find references to it in lineages elsewhere. Note also TAG 52: 176-7, 247.

30. NICHOLE D'AUBIGNY (126-30), m. (1) **ROGER DE SOMERY** (55-28).

31. MARGARET DE SOMERY (55-29), wid. of Ralph Basset of Drayton, slain 1265; m. (3) bef. 26 Jan. 1270/1, Ralph de Cromwell, d. bef. 18 Sep. 1289. (CP III 551).

32. RALPH DE CROMWELL, d. ca. 2 Mar. 1298/9. (CP III 551).

33. RALPH DE CROMWELL, d. 1291/2; m. Joan de la Mare, d. 9 Aug. 1348. (CP III 551).

34. RALPH DE CROMWELL, of Cromwell and West Hallam, d. bef. 28 Oct. 1364; m. 1351, Amice, dau. of Roger de Bellers. (Ibid.)

35. SIR RALPH CROMWELL, Lord Cromwell of Tattershall, co. Lincoln, M.P. 1375-1397, d. 27 Aug. 1398; m. bef. 20 Jun. 1366, **MAUD BERNAKE** (218-32), d. 10 Apr. 1419, dau. of John Bernake, and great-great-granddau. of Robert de Tateshall of Tattershall. (CP III 551-552; V 519; Banks I 168-170).

36. MAUD CROMWELL, m. Sir William Fitzwilliam, of Sproatsborough, Lord of Emley, d. 8 Apr. 1398. (CP V 519; Banks I 170).

37. SIR JOHN FITZWILLIAM, Knt., d. 5 Jul. 1417, Lord of Emley and Sproatsborough; m. Eleanor Greene, dau. of Sir Henry Greene of Drayton. (CP V 519; Clay 77). They were probably not the parents of No. 38. CP V, cit. does not mention dau. Jane. Paley Baildon's "Baildon and the Baildons" says Jane d.y. (p. 365). Thos. Bendish d. 1477. If Jane dau. Sir John she was 60+ when she m. Wm. Bradbury. (Credit: Dr. Alexander White III (UCLA). See also work of John Threlfall, who supplied many corrections and true identification of **PHILIPPA** (211-39).

* * *

38. JANE FITZWILLIAM, m. (1) Thomas Bendish, Esq., of Bowre Hall in Stephen Bumstead, d. 1477; m. (2) William Bradbury of Littlebury and Wicken Bonhunt, co. Essex. (NEHGR 71: 241-242). Not mother of No. 39. (See also Paley Baildon's "Baildon and the Baildons", p. 365 says Jane d.y. If Jane dau. of Sir John she was 60+ when m. Bradbury. Credit to Dr. Alexander White for this reference.)

* * *

39. PHILIPPA BRADBURY (211-39), d. aft. 14 Oct. 1530; m. (1) John Barley of Stapleford Abbotts, co. Essex.

40. MARGARET BARLEY, m. Edward Bell, Esq., of Writtle, co. Essex. They were the parents of Edward Bell, of St. Brevall, co. Gloucester, will made 16 Aug. 1649; Anne Bell who m. **SIR FERDINANDO GORGES** (209-39) (Mrs. Holman in TAG 18: 224-226;

Line 210 (cont.)

Noyes, Libbey and Davis: Gen. Dictionary of Maine and New Hampshire II 274). Not parents of No. 41. (Bradbury Memorial, pp. 31, 34-35, contains errors).

* * *

41. MARGARET BELL, m. William Whitgift of Clavering, co. Essex, gent. (will made 13 Jun. 1615, pro., London, 8 Nov. 1615), son of Henry and Anne (Dynewell) Whitgift, and own brother of John Whitgift, Archbishop of Canterbury (b. Great Grimsby, co. Lincoln, ca. 1530, will dated 27 Oct. 1602, pro. 31 Mar. 1604). (Bradbury Memorial, 34-35, 47-48 (from here down this book is useful); Gen. Dict. of Me. and N.H., II 274; TAG 18: 224-226: CCN 1060).

42. ELIZABETH WHITGIFT, b. Clavering, Essex, Mar. 1574, d. 26 Jun. 1612, ae. 38 yrs., bur. Croydon, Surrey; m. (1) Richard Coles of Leigh, co. Worcester, d. Nov. 1600; m. (2) Francis Gill of London, d. 1605; m. (3) **WYMOND BRADBURY** (246-40), bapt. Newport Pond, 16 May 1574, d. Whitechapel, co. Middlesex, ca. 1649; resided, London, 17 Oct. 1628-1649. Their dau. Anne (Bradbury) Stubbs was appointed admx. on her father's estate, 20 Nov. 1650, "as her brother Thomas was overseas." (Bradbury Memorial, 32-35, 47-48; Gen. Dict. of Me. and N.H., II 104; Mrs. Holman in TAG 18: 224-226; Morant: Hist. of Essex, II 587; DNB 16: 361; 37: 374-376; 56: 359-362; CCN 351).

43. CAPTAIN THOMAS BRADBURY, gent., 2nd son, bapt. Wicken Bonhunt, Essex, 28 Feb. 1610/11, d. Salisbury, Mass., 16 Mar. 1695, will made 14 Feb. 1694/5; came to N.E. 1634, as agent for **SIR FERDINANDO GORGES** (209-39); m. 1636, Mary Perkins, d. 20 Dec. 1700. Their eldest son was Wymond Bradbury. (Bradbury Memorial 59-66: Gen. Dict. of Me. and N.H., II 104). William Bradbury, another son, m. Rebecca Wheelwright, dau. of the Rev. John Wheelwright.

Line 211

38. MARGARET ROKELL, prob. gr.dau. Thomas, the "sick and aged" coroner of Herts. 1427, m. William Bradbury of Littleton & Wicken Bonhunt, co. Essex, son of Robert of Olerset, co. Derby. (Feet of Fines, Essex, IV: 80; Close Rolls, Bradbury Memorial) (provided by John B. Threlfall).

39. PHILIPPA BRADBURY, d. aft. 14 Oct. 1530; m. (1) John Barley; m. (2) aft. 7 Jul. 1502, John Josselyn, d. July 14, 1525, son of George & Maud (Bardolf) Josselyn, of Newell Josselyn and Hide Hall in Sawbridgeworth, Herts, and High Roding, Essex. (TAG 52: 177; NEHGR 71: 241-242).

40. SIR THOMAS JOSSELYN, K.B., of Hide Hall, Sawbridgeworth, and Newell Josselyn, High Roding, b. ca. 1507, d. 24 Oct. 1562, bur. at Sawbridgeworth; Knight of the Bath, 1547/8; m. 1524, Dorothy Gates, d. 11 Feb. 1582/3, dau. of Sir Jeffrey Gates, Knt., and Elizabeth Clopton, dau. of Sir William Clopton,

Line 211 (cont.)

Knt., of Kentwell, co. Suffolk. (NEHGR 71: 243-245).

41. HENRY JOSSELYN, b. Willingale-Doe, co. Essex, ca. 1540, bur. there 25 Aug. 1587; m. ca. 1562, Anne Torrell, b. ca. 12 Dec. 1542, d. 30 May 1589, dau. of Humphrey and Alice (Leventhorpe) Torrell of Torrell's Hall in Willingale-Doe. (NEHGR 71: 245-246).

42. SIR THOMAS JOSSELYN, Knt., of Torrell's Hall, ca. 1567, Knt., 1603; appointed by **SIR FERDINANDO GORGES** (209-39) deputy-governor of his possessions in N.E.; arriv. Black Point, Me., 14 Jul. 1638, returned to Eng., 3 Sep. 1639; m. (2) ca. 1603, Theodora (Cooke) Bere, bur. Boxley, Kent, 13 Aug. 1635, dau. of Edward and Elizabeth (Nichols) Cooke. (NEHGR 71: 248-250).

43. HENRY JOSSELYN, b. ca. 1606, d. Maine, bef. 10 May 1683, Corpus Christi Coll., Camb., 1623; sett. Black Point, Me. 1634, later at Pemequid; dep. gov. of Maine 1645; m. Margaret Cammock, living 12 May 1680. (NEHGR 71: 249).

43. JOHN JOSSELYN, b. ca. 1608, d.s.p. aft. 1675; sett. Black Point, Me., 1638; traveller, writer and naturalist; published New Rarities Discovered and An Account of Two Voyages to New England. (NEHGR 71: 249-250; Publications, Colonial Soc. Mass., 28: 24-36. Weis states that Thomas Josselyn (Joslin), 1591-1661, of Lancaster, Mass., was fifth cousin to Henry and John above.

Line 212

30. MILICENT DE CANTELOU (66-30, 200-30), d. ca. 1299; m. **EUDO LA ZOUCHE** (38-29), d. 1295, of Haryngworth.

31. WILLIAM LA ZOUCHE of Haryngworth, b. Haryngworth, 1276, d. Mar. 1351/2, Knt. 1306, M.P. 1308-1348; m. before 15 Feb. 1295/6 Maud, dau. of **JOHN**, 1st Lord Lovel (215-29) by his 1st wife, Isabel de Bois. (CP XII pt. II 97, 938-40).

32. EUDO LA ZOUCHE of Haryngworth, m. Joan, dau. of William Inge, Chief Justice, 1325/6. (Old-CP VIII 223-224).

33. WILLIAM LA ZOUCHE of Haryngworth, b. 1322, d. 23 Apr. 1382, M.P. 1348-1351; m. Elizabeth. (Ibid.)

34. WILLIAM LA ZOUCHE of Haryngworth, b. ca. 1342, d. 13 May 1396, M.P. 1382/3; m. Elizabeth, d. ca. 1408 (perhaps dau. of Thomas, Lord Ros). (Ibid.)

35. WILLIAM LA ZOUCHE of Haryngworth, K.G., b. ca. 1374, M.P. 1396, K.G. 1415, d. 3 Nov. 1415. (Ibid.)

36. WILLIAM LA ZOUCHE of Haryngworth, b. 1402, M.P. 1425/6; m. 1424, **ALICE ST. MAUR** (or Seymour) (213-34). (CP XI 362).

36A. WILLIAM LA ZOUCHE, Lord Zouche, b. ca. 1432, ae. 30+ at father's death, d. 15 Jan. 1467/8, MP 1455/6, m. (1) Katharine (dau. Sir Rowland Lenthall, by Lucy, aunt and in her issue coh. Henry Grey, 7th Lord Grey of Codnor, dau. Richard, 4th Lord Grey); m. (2) Katharine Plumpton.

37. JOHN LA ZOUCHE of Haryngworth, M.P. 1482/3; m. bef. 26 Feb. 1486/7 **JOAN DYNHAM** (214-36), d. aft. 1507. (CP IV 381; Gens. 30-37, CP XII pt. 2, pp. 937-947).

30. ELENA LA ZOUCHE (31-30), m. (1) Apr. 1314, Nicholas de St. Maur (Seymour), d. 8 Nov. 1316, M.P. 1314/5, Knt. of the Shire for Gloucester, 1312/3, Lord St. Maur. (CP XI 356-362).

31. NICHOLAS DE ST. MAUR (Seymour), d. 8 Aug. 1361, Lord St. Maur, Knt. 1346, J.P. for Somersetshire 1351, M.P. 1351-1360; m. Muriel Lovel, d. bef. 1361, dau. of James Lovel and granddau. of Robert, d. 1350/1, 1st Lord Lovel of Castle Cary.

32. RICHARD SEYMOUR, d. 15 May 1401, Lord St. Maur and Lovel, M.P. 1380-1400, Knt. 1382; m. aft. 1374, Ela de St. Lo, d. 1409/10, dau. of Sir John de St. Lo.

33. RICHARD SEYMOUR, d. Jan. 1408/9, Lord St. Maur and Lovel, J.P. 1405, M.P. 1402-1407; m. Mary (Peyvre) Broughton, dau. of Thomas Peyvre of Toddington, and Margaret, dau. of Sir Nele Loring, K.G.

34. ALICE SEYMOUR (St. Maur), b. 24 Jul. 1409, d. 1425/6; m. bef. 8 Mar. 1423/4, **WILLIAM LA ZOUCHE** (212-36), d. 1463, Lord Zouche of Haryngworth. (Generations 30-34: CP XI 356-362).

21. ERMENGARDE of Anjou (121-21); m. ca. 980, Conan I, Count of Rennes, Duke of Brittany.

22. GEOFFREY, b. ca. 980, d. 1008, Duke of Brittany; m. 996, Hawise, d. 21 Feb. 1034, dau. of Richard I, Duke of Normandy. (CP X 779).

23. EUDES, b. 999, d. 7 Jan. 1079, Count of Brittany, and Count of Penthièvre, 1034; m. Agnes (perh. dau. of Alan of Cornwall). (CP X 779-780).

24. STEPHEN I, d. 21 Apr. 1135 or 1136, bur. in the quire of St. Mary's, York, Count of Brittany, held honour of Richmond in England, founder of Augustinian abbey of Ste. Croix at Guincamp ca. 1110, founder of Cistercian abbey of Begard; m. Hawise (said to have been the Countess of Guincamp, which is doubtful). (CP X 786-787).

25. ELEANOR OF PENTHIEVRE, m. Oliver II, d. ca. 1150, Lord of Dinan, son of Geoffrey, Sire of Dinan in Brittany. (CP IV 369).

26. OLIVER III, d. aft. 1173, Lord of Dinan. (CP IV 369).

27. GEOFFREY DE DINAN. (CP IV 369; Generations 22-26: Brandenburg).

28. OLIVER DE DINAN, d. bef. 28 Jun. 1221. (CP IV 369).

29. SIR GEOFFREY DE DINHAM, d. bef. 26 Dec. 1258. (CP IV 369).

30. SIR OLIVER DE DINHAM, b. 1234, d. 26 Feb. 1298/9, Constable of Exeter and Taunton Castles. (CP IV 370-371).

31. SIR JOSCE DE DINHAM, d. 30 Mar. 1300/1; m. bef. 23 Apr. 1292, Margaret de Hydon, d. 15 May 1357, dau. of Sir Richard de Hydon of Clayhidon, Devon. (CP IV 371-372).

32. SIR JOHN DE DINHAM, b. Nutwell, 14 Sep. 1295, d. 14 Apr. 1332, ae. 36; m. Margaret, d. 28 Mar. 1361. (CP IV 372-373).

33. SIR JOHN DE DINHAM, Knt., d. 7 Jan. 1382/3, ae. 64; m. Muriel, d. bef. 12 Aug. 1369, dau. of Sir Thomas de Courtenay and Muriel, dau. of John de Moels, and granddau. of **SIR HUGH DE COURTENAY** (51-31) and **AGNES ST. JOHN** (262-32). (CP IV 373-374).

34. SIR JOHN DE DINHAM, b. 1359/60, d. 25 Dec. 1428, ae. 69; m. (3) aft. 1 Nov. 1402, **PHILIPPA** (215-34), dau. of Sir John Lovel of Titchmarsh. (CP IV 374-377).

35. SIR JOHN DYNHAM, Knt., Lord Dynham, d. 25 Jan. 1457/8; m. bef. 12 Jul. 1434, Joan, d. 1497, dau. of Richard de Arches and Lucy. (CP IV 377-378).

36. JOAN DE DYNHAM, d. aft. 1507; m. **JOHN** (212-37), Lord Zouche of Haryngworth. (CP IV 377, 381; Old-CP VIII 223-224).

37. JOHN LA ZOUCHE of Haryngworth, b. ca. 1485, d. 1550/1, M.P. 1529; m. bef. 1510, Dorothy, dau. of Sir William Capell, Lord Mayor of London, and Margaret, dau. of Sir Thomas Arundel of Lanherne, co. Cornwall. (Old-CP VIII 223-224).

38. RICHARD LA ZOUCHE of Haryngworth, b. ca. 1510, d. 1552, M.P. (CP VI 186-187; Old-CP VIII 223-224).

39. DOROTHY (nat. dau. of Richard la Zouche of Haryngworth); m. ca. 1553, Sir Arthur Grey. (CP VI 186-187).

Line 215

24. ISABEL DE VERMANDOIS (50-24), d. 1131; m. (1) Sir Robert de Beaumont, Earl of Leicester.

25. MAUD (Matilda or Alberade) **DE BEAUMONT**, d. aft. 1189; m. William de Lovel, d. 1166/70, Lord of Ivry and Brival. (CP VIII 211-212).

26. WILLIAM DE LOVEL, Crusader, d. 1212/3, Lord of Elcombe; m. bef. 1190, Isabel. (CP VIII 213-214).

27. JOHN LOVEL, d. bef. 23 Dec. 1252; m. bef. Aug. 1216, Katherine, dau. of Alan Basset and Aline. (CP VIII 214).

28. JOHN LOVEL, b. 1222, d. 1287; m. Maud de Sydenham, dau. of Sir William de Sydenham. (CP VIII 215).

29. SIR JOHN LOVEL, Knt., Lord Lovel, b. 1252, d. bef. 1 Oct. 1310, M.P. 1298-1307; m. (1) Isabel, dau. of Arnold de Bois; m. (2) Joan, d. 13 Oct. 1348, dau. of **ROBERT DE ROS** (89-29) and Isabel, granddau. of William d'Aubigny, M.C. 1215. (CP VIII 215-217; XI 95-96). No. 30 was son by (2).

30. JOHN LOVEL, Lord Lovel, b. 1288, killed at Bannockburn 24 Jun. 1314, M.P. 1311-1314; m. Maud, b. 1290, d. 17 May 1341, dau. of Sir Philip Burnell and Maud, dau. of **JOHN FITZ ALAN** (149-29), and sister of **RICHARD FITZ ALAN** (28-31), Earl of Arundel. (CP VIII 217-218).

31. SIR JOHN LOVELL, Lord Lovel, b. ca. Sep. 1314, d. 3 Nov. 1347; m. bef. 1340, Isabel, d. 2 Jul. 1349. (CP VIII 218-219).

32. SIR JOHN LOVEL, K.G., Lord Lovel, d. 10 Sep. 1408, Knt., K.G. 1405, M.P. 1375-1407; m. ca. 1372, **MAUD DE HOLAND** (47A-33), d. 7 May 1423, dau. of Robert de Holand, and granddau. of

Line 215 (cont.)

Robert, Lord Holand, d. 16 Mar. 1372/3. (CP VIII 219-221).
   33. JOHN LOVEL, Lord Lovel of Titchmarsh, d. 19 Oct. 1414, M.P. 1409-1414. (CP VIII 221).
   34. PHILIPPA LOVEL, m. **SIR JOHN DE DYNHAM** (214-34).

Line 216

   28. EDWARD I (1-28), King of England, b. 1239, d. 1307.
   29. JOHN DE BOTETOURTE, son of King Edward I, first Lord Botetourte, admiral, governor of Famlingham Castle 1304, M.P. 1305-1324, d. 25 Nov. 1324; m. 1285/92, **MAUD FITZ THOMAS** (122A-31), living 28 May 1329, dau. of Thomas Fitz Otes of Mendelsham, Suffolk, and Beatrice de Beauchamp, dau. of William de Beauchamp of Bedford. (CP II 233-234. For proof that John de Botetourte was an illeg. son of King Edward I, see Hailes Abbey Chronicle. The family tree of Botetourte here given is considered in this case to be completely reliable by Mr. H.C. Richardson, the authority on this line and agreed by Sir Anthony Wagner, College of Arms. Though questioned by some, due to an apparent erasure in the parchment, the Librarian, in whose care it resides, states that there are several other erasures and corrections, all apparently contemporary with the preparation of the original document and apparent corrections made at that time by the author. For a possible identification of his mother, see NEHGR 120: 259).
   30. THOMAS DE BOTETOURTE, perh. named after Thomas de Clare, d.v.p. 1322; m. Joan de Somery, living 18 Jan. 1326/7, sister and coh. of John, Lord Somery and dau. of **ROGER DE SOMERY** (81-30). (CP II 234-235).
   31. JOHN DE BOTETOURTE, Lord Botetourte of Weobley Castle, b. 1318, d. 1385, M.P. 1342-1385; m. (1) 1344/5 Elizabeth d.s.p. (sister of wife (2), m. (2) bef. 31 May 1347, **JOYCE LA ZOUCHE DE MORTIMER** (98-32), living 4 May 1372. (CP II 234-235; Generations 29-31: DNB V 447).
   32. JOYCE DE BOTETOURTE (98-33), b. 1367/8, d. 12 Aug. 1420; m. (1) **SIR BALDWIN FREVILLE** (230A-33), b. 1350/1, of Tamworth Castle, co. Warwick, d. 1387/8, m. (2) Sir Adam de Peshale, d. 1419. (CP V chart 332, 357 note a). By (1) she was mother of No. 32A.
   32A. SIR BALDWIN FREVILLE III of Tamworth Castle, b. Woebley Castle, Worcs. 1368, d. 1401, m. (1) Joan d.s.p., dau. Sir Thomas Greene; m. (2) Maud, d. 1397. By (2) he had Elizabeth No. 33. (Gen. Mag. 21, No. 6, pp. 373-375).
   33. ELIZABETH FREVILLE, b. ca. 1393/4, ae. 24 in 1418; m. **THOMAS FERRERS**, Esq. (11-35), d. 6 Jan. 1458/9. (CP V chart 332, 357 note a).

32. SIR WILLIAM PROUZ, Knt. (52-32), d. 1270, of Gidley Castle, Devon; m. (2) Alice Ferrers, dau. of Sir Fulk fitz Gilbert de Ferrers. (Crispin: Falaise Roll, Table IX; Vivian: Visitations of Devon, 1895, p. 626; W.H. Hamilton Rogers: Antient Sepulchral Effigies and Monumental and Memorial Sculptures of Devon, Exeter, 1876, pp. 34, 41, 188-189, 279; references under 52-32).

33. SIR RICHARD PROUZ, of Ashton (Ashreston), 2nd son, fl. 1340. (Rogers 29, 34, 188; Vivian 189, 597, 626).

34. THOMASINE PROUZ, m. well bef. 1340, Sir John Chudleigh, Knt., son of John Chudleigh. (Ibid.)

35. JOHN CHUDLEIGH, of Broadclist; m. **JANE BEAUCHAMP** (246B-32), dau. of Sir John Beauchamp of Ryme by Alicia, dau. of Sir Roger Nonant, Lord of Broadclist. (Ibid.).

36. SIR JAMES CHUDLEIGH, Knt., 1358 held Ashton as a minor. In 1361 of age, b. betw. 1337-1340; d. 1401 or later; m. as (1) husb. Agnes, d. aft. 1433, dau. Sir Richard Champernoun. She m. (2) by 1403/4 John de Courtney said to have d. by 29 July 1406.

37. JAMES CHUDLEIGH, of Ashton, d. 8 Feb. 1456/7, Inq.p.m. 36 Henry VI; m. Radigond. (Vivian 189, 597; see Devon and Cornwall N. & Q. XII pt. VIII, Oct. 1923, pp. 340-342).

38. PETRONELL CHUDLEIGH, m. Anthony Pollard of Waye and Horwood, s. and h. of Richard Pollard of Waye by Margaret, dau. of John Cockworthie. (Vivian 25, 189; Rogers 148-149, 289-290).

39. JOANNA POLLARD, named in the Inq.p.m. of her husband, whom she survived; m. Nicholas Ashe vel Esse of Clistformison, Devon, d. 4 Apr. 1552, Inq.p.m., will 3 Apr. 1552, pro. 8 Jun. 1555 at Exeter, son of John Ashe and Thomasine Maynard and great-great-grandson of Sir Oliver de Esse and Richard Formison. (Vivian 25, 597; Rogers 289-290).

40. RICHARD ESSHE vel Ashe, b. ca. 1531, s. and h., ae. about 24 yrs. and named in his father's will, buried at Sowton, 12 Sep. 1591; m. Prudence Rudgley, dau. of John Rudgeley of London, who was bur. at Sowton, Devon, 25 Aug. 1591. (Sowton Parish Registers; Vivian 25; original visitation sworn to 1620, signed Henrie Aysshe; Rogers 290).

41. HENRY ESHE, gent., of Clist-formison and Sowton, Devon, 1620, bur. Sowton, 8 Jun. 1640; m. Loveday Moyle, bur. Sowton, 27 Jan. 1628/9, dau. of Richard Moyle of St. Austle, Cornwall. (Sowton Parish Registers; Vivian 25, original, signed by H.E. above, 1620; Rogers 290; NEHGR 79: 110-111; Generations 39-42: John Tuckett: Devonshire Pedigrees Recorded in the Herald's Visitation of 1620, p. 80).

42. PRUDENCE ESSE, bapt. Sowton, 23 Dec. 1599; m. 1618, Oliver Mainwaring, gent., d. 14 Mar. 1672. (Sowton Parish Registers; Vivian 25; NEHGR 79: 110-111).

43. OLIVER MAINWARING, of Salem and New London, mariner, bapt. Dawlish, Devon, 16 Mar. 1633/4, d. New London, Conn., 3 Nov. 1723, ae. 89. (Hempstead's Diary; NEHGR 79: 110-111. This line was called to the attention of Mr. Weis by Mr. George Andrews Moriarty).

27. RICHARD FITZ ROY (26-27), nat. son of King John by a dau. of the Earl of Warenne (perh. a dau. of **HAMELIN PLANTAGENET** (123-26)); m. Rohese, d. 1264/5, dau. of Fulbert of Dover. (CP II 127; VIII 518; Genealogist, n.s. 22: 105-110, cf. 109).

28. LORETTE DE DOVER, m. 1248, Sir William de Marmion, d. by 1276, son of Robert de Marmion, the younger, and Avice de Tanfield; received Budington and Northampton by right of his wife. (CP VIII 518).

29. SIR JOHN DE MARMION, d. bef. 7 May 1322, Baron Marmion, M.P. 1313-1322; m. Isabel. (CP VIII 518-520).

30. JOHN DE MARMION, b. ca. 1292, d. 30 Apr. 1335, Lord Marmion, M.P. 1326; m. Maud, living 1343, dau. of Thomas, Lord Furnival by his first wife Joan (m. bef. Jan. 1272/3), dau. of Sir Hugh de Despenser of Ryhall and Aline, dau. and h. of Sir Philip Basset (see 72-31). (CP V 581-582; VIII 520-521).

31. JOAN MARMION, m. Sir John Bernacke. (CP VIII 518).

32. MAUD BERNACKE, d. 10 Apr. 1419; m. bef. 20 June 1366, **SIR RALPH CROMWELL** (210-35).

30. JOHN DE MARMION (218-30), m. Maud de Furnival.

31. AVICE DE MARMION, m. as his 2nd wife, **SIR JOHN DE GREY** (30-30), 1st Lord Grey of Rotherfield. (CP VIII 522). Their dau. **MAUD DE GREY** (30-31), m. (1) John de Botetourt; m. (2) **SIR THOMAS DE HARCOURT**, Knt. (50-35).

32. SIR ROBERT DE GREY (took the name of Marmion), d. bef. 30 Nov. 1367; m. Lora, dau. of Sir Hubert de St. Quenton of Brandesburton in Holderness. (CP V 424; VIII 522).

33. ELIZABETH DE MARMION, d. Dec. 1427; m. Henry, Lord Fitz Hugh, K.G., b. ca. 1358, d. Ravensworth, 11 Jan. 1424/5, ae. 60, son of Henry Fitz Hugh by Joan, dau. of Sir Henry Lescrope of Masham. (CP V 420-425; VIII 522).

34. WILLIAM FITZ HUGH, Lord Fitz Hugh, b. ca. 1399, d. 22 Oct. 1452, M.P. 1429-1450; m. bef. 18 Nov. 1406, Margery, d. bef. 1452, dau. of William de Willoughby, Lord Willoughby of Eresby, by Lucy, dau. of Sir Roger Lestraunge of Knockin, Salop. (CP V 426-427).

35. HENRY FITZ HUGH, d. 8 Jun. 1472, Lord Fitz Hugh; m. **ALICE DE NEVILLE** (78-36). (See also 78-37 and 201-37).

41. CAPTAIN JEREMY CLARKE (11-41), m. Frances (Latham) Dungan.

42. MARY CLARKE, m. 3 Jun. 1658, Governor John Cranston (son of Rev. James Cranstoun, A.M., of St. Saviour's, Southwark, London; chaplain to King Charles I), b. 1624, came to N.E. 1638, ae. 12 yrs., with Captain Jeremy Clarke, his future father-in-law; Deputy-Gov. of Rhode Island 1672-1678; Major; Gov. of R.I. 1678-

1680; d. Newport, R.I., 12 Mar. 1680.
   43. GOVERNOR SAMUEL CRANSTON, b. Newport, R.I., Aug. 1658; Gov. of R.I. 1698-1717; m. 1680, Mary Hart, a granddau. of Rev. Roger Williams of R.I. (Generations 41-43: NEHGR 79:57-66).

Line 221

   36. JOHN DE SUTTON, K.G. (81-36), b. 1400, d. 1487, Baron Dudley; m. aft. 1422, Elizabeth Berkeley.
   37. ELEANOR SUTTON, m. **SIR HENRY BEAUMONT**, Knt. (17-35), of Wednesbury, d. 16 Nov. 1471, Sheriff of Staffordshire. They were ancestors of Elizabeth Marshall who m. Thomas Lewis of Saco, Me. (See Walter Goodwin Davis. This connection was suggested by Mr. David Humiston Kelley).

Line 222

   25. HENRY I (121-25), b. latter half of 1068, d. 1 Dec. 1135, King of England 1100-1135. By an unknown mistress he had the following child. (CP XI App. D, 109-110 note; Brandenburg; Sanders, English Baronies, p. 20; Powick & Fryde, Handbook of British Chronology, p. 31).
   26. WILLIAM DE TRACY, born after 1090, almost certainly being younger than his half brother Robert de Caen, Earl of Gloucester, d. ca. 1135, soon aft. his father; granted during his father's lifetime the escheated estates of William Capra in Devonshire including the barony of Bradninch, Devon. By an unknown wife, William de Tracy had two identifiable children: Sir William de Tracy (his father's heir), b. say 1135, living 1170, who was one of the four murderers of Thomas à Becket, Archbishop of Canterbury, and a daughter, md. Gervase de Courtenay. (CP XI App. D, 109-110; Sanders, English Baronies, p. 20; Devon & Cornwall N&Q XIX 194-201; DNB XIX 1069-1070 (for biography of Sir William de Tracy, Becket's murderer); Family History (an English periodical), 13: 3-36, for discussion of Sir William de Tracy, Becket's murderer).

* * *

   27. GRACE DE TRACY, parentage unknown, m. by 1130, **JOHN DE SUDELEY** (235-23), of Sudeley Castle and Toddington, co. Gloucester, appears in the 1130 pipe roll. (Atkins: Gloucestershire 369; VCH Warwick V 70; Hist. Mon. St. Peter, Glouc, ii 180; Sanders, English Baronies, pp. 85-86).
   Note: Grace is given in all standard sources as the dau. and h. of William de Tracy of Devonshire. However, recent research reveals that William de Tracy, d. ca. 1135, was succeeded in his lands by 1165 by another William de Tracy who was apparently his son. This second William de Tracy was not Grace's son as commonly claimed even though she had a son with this name. Grace's son William de Tracy was an adult by the 1140s and he seems to have held only the

manor of Toddington, Gloucester, of the honour of Sudeley. Chronology suggests that Grace herself was likely of the same generation as King Henry's bastard son, William de Tracy. In any event she was probably not William's daughter and certainly not his heir.

28. RALPH DE SUDELEY, of age 1135, d. 1192, held 3 knights fees 1166, (brother of William de Tracy of Toddington, ancestor of the Vicounts Tracy); m. Emma, dau. of William de Beauchamp (d. 1170). (Authorities as before).

29. RALPH DE SUDELEY, paid 300 marks for livery of his lands 1198/9, d. 1221/2; m. Isabel, living 1241/2. (Ibid.; Generations 25-29: CP XII pt. 1, 413-414).

30. RALPH DE SUDELEY, of Great Dassent, later Burton Dassent, d. on or bef. 19 Mar. 1241/2; m. Imenia, living 1247. (VCH Warwick V 70; Atkins 369).

31. BARTHOLOMEW DE SUDELEY, Knt. of Chipping Dassett 1269, Sheriff of Hereford 1272, M.P. 1278, Gov. of the Castle of Hereford, temp. Henry III, d. ca. 29 Jun. 1280; m. Joan, living 1298. (CP XII pt. 1, 415).

32. JOHN DE SUDELEY, 1st Lord Sudeley, M.P. 1299-1321, d. 1336; was a soldier, temp. Edward I, Lord Chamberlain, served in the French and Scottish wars. (Ibid.)

33. BARTHOLOMEW DE SUDELEY, d. 1327, in his father's lifetime; m. Maud, dau. of John de Montfort, Baron Montfort, d. 1296, and wife, Alice de la Plaunche. (VCH Warwick V 70; CP IX 128).

34. JOHN DE SUDELEY, 2nd Lord Sudeley, b. 1305, d. 1340; m. Eleanor (or Isabelle), d. 1361, dau. of Robert, Lord Scales (prob. Robert de Scales, 2nd Lord Scales, b. ca. 1279, d. 20 Mar. 1324/5, M.P. 1306-1321/22 (son of Robert de Scales, M.P., and Isabel de Burnell) who m. Egeline, d. ca. 1 Oct. 1335, dau. of **SIR HUGH DE COURTENAY** (50-30) and Eleanor Le Despenser). (CP XI 499-501; VCH Warwick V 70; Atkins 369).

35. JOAN DE SUDELEY, co-heiress; m. as 2nd wife, ca. 1354, **WILLIAM LE BOTILLER** (77-32), 2nd Baron of Wemme, by whom mother of Thomas le Botiller, Lord Sudeley. (CP XII, pt. 1, 414-417; Generations 30-35; The Gen. Mag. 13:173-174; Wm. Salt Soc. n.s. vol. (1945-6) 41-42). Note: The assistance of Douglas Richardson in revising this line is gratefully acknowledged.

Line 223

33. ELIZABETH DE SEGRAVE (16-31), b. 1338, d. 1368; m. 1353, John de Mowbray, Lord Mowbray, b. 1340, d. 1368. (CP IX 384).

34. JANE DE MOWBRAY, m. Sir Thomas Gray of Wark. (NEHGR 104: chart betw. pp. 270 and 271, as corrected by vol. 105, p. 155, which also corrects CP, Clay, and other established references).

35. MAUD GREY, living 22 Aug. 1451; m. ca. 21 May 1399, Sir Robert Ogle, Knt., b. 1369/73, d. 12 Aug. 1436, warden of Roxborough Castle. (CP VI 488; X 28-29; Clay, op.cit.)

36. ELIZABETH OGLE, m. (1) disp. 13 Jan. 1411/12, Sir William Heron, Knt., of Ford, b. Nov. 1400, d. 1425, knighted Feb. 1421/2, Justice of Northamptonshire 1422, Sheriff of same 1425; m. (2) Sir John Middleton. (CP VI 487-488; Clay 152-153 as corrected by Surtees; See Surtees Soc. Pub. 45:321; disp. 13 Jan. 1411/12 permits Elizabeth, dau. of Robert Ogle to marry her cousin William Heron (Hunt).)

37. ELIZABETH HERON, b. 1422; m. her cousin, under dispensation, 11 Jul. 1438, Sir John Heron, Knt., son of William and Isabel (Scott) Heron, b. 1415/18, Sheriff of Northumberland 1440-1441, 1451-452, 1456-57, slain at the battle of Towton, 29 Mar. 1461. (CP VI 488-489; v.Redlich 212; Harl. Soc. Pub. 52:946; Foster, op.cit. III 860-861, gives her line back to King Edward I). No evidence that gen. 38 is dau. of gen. 37.

* * *

38. ELIZABETH HERON, m. **SIR ROBERT TAILBOYS,** Knt. (224-37), Lord Kyme, M.P. 1472-1478, d. 30 Jan. 1494/5; ancestors of President George Washington. (CP VII 356, 361; Harl Soc. Pub. 52:946; v.Redlich 212).

39. MAUDE TAILBOYS, m. Sir Robert Tyrwhit, Knt., of Kettleby, b. 1482, knighted at Touraine 1513, High Sheriff of Lincolnshire, d. 4 Jul. 1548; he was a descendant of **MARGARET DE CLARE** (54-33). (CP VII 361 note h; Harl. Soc. Pub. 52: 1019).

40. KATHARINE TYRWHIT, m. Sir Richard Thimbleby of Irnham, Lord of the manor of East Bridgeford, Nottinghamshire, d. 28 Sep. 1590.

41. ELIZABETH THIMBLEBY, m. (1) John St. Paul of Nettleby; m. (2) 20 Jul. 1560, Thomas Welby of Moulton, d. Bath 1570. (Harl. Soc. Pub. reverses the correct order of these marriages).

42. RICHARD WELBY, of Moulton, 2nd son, bapt. 1564; m. ca. 1595, **FRANCES BULKELEY** (31-40).

43. OLIVE WELBY (31-41), b. ca. 1604, d. ca. 1691; m. ca. 1629, Dea. Henry Farwell, d. ca. 1670; came from England to Concord ca. 1635.

Line 224

28. ROGER DE QUINCY (53-28), Earl of Winchester, Constable of Scotland; m. **HELEN OF GALLOWAY** (38-27). (Generations 28-37: v.Redlich 211-212).

29. ELIZABETH DE QUINCY, m. **ALEXANDER COMYN** (114A-27), Earl of Buchan, Constable of Scotland, Justiciar, d. 1290, son of William Comyn and Margaret, Countess of Buchan. (CP I 148).

30. ELIZABETH COMYN, d. bef. 17 Feb. 1328/9; m. Gilbert de Umfreville, Earl of Angus, b. 1244, d. bef. 13 Oct. 1307, son of Gilbert de Umfreville and Maud, dau. of Malcolm, Earl of Angus. (CP I 148).

31. ROBERT DE UMFREVILLE, Earl of Angus, d. 12 Apr. 1325; m. (1) 1303, Lucy de Kyme, dau. of Philip, 1st Lord Kyme, M.P. 1295, d. bef. 2 Apr. 1323, and his wife, Joan Bigod, dau. of **SIR HUGH DE BIGOD** (69-29), Chief Justice of England. (CP I 148-150; VII 357).

32. ELIZABETH DE UMFREVILLE, m. Gilbert de Boroughdon of Boroughdon, Sheriff of Northumberland 1323-1324, 1339-1341. (CP VII 358).

33. ELEANOR, Baroness Kyme, m. Henry Tailboys, d. 23 Feb. 1368/9, son of William and Margaret Tailboys. (CP VII 358).

34. SIR WALTER TAILBOYS, Lord Kyme, Sheriff of Lincolnshire 1389, b. ca. 1351, d. Sep. 1417; m. Margaret. (CP VII 358).

35. WALTER TAILBOYS, Sheriff of Lincolnshire 1423, J.P. 1442-1443, Lord Kyme, b. 1391, d. 13 Apr. 1444; m. (1) unknown; m. (2) Alice, heiress of Stafford Earls of Devon, dead by 24 Apr. 1448, wid. of Sir Henry Cheyney, Knt., and dau. of Sir Humphrey Stafford. (CP VII 358-359).

36. SIR WILLIAM TAILBOYS, Knt., son of 1st mar. (received none of the inheritance of Alice Stafford), Lord Kyme, knighted 19 Feb. 1460/1, b. ca. 1415, beheaded 26 May 1464; m. Elizabeth Bonville, d. 14 Feb. 1490/1, dau. of William, Lord Bonville. (CP VII 359-361).

37. SIR ROBERT TAILBOYS, Knt., Lord Kyme, M.P. 1472, 1477-1478, Sheriff of Lincolnshire 1480, b. ca. 1451, d. 30 Jan. 1484/5; m. Elizabeth (not 223-38), dau. of John Heron. (CP VII 361).

Line 225

32. PHILIPPA PLANTAGENET (5-32), granddau. of King Edward III; m. 1368, **EDMUND DE MORTIMER** (29-34), 3rd Earl of March (DNB).

33. ROGER DE MORTIMER, 4th Earl of March, Earl of Ulster, Lord Mortimer, b. 11 Apr. 1374, d. 20 Jul. 1398; m. ca. 1388, Eleanor, d. Oct. 1405, dau. of **THOMAS DE HOLAND** (47-32), Earl of Kent. (v. Redlich 208; CP VII 156 note e).

34. ANNE DE MORTIMER, m. Richard Plantagenet, Earl of Cambridge, executed Aug. 1415, son of Edmund Plantagenet, Earl of Cambridge, Duke of York, K.G. (5th son of **EDWARD III** (1-30) and **PHILIPPA** (103-34)) and Isabel, yngst dau. & coh. of Pedro I, King of Castile & Leon. She m. (2) 1399 Sir Edward Charleton, Lord of Powys. (v. Redlich 208; DNB; CP).

35. RICHARD PLANTAGENET, K.G., Earl of Cambridge, Duke of York, d. 30 Dec. 1460; m. Cecily, dau. of **RALPH DE NEVILLE** (207-34), 1st Earl of Westmoreland, K.G. They were parents of Kings Edward IV and Richard III. (v.Redlich 208; Blore: Monumental

Remains, section 21, pp. 1-5; DNB).

36. SIR GEORGE PLANTAGENET, K.G., Duke of Clarence, b. 21 Oct. 1449; m. 11 Jul. 1467, Isabel Neville, dau. of Sir Richard Neville (see 78-36), Earl of Salisbury and Warwick, "the King Maker," b. 22 Nov. 1428, d. 14 Apr. 1471, by wife Anne, dau. of Richard Beauchamp, Duke of Warwick. (CP VI 656 note e; XI 398-399; Blore, op.cit. 21, pp. 1-5; DNB).

37. MARGARET PLANTAGENET, Countess of Salisbury, b. Aug. 1473, executed 28 May 1541; m. 1491/4, Sir Richard Pole, K.G., d. bef. 18 Dec. 1505, son of Sir Geoffrey Pole, K.G., of Medmenham and Ellesborough, Bucks, by first wife, Edith St. John, dau. of Sir Oliver St. John by **MARGARET BEAUCHAMP** (85-35), sister and h. of Sir John Beauchamp of Bletso. (CP VI 656 note e; XI 399-402; CCN 815; Blore 21: 1-5).

38. SIR HENRY POLE, Lord Montagu (brother of Reginald, Cardinal Pole); m. Jane Neville, dau. of Sir George Neville, Lord Abergavenny. (CP V 656 note e; Blore 21: 1-5).

39. CATHERINE POLE, d. 23 Sep. 1576; m. 1532, Sir Francis Hastings, K.G., 2nd Earl of Huntingdon, b. ca. 1514, d. 23 Jun. 1560, ae. 47 yrs. (CP VI 655-656; VII 694).

40. CATHERINE HASTINGS, b. 11 Aug. 1542; m. Sir Henry Fiennes, K.B. (or Clinton), 2nd Earl of Lincoln, M.P. 1571-1585, d. 29 Sep. 1616, son of Sir Edward Fiennes de Clinton, Earl of Clinton and Saye, Earl of Lincoln, Lord High Admiral 1550, by his 2nd wife, m. ca. 1541, Ursula Stourton, dau. of William, Lord Stourton, by Elizabeth, dau. of Edmund Dudley (Sutton), and sister of John, Duke of Northumberland. (CP VII 692-694; I Proc. Mass. Hist. Soc. II: 212; CCN 260).

41. THOMAS FIENNES (or Clinton), 3rd Earl of Lincoln, A.M., Christ Ch. Coll., Oxford 1588, M.P. 1601, 1604-1610, b. 1568, d. 15 Jan. 1618/19; m. ca. 21 Sep. 1584, Elizabeth Knyvett, d. aft. 1619, dau. of Sir Henry Knyvett of Charlton, Wilts. (CP VII 695-696; Proc. Mass. Hist. Soc. as before).

42. SUSAN FIENNES (or Clinton), d.s.p.; m. Maj.-Gen. John Humphrey, of Chaldon, Dorset, b. 1595, d. 1661, of Dorchester, England; Dep.-Gov. of Mass., came with his wife to New England, July 1634, founder of Lynn; memb. Artillery Co. 1640; Sergt.-Maj.-Gen. 1641; returned to Sandwich, England, 26 Oct. 1641 (see 228-40). (CP VII 696 note c; I Proc. Mass. Hist. Soc. 11: 212; Am. Antiquarian Soc., Coll. 3: 1, lxxxvi; Farmer 154; Jones: Thos. Dudley 46; Winthrop: Journal I 15, 127; II 83).

42. ARBELLA FIENNES (or Clinton), sister of Susan above, d.s.p. Salem Aug. 1630; m. Isaac Johnson, Esq., d. Boston, 30 Sep. 1630, son of Abraham Johnson of Chilsam, Rutlandshire, by his wife, a dau. of Dr. Chadderton, Master of Emmanuel College, Cambridge, and one of the translators of the King James version of the Bible. Governor Winthrop's flagship, the "Arbella," was named for Lady Arbella. (CP VII 696 note c; Winthrop: Journal I 15, 26, 52; Capt. Edward Johnson: Wonder Working Providence 56, 65; Am. Antiquarian Society, Collections III lxvii-lxviii, 87).

23. EUDES, Count of Brittany (214-23), b. 999, d. 7 Jan. 1079; also Count of Penthièvre 1034. (CP X 779-780).

24. BARDOLF (nat. son of Eudes), ancestor of the Lords Fitz Hugh of Ravensworth; brother of Bodin who held Ravensworth, Mickleton, Romandkirk, etc., in Domesday Book 1086. (CP V 416-417 note d; Yorkshire Archaeological Society Publications iv, v, "Early York Charters," v 196-200, 316-321).

25. AKARIS FITZ BARDOLF of Ravensworth. (CP V 416-417, note d).

26. HERVEY of Ravensworth, forester of the New Forest and Arkengarthdale, co. York, by grant of Conan, Duke of Brittany. (CP V 416).

27. HENRY FITZ HERVEY of Ravensworth, Cotherstone, Hinton, etc., Lord of Ravensworth, living 16 Mar. 1212; m. Alice, dau. of Randolf Fitz Wauter of Greystoke. (CP V 416 note d).

28. AGATHA OF RAVENSWORTH, m. **SIR MICHAEL LE FLEMING III** (34-27), b. 1197.

24. STEPHEN I (214-24), d. 21 Apr. 1135 or 1136, Count of Penthièvre and Richmond; m. Hawise (or Hedwig). (CP X 786-787).

25. ALAN II, d. 15 Sep. 1146, Earl of Richmond; m. ca. 1137, **BERTHA** (119-26) of Brittany. (CP X 780, 788-791).

38. ANNE KNOLLYS (1-38); m. **THOMAS WEST** (18-38), Lord de la Warre.

39. ELIZABETH WEST, b. 11 Sep. 1573; m. as his 2nd wife, Wherwell, Hants, 12 Feb. 1593/4, Herbert Pelham, of Fordingham, co. Dorset, and Hellingly, Sussex (father by his first wife of Herbert Pelham (1580-1624) who m. **PENELOPE WEST** (1-39), sister of Elizabeth West above).

40. ELIZABETH PELHAM, b. Hellingly, 27 Apr. 1607, d. 1 Nov. 1628; m. Salisbury, 4 Sep. 1621, Col. John Humphrey, gent., of Chaldon (ae. 25 in 1621), who m. (3) 1630/4, **SUSAN FIENNES** (225-42).

41. ANNE HUMPHREY, only surviving child, bapt. Fordingham, Dorset, 17 Dec. 1625; m. (1) William Palmes; m. (2) Rev. John Miles of Swansea, Mass. (Generations 38-41: Meredith B. Colket, Jr. in TAG 15: 123-124).

42. REV. SAMUEL MYLES, A.M. (H.C. 1684), was Rector of King's Chapel, Boston 1689-1728. (Weis: Colonial Clergy of New England 148).

40. PENELOPE PELHAM (dau. of Herbert Pelham and **PENELOPE WEST** (1-39), and sister of **HERBERT PELHAM** (1-40), 1st wife), b. ca. 1619, d. 28 May 1702; m. 9 Nov. 1641, Richard Bellingham, b. Boston, co. Lincoln, ca. 1592, d. 1672, son of William and Frances (Amcotts) Bellingham of Manton and Bromby, co. Linc.; M.P. 1628-1629, came to Mass. 1634, Gov. of Mass. 1641, 1654, 1665-1672 (no issue by this marriage). (TAG 18: 138; "Linc. Pedigrees" Harl. Soc. Pub. 50: 118).

* * *

41. CAPT. EDWARD PELHAM, gent. of Newport, R.I. (son of **HERBERT PELHAM** (1-40) by 2nd wife), b. ca. 1650, d. 20 Sep. 1730; m. 18 Apr. 1682, Freelove Arnold, b. 20 Jul. 1661, d. 8 Sep. 1711, dau. of Gov. Benedict Arnold of R.I. (Colket in TAG 18: 144-145).

30. SIR PETER DE ARDERNE, Knt. (150-30), of Alford, Alvanley and Alderley, bore arms 1289, d. ca. 1292; m. Margery. (Inq.p.m. 1292; Earwaker: East Chester I 473).

31. SIR JOHN DE ARDERNE, Knt., of Alford, Alvanley, Alderley and Elford, b. 1266, d. 1308; m. bef. 1299, Margery, dau. of Griffin ap Madog, lord of Bromfield. (Ibid.)

32. SIR JOHN DE ARDERNE, Knt., of Alford and Elford, etc., d. ca. 1349, Knight of the Shire of Stafford 1324; held manors of Stockport, Poynton and Woodford; m. (1) 1307/8, Alice, dau. of Hugh de Venables, Baron of Kinderton. (Ibid. 474; Inq. p.m. 1349).

33. PETER DE ARDERNE of Alvanley and of Harden, b. 1327, d. bef. 1378/9; m. Cicely, dau. of Adam de Bredbury, and Cicely his wife. (Ibid., 474).

34. HUGH DE ARDERNE of Harden and Alvanley, fl. 1385, 1419, d. bef. 1423; m. (2) Cicely, dau. of Ralph de Hyde, living 1378/9. (Ibid., 474).

35. ALICE ARDERNE, m. ca. 1414/5, Christopher Davenport, Esq. of Woodford, b. ca. 1394, d. ca. 1488, son of Nicholas Davenport of Woodford, and his wife, Ellen, living 1371, wid. of Edward Massey. (Ibid. I 474; II 411).

36. JOHN DAVENPORT of Woodford, living 1476, d. bef. his father, ca. 1480; m. Alice, dau. of Ralph Prestwick. (Ibid.)

37. NICHOLAS DAVENPORT, Esq., of Woodford, succeeded his grandfather 1488, d. bef. 9 Feb. 1522; m. ca. 1459/60, **MARGARET DAVENPORT** (231-36), dau. of John Davenport, Esq., of Bramhall. (Ibid. I 436; II 411).

38. CHRISTOPHER DAVENPORT, of Lowcross in Malpas Parish, Cheshire, said to be founder of the branch of the Davenport family in Coventry; m. Emma, dau. of John Blunt of Stafford. (Earwaker: East Chester I 436; II 411; Harleian MSS 1535,2094,2119: Visitation of the County of Warwick in the Year 1619 in Harl. Soc. Pub. XII (London 1877), 373; Isabel MacB. Calder: Letters of John Davenport, Puritan Divine, New Haven, 1937, pp. 1, 13-14, notes 4 and 5).

* * *

39. EDWARD DAVENPORT, ancestry unknown, Mayor of Coventry, 1551; m. Margery, dau. of John Harford, alderman of Coventry. (Ibid.)

40. HENRY DAVENPORT, Mayor of Coventry 1613, alderman for life 1621, d. Coventry, Warwickshire, by 1627 (his brother Christopher Davenport, d. 1627/9, was alderman, and assisted in the education of his nephew, John); m. (1) **WINIFRED BARNABY** (230A-40), d. by 1619, dau. of Richard Barnaby (mother of Rev. John); m. (2) Elizabeth Bennett (whose only child, Henry Davenport, d. by 1627). (Calder, op.cit. I 13-14).

41. THE REVEREND JOHN DAVENPORT, B.D. (Oxford, 1625), bapt. Coventry, 9 Apr. 1597, d. Boston, Mass., 15 Mar. 1669/70; a founder of New Haven Colony, minister there and at the First Church in Boston; m. bef. 1619, Elizabeth Wooley. (Weis: Colonial Clergy of New England, 69; CCN 310; Calder, op.cit.; Boston Evening Transcript, "H.B." in answer to ALOL 8670, 19 Jun. 1929).

Line 230A

33. JOYCE DE BOTETOURT (216-32), b. 1367/8, d. 12 Aug. 1420, m. (1) Sir Baldwin Freville, of Tamworth Castle, b. 1350/1, d. 1387/8. (Gen. Mag. 21, No. 6, 373-375).

34. MARGARET FREVILLE, m. (1) Sir Hugh Willoughby, of Middleton, co. Warwick, Knt., m. (2) Sir Richard Bingham, Knt. (Dugdale, Antiquities of Warwickshire; Willoughby ped. in Visitations of Nottinghamshire, 1569 and 1614, pub. by Harl. Soc; Gen. Mag. cit.)

35. ELEANOR WILLOUGHBY, m. John Shirley, d. 1486, of Eatington and Shirley, co. Warwick. (Stemmata Shirleiana (London, 1873) 53f.; TAG 23: 109).

36. HUGH SHIRLEY, 4th son, b. say 1467, m. Anne, wid. (d. seized of Clyberry 17 Sep 1510), dau. & coh. John Hevyn of Hevyn, psh. of Dilwyn, co. Hereford, and of Clyberry, co. Salop. (Stemmata Shirleiana 54 and Table II; Visitations of Shropshire 1623 (Harleian Sco. v. 28) 83, 153).

37. THOMAS SHIRLEY, d.v.p., m. Margaret, dau. John Wroth of Durance, psh. of Enfield, co. Middlesex. (Stemmata Shirleiana 54, Table II misidentifies him as "John" Shirley).

38. JOYCE SHIRLEY, only surviving dau. & h., m. (1) Richard Abington or Habington, of Brockhamton, co. Hereford, m. (2) Thomas Blount of Sodington, co. Worcs., as (2) wife. She had 3 daus., cohs. of father, by (1), and 2 sons by (2). (Stemmata Shirleiana 54, Table II misidentifies 2 husb. as "Richard", though "Thomas" in text; Harleian Soc. 27, Visitations of Worcs. 1569, 18, 22, 63; Nash: Hist. of Worcs, 2nd ed. I ped. facing p. 588).

39. MARY ABINGTON (or Habington), eldest dau. & coh. of father Richard, d. 9 July 1574, inherited Brockhampton, m. by 1555 Richard Barnaby, bur. widower 4 Dec. 1597, of Acton and the Hull, co. Worcs, Esq., son & h. of Thomas Barnaby of the Hull and Joyce,

Line 230A (cont.)

dau. & h. of Walter Acton of Acton, co. Worcs. (Nash cit. I: 115-118; Visitations of Worcs. 1569 cit. 14; Weaver: Visits. of Hereford (London 1884) 2; TAG 52:216-217).

40. WINIFRED BARNABY, 3rd of 4 daus., b. 1569, bur. Holy Trinity, Coventry, co. Warwick, 12 Apr. 1597; m. ca. 1585 as (1) wife **HENRY DAVENPORT** (230-40), b. say 1555, draper, alderman, Mayor of Coventry, bur. Holy Trinity 29 May 1627. (Visit. of Warwick 1619, cit. 373; parish registers of Holy Trinity, Coventry, in Warwick Co. Record Office, Warwick.) (This information supplied by Gary Boyd Roberts.)

Line 231

29. WILLIAM DE WARENNE (83-29), m. 1283, **JOAN DE VERE** (60-30).

30. JOHN DE WARENNE, 8th and last Earl of Surrey of this family, b. 30 Jun. 1286; d. without legitimate issue.

31. SIR EDWARD DE WARENNE, Knt. (nat. son of John de Warenne, by Maud of Nerford), living 1347, d. bef. 1369; m. Cicely de Eton, dau. of Sir Nicholas de Eton, Knt., of Poynton and Stockport.

32. SIR JOHN DE WARENNE, Knt., b. ca. 1343, d. 1387 (Inq.p.m. 1392), of Poynton and Stockport; m. 1371, Margaret, d. 6 Apr. 1418, (Inq.p.m. 1418), dau. of Sir John de Stafford, Knt., of Wickham.

33. NICHOLAS DE WARENNE, b. 1378, d. 1414, of Poynton and Stockport; m. Agnes, living 1417, dau. of Sir Richard de Wynnington of Wynnington, co. Chester, Knt.

34. SIR LAWRENCE DE WARENNE, Knt., b. ca. 1394, d. 1444, of Poynton and Stockport; m. Margaret, dau. of Richard Bulkeley and Margery Venables.

35. CICELY DE WARENNE, m. ca. 4 Jan. 1435, John de Davenport, bapt. Stockport, 3 May 1419, d. Oct. 1478 (Inq.p.m.), of Bramhall, Esq.

36. MARGARET DAVENPORT, of Bramhall, m. ca. 1459/60, **NICHOLAS DAVENPORT,** Esq. (230-37), of Woodford. (J.P. Earwaker: East Chester I 436, Davenport of Bramhall: II 286, Warenne of Poynton; II 411, Davenport of Woodford).

Line 232

28. MAUD MARSHALL (69-28), d. 1248; m. (1) 1207/12, Hugh Bigod, d. 1224/5, Earl of Norfolk, Magna Charta Surety 1215. (Parkin IV 306).

29. SIR SIMON LE BIGOD, 3rd son, living 1236, d. bef. 1242; m. Maud de Felbrigg, a wid. seen 1242 and 1275, only dau. and eventual sole h. of Richard de Felbrigg, and granddau. of Roger de Felbrigg of Felbrigg, co. Norfolk, and his wife the dau. of Gilbert de Norfolk, Lord of Beeston. (Parkin IV 305-307).

30. SIR ROGER LE BIGOD, living 1275, 1281 and 1295; m. Cecilia, living 1295. (Op. cit., IV 306).

31. SIR SIMON LE BIGOD, alias Felbrigg, of Felbrigg, Knt., living 1310, Lord of the Manor of Felbrigg 1316-1349; m. Alice, dau. of Sir George de Thorpe, Knt., Lord of the Manor of Breisworth, co. Suffolk. (Op. cit., IV 305-307).

32. SIR ROGER LE BIGOD, alias Felbrigg, of Felbrigg, Lord of the Manor of Felbrigg 1352-1368; m. Elizabeth de Scales (CP XI 507), dau. and h. of Robert de Scales, 3rd Lord Scales (b. ca. 1311, d. 13 Aug. 1369, M.P. 1341-1369, Lord of the Manor of Worlington) and his wife, Catherine de Ufford, dau. of Robert de Ufford, 1st Earl of Suffolk, and Margaret, dau. of Sir Walter de Norwich. (CP XI 501-502, 507; DNB XLI 230; LVIII 13). Robert, Lord Scales III, was son of Sir Robert de Scales, Knt., 2nd Lord Scales (b. ca. 1279, d. 20 Mar. 1324/5, M.P. 1306-1322, Knt. 1306, Lord of the Manor of Worlington) by his wife, Egeline, d. 10 Oct. 1335, prob. dau. of **SIR HUGH COURTENAY** (50-30), Baron of Oakhampton, co. Devon. (CP XI 500-502, 507; Parkin IV 305-307; J.J. Muskett: Suffolk Manorial Families I 153).

33. SIR SIMON DE FELBRIGG, of Felbrigg, alias Bigod, K.G., Lord of the Manors of Felbrigg, co. Norfolk, and of Breisworth, co. Suffolk and Lord of Beeston Regis, co. Norfolk, K.G. 1422, standard bearer to Richard II, fl. 1395, 1399, will made Sep. 1431, pro. 1443; m. (1) Margaret, d. 1413 (possibly dau. of Prezemysl I Nosak, Duke of Teschen and Glogau, prob. illeg., (son of Kazimierz I by Eufemie, dau. of Trojden I of Masovia). He had m. (1) Elska, dau. of Boleslaw of Beuthen-Kosel). He m. (2) Katherine said to be dau. of Sir Anketil Malory "of Winwick", wid. of Ralph Greene of Drayton. Perh. she was dau. of **SIR ANKETIL MALORY** of Kirkby (16A-32). (Erroneous statements appear in Parkin: History of Norfolk IV 305-307; Muskett: Suffolk Manorial Families I 153; Weever 856; See discussion in Chas. Evans' "Margaret, Lady Felbrygge" in Blackmansbury II (Apr. 1965), pp. 207).

34. HELENA DE FELBRIGG, dau. by (1), (h. of her brother, Thomas de Felbrigg, to the Manor of Breisworth in Suffolk); m. Sir William Tyndal of Dene, co. Northants., d. 1426. (Parkin IV 205-207; Muskett I 153).

35. SIR THOMAS TYNDAL, of Dene and Redenhall, co. Norfolk, Lord of the Manor of Breisworth in Suffolk, d. 1448; m. Margaret, dau. of Sir William Yelverton, Justice of the King's Bench 1471. (Muskett I 153).

36. SIR WILLIAM TYNDAL, K.B., of Dene and Hockwold, co. Norfolk, K.B. 1473, d. ca. 1488 (Inq.p.m. 13 H VII), inherited Worlington manor 1484, as one of the heirs of Thomas, Lord Scales, being a descendant of Elizabeth (Scales) Felbrigg (see No. 32 above). (CP XI 507), and he was declared h. by inheritance through his great-grandmother Margaret (see No. 33 above) to the Kingdom of Bohemia; he m. Mary, dau. and h. of Sir Osbert Mondeford of Feltwell, co. Norfolk, Esq., by Elizabeth Berney. (Muskett I 153).

Line 232 (cont.)

37. SIR JOHN TYNDAL, K.B., of Hockwold, sold his Suffolk manor 1524; m. Amphillis, dau.of Sir Humphrey Coningsby. (Muskett I 153; Ormerod (Helsby): Cheshire 711-713).

38. SIR THOMAS TYNDAL, of Hockwold and Great Maplestead, co. Suffolk, High Sheriff of the counties of Norfolk and Suffolk 1561; will made 18 Apr. 1583; m. (2) ca. 1533, Anne, dau. of Sir Henry Fermor of East Bersham, co. Norfolk. (Muskett I 153).

39. SIR JOHN TYNDAL, Knt., of Great Maplestead, Knt. 1603, will made 17 Jan. 1615/16; murdered 12 Nov. 1616; m. Anna (Egerton) Dean, will made 14 Jun. 1620, d. Jul. 1620, dau. of Thomas Egerton, Esq., of Wallegrange, co. Suffolk, and London. (Muskett I 153).

40. MARGARET TYNDAL, b. ca. 1591, d. Boston, Mass., 14 Jun. 1647, ae. 56; m. 28 Apr. 1618, as his 3rd wife, John Winthrop, Esq., of Groton, co. Suffolk, Governor of Massachusetts 1630-1634, 1637-1640, 1642-1644, 1646-1649, b. Groton, Suffolk, Eng., 12 Jan. 1587, d. Boston, Mass., 26 Mar. 1649. (See abundant material about the last several generations in Winthrop Papers (M.H.S.) 1929, 1931, 1943, 1944, 1947, 1952, etc.; Lawrence Shaw Mayor: The Winthrop Family in America, 1948: Muskett I 153, etc.)

41. COL. STEPHEN WINTHROP (1619-1658), m. Judith Rainsborough.

41. ADAM WINTHROP (1620-1652), m. Elizabeth Glover.

41. DEANE WINTHROP (1623-1704), m. Sarah Glover.

41. CAPT. SAMUEL WINTHROP (1627-1674, H.C. 1646); m. Jun. 1648, Elizabeth; Dep.-Gov. of Antigua, W.I., 1667-1669, etc.

Line 233

36. SIR THOMAS STANLEY, K.G., of Lathom (57-36); m. **JANE GOUSHILL** (20-33).

37. KATHERINE STANLEY, m. Sir John Savage of Clifton, d. 22 Nov. 1495, ae. 73 yrs. (son of Sir John Savage of Clifton, d. 29 Jun. 1463, ae. 53 yrs., son of Sir John Savage of Clifton, Knt., d. 1 Aug. 1450, fought at Agincourt 1415, Knt. 1416), by **MAUD DE SWYNNERTON** (32-33), q.v. (see Visitations of Cheshire 1580, pp. 203, 204; Peter Leycester: Hist. & Antiq. pp. 231, 232; note: some of these ages at death are certainly in error).

38. KATHERINE SAVAGE, m. (lic. 4 Nov. 1479) Thomas Legh, Esq., of Adlington, co. Chester, b. 1452, d. Adlington, 8 Aug. 1519 (Inq.p.m.; will dated 4 May, pro. 15 Sep. 1519), son of Robert de Legh of Adlington and Ellen, dau. of Sir Robert Booth, of Dunham Massey, Knt.

39. GEORGE LEGH of Adlington, Esq., b. 1497, d. Fleet Prison, 12 Jun. 1529 (Inq. p.m.; will made 11 Jun. 1529); m. ca. 1523, Joan, dau. of Peter Larke of London and co. Hunts; she m. (2) George Paulet.

40. THOMAS LEGH of Adlington, Esq., b. ca. 1527, d. Eaton, co. Chester, 17 May 1548 (Inq.p.m.); m. Mary, dau. of Richard Grosvenor of Eaton, Esq.; she d. 26 Mar. 1599, will dated 18 Oct. 1597.

41. THOMAS LEGH of Adlington, Esq., b. 1547, d. 25 Jan. 1601/2 (Inq.p.m.; will 20 Nov. 1600); he rebuilt Adlington Hall 1581; High Sheriff of Cheshire 1588; m. Cheadle, 29 Jun. 1563, Sybil, dau. of Sir Urian Brereton of Handford, Knt. (her will was dated 6 Jun. 1608, and she was buried 19 Feb. 1609/10).

42. SIR URIAN LEGH of Adlington, Knt., bapt. Cheadle 1566, knighted 26 Jun. 1596, High Sheriff of Chester 1613, d. 2 Jun., bur. 4 Jun. 1627 (Inq. p.m.); m. (settlement 9 Sep. 1586) Margaret, dau. of Sir Edmund Trafford, of Trafford, co. Lancaster, Knt. (J.P. Earwaker: East Chester II 251-252).

43. LUCY LEGH, bapt. Manchester, 12 Jul. 1596, bur. 5 Mar. 1643/4; m. Col. Alexander Rigby of Middleton, co. Lancaster, Esq., b. 1594, d. 18 Aug. 1650, son of Alexander and Anne (Asshaw) Rigby of Wigan, co. Lancaster; lawyer, Col. in the Parliamentary Army, Baron of the Exchequer; adm. Grey's Inn 1610, M.P. 1639-1640; Dept.-Lieut. for Lancashire 1641-1642, Col. 1643-1644, purchased the Plough Patent (Organized by the Rev. Stephen Bachiller) which included the province of Lygonia in Maine between the Sagadohoc and Kennebeck Rivers, 7 Apr. 1643, Dept.-President of Lygonia 1643-1644.

44. EDWARD RIGBY, succeeded to his father's rights in Maine; his bro., Alexander Rigby, bapt. at Prestbury, 26 Aug. 1620; there were four children by Lucy (Legh) Rigby. (J.P. Earwaker: East Chester II 250-252; Genealogical Dict. of Me. and N.H. II 587; 4th series Collections of the Massachusetts Historical Society VII pp. 90-91 note, and ff.).

Line 234 Original line, published years ago, no longer sound. Read the following discussion.

The ancestry of John Drake has been widely questioned for several reasons, which will not be discussed here. As a result of these questions, it was dropped from the 3rd edition of this work. Since that time, Mrs. J.J. Kiepura, of Soledad, Calif., has published a study, demonstrating that the identification of John Drake's parentage is probably sound, and which was accepted by Donald Lines Jacobus at the time it was published. However, the line as published in the earlier editions, running through Grenville, though probably correct in substance if not in detail, has some inconsistencies in dates. The following line which replaced it in subsequent editions, also contains errors. Those wishing to see the proofs of John Drake's parentage are referred to The American Genealogist, vol. 41, pp. 239-244.

30. JOHN OF GAUNT (1-31), Duke of Lancaster, by his (3) wife, Katharine (Roet) Swynford. (DNB; Armitage-Smith: John of Gaunt; TAG 32:9-10).

31. HENRY BEAUFORT, Bishop of Lincoln, Bishop of Winchester, Cardinal of St. Eusebius, b. ca. 1375, d. Winchester 11 Apr. 1447, bur. Winchester Cathedral; in his youth had an affair with

Lady Alice fitz Alan, b. ca. 1373-5, d. unknown, dau. of **SIR RICHARD FITZ ALAN** (60-32); m. by Mar. 1392, Sir John Charlton, 4th Baron Charlton of Powis who d.s.p. 19 Oct. 1401. His bastard dau. Jane (or Joan) and her husband, Sir Edward Stradling, are mentioned in Cardinal Beaufort's will dated 20 Jan. 1446/7. (DNB; John of Gaunt, esp. pp. 389, 462; TAG 32: 10-11).

    32. JOAN BEAUFORT, b. prob. winter 1391/2; m. Sir Edward Stradling, Knt. of St. Donat's Castle, co. Glamorgan, b. ca. 1389, ae. 22+ on 23 Nov. 1411, son of Sir William of same, by Isabel St. Barbe. On pilgrimage to Jerusalem 9 Hen. IV (1407-8) and returned, d. 1453. (TAG 32: 11).

* * *

    33. WILLIAM STRADLING, yr. brother (not son) of Sir Edward, gen. 32, (Vis. Gloucs. p. 133; refs. cited in TAG 32: 11; Richard Llwyd's "History of Wales" (1832) p. 108; Trahern, "Stradling Correspondence" (1840) xviii, xix; "Genealogies of Glamorgan" 435).

    34. GWENLIAN STRADLING, m. Sir Anthony Woodville, d. 1483. (Vis. Gloucs. 133).

    35. MARGARET WOODVILLE, m. Sir Robert Poyntz, Knt., ae. 17 in 1466, d. 1520. (Vis. Gloucs. 133). They were not parents of No. 36. Line breaks at this point. Gen. 36 not son of Gen. 35. See 234A, Gen. 35 for correct parentage of No. 36.

* * *

    36. HUMPHREY POYNTZ (234A-36), b. bef. 1450, could not be son of No. 35, m. Elizabeth Pollard. (Vivian's Visit. of Devon 57, 597; Harl. Soc.: Vis. of Devon 215; Maclean: Hist. & Gen. Mem. of the Fam. of Poyntz 95, 256; Trans. Bristol & Gloucs. Arch.Soc. XII: 151).

    37. CATHARINE POYNTZ, m. as (2) wife, Fulk Prideaux. (Vivian 615; Harl. Soc. 219).

    38. HUMPHREY PRIDEAUX, b. 1486, d. 1550; m. Elizabeth Hatch, d. 1571, will dtd 13 Jul 1571. (Vivian 616,293; Harl.Soc. 93:4).

    39. ELIZABETH PRIDEAUX of Theuborough, Devon; m. Robert Drake (2nd son of John Drake of Ashe by his wife Amy Grenville) of Wiscombe Park, Devon. (GS of Robert, bur. Southleigh Church, 30 Mar. 1600; Rogers: Ant. Sepul. Effigies of Devon 207; Vivian 293).

    40. WILLIAM DRAKE, of Wiscombe Park, bur. Southleigh, will 4 Dec. 1619, pro. 19 May 1625; m. Philippa (will 16 Jul. 1647, pro. 5 Oct. 1655), dau. of Sir Robert Dennys, of Holcombe-Burnell, Knt. (will of Sir Robert, 15 Jul. 1592, pro. 22 Sep. 1592). (Rogers, op. cit. 207; Vivian: Devon 280, 293).

    41. JOHN DRAKE, b. at Wiscombe 1585, came to New England 1630; settled in Windsor, Conn.; mentioned in Vivian: Visitations of Devonshire 293, as "emigrated to New England." (For John Drake's children, see Frank B. Gay: The Descendants of John Drake of Windsor, Connecticut, Rutland, Vt. 1933. Pages xii to xxii supply data on generations 39 to 41.)

25. ROBERT MALET, mentioned in connection with Warminster, Wilts in 1130, held the barony of Curry Malet, Somerset by 1135, which previously had been held by the de Courcelles family, d. by 1156; widely believed to be a grandson of William Malet (d. 1071) of Graville-Saint Honorine, Normandy, who was a companion of William I the Conqueror at the Battle of Hastings in 1066, and afterwards served as Sheriff of York in 1068; m. Hesilia Crispin, quite possibly great-granddau. of Richard I, Duke of Normany. Malet family arms were, Azure, three escallops or. (Arthur Malet, Notices of an English Branch of the Malet Family, 1-73; Sanders, English Baronies, 38-39; Arthur Malet, "Notes on the Malet Family", Somerset Arch. and Nat. Hist. Soc. xxx, 74-75; Wagner, English Genealogy (2nd ed.), 66; Dugdale, Baronage, I 110-111; Falaise Roll, Tables III & V).

26. WILLIAM I MALET, died 1169, steward and favorite of King Henry II, held barony of Curry Malet, Somerset and other lands in Kent, Cambridge and Sussex; one of the recognitors of the Constitutions of Clarendon in 1164. (Sanders, op. cit.; Dugdale, op. cit.; VCH Cambridge VI 159-160 (manor of Dullingham, a Malet property); Arthur Malet, Notices of an English Branch of the Malet Family 73-74).

27. GILBERT MALET, d. ca. 1194, held barony of Curry Malet, Somerset, steward during reign of King Henry II, in which capacity he witnessed the treaty in 1174, between Henry II and William, King of Scotland; m. Alice, dau. of Ralph Picot. (Malet, op. cit. 75-76; Sanders, op. cit.; Dugdale, op. cit.; VCH Cambridge op. cit.

28. WILLIAM II MALET, adult by 1196, d. ca. 1216, held barony of Curry Malet, Somerset, Sheriff of Somerset and Dorset, 1209, Magna Charta surety, 1215, m. Alice, d. ca. 1263, dau. and coh. of Thomas Basset (d. 1220), lord of Headington, Oxford and of Colynton and Whitford, Devon, by his wife, Philippa Malbank. Alice's maritagium was the manor of Deddington, Oxford. She m. (2) by 1223 John Bisset (or Biset) who died in 1241. The Basset family arms were, Or three bars wavy gules. (Sanders, op. cit. 38-39, 51-52; Malet, op. cit. 77-83; VCH Cambridge op. cit. VI 159-160; DNB XII 865-866; Dugdale, op. cit.; VCH Somerset V 97-98 (manor of Kilve, a Malet property); CP X 672, esp. footnote g.)

29. HAWISE MALET, dau. and coh. to barony of Curry Malet, Somerset, living 4 May 1287, m. (1) bef. 23 Mar. 1216/7, Sir Hugh Poyntz, adult by 1210, d. shortly bef. 4 Apr. 1220, son and h. apparent of Nicholas Poyntz (dead by 2 Nov. 1223), lord of Tockington, Gloucester, by his first wife, Juliane, dau. of Hugh Bardolf. With his father, Hugh joined the Barons against King John, and was captured 17 July 1216, at Worcester and imprisoned. The Poyntz family arms were, Barry of eight or and gules. Hawise m. (2) bef. 11 Feb. 1220/1, Robert de Muscegros of Charlton, Somerset who d. shortly bef. 29 Jan. 1253/4. (CP X 672; Sanders, English Baronies 38-39; Sir John Maclean, Historical and Genealogical Memoir of the Family of Poyntz, esp. charts pp. 28-29; VCH Cambridge op. cit.; Cal. Inq.p.m. I 82).

192

30. SIR NICHOLAS POYNTZ, b. ca. 1220, d. shortly bef. 7 Oct. 1273, lord of Tockington and Swell, Gloucester. In 1225, he was, through his grandmother, a coh. of Robert Bardolf, and on his stepfather's death in 1253/4, he entered into possession of his mother's portion of half the barony of Curry Malet, Somerset with its 1/3 share of the Basset inheritance. Although his wife's name has not been confirmed, the 1552 Visitation of Essex calls her Elizabeth, daughter of Timothy Dyall. The Inq.p.m. of Nicholas Poyntz, dated 1273, shows that he held the manors of Curry Malet, Somerset; Hoo, Kent; and Sutton, Dorset; and that prior to his death, he had given the manor of Tockington, Gloucester and a moiety of the manor of Dullingham, Cambridge to his son, Hugh. (CP X 673; Sanders, op. cit.; VCH Gloucester VI 167 (manor of Swell, a Poyntz property); VCH Cambridge op. cit.; Maclean, op. cit.)

31. SIR HUGH POYNTZ, b. 25 Aug. 1252, d. shortly bef. 4 Jan. 1307/8, first Lord Poyntz, held manors of Curry Malet, Somerset (including a moiety interest in the barony), Tockington, Gloucester, Hoo St. Werbergh and Lullingstone, Kent; Dullingham, Cambridge; and Sutton, Dorset. Maclean, Bristol and Glouc. Arch. Soc. Trans. XII 129 suggests wife of Sir Hugh Poyntz was Margaret, daughter of Sir William Paveley. (CP X 673-674; Sanders, op. cit.; Knights of Edward I, IV 89-90; VCH Cambridge VI 159-160 (manor of Dullingham); Maclean, op. cit.)

32. SIR NICHOLAS POYNTZ, 2nd Lord Poyntz, b. ca. 1278 (ae. 30+ in 1308), d. shortly bef. 12 July 1311, conservator of peace, Dorset, 1307, supervisor of array, Somerset and Dorset, 1311; held manors of Curry Malet, Somerset (including a moiety interest in the barony); Tockington, Gloucester; Hoo and Lullingstone, Kent; Dullingham, Cambridge; and Sutton and Stoke St. Edwald, Dorset; m. (1) by 20 Jan. 1287/8, **ELIZABETH LA ZOUCHE** (253-30), living 1297, dau. of Eudo La Zouche of Harringworth, Northants by Milicent, dau. and eventual h. of Sir William de Cauntelo; m. (2) by 9 Feb. 1308/9, to Maud (or Matilda), d. 15 Aug. 1361, dau. & eventual h. of Sir John II de Acton (d. 1312) of Iron Acton, Gloucester, Sheriff of Gloucester 1311, by his first wife, Helen. Maud m. (2) by 12 Apr. 1315, Sir Roger de Chaundos (or Chandos), first Lord Chaundos, adult by 1303, d. 24 Sep. 1353, lord of Snodhill, Wellington and Fownhope, co. Hereford, Sheriff of Hereford, Glamorgan and Morganwg, Keeper of Caerphilly Castle, son of Robert de Chaundos by his wife, Alice. The Acton family arms were, Quarterly per fesse indented argent and azure. (Sanders, op. cit.; CP X 674-675; III 147-148; VCH Cambridge op. cit.; Vis. of Gloucs. 1623 (Harl. Soc. Pub., XXI 128-133) (for Poyntz and Acton pedigrees); Maclean, op. cit.; List of Sheriffs for England and Wales, Lists & Indexes, no. IX, p. 49).

33. SIR JOHN POYNTZ, son by (2), b. say 1310, d. 24 Feb. 1376, lord of Iron Acton, Winston and Elkstone, Gloucester which he received in 1343, by an agreement with his first cousin, Sir John de Acton; Sheriff of Gloucester 1368; m. (1) by 1343, Elizabeth, dau. and coh. of Sir Philip de Clanvowe by his wife, Philippa. The Clanvowe family arms were, Paly of six or and azure, on a fess gules three mullets argent. (VCH Gloucester VII 212 (manor of Elkstone, an Acton property); Maclean, op. cit. 51-53, and charts pp. 29, 94; Vis. of Gloucs. 1623 (Harl. Soc. Pub., XXI 128-133) (for Poyntz and Clanvowe pedigrees); Cal. Inq.p.m. XIV 303-304; XV 19-20; List of Sheriffs for England and Wales, Lists & Indexes, no. IX, p. 49).

34. ROBERT POYNTZ, Esq., b. 15 Jun 1359 at Deuchurch in Irchinfeld, co. Hereford, d. 15 June 1439, bur. Iron Acton, Gloucester; lord of Iron Acton, Winston, Elkstone and Acton Ulgar, Gloucester, and, in right of his wife, lord of Hull alias Hill and Nympsfield, Gloucester; Escheator of Gloucester, 1395, 1399, 1402, and 1415; Sheriff of Gloucester, 1396; m. (1) Anne, parentage unknown, by whom he had no issue, m. (2) Katherine Fitz Nichol, b. ca. 1378 (ae. 40+ in 1418), living 8 Feb. 1441, dau. and coh. of Sir Thomas Fitz Nichol, b. ca. 1354, d. 1418, of Hull alias Hill and Nympsfield, Gloucester, Sheriff of Gloucester 1382, by his first wife, Margery. Sir Thomas Fitz Nichol was 8th in descent from Robert Fitz Harding, d. 1170/1, first feudal Lord Berkeley who was granted Berkeley Castle, co. Gloucester by King Henry II ca. 1153-4. For Sir Thomas' lineage back to Robert Fitz Harding, see John Smyth: The Lives of the Berkeleys I 43-50. The Fitz Nichol family arms were, Quarterly gules and or, a bend(let) argent. Sir Thomas' wife, Margery, was probably closely related to Edmund Blount (b. 1352, d. 1381) of Filton, Gloucester as Sir Thomas and Margery enfeoffed Edmund and his wife Margaret ca. 1379-80, with moieties of the manors of Filton and Harry Stoke (or Stoke Harris), Gloucester in return for 16 marks yearly payment. Smyth, op. cit. I 48, states that Margery was herself heiress to moieties of these manors but does not give her parentage. (Maclean, op. cit. 54-57, and chart p. 94; Vis. of Gloucs. 1623 (Harl. Soc. Pub. XXI 128-133) (for Poyntz and Fitz Nichol pedigrees); VCH Gloucester VII 212 (manor of Elkstone); Cal. Close Rolls, Henry V, I A.D. 1413-1419, 493-494; Henry V, II, A.D. 1413-1422, 158-159; Cal. Fine Rolls, XIV, A.D. 1413-1422, 269-270; List of Escheators for England and Wales, List and Index Society, 72: 53-54; CP II: 125-125 (re Robert Fitz Harding, first Lord Berkeley); Cal. Inq.p.m. XV: 124-126, 184); List of Sheriffs for England and Wales, Lists & Indexes, no. IX, p. 50).

35. SIR NICHOLAS POYNTZ, son by (2), adult by 1411, d. shortly bef. 20 Sep. 1460, lord of Iron Acton, Tockington, Swell, Nympsfield, Winston, and Elkstone, co. Gloucester; Escheator for Gloucester, 1424, 1434; m. (1) Elizabeth, dau. of Sir Edward Mill of Harescombe, co. Gloucester (the Mill family arms were, Ermine a millrind azure); m. (2) by 17 Sep. 1450 (and probably much earlier), Elizabeth, living 7 Dec. 1470 when her dower rights were assigned to her, dau. of Sir Henry Hussey of Harting, Sussex. (Maclean, op. cit. 57-59, and charts pp. 94-95; Vis. Gloucs. 1623, op. cit. 72:36; VCH Gloucester op. cit.; List of Escheators for England and Wales, op. cit. 72: 54; Cal. Close Rolls, Edward IV II, A.D. 1468-1476, 57, 149).

36. HUMPHREY POYNTZ, son by (1), b. say 1430, d. 10 Oct. 1487, lord of Elkstone, Gloucester and, in right of his wife, lord of Over Woolacome and East Ansty (alias Ansty Cruse), Devon;

Line 234A (cont.)

Escheator of Devon, 1460; living 1461, Tawstock, Devon; living 1484, Womberlegh and Langlegh, Devon; m. by 1466 Elizabeth, living 1486, dau. and sole h. of Richard Pollard by his wife, Thomasin, dau. and coh. of William (or Robert) Cruse. The Pollard family arms were, Argent, on a chevron Sable between 3 escallops gules. (Maclean, op. cit. l.c. g; Vis. Gloucs. 1623 op. cit. 72:36; J.L. Vivian: Vis. Devon 59, 256 and 597 (for Pollard and Cruse pedigrees); VCH Gloucester op. cit.; List of Escheators for England and Wales, op. cit. 72:36; Inq.p.m. of Fulk Prideaux, 22 Henry VIII (A.D. 1530), Chanc. Ser. II; Cal. Fine Rolls, XIX, A.D. 1452-1461, 39-40; op. cit. XXII, A.D. 1485-1509, 84; Sir William Pole, Collections towards a Description of the County of Devon, 420 (East Ansty, a Pollard property).

37. KATHERINE POYNTZ, m. by 1486, as his (2) wife to Fulk Prideaux, Esq., d. 14 Jan. 1529/30, held manors of Blacheburgh, Yew, Middelmerwode, North Ludbroke, moieties of Overwollacomb and Theuborough, and 1/2 of 1/3 of Curreworthy and Esse Rafe, all in Devon; son of William Prideaux of Adeston in parish of Holbeton, Devon, by his third wife, Alice (d. 1511/2), dau. and coh. of Stephen Gifford of Theuborough, Devon. (J.L. Vivian, op. cit. 618 (for Prideaux pedigree); Transactions of the Devonshire Association XXXII, chart p. 214A (descent of manor of Esse Rafe through the families of Esse, Gifford and Prideaux); Pole, op. cit., 308-309 (Adeston, a Prideaux property); Abstract of Inq.p.m. for Fulk Prideaux, 22 Henry VIII (A.D. 1530), Chancery Ser. II, Vol. 51, no. 12 on file at Devon Record Office, Exeter, Devon).

38. HUMPHREY PRIDEAUX (234-38), b. ca. 1486 (ae. 44 in 1530), d. 8 May 1550, will dtd 4 July 1549, pro. 10 Jan. 1550/1 (PCC 15 Code), of Theuborough, Devon, Escheator of Devon, 1534; m. as his (2) wife, Edith, dau. of William Hatch of Aller, Devon, by his wife, Margaret, dau. and sole h. of Thomas Horton of South Molton, Devon. Edith left a will dtd. 23 Dec. 1562, pro. 13 July 1571, P.R. Exeter. (J.L. Vivian, op. cit. 618 and 455 (for Hatch pedigree); List of Escheators for England and Wales, op. cit. 72: 38).

Line 235

19. AETHELRED II (1-19), King of England 979-1016; m. (2) Emma of Normandy, dau. of Richard I, the Fearless, Duke of Normandy, and Gunnora. She d. 1052. (CP VI 466; XI App. D 109-110 note 1; XII pt. 1, 411-412).

20. GODGIFU, d. 1055; m. **DREUX** (250-20), Count of Vexin, d. 1035.

21. RALPH DE SUDELEY of Sudeley and Toddington, co. Gloucs. and Chilvers Coton, co. Warwick, d. 21 Dec. 1057; m. Getha. (CP XII pt. 1, op.cit.).

22. HAROLD DE SUDELEY, held as above, with Burton Dasset, co. Warwick. (CP cit. 412-413).

23. JOHN DE SUDELEY m. **GRACE DE TRACY** (222-27). (CP XII pt. 1 413-414; VI 466).

7. LLEWELLYN AP IORWERTH (176-7), Prince of Wales, m.
JOAN (27-27), dau. King John.
8. HELEN, m. (1) John le Scot, Earl of Huntingdon; m. (2)
ROBERT DE QUINCY of Colne Quincy, co. Essex, 3rd son of **SAIRE
DE QUINCY** (53-27), (CP III; Clay 228). He was the 2nd son named
Robert, the first d.s.p. 1217. (CP XII pt. 2, 748 note g).
9. HAWISE DE QUINCY, m. as (2) wife, Baldwin Wake, b. 1236,
d. 1281/2, son of Hugh Wake by his wife Joan (m. 1229) eldest dau.
and coh. Nicholas de Stuteville of Liddell, co. Cumb., by Devorgilla,
dau. **ROLAND OF GALLOWAY** (38-25). (Baldwin's first wife was
Ela, dau. William Beauchamp, Baron of Bedford, by wife Ida (dau.
WILLIAM LONGESPEE (30-26).) She d. 10 Jan. 1266/7. He d. by 10
Feb. 1281/2, she (b. ca. 1250) d. by 27 Mar. 1284/5. (CP XII pt. 2,
295 ff.; Clay: Early Yorkshire Charters XI 18-23, chart fac. p. 1).
10. JOHN WAKE, 1st Baron Wake, d. 1300; m. Joan, dau. Sir
John fitz Bernard of Kingsdown, co. Kent, d. 1310. (CP, op.cit.;
Clay 228-9).
11. MARGARET WAKE, b. ca. 1299, d. 29 Sep. 1349; m. (1) John
Comyn of Badenoch; m. (2) ca. 25 Dec. 1325, **EDMUND OF
WOODSTOCK** (155-31).
12. JOAN, "Fair Maid of Kent", m. (1) William Montacute, Earl
of Salisbury, div.; m. (2) **SIR THOMAS DE HOLAND,** K.G. (47-31),
who assumed Earldom of Kent j.u.; m. (3) 10 Oct. 1361, Edward, the
Black Prince, by whom mother of Richard II of England. She d. 7
Aug. 1385. (CP, op.cit.; DNB, etc.)

Line 237

4. SIBYL DE NEUFMARCHÉ (177-4, 193-4), great-granddau. of
Griffith I ap Llewellyn, Prince of North Wales; m. 1121, Miles Fitz
Walter, of Gloucester, Constable, Earl of Hereford 1141, d. 1143,
son of Walter Fitz Roger. (CP V 465 note d).
5. LUCY OF HEREFORD, dau. and coh., living 1219 or 1220,
Lady of Blaen Llyfni and Bwlch y Dinas, co. Brecknock, bur. Chapter
House of Lanthony, near Gloucester, heir to a 1/3 interest in the
barony of Miles of Gloucester, her father; m. by 1196 **HERBERT
FITZ HERBERT** (262-28), adult by 1165, d. sh. bef. Jun. 1204, son
and eventual h. of Herbert Fitz Herbert, dead by 1155, by his wife,
Sibyl Corbet.
6. PIERS FITZ HERBERT (262-29), son and eventual h., adult by
1204, d. sh. bef. 6 June 1235, bur. at Reading, heir through his
mother to a 1/3 interest to the barony of Miles of Gloucester, Earl
of Hereford; m. (1) (marriage settlement 28 Nov. 1203), **ALICE DE
WARKWORTH** (246D-28), dau. of Robert Fitz Roger, 2nd Baron of
Warkworth and sister of John Fitz Robert. Magna Charta Surety
1215.
7. LUCY FITZ PIERS, living 1266; m. **SIR WILLIAM DE ROS**
(170-26), b. aft. 1192, d. ca. 1264. (Generations 4-7: CP V 465 note
d).

(Magna Charta Line)

6. JOAN DE HUNTINGFIELD (187-6); m. Sir Richard Basset, Lord Basset.

7. RALPH BASSET, 2nd Lord Basset of Weldon, b. 27 Aug. 1300, d. ca. 4 May 1341; m. Joan Stordon, of Winterbourne, co. Gloucester. (CP II 10-11).

8. ALIAÑORE BASSET, m. Sir John Knyvet of Winwick, Northants, Chief Justice of the King's Bench, Lord Chancellor of England, d. 1381.

9. JOHN KNYVET, Esq., M.P. for Huntingfield 1397/8, d. 1418; m. Joan, dau. of John Botetourt of Mendlesham, Suffolk. (CP II 13).

10. SIR JOHN KNYVET, Sheriff of Northamptonshire 1427, d. 1446; m. Elizabeth, b. ca. 1392, dau. of Lord Clifton of Buckenham. (CP III 308).

11. MARGARET KNYVET, b. ca. 1412, d. 1458; m. Richard Chamberlayne, of Tilsworth, Bedfordshire, b. ca. 1392, d. 1439. (VCH Bedford, III 433; VCH Bucks, IV 340).

12. WILLIAM CHAMBERLAYNE, gent. b. ca. 1436, d. bef. 1471; m. Joan, living 1477. (Colket: Marbury Ancestry 42).

13. RICHARD CHAMBERLAYNE, of Sherbourne Castle, Oxfordshire, d. 28 Aug. 1497; m. Sybil, d. 1525, dau. of Richard Fowler of Sherbourne, Chancellor of the Duchy of Lancaster.

14. ANNE CHAMBERLAYNE, m. **SIR EDWARD RALEIGH**, Knt. (14-37). (Generations 6 to 14: Meredith B. Colket, Jr.: Marbury Ancestry, 1936, 41-42).

Line 239 (Prepared by David H. Kelley)

1. BRIAN BORU (175-1), m. Gormflaith, by whom he had a son **DONNCHAD** (175-2), who may have m. Druella, dau. of Godwin, Earl of Kent, and sister of King Harold. Donnchad was father of **DARB FORGAILL** (175-3), but not by Druella. Gormflaith m. again, Olaf Kvaaran, King of Dublin. Brian's dau. (not by Gormflaith) was

2. SLANI m. Sihtric of the Silken Beard, King of Dublin (son of Olaf Kvaaran, King of York and Dublin, d. in Iona abt. 981, by his wife Gormflaith, dau. of Murchad, King of Leinster, and wife of Brian. Sihtric went on pilgrimage to Rome 1028, and d. 1042.

3. OLAF, of Dublin, prob. the Olaf slain by the "Saxons" while en route to Rome on pilgrimage 1034; m. Maelcorcre, dau. of Dunlang, King of Leinster, who d. 1014.

4. RAGNAILLT m. Cynan ap Iago, Prince of North Wales, exiled in Dublin.

5. GRIFFITH, b. Dublin 1055, d. 1137, Prince of North Wales; m. ca. 1095, Angharat of Tegaingl, dau. Owain ap Edwin.

6. OWAIN I GWYNEDD, b. ca. 1100, d. 1170, Prince of North Wales; m. (1) **GLADYS** (176-5); m. (2) Christina (his cousin), dau. Gronw ap Owen ap Edwin. (Arthur Jones: The History of Gruffydd ap Cynan, Manchester, 1910, a translation and analysis of a twelfth century biography of Griffith, is the source for this pedigree, with details verified and amplified from the Irish Annals, especially the Annals of Innisfallen, of Ulster, and of the Four Masters).

MEROVINGIAN KINGS

OF FRANCE

Line 240 (See David H. Kelley in <u>NEHGR</u> 101: 109-112).

10. DAGOBERT II, King of Austrasia 676-680. (Generations 1 to 10 (questionable and omitted): Larousse, <u>Hist. de France</u> I 49).

11. ADELA, accepted by Eckhardt as dau. of Dagobert II but believed by Hlawitscha to be dau. of Hugobert and Irma; mother of Aubri I, Count of Blois. (Identification of Adela's parents depends on a forged charter.)

12. AUBRI I, Count of Blois, son of Adela and father of Aubri II.

13. AUBRI II, Count of Blois, son of Aubri I and father of Theidlindis.

14. THEIDLINDIS, dau. of Aubri II, Count of Blois; m. Count Gainfroi, fl. 795, son of Mainier, Count of Sens, Duke of Austria 791-796, d. 800, and his wife, a dau. of Duke Haudre.

15. GISELBERT, Count in the Massgau (the valley of the Meuse river) 839-842; prob. m. a sister of Echard, Count of Hesbaye.

16. GISELBERT, Count of Darnau 846-863; m. **HELLETRUDE** of Lorraine (also called Ermengarde), dau. of the Emperor **LOTHAIR I** (140-15).

17. RÉGNIER I (140-17), b. ca. 850, fl. 877-886, d. aft. 25 Oct. 915, bef. 19 Jan. 915/6, Count of Hainaut, lay Abbot of Echternach (Luxembourg) 897-915; m. (1) **HERSENT**, dau. of **CHARLES II** (148-15); m. (2) Alberade, d. 916 (of Mons ?). (Generations 10-18: G.A. Moriarty, in TAG 26: 188-189; 28: 23-25; Chaume I 548-549).

18. RÉGNIER II (son by first wife), b. ca. 890, d. 932, Count of Hainaut; m. Adelaide, dau. of Richard of Burgundy.

18. GISELBERT (140-18) (son by first wife), d. 2 Oct. 939, Duke of Lorraine, lay Abbot of Echternach 915-939; m. 929, Gerberga, d. 5 May 984, dau. of **HENRY I** (141-18), the Fowler, Emperor of Germany. (Ibid.)

From these two brothers are descended the later kings of England, Scotland, France, Spain, Portugal, many of the German emperors, the Dukes of Brabant, Burgundy, Warwick, Northumberland and Lorraine, the Earls of Chester, Clare and Pembroke, the Counts of Roucy, Vermandois, Barcelona, Provence, Nevers, Poitou, Burgundy and Savoy, and the families of Cantelou, Courtenay, Zouche and many others.

RURIK

GRAND PRINCE OF KIEV

Line 241

1. RURIK, prob. a Danish Viking, Grand Prince of Kiev, d. 879.

2. IGOR, Grand Prince of Kiev, d. 947; m. 903, St. Olga, d. 969.

3. SVATISLAV I, Grand Prince of Kiev, d. 973; m. Maloucha.

4. ST. VLADIMIR, Grand Prince of Kiev, d. 15 Jul. 1015; m. aft. 1011, a dau. (d. 14 Aug. 1014) of Kuno, Count of Ohningen, by Richilde, dau. of **OTTO I,** the Great (147-19); m. also Rogneide, dau. of Rognald of Polotzk.

5. DOBRONIEGA (dau. of St. Vladimir by the dau. of Kuno), b. aft. 1011, d. 1087; m. 1038 **CASIMIR I** (147-23), b. 28 Jul. 1016, d. 28 Nov. 1058, King of Poland.

5. JAROSLAV I (son of St. Vladimir by Rogneide), Grand Prince of Kiev, d. 20 Feb. 1053/4; m. (2) 1019, Ingeborg, d. 10 Feb. 1050, dau. of Olof Skötkonung, King of Sweden, b. prob. in 960s, d. ca. 1020, son of Erik Segersäll, King of Sweden, d. ca. 994, and Sigrid Storråda, dau. of Skoglar-Toste. Olof's wife is unknown. (Supplied by Nils William Olsson; sources: Svenska män och kvinnor (Stockholm 1942-1955); Brenner; Beckman "Tre konungaätter och deras jordegendommer i Sverige", Personhistorisk tidskrift, XIV, no. 1, pp. 1-19 (Stockholm 1913)).

6. ANNE OF KIEV, d. 1075; m. 20 or 29 Jan. 1044, **HENRY I** (53-22, 101-22), d. 1060, King of France.

6. ISIASLAV I, Grand Prince of Kiev, son of Jaroslav I, b. 1025, d. 3 Oct. 1078; m. ca. 1043 Gertrude, d. 4 Jan. 1107, dau. Mieszco, King of Poland (see 147-22). (Generations 1-6: G. Andrews Moriarty and Walter L. Sheppard, Jr. in TAG 28: 91-95, cf. 93).

7. SVIATOPOLK II (Michael), Grand Prince of Kiev, b. 1050, d. 16 Apr. 1113, by (1) a mistress d. bef. 1094; m. a dau. of Tougor Khan, a princess of Coumanie, who d. by 1103.

8. ZBYSLAVA (mother uncertain), d. 1113, m. 1103 **BOLESLAS III** (147-25). (Baumgarten: Tables I & II).

Line 242

5. JAROSLAV I (241-5), m. (2) 1019, Ingegard of Sweden.

6. WSEVOLOD I, Grand Prince of Kiev, b. 1030, d. 13 Apr. 1093; m. (1) 1046, a Monomacha, who d. 1067.

7. VLADIMIR II, Monomachus, Grand Prince of Kiev, b. 1053, d. 19 May 1125; m. (1) ca. 1070, **GYTHA** (1B-24), dau. of Harold II, the Saxon, King of England.

8. MSTISLAS II, Grand Prince of Kiev, b. 1076, d. 15 Apr. 1132; m. (2) 1122, the dau. (d. 1168) of Dmitri I of Novogorod.

9. EUPHROSINE, b. ca. 1130, d. 1175/86; m. 1146, Geza II, King of Hungary (Bela II[9], Almos[8], Geza I[7], BELA I (243-6), q.v.)
10. BELA III, b. 1148, d. 18 Apr. 1196, King of Hungary; m. ca. 1171, **AGNES DE CHÂTILLON** (103-27). (TAG 28: 93; Baumgarten Table V).

Line 243

5. VASUL, King of Poland, dead 1038. Two sons successively Kings of Hungary, Bela I and Andrew I.
6. BELA I, d. ca. 1063, King of Hungary; m. Rixa, living 1051, dau. of Miesco II (see 147-22).
7. SOPHIA, d. 18 Jun. 1095; m. Magnus, Duke of Saxony (see 166-24), b. bef. 1045, d. 23 Aug. 1106.
8. WULFHILDA of Saxony, b. ca. 1075, d. 29 Dec. 1126; m. 1095/1100, **HENRY I** (166-24), Duke of Bavaria. (Brandenburg). See note under Line 245.

Line 244

5. VASUL (243-5), King of Poland.
6. ANDREW I, d. 1060, King of Hungary; m. ca. 1046, Anastasia, living 1064, dau. of **JAROSLAV I** (241-5) and Ingegard.
7. ADELAIDE, d. 27 Jan. 1061/2; m. ca. 1058, Wratislav, b. ca. 1035, d. 14 Jan. 1092 (Wagner says d. 1085), King of Bohemia.
8. JUDITH, d. 25 Dec. 1085; m. ca. 1080, **VLADISLAV I** (147-24), b. ca. 1043, d. 4 Jun. 1102, King of Poland. (TAG 28: 93).
Note: As printed in the past, Bela I and Andrew I, brothers and successive Kings of Hungary, were shown as sons of Ladislas I, King of Hungary, by Premyslava, dau. of St. Vladimir (241-4) based on Table I of Baumgarten. However the chronology can now be shown to be in error for Premyslava, and Moriarty's The Plantagenet Ancestry shows the brothers of be children of Vasul, King of Poland, dead 1038, by an unknown wife. Vasul was the son of Mihaly (Michael), a regent in Poland. Isenenburg (1976 ed.) confirms all this (Table 104, Europäische Stammtafeln) and shows Michael as bro. of Geza and son of Taksony, d. 972.

Line 244A

6. BELA I, d. ca. 1063, King of Hungary, m. Rixa.
7. ST. LADISLAS, King of Hungary 1077, d. 27 July 1095; m. ca. 1079 Adelaide, prob. dau. Berthold I, "the Bearded", of Zahringen, Count, d. 1090.
8. PRISCA (IRENE) OF HUNGARY, b. ca. 1088, d. Bethinia 13 Aug. 1134, m. ca. 1104, **JOHN II COMNENUS** (105A-25), Basileus (Emp.) of the East, b. 1088, d. 8 Apr. 1134.

ADDITIONAL LINES

Line 245

40. REV. EDWARD BULKELEY, D.D. (31-39); m. Olive Irby.

41. SARAH BULKELEY, b. 1580, d. 1611; m. 1597, Sir Oliver St. John (see 85-40) of Keysoe, co. Bedford, b. ca. 1575, d. Keysoe, 23 Mar. 1625/6, will made 13 Mar. 1625/6, son of Henry and Jane (Neale) St. John. (Note: Proof of Sir Oliver St. John's descent from the Bletsoe St. John family has not been established).

42. ELIZABETH ST. JOHN (85-41); m. 6 Aug. 1629, Rev. Samuel Whiting, minister at Lynn, Massachusetts, 1635-1679.

43. REV. SAMUEL WHITING, Jr., A.M. (85-42).

43. REV. JOSEPH WHITING, A.M. (85-42). (For authorities and further data, see Line 85, Generations 39-42).

Line 246

22. ADÈLE (ALIX) DE ROUCY (151-22); m. 1031, Hildouin de Rameru, d. ca. 1062, Count of Montdidier and Roucy.

23. MARGARET DE ROUCY, m. ca. 1080, Hugh, d. 1101/3, Count of Clermont in Beauvais. (CP X 348).

24. ADELAIDE DE CLERMONT, m. GILBERT FITZ RICHARD (184-3), b. bef. 1066, Earl of Clare, Lord of Tunbridge. (CP X 348).

25. ALICE DE CLARE, m. Aubrey de Vere II, slain at London, 15 May 1141, of Great Addington and Drayton, co. Northampton, Sheriff of London and Middlesex 1121, 1125, Justice, and Master Chamberlain of England 1133. (CP X 195-213).

26. AUBREY DE VERE, d. 26 Dec. 1194, 1st Earl of Oxford; m. (3) 1162/3, Agnes, dau. of Henry of Essex, Lord of Rayleigh and Haughley (son of Robert Fitz Suein of Essex and Gunnor Bigod) by his wife, Cicely. (CP X 210.

27. ROBERT DE VERE, M.C. (see 60-28), b. prob. bef. 1164, d. bef. 25 Oct. 1221, Magna Charta Surety 1215; m. Isabel, d. 2 or 3 Feb. 1245, dau. of Hugh II de Bolbec (son of Walter I), and wid. of Henry de Nonant. (CP X 210-216, cf. 213 note b; Philip Morant: Hist. of Essex, 1768, II 159, 179-182).

28. ELEANOR DE VERE, m. as (1) wife, Sir Ralph de Gernon, d. 1274 (Inq.p.m. 2 Edw. I), Lord of the Manors of East Thorpe and Great Birch, co. Camb., son of William Gernon (d. Dec. 1258, Inq.p.m. 43 Henry III), Marshall of the King's household. (CP X 213 note b: Waters: Chester of Chicheley I 193-194, 199). Ralph m. (2) Hawise, sis. and coh. Nicholas Tregoz of Tolleshunt. (The pedigree as it appears in editions prior to the 5th edition shows the wife of

William Gernon as Beatrix, dau. Henry de Theydon. The source of this is Morant's Essex. This is proven incorrect in Chester of Chicheley (cit). The Gernon pedigree is there developed as follows: William's wife was unknown. His father was Ralph, the grantee of East Thorpe & Birch from King John, founder of Lees Priory 1230, acquired Theydon Girnon 1207, d. 1247. He was son of Ralph who received Bakewell in Derby from Richard I and m. a sister of William de Briwer, the founder of Dunkeswell Abbey. This Ralph's father was Matthew of Downham, j.u. of Mont-Bures, Essex, seen 1161, whose wife was Hodierna, sis. & h. of William de Sackville. (Refs.: pp. 189-193).

29. WILLIAM GERNON, s. and h. ae. 24 in 1274, of Bakewell, East Thorpe, etc., d. 1327. (Inq.p.m. 7 Edw. III). (Chester of Chicheley, cit. I 194).

30. SIR JOHN GERNON, s. and h. ae. 30+ in 1327, m. very young to Isabel Bigot who d.s.p. ae. 13 in 1311, bur. Messing, Essex; m. (2) Alice, wid. of Guy Gobaud, dau. event. coh. in her issue Roger, Lord Colville, of Bytham, Lincolnshire (by whom father of No. 31). He m. (3) bef. 1331/2, Margaret, dau. and h. Sir John de Wygeton, Knt. of Wigton, co. Cumb., who d. 1315, and wid. John de Crokedayk, d.s.p. 1323. Sir John Gernon d. betw. Apr. 1332 and 28 Mar. 1333/4. His wid. m. (3) bef. 1337, Sir John de Weston, Knt., and d.s.p. 1347. (Chester of Chicheley I 194-195; CP III 374). (The wife of Roger de Coleville, of Bytham, and mother of Alice, was Margaret (or Margery) de Braose, dau. of Sir Richard de Braose of Stinton, Norf., by Alice, dau. & h. of William le Rus of Stinton). Richard was a yr. son of John de Braose, lord of Gower (by his wife Margaret, m. 1220, dau. of Llewellyn ap Jorwerth and Princess Joan), son of William de Braose, lord of Gower and his wife Maud de Clare, dau. of Richard de Clare and **AMICE** (63-27), Countess of Gloucester. (CP V 736; I 22; II 302-304; III 374; Farrer: Honours & Knts. Fees III 440; Moriarty, Notebooks, 15: 147, 149, 161, 163; Lipscomb, 2: 558; Farrer, Early Yorkshire Charters, p. 481).

31. SIR JOHN GERNON, b. 1314; ae. 40+ in 1369/70; m. 1332 at 18, to Alice Bygot, wid. of John Bygot who was nephew of Isabel, his father's childless first wife. He m. (2) at unknown date, one Joan who survived him. He d. 13 Jan. 1383/4. Children were by 1st wife, Alice. (Chester of Chicheley I 196, 198; CP 375 note d).

32. MARGARET GERNON, ae. 34 in 7 Richard II (1383/4), b. ca. 1350, d. a wid. 6 Jun. 1413, bur. Wicken, Cambs. (Inq.p.m. 2 Henry V), m. Sir John Peyton, Knt., of Peyton Hall in Boxford, co. Essex. He held j.u. East Thorpe and Wicken (Inq.p.m. 7 Richard II), son of Sir John de Peyton, Knt., M.P. 29 Edw. I, Knt. of the Shire, Lord of Peyton Hall in Boxford, and a descendant of Reginald de Peyton who held Peyton Hall in Suffolk 1135. (Morant II 159, 179-182; Augustine Page; Topographical and Gen. Hist. of Suffolk, Ipswich, 1847, pp. 155, 919-920; Harl. Soc. 71: 3; Burke: Ext. and Dor. Baronet. 408).

33. JOHN PEYTON of Peyton Hall and Wicken, d.v.p. 1403/4; m. Joan, dau. of Sir Hamon Sutton of Wickshoo, co. Suffolk. (Morant II 179-182; Page 155, 904, 919-920; Harl. Soc. 71:3; Burke op. cit.

408).
34. JOHN PEYTON, Esq., b. 1392, ae. 12 in 1404, ae. 15 in 1407,
d. 6 Oct. 1416, ae. 24. (Inq.p.m. 4 Henry V), Lord of the Manor of
East Thorpe 1414-1417; m. Grace, d. 6 Henry VI, dau. of John
Burgoyne, Esq. of Drayton in co. Cambridge; she m. (2) Richard
Baynard of Messing. (Morant II 179-182; Harl. Soc. 71: 3; Burke
408).
35. SIR THOMAS DE PEYTON, 2nd son and event. h., b. and
bapt. at Dry-Drayton, 14 Feb. 1416/17, d. 30 Jul. 1484, Sheriff of
the counties of Camb. and Hunts (21 and 31 Henry VI) 1443, 1453; m.
(1) Margaret, eldest dau. and coh. of Sir John Bernard, Knt., of
Iselham, co. Camb; m. (2) Margaret Francis, wid. of Thomas Garneys
and dau. of Sir Hugh Francis of Giffords Hall in Wickenham, co.
Suffolk. His great-grandson, Robert Peyton, sold the Manor of East
Thorpe and the Hundred of Lexton on 1 Oct. 1536. (Morant II 179-
180; Burke 409; Harl. Soc. 71: 4; William Camden: Visitation of
Warwick, 1619, in Harl. Soc. 12: 379-380).
36. FRANCIS PEYTON, d. 1529, bur. Church of St. James, co.
Suffolk (Bury St. Edmunds), yr. son of the 2nd wife, of Bury St.
Edmunds, co. Suffolk, h. to his mother; m. Elizabeth, dau. of
Reginald Brooke, Esq., of Aspall Stoneham, co. Suffolk. (Camden in
Harl. Soc. 12: 379; see Waters' Chester of Chicheley 202-203).
37. CHRISTOPHER PEYTON, Esq., of St. Edmunds Bury; m.
Joanne Mildmay, sister of Sir Walter Mildmay (b. 1520, d. Hackney,
31 May 1589, founder of Emmanuel Coll., Camb.). Morant: Hist. of
Essex II 587; Bradbury Memorial 32-33; DNB 56: 359-362; CCN 351).
38. MARGARET PEYTON (7th of 10 children); m. Richard Eden,
Esq., of Bury St. Edmunds; said to have been the first publisher of
charts of the early voyagers. (Bradbury Memorial 31-33, etc.; Wm.
Camden: Visit. of Warwickshire, 1619 in Harl Soc. 12: 379-380, for
generations 34 to 38 above).

* * *

39. ANN EDEN, dau. of Henry Eden, cousin of Richard Eden (38)
above, bur. at Wicken 8 Feb. 1611/12; m. William Bradbury, Esq., of
Wicken Bonhunt, b. 1544, d. Wicken 30 Nov. 1622, will dated 19 Apr.
1622, pro. 6 May 1623, son of Matthew and Margaret (Rowse)
Bradbury of Wicken Bonhunt. (Bradbury Memorial 32-33, etc. That
William Bradbury's wife was not a descendant of the Peytons was
noted by Mrs. Margaret Buxton, of Albuquerque, New Mexico).
40. WYMOND BRADBURY (246A-41) bapt. Newport Pond 16
May 1574, d. Whitechapel, Middlesex, 1649/50; m. **ELIZABETH
WHITGIFT** (210-42), b. ca. Mar. 1574, d. 26 June 1612, ae. 38 yrs.
(Bradbury Memorial 32-35, 47-48).

22. ALBERT III (149-22), Count of Namur, first mentioned in 1035 next to his father, prob. as a child, next in 1062; d. 22 June 1102; m. ca. 1067 Ida, d. 31 July 1102, prob. widow of Frederic of Luxembourg, Duke of Lower Lotharingia, d. 28 Aug. 1065, and dau. of Bernard, Duke of Saxony, b. ca. 995, d. 1059, by his wife Elica (or Eilika), dau. of Henrich, Margrave von Schweinfurt. (Moriarty, The Plantagenet Ancestry; Felix Rousseau: Actes des Comptes de Namur de la Première Race 946-1195 (Bruxelles) 1936; L'Art de Verifier les Dates des Faits Historiques (Paris) 1787).

23. GODFREY OF NAMUR, b. 1067 or 1068, d. 19 Aug. 1139 as a lay brother in the abbey of Floreffe, m. ca. 1087 Sibylle, dau. Count Roger of Château-Porcien, which marriage ended in divorce or annullment because of her affair with a neighbor while Godfrey was away waging war. (Ibid.)

24. ELIZABETH OF NAMUR (or Isabell), m. (1) Gervais, Count of Rethel, d. 1124, 3rd son of Hugh and Milicent, archdeacon of Rheims, resigned on the death of his father and succeeded him as count of Rethel, m. (2) Clarembald de Rosoy. (Ibid.; Chronicon Alberici; TAG 20: 255-6).

25. MILICENT OF RETHEL, m. (1) Robert Marmion, b. prob. 1090-1095 in Normandy, killed 1143 or 1144 at Coventry, son of Roger; first appears in the Lindsey Survey of Lincolnshire 1115-1118, m. (2) Richard de Camville. (C.F.R. Palmer: Hist. of the Baronial Family of Marmion (1875); TAG ibid.; Dugdale: Monasticon Anglicorum; G. Saige: Cartulaire de Fontenay de Marmion (1895); J.H. Round: Calendar of Documents Preserved in France.)

26. ROBERT MARMION, b. bef. 1133, d. ca. 1185. (Ibid; CP VIII 505-522; Société des Antiquaires de Normandie, Tome 7; Gallia Christiana, Vol. XI; Salter: Boarstall Cartulary pub. by Oxfordshire Hist. Soc. 1930).

27. WILLIAM MARMION, b. prob. 1155-1160, d. in or bef. 1220, acquired lordship of Checkenden in Oxfordshire through a series of deeds from his father and brother Geoffrey. (Ibid.; Thame Cartulary, edited by Salter, 1948; Abbreviatio Placitorum).

28. GEOFFREY MARMION, b. ca. 1198, d. betw. Oct. 1246 and 1255, m. Rosamund, d. betw. 25 Apr 1273 and 2 Feb. 1273/4. (Ibid.; M.T. Pearman, Notices of Checkenden 1898).

29. WILLIAM MARMION, b. ca. 1229 at Checkenden, d. ca. 1266, m. Matilda. (Ibid.; The Goring Charters, vols. 13 & 14, Oxfordshire Record Society, 1931).

30. JOHN MARMION, b. ca. 1260 at Checkenden, d. 1330-31, m. ca. 1273 (an arranged child marriage) Margery, dau. of Henry de Nottingham, his guardian. (Ibid.)

31. THOMAS MARMION, b. ca. 1285-90, m. Agnes. (Ibid.)

32. ALICE MARMION, b. ca. 1320, d. bef. 1367, m. bef. 1353 William Harlyngrugge of Checkenden. (Ibid.)

33. CECILIA HARLYNGRUGGE, b. prob. 1340-46 at Checkenden, d. 20 May 1428, m. John Rede, d. 20 May 1404, elaborate brass to him in the Checkenden church, brass inscription to her, Rede and Marmion arms, appointed Serjeant-at-law 1396,

Line 246A (cont.)

possibly son of John and Margery Rede of Ascote in the parish of Winkfield, Berkshire. (Ibid.)

34. JOAN REDE, m. (2) as his (2) wife, Walter Cotton, b. ca. 1376 at Cambridge, d. 13 May 1445 per Inq.p.m. (14 May per former brass), a mercer of London, bought Landwade estate in Cambridgeshire, rebuilt the Landwade church (his tomb is there, Cotton-Rede/-Marmion arms in original stained glass window) son of John and Margaret, his father Mayor of Cambridge in 1378. (TAG 57: 35-36).

35. WILLIAM COTTON, b. 1410-11, killed 22 May 1455 in Battle of St. Albans, the beginning of the War of the Roses, his tomb and brass epitaph at Landwade, a London mercer, Vice Chamberlain to Henry VI, m. Alice Abbott, d. 21 Nov. 1473, dau. of John and Agnes Abbott. (TAG 56: 13-29; 57: 35-56).

36. CATHERINE COTTON, eldest dau., m. Thomas Heigham V, b. 1431 per Inq.p.m., living 1494, of Heigham Hall in Gazeley, Suffolk. (TAG 57: 35-44; 58: 168-180).

37. CLEMENT HEIGHAM of Lavenham, Suffolk, d. 26 Sept. 1500, m. Matilda (or Maud), dau. of Lawrence Cooke of Lavenham. (TAG 58: 168-180).

38. CLEMENT HEIGHAM of Barrow Hall, Suffolk, d. 9 Mar. 1570/71, knighted by Queen Mary, m. (1) Anne Munnings of Bury St. Edmunds, d. betw. 26 May and 22 Aug. 1540, dau. of Thomas and Margaret. (TAG 55: 151-155; 58: 168-180).

39. ELIZABETH HEIGHAM, m. (1) Henry Edon of Barningham, Suffolk, d. 30 Jan. 1545/6, son of Thomas and Joan Edon of Bury St. Edmunds, m. (2) Robert Kempe of Spain Hall in Finchingfield, Essex. (TAG 55: 5-16).

40. ANN EDON, b. ca. 1542, bur. at Wicken Bonhunt, Essex, 8 Feb. 1611/12, m. William Bradbury, Esq., b. ca. 1544, d. 30 Nov. 1622, son of Matthew and Margaret (Rowse) Bradbury. (TAG ibid.)

41. WYMOND BRADBURY (246-40), bapt. Newport Pond, Essex, 16 May 1574, d. Whitechapel, London, ca. 1649, m. as (3) husb. **ELIZABETH WHITGIFT** (210-42), b. Clavering, Essex in March 1574, d. 26 June 1612 ae. 38 yr. 3 mo., buried Croydon, Surrey, dau. of William and Margaret (Bell) Whitgift; she m. (1) Richard Coles of Leigh, Worcestershire, m. (2) Francis Gill of London. Her uncle John Whitgift became Archbishop of Canterbury. (Bradbury Memorial 32-35, 47-48; TAG 18: 220-226; Morant: Hist. of Essex II: 587; DNB 16: 361; 37: 374-6; 56: 359-62; CCN 351; Visitation Pedigrees pub. by Harleian Soc.; Ducarel: History of Croydon 1786; NEHGR 23: 262). Note: at Croydon is a portrait of her sister Jane who m. his brother Matthew, recently correctly so identified.

42. THOMAS BRADBURY, Capt., gent., 2nd son, bapt. Wicken Bonhunt, 28 Feb. 1610/11, d. Salisbury, Mass. 16 Mar. 1694/5, came to New England 1634 as agent for Sir Ferdinando Gorges (209-39), m. 1636 Mary Perkins, bapt. 3 Sept. 1615 at Hillmorton, Warwickshire, d. 20 Dec. 1700, convicted of witchcraft, but eventually freed, dau. of John and Judith (Gater) Perkins. A son William Bradbury m. Rebecca Wheelwright, dau. of the Rev. John Wheelwright. (This line was supplied by John B. Threlfall.)

24. **ADELIZA** (or Adelaide) **DE CLERMONT** (246-24), m. (1) **GILBERT FITZ RICHARD** (184-3), b. bef. 1066, d. 1114 or 1117, Lord of Clare, co. Suffolk, and Tonbridge, co. Kent, founder of the Priory of Clare, 1090, Lord of Cardigan, 1107-1111, son of Richard Fitz Gilbert, Lord of Clare and Tonbridge, by his wife Rohese (or Rose), dau. of Walter Gifford, the elder. (CP III 242-243; Sanders, English Baronies 34-35, 62-63; Round, Feudal England 468-474).

25. **RICHARD FITZ GILBERT** (also styled de Clare), son and h., Lord of Clare, co. Suffolk, slain by the Welsh near Abergavenny, 15 Apr. 1136, bur. Gloucester; m. Adeliz (or Alice), dau. of **RANULPH** (styled le Meschin) (132A-26), Earl of Chester by Lucy, widow, (1) of Ivo Taillebois and (2) of Roger Fitz Gerold. (CP III 243; Sanders, op. cit.)

26. **ROGER (DE CLARE)**, adult by 1155/6, d. 1173, Earl of Clare or Hertford; m. Maud, dau. and h. of James de St. Hilary, lord of Field Dalling, Norfolk, by his wife, Aveline. (CP V 124-125; VI 499-501; Sanders, op. cit.)

27. **AVELINE DE CLARE**, living 1220 but dead by 1225, m. (1) William de Munchanesy of Swanscombe, Kent; Winfarthing and Gooderstone, Norfolk who d. shortly bef. 7 May 1204; m. (2) by 29 May 1205, as (2) wife, Geoffrey Fitz Piers, adult in 1184, died 14 Oct. 1213, bur. Shouldam Priory, Earl of Essex (in right of his first wife), Justiciar of England, 1198-1213, son of Piers de Lutegareshale by his wife Maud. (CP V 122-125).

28. **HAWISE FITZ GEOFFREY**, dead 1243, received manor of Streatley, Bedford, from her half-brother, William de Mandeville, Earl of Essex; m. by 1227, as his (1) wife, **SIR REYNOLD DE MOHUN** (143-28), b. say 1206, minor in 1213 and 1222, adult by 1227, d. 20 Jan. 1257/8, at Torre Mohun, Devon, bur. Newenham Abbey; Lord of Dunster, Somerset, Justice of Common Pleas, Chief Justice of Forests South of the Trent, son of Reynold de Mohun, Lord of Dunster, by his wife, Alice, 4th dau. and eventual coh. of Sir William de Briwere, lord of Horsley, Derby (d. 1226) by his wife, Beatrice de Valle. (Sanders, English Baronies, 144, 122-3; CP IX 19-20; V 433, footnote e; George Oliver: "Monasticon Dioecesis Exoniensis" 173-174, 190-191; VCH Berkshire III 512; Sir H.C. Maxwell Lyte: "History of Dunster and of the Families of Mohun and Luttrell", Part I 15-34).

29. **ALICE DE MOHUN**, living 1282 but dead by 1284, m. (1) as as young child to William de Clinton, the younger, d. by 1237; m. (2) by 1246 Robert IV de Beauchamp, adult by 1244, living 1262-3, dead by 1265-6, Lord of Hatch, Somerset, Justice in Eyre for the Western Counties, son of Robert III de Beauchamp (also styled Fitz Simon), Lord of Hatch, Somerset by his probable wife, Juliana (Brett?). (Somersetshire Arch. and Natural History Society 36: 23-34 (Beauchamp of Hatch); Sanders, English Baronies 51; CP II 48; Maxwell Lyte, op. cit. Part I 32; NEHGR 139: 286-287; Cal. Inq.p.m. I: 19; Cal. Close Rolls, Henry III 3: 505).

30. **SIR HUMPHREY DE BEAUCHAMP**, Knt., younger son, adult by 1274, apparently alive 1316 but dead by 1317, lord of Ryme

Intrinseca, Dorset and of Oburnford, Oulescombe, Teinghervy, and Buckerell, Devon; m. (1) by 1280 Sibyl Oliver, living 1306, dau. and sole h. of Walter Oliver, lord of Wambrook, Somerset, from whom he was divorced betw. 1287 and 1290; m. (2) after 10 Aug. 1300 Alice, d. shortly bef. 20 Oct. 1317 as wid. of Peter Corbet. With Alice Sir Humphrey held the manor of Silferton, Devon in dower for the term of their lives. (Somerset Arch. and Natural History Society 36: 33; VCH Somerset 4: 224; "Knights of Edward I" I 71; Coker: "Survey of Dorsetshire" 125-126; Hutchins: "History and Antiquities of the County of Dorset" 491; Cal. Inq.p.m. 6: 75; Cal. Patent Rolls, Edward I, A.D. 1272-1281, 46; NEHGR 139: 286-287; CP III 417; E.A. Fry and G.S. Fry, ed., Dorset Records, V 234 (being Dorset Feet of Fines from Richard I).

31. SIR JOHN BEAUCHAMP, Knt., younger son but eventual h., almost certainly by (1), b. say 1285, living 1337 when witness to a charter of John, Bishop of Exeter, lord of Ryme, Dorset and of Oburnford, Oulescombe, Teignhervy and Buckerell, Devon; probably d. by 1346 when son John was probably the John Beauchamp holding his manors of Ryme, Dorset and Oburnford, Devon; m. by 1311/2 Joan, surname not known, at which time his father settled lands on him in Oburnford, Devon. Coker, Risdon and Pole all state however that Sir John m. Alice, dau. and coh. of Sir Roger de Nonant, Lord of Cliston or Brode Clist, Devon. Alice was reportedly living 17 Edward III (A.D. 1343-4). (Index of Placita de Banco, A.D. 1327-1328, Part I, 116; Inq. Ad Quod Damnum, Part I, 125; Cal. Inq.p.m. Vol. 7, 314-315; Dugdale: "Monasticon", Vol. 3, 60; Coker: "Survey of Dorsetshire" 125-126; Hutchins, "Hist. of the Co. of Dorset: 491; Notebook of Tristram Risdon 124-125; Sir William Pole: "Collections towards a Description of the County of Devon" 169-170, 255; "Feudal Aids" Vol. 1, 432; Vol. 2, 59).

32. JANE (or Joan) **BEAUCHAMP**, m. **JOHN CHUDLEIGH** (217-35), lord of Cliston or Brode Clist, Devon. (Pole, op. cit.)

Line 246C (Prepared by Douglas Richardson)

27. AVELINE DE CLARE (246B-27), living 1220 but dead by 4 June 1225, m. (1) William de Munchanesy of Swanscombe, Kent, Winfarthing and Gooderstone, Norfolk who d. shortly bef. 7 May 1204; m. (2) by 29 May 1205, as (2) wife, Geoffrey Fitz Piers, adult in 1184, d. 14 Oct. 1213, bur. Shouldham Priory; Earl of Essex (in right of his first wife), Justiciar of England, 1198-1213, son of Piers de Lutegareshale by his wife Maud. (CP V 122-125).

28. SIR JOHN FITZ GEOFFREY, adult by 1227, d. 23 Nov. 1258, Justiciar of Ireland, 1245-1256, of Fambridge, Essex, m. after 1230 **ISABEL BIGOD** (72-29), widow of Gilbert de Lacy of Ewyas Lacy, and dau. of Hugh Bigod, Earl of Norfolk. (CP V 433-434, 437).

24. ADELIZA (or Adelaide) **DE CLERMONT** (246-24), m. (1) Gilbert Fitz Richard, b. bef. 1066, d. 1114/7, Lord of Clare and Tonbridge, founder of the Priory of Clare, 1090, Lord of Cardigan, 1107-1111, son of Richard Richard Fitz Gilbert, Lord of Clare and Tonbridge, by his wife Rohese (or Rose), dau. of Walter Giffard, the elder. (CP III 24-243).

25. ADELIZA (or Alice) **DE CLARE**, d. ca. 1163, m. Aubrey de Vere II, b. prob. bef. 1090, slain in London, 15 May 1141, of Great Addington and Drayton, Sheriff of London and Middlesex, Justice and Master Chamberlain of England, 1133, son of Aubrey I de Vere by his wife, Beatrice. (CP X 193-199, App. J, 110-112).

26. ALICE DE VERE, b. bef. 1141, living 1185, m. (1) as his (2) wife, Robert de Essex, Lord of Rayleigh; m. (2) Roger Fitz Richard, adult by 1157, d. by the end of 1177, first Lord of Warkworth, co. Northumberland, son of Richard by his Jane, dau. of Roger Bigod. (Sanders, English Baronies, p. 150; CP X, App. J, 113-116; Sir Charles Day, Archaeologia Aelieana 4th ser. vol. 32).

27. ROBERT FITZ ROGER, b. bef. 1177, adult by 1199, d. 1214, second Baron of Warkworth, Lord of Clavering, Sheriff of Northumberland, m., as her (2) husb., Margaret (or Margery) de Chesney, widow of Hugh de Cressi and dau. and h. of William de Chesney (styled de Norwich) of Horsford, Norfolk, Sheriff of Norfolk and Suffolk. (Sanders, English Baronies p. 150; CP X, App. J, 117; Sir Charles Clay, Archaeologia Aeliana 4th ser. vol. 32; Landon, Norfolk & Norwich Arch. Soc. XXIII: 156-159).

28. ALICE FITZ ROGER DE WARKWORTH, d. by 1225, m., as his (1) wife, by settlement dated 28 Nov. 1203, **PETER FITZ HERBERT** (262-29), adult by 1204, d. ca. May 1235, son of Herbert Fitz Herbert, by his wife, Lucy, Lady of Blaen Llyfni, co. Brecknock, dau. of Miles, Earl of Hereford. (CP V 265; Sanders, English Baronies pp. 8-9; Clay, Antiquities of Shropshire VII: 148, 150-154).

31. SIR JOHN BEAUCHAMP, Knt. (246B-31), b. say 1285, living 1337, and presumed dead by 1346, lord of Ryme, Dorset and of Oburnford, Oulescombe, Teignherby and Buckerell, Devon; m. (1) by 1311/2 to Joan, maiden name unknown; also apparently m. (2) by 1344 Alice de Nonant, dau. and coh. of Sir Roger de Nonant, lord of Cliston or Brode Clist, Devon. (Refs as cited).

32. SIR JOHN BEAUCHAMP, Knt., son and h., perhaps by (1), b. sah 1315, d. 8 Apr. 1349, lord of Ryme, Dorset and of Oburnford, Oulescombe, Teignhervy and Buckerell, Devon; m. say 1340 Margaret Whalesburgh, dau. of John Whalesburgh. She m. (2) by 23 Oct. 1353 Richard de Branscombe, Sheriff of Devon in 1358, 1866 and 1874. The arms of Whalesburgh were, Argent, three bendlets, gules, a bordure sable charged with 8 besants. (Hutchins, History & Antiquities of the County of Dorset, p. 491; Coker, Survey of Dorsetshire, pp. 125-126; Cal. Inq.p.m. IX: 262-263, 387, X: 228; List of Sheriffs for England and Wales (Lists and Indexes), IX: 35; Cal.

Close Rolls, Edward III, X 1354-1360, pp. 242-243; Cal. Fine Rolls, Edward III, VI: 381; Harleian Add. MS 28649, fo. 518).

33. ELIZABETH BEAUCHAMP, dau. and event. coh., b. by 1349, living 1410, Whympston in parish of Modbury, Devon; m. (1) Richard, son of Adam de Branscombe; m. (2) by 1394, and prob. much earlier, William Fortescue, lord of Whympston, Devon, b. say 1345, living 1410, son of William Fortescue, lord of Whympston, Devon, by his wife, Alice, dau. of Walter de Strechlegh. In 1401, William and Elizabeth sued her sister, Joan's husband, Sir Robert Challons, regarding tenements in Oulescombe and Buckerell, Devon which had been possessed by Elizabeth's brother, Sir Thomas Beauchamp. In 1410, license for an oratory was granted by Bishop Stafford to William Fortescue, senior, and Elizabeth, his wife, and also to William Fortescue, junior, and Matilda, alias Mabilla, his wife, for the mansion of the said William (senior) at Whympston. The arms of Fortescue were, Azure, a bend engrailed Argent, cotised Or. (Cal. Close Rolls, Henry IV, I: 480; J.L. Vivian, The Visitations of the County of Devon, p. 352; Thomas (Fortescue), Lord Clermont, A History of the Family of Fortescue, pp. 1-9, 484; Devon & Cornwall N & Q, XXI, pt. VI, pp. 249-255; Sir Egerton Brydges, Collin's Peerage of England, V: 335-343; The Register of Bishop of Edmund Stafford, p. 275.)

34. WILLIAM FORTESCUE, son and h., b. say 1385, m. by 1410, Matilda, alias Mabilla, dau. and h. of John Falwell or Fawell; both were mentioned in the license for an oratory granted in 1410 by Bishop Stafford to William's father mentioned above. The Fortescue family later quartered the Falwell arms, they being, Gules, on a bend argent, 3 water bougets sable. (Refs. as cited; also Harleian MS 1567, fo. 46; Harleian MS 1091, fo. 58; Harleian MS 889, fo. 10v, all of which show Fortescue quartering the Falwell arms).

35. JOHN FORTESCUE, son and h., born say 1420, d. 11 Mar. 1480/1, Inq.p.m. taken 4 Nov. 1481, lord of Whympston, Devon; m. by 1450, Joan, dau. and sole h. of John Prutteston of Prutteston (or Preston) in the parish of Ermington, Devon. Joan is mentioned in the Inq.p.m. taken on her father's lands dated 1468. She d. 23 May 1501, Inq.p.m. taken 26 Oct. 1501. The Fortescue family later quartered the Prutteston arms, they being, Or, on a bend azure, 3 crosses patty fitchy argent. John Fortescue is sometimes confused with his first cousin, Sir John Fortescue, the eminent lawyer who became lord chief justice in England (for his biography, see DNB VII: 482-485). (Refs as cited; also Harleian MS 1567, fo. 40 and 57v; Harleian 5871, fo. 15v, all of which show Fortescue quartering the Prutteston arms; Abstracts of Inq.p.m. for John Fortescue (Year:1481) and for John Prutteston (Year:1468) on file with the Devon Record Office, Exeter, Devon; Cal. Inq.p.m., Henry VII, II: 264-265).

36. JOANE FORTESCUE, b. say 1450, living 1524 but dead by 1525, Staverton, Devon, m. say 1470-5, Thomas Hext, gentleman, of Kingston in the parish of Staverton, Devon, d. sh. bef. 8 May 1497, when a writ for an Inq.p.m. on his estate was issued to the escheator of Devon. He is referred to as being deceased in the Inq.p.m. taken on his mother-in-law, Joan Fortescue's estates in 1501. The Hext family arms were, Or, a tower (castle) with three battlements port open between 3 battle-axes Sable. (J.L. Vivian, The Visitations of the County of Devon, p. 484; Harleian MS 1091, fo. 58; Harleian MS 1194, fo. 108v; Harleian MS 1562, fol. 23v; Harleian MS 5871, fo. 7v, all of which show Thomas Hext's wife, Joane Fortescue, as the daughter of John and Joan (Prutteston) Fortescue of Whympston; Cal. Fine Rolls, Henry VII, XXII: 244; Devon Lay Subsidy Rolls 1524-7, ed. T.L. Stoate, pp. 212-213, in which Joan Hext, widow, appears on the 1524 list but was deleted from the 1525 list.)

    37. THOMAS HEXT, younger son, b. say 1475-80, bur. 1 Dec. 1555, Georgeham, Devon, residing at Pickwell in the parish of Georgeham at his death, Escheator of Devon 1525; m. say 1510, Wilmot (Poyntz) Hyllinge, a widow, born by 1487, d. 15 Apr. 1558, dau. of **HUMPHREY POYNTZ** (234A-36), d. 1487, of Iron Acton, Gloucester and Womberlegh and Langley, Devon, Escheator of Devon 1460, by his wife Elizabeth, dau. and sole h. of Richard Pollard. The Poyntz family can be traced directly back to Sir Hugh Poyntz (d. 1220) whose wife Hawise was a dau. of William Malet, a Magna Charta baron (see Historical and Genealogical Memoir of the Family of Poyntz by Sir John Maclean, especially charts on pages 29, 94 and 95 for particulars. The Poyntz family arms were, Barry of eight or and gules. (J.L. Vivian, The Visitations of the County of Devon, p. 484; Cal. Fine Rolls, Henry VII, XXII: 69, 84; Abstract of the Inq.p.m. for Wilmot (Poyntz) Hyllinge Hext (Year:1560 and 1561/2) on file with the Devon Record Office, Exeter, Devon; Parish Records of Georgeham, Devon; Chancery Proceedings, C3/91/77, Edward Hext, Plaintiff vs. Hugh Hext, Defendant regarding lands held by Thomas and Wilmont Hext; F.T. Colby, ed., Visitation of the County of Somerset 1623, Harleian So. Pub. XI: 49-50; List of Escheators for England and Wales (List and Index Society), 72: 36, 38; Cal. Patent Rolls, Elizabeth I, III: 302).

    38. MARGERY HEXT, b. say 1510, bur. 22 Aug. 1551, Braunton, Devon, m. say 1532, John Collamore, b. say 1500, bur. 17 Apr. 1555, being of Luscott, in the parish of Braunton, Devon, son of Peter and Isabel (Cushe) Collamore. The Collamore family arms were, Gules, three crescents between nine billets or. (J.L. Vivian, The Visitations of the County of Devon, pp. 216-217 re Collamore and p. 484 for Hext, but Vivian errs in the Hext pedigree by placing Margery Hext in the wrong generation; Harleian MS 1163, fol. 190 which identifies John Collamore's wife as the dau. of . . . . Hext of Pickwell in the parish of Georgeham, Devon; Parish Records of Braunton, Devon).

    39. HENRY COLLAMORE, second son but event. h., chr. 12 Jan. 1541/2, Braunton, Devon, bur. 15 June 1625, Bishop's Tawton, Devon, m. by 1563, place unknown, Margaret Blight, b. say 1545, bur. 27 Nov. 1626, Bishop's Tawton, Devon. (Parish Records of Braunton, Devon and of Bishop's Tawton, Devon; J.L. Vivian, The Visitations of the County of Devon, pp. 216-217).

40. ELIZABETH COLLAMORE, chr. 2 Sept. 1566, Bishop's Tawton, Devon, bur. 7 Dec. 1647, Barnstaple, Devon, m. 18 Jan. 1586/7, Braunton, Devon to Bartholomew Harris, yeoman, Mayor of Barnstaple, Devon, 1602, b. say 1560, bur. 10 Oct. 1615, Barnstaple, Devon. Bartholomew's parentage has not been established but he was probably related in some manner to John Harris, Mayor of Barnstaple 1578 and 1596 whose will dated 1600, prob. 1602 (P.C.C. 2 Montague) names Bartholomew Harris as a co-executor of John Harris' estate. (Parish Records of Bishop's Tawton, Devon, of Braunton, Devon and of Barnstaple, Devon; Abstract of probate (administration) of Bartholomew Harris, dated 1615, on file with the Oswyn Murray Collection at the Devon Record Office, Exeter, Devon; Will of Elizabeth (Collamore) Harris, dated 1647, prob. 1649, P.C.C. 9 Fairfax).

41. AGNES HARRIS, chr. 6 Apr. 1604, Barnstaple, Devon, living 1680, Hartford, Connecticut, m. (1) say 1634, prob. Cambridge, Massachusetts, William Spencer, chr. 11 Oct. 1601, Stotfold, Bedford, d. 1640, Hartford, Connecticut, Deputy to Massachusetts General Court, 1634 through 1637, and representative to Connecticut General Court, 1639-1640, son of Gerard and Alice (Whitbred) Spencer; m. (2) 11 Dec. 1645, Hartford, Connecticut, William Edwards, chr. 1 Nov. 1618, St. Botolph without Aldgate, Middlesex, England, living 1680, Hartford, Connecticut, son of Rev. Richard Edwards, B.A., by his wife, Anne, dau. of Mrs. Julian Munter. Agnes' identity is proven by the wills of her mother Elizabeth Harris, 1649 (P.C.C. 9 Fairfax), her sister Priscilla Harris 1651 (P.C.C. 173 Grey), and her brother Richard Harris 1665 (P.C.C. 50 Hyde), all of which mention her. (Parish Records of Barnstaple, Devon; Jacobus and Waterman, Hale, House and Related Families, pp. 524-529; TAG 42: 65-76; Lucius R. Paige, History of Cambridge, Massachusetts, p. 659).

Line 246F

35. JOHN FORTESCUE (246E-35), b. say 1420, d. 11 Mar. 1460/1, lord of Whympston, Devon, m. by 1450, Joan, dau. and sole h. of John Prutteston of Prutteston (or Preston) in the parish of Ermington, Devon, mentioned in the Inq.p.m. taken on her father's lands dated 1468, d. 23 May 1501. (Refs. as cited for Line 246C-35).

36. WILLIAM FORTESCUE, second son and h. to a part of his mother's lands, b. say 1460, d. 1 Feb. 1519/20, Inq.p.m. taken 21 Apr. 1520, of Preston in the parish of Ermington, Devon, m. Elizabeth Champernowne, b. ca. 1465, d. bef. 1518, dau. and coh. of Richard Champernowne of Inworthy, Cornwall, by his wife, Mary, dau. and coh. of Sir John Hamley. The Fortescue family later quartered the Champernowne arms, they being, Gules, a saltire vair between 12 billets or. (Cal. Inq.p.m. Henry VII, II: 264-265; J.L. Vivian, The Visitations of the County of Devon, p. 162 for Champernowne and p. 353 for Fortescue; Thomas (Fortescue), Lord Clermont, A History of the Family of Fortescue, pp. 1-10; Harleian MS 1567, fol. 46; Har-

Line 246F (cont.)

leian MS 1091, fo. 58; Harleian MS 889, fol. 10v, all of which show Fortescue quartering Champernowne; Abstract of the Inq.p.m. for William Fortescue (Year:1520) on file with the Devon Record Office, Exeter, Devon).

37. JANE FORTESCUE, b. say 1485, dead by 12 May 1527, m. ca. 1501, as (1) wife, **JOHN COBLEIGH** (25-35), b. ca. 1479, d. 24 Oct. 1540, Inq.p.m. taken 4 Oct. 1541, lord of Brightley, Stowford Carder, Bremridge, Wollacombe Tracy, Snape, Stowford, and Nymet St. George, all in Devon, son of John Cobleigh by his wife, Alice, dau. of John Cockworthy of Harnscombe, Devon, Escheator of Devon in 1430 and 1440. (Thomas (Fortescue), Lord Clermont, A History of the Family of Fortescue, pp. 1-10; J.L. Vivian, The Visitations of the County of Devon, pp. 353 and 357; Abstract of the Inq.p.m. for John Cobleigh (Year:1541) on file with the Devon Record Office, Exeter, Devon; Devon N & Q I: 210-214; Devonshire Association, 34: 689-695; List of Escheators for England and Wales, List and Index Society, 72: 35).

Line 247

20. MALDRED (172-20), slain in battle 1045, Lord of Carlisle and Allendale; m. ca. 1030/40, **EALDGYTH** (34-21), b. ca. 1010/15, dau. of Uchtred, Earl of Northumberland, and granddau. of **AETHELRED II,** the Redeless (1-19), King of England.

21. MALDRED, b. ca. 1045, held the Manor of Winlaton 1084, undoubtedly son of Maldred and Ealdgyth, and certainly father of Uchtred. (NEHGR 106: 186-190; G. Andrews Moriarty: Origin of Nevill of Raby; Sir William G. Gibson: The Manor of Winlaton).

22. UCHTRED FITZ MALDRED, b. ca. 1075/80, d. 1128/9, Lord of Raby, co. Durham. (CP IX 494; NEHGR 106: 190).

23. DOLFIN FITZ UCHTRED, Lord of Raby, "a turbulent baron", b. ca. 1100/10, noted 1128/9, 1131; d. ca. 1136; held lands in England and Scotland; granted Staindrop and Staindropshire 1131; m. Alice, dau. of Walcher, Bishop of Durham. (CP IX 494; NEHGR 106: 190).

24. MALDRED FITZ DOLFIN, Lord of Raby, b. ca. 1135, witness, ca. 1140, d. ca. 1183; m. ca. 1170/3, the dau. of John de Stuteville, of Long Lawford, Newbold-on-Avon and Cosford, co. Warwick, a yr. son of Robert de Stuteville and Emberga. (CP IX 494; NEHGR 106:190).

25. ROBERT FITZ MALDRED, Lord of Raby and Brancepeth, co. Durham, 1194/5-1242/8; b. ca. 1070/4, d. betw. Aug. 1242 and 26 May 1248; went overseas in the King's service 1230, commissioner in Northumberland 1235, in Durham 1238, in an expedition against Wales Aug. 1242; m. Isabel de Neville, d. May 1254, dau. of Geoffrey de Neville and Emma de Bulmer. (CP IX 485, 494-495; NEHGR 106: 190).

26. GEOFFREY DE NEVILLE, of Raby Castle, Sheriff of Northumberland 1258, Justice of the King's Forests; m. Joan, living 1247, prob. dau. of John of Monmouth. (CP IX 485).

27. GEOFFREY DE NEVILLE, of Hornby Castle, d. ca. 26 Mar. 1285; summoned to Shrewsbury 1285, Chief Justice of the King's Forest; m. ca. 1267, Margaret de Lungvilliers, d. ca. Feb. 1318/9, dau. of John de Lungvilliers, and a descendant of Aleric, Lord of Hornby 1066. (CP IX 487-488; VCH Lanc. VIII 192-193).

28. ROBERT DE NEVILLE, of Hornby Castle, living 1313, was with the King of Scots 1296; m. Isabel de Byron, dau. of Robert de Byron of Melling Manor, Melling Parish, 1280. (CP IX 486; VCH Lanc. III 210).

29. SIR ROBERT DE NEVILLE, Knt. of Hornby Castle, living Jul. 1373, knighted 1344, was at the siege of Amiens, fought at Crecy, 26 Aug. 1346, commissioner for Lancashire 1344, 1346, J.P. for Yorkshire 1353, summoned to Council at Westminster 25 Feb. 1341/2; m. Joan de Atherton, living 1348, dau. of Henry de Atherton of Atherton and Emma de Aintree, and a descendant of William de Atherton of Atherton, 1212. (CP IX 489; VCH Lanc. III 436-437; IV 146; VIII 192-193).

30. SIR ROBERT DE NEVILLE, of Hornby Castle, b. ca. 1321, d. 4 Apr. 1413, served in Gascony, M.P. for Yorkshire 1358, 1377, Sheriff of Yorkshire 1378-1379; m. ca. 1344, Margaret de la Pole, d. 1366, dau. Sir William de la Pole, Knt., Earl of Suffolk, and Katherine of Norwich. (CP IX 490-491; VCH Lanc. VIII 192-193).

31. MARGARET DE NEVILLE, d. bef. 1387; m. SIR WILLIAM DE HARRINGTON, K.G. (35-34), of Farleton and Chorley, co. Lancaster. (CP V 204 note b; IX 490-491; VCH Lanc. VIII 194-202. Mr. Moriarty has revealed the one missing link in the Neville ancestry for which many have long been searching. The proof is partly circumstantial, partly factual. The holding of lands both in Scotland and England; extensive land holdings for many centuries by the same family; unusual repetition of names, especially that of Maldred; and a sound chronological succession, taken together, are conclusive.

Line 248

34. WILLIAM DE FERRERS (11-34), bapt. Luton, co. Bedford, 25 Apr. 1372, d. 18 May 1445, 5th Lord Ferrers of Groby; m. (1) aft. 10 Oct. 1388, Philippa (dau. ROGER DE CLIFFORD (26-32), Lord Clifford, and Maud de Beauchamp), living 4 Jul. 1405; m. (2) Margaret, dau. John de Montague, Earl of Salisbury by Maud, dau. Sir Adam Franceys; m. (3) Elizabeth, dau. Sir Robert de Standisshe, wid. of John de Wrottesley and Sir William Botiller. (CP V 354-356).

35. ELIZABETH FERRERS, apparently eldest dau. by (1); m. Sir William Colpepper, d. 20 Jul. 1457, will 17 May 1445. (Walter G. Davis: Ancestry of Abel Lunt 238-239).

36. RICHARD COLPEPPER, b. ca. 1430; m. (1) Sybil; m. (2) 1480, as 1st husb., Isabel Worsley, dau. of Otewell Worsley, b. ca. 1460, d. 1527; m. (2) Sir John Leigh, son of Ralph, of Stockwell, psh. of Lambeth, Surrey. (Davis: Ancestry of Mary Isaac 343-348).

37. **JOYCE COLPEPPER** (by (1)), b. ca. 1480, d. aft. 1527; m. (1) by 1492, Ralph Leigh of Stockwell, yr. bro. of Sir John Leigh, mother's 2nd husb., will dated 9 Sep. 1509, pro. 1 Feb. 1509/10; she m. (2) aft. 1509, Lord Edmund Howard, yr. son of Thomas, 2nd Duke of Norfolk, d. 16 Feb. 1572/3. (Mary Isaac op. cit. 348-350).

38. **ISABEL LEIGH**, m. as 2nd wife, ca. 18 Jan. 1531/2, Sir Edward Baynton, d. 27 Nov. 1544, son of John, Knt. of Bromham, Wilts., b. ca. 1480; m. (1) ca. 1505, Elizabeth, dau. Sir John Suliard. After his death, Isabel m. (2) Sir James Stumpe of Malmesbury, Wilts., d. 1563, and m. (3) Thomas Stafford. (Mary Isaac op. cit. 352-353; Davis: Ancestry of Abel Lunt 229-237).

39. **HENRY BAYNTON** of Chelsea, co. Mdsx., b. ca. 1536; m. Anne, dau. Sir William Cavendish. (Lunt op. cit. 244-246).

40. **FERDINANDO BAYNTON**, bapt. Bromham, 28 May 1566, living 4 Nov. 1616; m. ca. 1598 as 2nd husb., Joan Weare alias Browne, dau. John Weare alias Browne of Calne, wid. John Hinckley of Salisbury. (Lunt op. cit. 246-247).

41. **ALICE BAYNTON**, b. 23 Sep., bapt. 30 Dec. 1602, will (Boston, Mass.) 14 Mar. 1678/9, pro. 21 May 1679; m. by lic. 12 Oct. 1629, Christopher Batt, son of Thomas, bapt. 6 Jul. 1601, d. Boston, Mass., 10 Aug. 1661, will 19 Nov. 1656, pro. 19 Sep. 1661. (Lunt op. cit. 247, 183-185).

Line 249

30. **NICHOLE DE AUBIGNY** (126-30); m. **ROGER DE SOMERY** (55-28), d. 26 Aug. 1273. (CP XII pt. 1, 113).

31. **JOAN DE SOMERY**, d. 1282; m. **JOHN LE STRANGE IV** (255-31) of Knockin, dead 26 Feb. 1275/6. (CP XII pt. 1, 353; H. LeStrange: LeStrange Records 154-176, 154-155 chart, 159).

32. **JOHN LESTRANGE V**, of Knockin, 22+ at father's death, dead 8 Aug. 1309; m. (2) Maud de Walton. (CP XII pt. 1, 353, 354; C. L'Estrange Ewen: Observations on the LeStranges (1946), chart opp. p. 1; LeStrange Records, 184-254).

33. **ELISABETH LESTRANGE**, b. 1298; m. 8 Jul. 1304, Gruffyd ap Madog ap Gruffyd Maelor of Rhuddailt & Glyndyfrdwy, b. 23 Nov. 1298. (Bridgeman: Princes of South Wales 252; LeStrange Records 215-216).

34. **GRUFFYD FYCHAN** of Glyndyfrdwy; m. **ELEN FERCH THOMAS AP LLEWELLYN** ap Owen (254-34). (Bridgeman op. cit.) (To this point, see TAG 32: 72, generations 7-11). (Note: Charles Evans doubts that Elen existed. Question not resolved at this date.)

35. **LOWRI FERCH GRUFFYD FYCHAN**, m. Robert Puleston of Emral, b. ca. 1358, d. 1399. (J. E. Lloyd: Owen Glendower 24; Dwyn: Visitation of Wales II 150; Bryan Cooke: Seize Quarters of the Family of Brian Cooke, Esq. (London, G. Barclay (1857), Puleston chart). (Proceedings at Scrope-Grosvenor trial show Puleston was Owen Glendower's brother-in-law).

Line 249 (cont.)

36. ANGHARAD PULESTON, m. Edwart (Iorwerth) Trevor ap Daffyd ap Ednyfed Gam, d. 1448. (Lloyd: Powis-Fadog IV 84; Grazebrook & Rylands: Visitations of Shropshire (1633) II 465; Davis: Ancestry of Mary Isaac, chart opp. p. 334, which chart shows Lowri with a different father, but otherwise as shown. See also Mr. Davis' footnote on the Trevor ancestry).

37. ROSE TREVOR FERCH EDWART ap Daffyd; m. ca. 1435, Sir Otewell Worsley of Calais, b. ca. 1410, d. 24 Mar. 1470. (Mary Isaac op. cit. 331-335).

38. MARGARET WORSLEY, d. 1515; m. ca. 1460, Adrian Whetehill, Comptroller of Calais, b. ca. 1435, d. 1503. (Mary Isaac op. cit. 275-278).

39. SIR RICHARD WHETEHILL, of Calais, b. ca. 1465, d. 1536/7; m. ca. 1491, Elizabeth Muston, d. 1542/3. (Mary Isaac op. cit. 280-292).

40. MARGERY WHETEHILL, m. by 24 Jun. 1544, Edward Isaac of Well Court, Kent, b. ca. 1510, d. 4 Mar. 1573. (Mary Isaac op. cit. 298, 30-38).

41. MARY ISAAC, b. ca. 1549, d. 1612/3; m. ca. 1568, Thomas Appleton, of Waldingfield Parva, Suffolk, b. ca. 1538, d. 1603. (Mary Isaac op. cit. 40-41; Davis: Ancestry of Phoebe Tilton 70-72).

42. SAMUEL APPLETON, bapt. 13 Aug. 1586, d. Rowley, Mass., Jun. 1670; m. 24 Jan. 1615/6, Judith Everard, dau. of John Everard. (Mary Isaac, op. cit. 41: Phoebe Tilton 75-77).

Line 250

The following line, not completely supported, appears in Additions and Corrections (1954), page 14.

15. GISELE (146-15), dau. of Louis I and granddau. of Charlemagne, m. **EBERHARD** (191-16), Margrave of Friuli, d. 864/866.

16. HELWISE OF FRIULI, m. (Hucbold, Count of Osrevant ?) d. 895.

* * *

17. RAOUL DE GOUY, Count of Ostrevant and Amiens and of Valois and the Vexin, d. 936 (his mother was a Heiliwich, very doubtful if identical with No. 16), m. Eldegarde, (dau. or niece of Ermenfroi, Count of Amiens ?, prob. a Carolingian princess), who m. (2) Waleran, a count who has been misidentified as father of No. 18.

18. WALTER I, Count of Amiens, Valois and the Vexin, d. 992-998; m. Adele, dau., perh. of Fulk I, Count of Anjou. (Walter I was son of Ralph, Count of Valois, which Ralph is either identical with No. 17, or a son of No. 17 with the same name. Turton in error calls Walter I son of Waleran).

Line 250 (cont.)

19. WALTER II, the White, Count of Amiens, Valois, and the Vexin, d. 1017/1024; m. Adèle. (Perhaps the son of No. 18's brother, Raoul, Count of Valois, d. 940, rather than son of No. 18.)

20. DROGO (DREUX), Count of the Vexin, d. 1035; m. **GODGIFU** (235-20), d. 1055, dau. of Aethelred II, King of England, and Emma, dau. of Richard I, the Fearless, Duke of Normandy.

21. RALPH (235-21), the Timid, Earl of Hereford, d. 1057; m. Gytha (see also Round: Peerage and Family History; Bannister: History of Ewias-Harold; Seversmith: Ancestry of Roger Ludlow 2465-2474).

From No. 17 down, it appears to be correct (proven by Grierson). The parentage of Raoul No. 17 is in doubt. His mother was a Heiliwich who m. (2) Waleran, Count of Laon. David H. Kelley, from his studies (soon to be published) thinks it more likely that his father was Count Theuderic, prob. of Valois, Vexin, pos. of Amiens, who was of the male line of Childebrand, germanus of Karl Martel. Count Theodoric, the Nibelung, did have a son, Count Radulph or Raoul, prob. of Valois, who could well be this Raoul. If the Heiliwich is daughter of Eberhard of Fruili, then, and only then, is the father of Raoul Hucbold, Count of Ostrevant. The fact that Raoul may have borne the title of Count of Ostrevant is not necessarily significant, since such titles were not necessarily hereditary in this period, and there is no proof that Raoul's mother was Eberhard's daughter.

The identification of the parentage of Eldegard, wife of Raoul, as dau. or niece of Ermenfrid (Erminfroi) rests on Walter's statement that he was his heir. However, it is equally possible that Erminfrid was Raoul's brother.

Line 251

34. GRUFFYDD FYCHAN (249-34); m. **HELEN** or Ellen (254-34), dau. of Thomas ap Llewellyn ap Owen. (Her existence is doubted by Charles Evans, and this has not been resolved at this date.) (They were also the parents of Owen Glendower.) (TAG 32: 72).

35. TUDOR (or TWDR) AP GRUFFYD FYCHAN, m. Maud, dau. of Ienaf ap Adda. (TAG cit.) He was ae. 24+ at Scrope-Grosvenor trial, seen 1400, killed in battle, May 1405 at Pwll Melyn. (cit. 76).

36. LOWRI, only dau. and h.; m. (2) Gruffyd ap Einion of Gwyddelwern ap Gruffyd ap Llewellyn ap Cynrig ap Osbern Wyddel of Cora y Gedol. (TAG cit.)

37. ELISSAU AP GRUFFYD, m. Margaret, dau. and coh. of Jenkyn of Allt Llwyn ap Ienen ap Llewellyn ap Gruffyd Lloyd. (TAG 32: 73).

38. DAVID LLOYD, m. Gwenhwyfar, dau. of Richard Lloyd ap Robert Lloyd of Llwyn y Maen. (TAG 32: 73).

39. JOHN WYNN or Ial, of Plas yn Ial; m. Elizabeth, dau. of Thomas Mostyn. The mother of his illeg. son David Yale was Agnes

Line 251 (cont.)

Lloyd. (TAG cit. TAG 50:246).
    40. REV. DAVID YALE, D.L.C., d. 1626, illeg. son by Agnes
Lloyd; m. Frances, dau. of John Lloyd ap Davis Lloyd. (TAG cit.;
Dict. Welsh Biog. 1110).
    41. THOMAS YALE, m. Ann, dau. the Rt. Rev. George Lloyd, d.
1615, Bishop of Chester. She m. (2) Theophilus Eaton, Gov. New
Haven Colony. (TAG cit.; Dict. Welsh Biog. 579, 1110); to New
Haven 1638, Gov. 1639-1658. She came with him, with her children,
incl. David, father of Elihu, (for whom Yale University is named) and
Thomas, ancestor of the family of Yale in America.

Line 252

    26. DAVID, Earl of Huntingdon (93-26), b. ca. 1144, d. at
Jerdelay, 17 Jun. 1219; m. 26 Aug. 1190, **MAUD** (131-29), dau. and in
her issue coh. of Hugh de Kevelioc, Earl of Chester. (For a chart of
their ancestry, see Geo. F. Farnham: Leicester Medieval Pedigrees
11). They had with others, Margaret, who m. 1209, **ALAN** (38-26),
Lord of Galloway, d. 1234, whose dau. Devorguilla m. 1236, John
Baliol of Barnard Castle and had with others, John Baliol, King of
Scots; Cecily m. **JOHN DE BURGH** (94-29); and **ELEANOR** (95-29),
m. **JOHN COMYN** (121A-24) of Badenoch. Also
    27. ISABELLA m. Robert Brus (or Bruce), Lord of Annandale, d.
1245 (for his ancestry, see SP II 429-432; Farrer: Early Yorkshire
Charters II 430-432).
    28. ROBERT BRUCE, Lord of Annandale, d. by 3 May 1294
(G.W.S. Barrow says d. at Lochmaben, Good Friday, 1295); m. in or
bef. 1240, Isabel, b. 1226, ae. 13 at mar., living 1264, 2nd dau. of
GILBERT DE CLARE (63-28), Earl of Gloucester and Hertford, and
his wife Isabel Marshall. (SP II 431-432; IX 55.)
    29. ROBERT BRUCE, eldest s. and h., Earl of Carrick, j.u., b.
Writtle July 1243, d. shortly bef. 4 Apr. 1304; m. as 2nd husb.,
MARJORIE (121C-30), d. 1292, bef. 27 Oct., wid. of Adam de
Kilconquhar, eldest dau. and h. of **NEIL** (121C-29), Earl of Carrick;
he m. (2) an Eleanor, seen 1305, who m. (2) 1306, Richard de
Waleys. (SP II 427, 432-433).
    30. ROBERT BRUCE, Lord of Annandale, s. and h. by Marjorie;
b. prob. at Turnberry Castle, 11 Jul. 1274; succeeded as Earl of
Carrick 9 Nov. 1292; crowned King of Scots (as Robert I) at Scone,
25 Mar. 1306, d. at Cardross, near Dumbarton, 7 Jun. 1329; m. ca.
1295 (1) Isabel (also called Matilda), d. bef. 1302, dau. of Donald, 6th
Earl of Mar; m. (2) 1302, Elizabeth, d. 26 Oct. 1327, dau. of
RICHARD DE BURGH (75-31), Earl of Ulster. (Donald, 6th Earl of
Mar was son of William, Earl of Mar, d. ca. 1281, by his 1st wife,
Elizabeth, d. 1267, daughter of **WILLIAM COMYN** (121A-26), Earl of
Buchan, j.u., by his 2nd wife, Countess of Buchan). Donald, Earl of
Mar, was knighted 1270, living 25 Jul. 1297, d. shortly thereafter.
His wife, and mother of Isabel, was Helen, widow of Malcolm, 7th
Earl of Fife, d. 1266, and daughter of **LLEWELLYN**, Prince of Wales
(176-7). Helen's first husband must have been an old man when she

married him, for he succeeded his uncle in 1228. When he died, his son and heir was Colban, the 8th Earl, then under age, who had been knighted in his teens in 1264. Colban was married in his nonage, for when he died in 1270, when he could not have been more than 24, his heir was his son Duncan, aged 8. (Mr. Balfour Paul believes Colban's wife Alice was one of the three daughters and co-heirs of Sir Alan Durward. If so, his issue shared with the Soulis family the descent from Alexander II of Scotland. However, since the line of his heir Duncan has died out, remaining descendants of this line would stem from younger children of Colban and Alice, if there were any.) The Helen, daughter of Llewellyn, who was successively the wife of Malcolm and of Donald, and mother of the children of both, appears clearly the daughter of **LLEWELLYN AP IORWERTH** (176-7) but must not be confused with his daughter **HELEN** (236-8), successively the wife of John le Scot, Earl of Chester, and of Robert de Quincy, whose mother was Princess **JOAN** (27-27). (Refs.: Mar; CP VIII 401-402 (William, 5th Earl), 402-403 (Donald, 6th Earl); SP V 576-578; Burke's Peerage (1953) p. 1397; Fife: CP V 373; SP IV 8-10).

    31. MARJORIE BRUCE, daughter by (1) and eventual heiress, b. bef. 1297; m. 1315, **WALTER** (75A-32), b. 1292, d. 9 Apr. 1327, 6th High Steward of Scotland. (His (1) wife is said by Douglas to have been Alice, dau. Sir John Erskine by whom a dau. Jean, m. to Hugh, Earl of Ross. No proof either of marriage or daughter, almost certainly wrong.) After the death of Lady Marjorie, Walter the Steward m. (2) or (3) Isabel, sis. Sir John Graham by whom he had issue.

    32. ROBERT II, King of Scots 1371-1390; b. 2 Mar. 1315/6; succeeded his uncle, King David II, 22 Feb. 1370/1; d. at Dundonald, Ayrshire, 19 Apr. 1390; m. (1) 1348/9 (disp. Pope Clement VI 22 Nov. 1347 (SP I, 15)) Elizabeth, dau. of Sir Adam Mure, of Rowallan; m. (2) Euphemia, dau. Hugh, Earl of Ross, wid. of John Randolph, Earl of Moray (disp. 2 May 1355), by whom issue.

    33. ROBERT III (named John, Earl of Carrick, but took name of Robert), by (1), King of Scots 1390-1406; b. ca. 1337 (legitimated through his parents' marriage, disp. 22 Nov. 1347), d. at Dundonald 4 Apr. 1406; m. ca. 1367, Annabella (d. 1401), dau. of Sir John Drummond of Stobhall.

    34. JAMES I, King of Scots 1406-1437; b. at Dunfermline, Dec. 1394, murdered at Perth, 21 Feb. 1436/7; m. 2 Feb. 1423/4 (post nuptial dispensation 21 Sept. 1439), Joan de Beaufort, d. at Dunbar, 15 Jul. 1445, dau. of **JOHN**, 1st Earl of Somerset (1-32) and his wife **MARGARET DE HOLAND** (47-33). She m. (2) 1439, Sir James Stewart, "The Black Knight of Lorn", issue.

    35. JAMES II, King of Scots 1437-1460; b. at Holyrood, 16 Oct. 1430, killed at the siege of Roxburgh Castle, 3 Aug. 1460; m. 3 Jul. 1449, Marie (d. 1 Dec. 1463 at Edinburgh), dau. of Arnulf, Duke of Gueldres.

    36. JAMES III, King of Scots 1460-1488; b. at Stirling, 10 Jul. 1451, assassinated 11 Jun. 1488; m. 13 Jul. 1469, Margaret (b. 23 Jun. 1456, d. 14 Jul. 1486), dau. of Christian I, King of Denmark by

Line 252 (cont.)

his wife Dorothea of Hohenzollern.

37. JAMES IV, King of Scots 1488-1513; b. 17 Mar. 1472/3, killed in action at Flodden Field, 9 Sep. 1513; m. 8 Aug. 1503 (disp. granted by Pope Alexander VI, Rome, 28 Jul. 1500), Margaret, d. 18 Oct. 1542, eldest dau. of Henry VII, King of England, by whom he had his successor, James V, ancestor of the later Kings of Scotland and England. After his death, she m. (2) Aug. 1514, Archibald Douglas, Earl of Angus, div. 1526; m. (3) 1526, Henry Stewart, Lord Methven. (References for Generations 30-37: G.W.S. Barrow: Robert Bruce and the Community of The Realm of Scotland, 1965, pp. 37-38, 92-93, 199, 212-213, 397, 444-445, 455-464; SP I 3-4, 7-8, 14-22; II 435; VII 44-45). By a mistress, Margaret (said to have died of poison, Apr. 1502), dau. of John, 1st Lord of Drummond, and his wife Elizabeth Lindsay, dau. of Alexander, 4th Earl of Crawford. King James IV had:

38. MARGARET, b. 1497; m. (1) Nov. 1512, John, Lord Gordon, Master of Huntly (d. 5 Dec. 1517), s. and h. of Alexander, 3rd Earl of Huntly. (Registrum Magni Sigilli Regum Scotorum: The Register of the Great Seal of Scotland, 1424-1513, p. 740, no. 3452; SP IV 532-533).

39. ALEXANDER GORDON, b. ca. 1516, d. 11 Nov. 1575, Bishop of the Isles 1553; Bishop of Galloway 1558, titular Archbishop of Athens, the only Scottish prelate to join the Reformers. (Dictionary of National Biography, XXII 159-161; SP IV 533). By a concubine, Barbara Logie:

40. JOHN GORDON, D.D., b. 1544, d. 1619, Bishop-Elect of Galloway; Dean of Salisbury 1604-19; legitimated by his cousin, Mary, Queen of Scots, 16 Sep. 1553; m. (2) Geneviève, dau. of Gideon Petau, Sieur de Maule, in France. (Dict. Natl. Biog. XXII 212-214: Reg. Mag. Sig. Reg. Scot., 1546-80, p. 190, no. 848; ibid., 1580-93, pp. 289-290, no. 900).

41. LOUISA (called also **LUCY**) **GORDON**, b. 1597, d. Sep. 1680; m. 16 Feb. 1613, Sir Robert Gordon, 1st Bart., of Gordonstoun, co. Moray (created 28 May 1625 — the premier Baronet of Scotland and Nova Scotia). He was b. 14 May 1580, d. Mar. 1656; son of Alexander, 11th Earl of Sutherland, by his 2nd wife, Lady Jean Gordon, dau. of George, 4th Earl of Huntly. (Will of Dr. John Gordon, 16 Sep. 1618, quoted by Capt. Edward Dunbar-Dunbar: Social Life in Former Days, 1865, pp. 284-285; Sir Robert Gordon, 1st Bart., of Gordonstoun: A Genealogical History of the Earldom of Sutherland, from its Origin to the Year 1630, p. 289 (continued to 1651 by Gilbert Gordon of Sallah, but not published until 1813); Dict. Natl. Biog. XXII 224-225; Francis W. Pixley: A History of the Baronetage, 1900, pp. 59-89 (the Latin text of Sir Robert Gordon's Patent creating him a baronet) and p. 154).

42. KATHERINE GORDON, b. 11 Jan. 1620/21, d. ca. 1663; m. 26 Jan. 1647/8, Col. David Barclay, 1st Laird of Urie, co. Kincardine (b. ca. 1610, d. 12 Oct. 1686). (Lt. Col. Hubert F. Barclay and Alice Wilson-Fox: A History of the Barclay Family, part III, 1934, pp. 3, 35-36; Alexander Gordon, "The Great Laird of Urie", Theological

Review, Oct. 1874, p. 537 (marriage contract of Col. David Barclay and Katherine Gordon)).

43. ROBERT BARCLAY, 2nd Laird of Urie, b. 23 Dec. 1648, d. at Urie, 3 Oct. 1690; the eminent Quaker "Apologist", Governor of East New Jersey, Sep. 1682-Oct. 1690; m. Christian Mollison (d. 14 Dec. 1722); ancestors of the later Lairds of Urie.

43. JOHN BARCLAY, b. ca. 1650, d. at Perth Amboy, N.J., Apr. 1731; settled in East Jersey ca. 1684, Member of the General Assemblies of the Province of East Jersey and of the later Province of New Jersey, Deputy Surveyor of East Jersey, Town Clerk of Perth Amboy, Receiver General and Ranger General of New Jersey, Clerk of the Governor's Council, J.P. for Middlesex and Somerset Cos., N.J., Surrogate of the Eastern Division of New Jersey; m. Katherine (Rescarrick ?), bur. 6 Jan. 1702/3, by whom he had two children: John Barclay (1702-86), of Cranberry, N.J. (whose descendants are traced in R. Burnham Moffat's The Barclays of New York, 1904, pp. 57-65); and Agnes Barclay. (Proofs of John Barclay's parentage and relationship to Gov. Robert Barclay: Documents abstracted in the New Jersey Archives, 1st series, vol. XXI, Calendar of Records, pp. 66, 76, 182, 201, and vol. XI, Newspaper Abstracts, vol. I, p. 243 (his obituary); King James II's confirmation in 1685 of the Barclay's possession of the Barony of Urie, naming Col. David Barclay, "Catharine Gordon his spouse", and all of their children, in The Acts of the Parliaments of Scotland, vol. VIII, 1821, p. 531. See also Milton Rubicam: "John Barclay of Perth Amboy: The Scion of an Illustrious House", Proceedings of the New Jersey Historical Society, Jul. and Oct. 1940, containing heavy footnote documentation).

Line 253

29. EUDO LA ZOUCHE (38-29), seen 1251, d. 28 Apr.-25 Jun. 1279; m. by 13 Dec. 1273, **MILICENT** (66-30), wid. John de Mohaut, and dau. of William de Cauntelo of Calne, Wilts (and h. to her bro. George de Cauntelo) by Eve, 3rd dau. and coh. of William de Briouze of Abergavenny. (CP I 22, 23; XII pt. 2, 937-938; X 674).

30. ELIZABETH LA ZOUCHE, living 1297; m. by 20 Jan. 1287/8, as a child, Sir Nicholas de Poyntz, Knt., 2nd Lord Poyntz, b. ca. 1278, d. sh. bef. 12 Jul. 1311; m. (2) by 9 Feb. 1308/9, Maud, d. 1361, dau. of John de Acton (d. 1312). She m. (2) by 1315, Roger de Chaundos, first Lord Chaundos. (CP X 674-675).

31. HUGH DE POYNTZ, eldest son and h. by (1), b. at Hoo, Kent, proved age 12 Feb. 1316/7, d. shortly bef. 2 May 1337; m. by 1 Jun. 1330, Margaret, prob. dau. of William Pavelley of Brooke, Wilts. (Coll. Topo. & Gen. VII 149; CP X 675-676).

32. NICHOLAS DE POYNTZ, s. and h., b. North Okenden, Essex, ae. 17+ in 1337, d. by Michaelmass 1376; m. (1) by 13 Oct. 1333, Eleanor Erleigh, said to be dau. of Sir John Erleigh; m. (2) by 30 Jan. 1367/8. (Dugdale: Baronage II 2: CP X 676).

33. MARGARET POYNTZ, dau. and coh. by (1), m. ca. 1370, John de Newburgh, b. ca. 1340, d. Bindon Abbey, 4 Jun. 1381. (CP X

Line 253 (cont.)

676 note k; J. Gardner Bartlett: Newberry Genealogy (Boston, 1914), p. 10).

34. JOHN NEWBURGH, s. and h., b. ca. 1370, d. soon aft. Feb. 1438/9; m. by 1400, Joan Delamere, dau. of Sir John Delamere, Knt. He lived in Dorset. (Newberry, cit. 11).

35. JOHN NEWBURGH, s. and h., b. ca. 1400, d. in Dorset, 1 Apr. 1484; m. (1) 1422, Edith, dau. Robert and Joan Attemore, no issue; m. (2) ca. 1435, Alice, wid. of John Westbury, dau. of William Carent of Toomer, co. Somerset, who brought him the manor of Berkley, Somerset. (Newberry, cit. 10, 11).

36. THOMAS NEWBURGH, b. ca. 1445, 3rd and youngest son, received manor of Berkley from his mother, d. 15 Mar. 1512/13; m. ca. 1584, one Alice, who m. (2) Thomas Kyrton, and d. 1525. (Newberry cit. 14-16).

37. WALTER NEWBURGH (or Newborough), 2nd son, b. ca. 1487, d. 12 Aug. 1517; m. ca. 1512, Elizabeth Birport, who m. (2) ca. 1520, George Strangeways and d. 1570/1 leaving a will, and chn. by both husbands. (Newberry, cit. 16-17).

38. RICHARD NEWBOROUGH (or Newburgh), only s. and h., b. ca. Jul. 1517, held manors in Dorset, d. at Othe Fraunces, Dorset by 30 Jan. 1568/9; m. ca. 1552, Elizabeth, dau. of William Horsey of Binghams, who m. (2) one Woodshaw after his death. (Newberry cit. 17-19).

39. RICHARD NEWBERRY (or Newburgh), 2nd son, b. ca. 1557, present at Netherbury, Dorset, d. ca. 1629 at Yarcombe, Devon.; m. 15 Jan. 1580/1, Grace Matthew, dau. of John Matthew. She bur. Yarcombe, 18 Dec. 1632. (Their children were b. and rec. in Yarcombe). (Newberry cit. 23-24).

40. THOMAS NEWBERRY, 4th son (6th ch.), b. Yarcombe, 10 Nov. 1594, to America Apr. 1634, to Dorchester, Mass., where d. Dec. 1635; m. (1) ca. 1619, Joan, b. ca. 1600, dau. of Christopher Dabinott of Yarcombe, d. Eng. ca. 1629; m. (2) ca. a Jane, who may have been Jane Dabinott, cousin of his (1) wife. She m. (2) 1637, as (2) wife, Rev. John Warham of Norwalk, Conn., where she d. 23 Apr. 1655. (Newberry cit. 35-44).

Line 254

28. JOAN, Princess of Wales (27-27); m. by 1206, **LLEWELLYN AP JORWERTH** (176-7), Prince of Wales.

29. ANGHARAD, m. Aelgwn Fychan, lord of Cardigan Is Ayron, d. 1257. (TAG 38: 180; Bridgeman: Princes of South Wales, pp. 203-204, 209; The Genealogist V (1881) p. 166).

30. ELENA FERCH MAELGWN FYCHAN, m. Maredudd ap Owain, d. 1265, lord of Cardigan Uch Ayron. (Bridgeman, cit. 209, 249; J.E. Lloyd: History of Wales (1954), II p. 768).

31. OWAIN AP MAREDUDD, d. 1275, m. Angharad ferch Owain ap Maredudd, lord of Kedowain. (Bridgeman, cit. 249; Lloyd, cit. 768).

32. LLEWELLYN AP OWAIN, lord of a moiety of Gwynnionith

Line 254 (cont.)

and of Caerwedros, d. 1309; m. a dau. of Sir Robert de Vale, Lord of Trefgarn. (Bridgeman, cit. 249; Lloyd, cit. 768).
33. THOMAS AP LLEWELLYN, lord of a moiety of Iscoed Uchirwern, b. bef. 14 Aug. 1343; m. **ELEANOR** (260-33) ferch Philip ap Ifor, lord of Iscoed. (Bridgeman, cit. 247, 249).

* * *

34. ELEN FERCH THOMAS AP LLEWELLYN, m. **GRUFFYDD FYCHAN** (249-34), lord of Glyndyfrdwy. (Bridgeman, cit. 249; J.Y.W. Lloyd: Hist. of Powys Fadog I 198). (Charles Evans doubts the existence of Elen, No. 34. This matter is not yet unresolved.)

Line 255

25. HAROLD DE EWYAS (235-22), Lord of Sudeley and Ewyas Harold, living 1115; wife's name is lacking. (Mis. Gen. Her., as above; Sanders: English Baronies (1960), p. 43).
26. ROBERT I DE EWYAS, d. post 1147, Lord of Ewyas Harold; wife's name lacking. (Ibid.)
27. ROBERT II DE EWYAS, d. 1198, Lord of Ewyas Harold; m. Pernel (Petronilla), liv. 1204. (Sanders, op. cit; CP XII pt. 2, p. 18).
28. SIBYL DE EWYAS, d. 1236; m. possibly in 1198, Robert I de Tregoz, d. 1213-14. Ibid.) Parents of both Robert II, No. 29, and Lucy, No. 30.
29. ROBERT II DE TREGOZ, d. Evesham 1265, of Ewyas Harold; m. by 1245, Juliane, living 1285 (sister of Thomas, Bishop of Hereford, d. 1282, canonized 1320 as St. Thomas of Hereford), dau. of William II de Cauntelo (d. 1251) and his wife Melicent (d. 1260), dau. of Hugh de Gournai. (CP XII pt. 2, p. 16 note d, 18-20; I 350-351; Sussex Arch. Cols. xciii 34-56; Bedfordshire Hist. Rec. Society V 213-214 and chart p. 215). Not parents of No. 30.
30. LUCY TREGOZ, dau. of Robert I (No. 29), m. John Lestrange III, d. by 1269, Lord Strange of Knockyn. (Topo. and Geneal. II 130; CP XII pt. 1, 350-351; Eyton: Antiquities of Shropshire X 262; Ewen: Observations on the Lestranges, Chart, p. 1).
31. JOHN LESTRANGE IV, d. 1275, Lord Strange of Knockyn; m. bef. 1254 **JOAN** (249-31), dau. of Roger de Somery and **NICHOLE D'AUBIGNY** (126-30). (CP XII pt. 1, p. 351; Eyton, op. cit. 263; Ewen, op. cit.)

Line 255A (Prepared by Douglas Richardson)

29. ROBERT II DE TREGOZ (255-29), d. 1265 at Evesham, held barony of Ewyas Harold co. Hereford; m. by 1245, Juliane de Cauntelo, dau. of William II de Cauntelo, d. 1251, by his wife Millicent, d. 1260, dau. of Hugh de Gournay. (Sanders, English Baronies 43; Beds. Hist. Rec. Soc. V 213-214, chart p. 215).
30. SIR JOHN DE TREGOZ, adult by 1271, d. shortly bef. 6 Sep. 1300, Lord Tregoz, lord of barony of Ewyas Harold, co. Hereford, m.

Line 255A (cont.)

(1) Mabel Fitz Warin, widow of William de Crevequer (d. 1263) and dau. of Sir Fulk Fitz Warin of Whittington, Salop. (CP XII, pt. II 20-22).

31. CLARICE DE TREGOZ, elder dau. and coh., inherited half the barony of Ewyas Harold, living April 1289, dead by 28 Aug. 1300, m. in or bef. 12 Sep. 1276 Sir Roger la Warre, 1st Baron la Warre, adult by 1279, d. 20 Jun. 1320, of Wickwar, Gloucester, Brislington, Somerset, etc., son of Sir John la Warre by Olympia, dau. of Sir Hugh de Fokinton. (CP IV 139-141).

32. JOHN LA WARRE, b. ca. 1276/7 (ae. 23 or 24 in 1300), d. 9 May 1347, 2nd Baron la Warre, m. soon after 19 Nov. 1294 **JOAN DE GRELLE** (99-31), d. 20 or 21 Mar. 1352/3. (CP IV 141-143).

Line 256

33. ROBERT III, King of Scots (252-33), b. ca. 1337 (legitimated through his parents' marriage), d. 4 Apr. 1406; m. ca. 1367, Annabella, d. 1401, dau. of Sir John Drummond of Stobhall. (SP I 17-18).

34. MARY STEWART, d. in 1458; m. (1) George Douglas, Earl of Angus (marriage contract dated 24 May 1397). He was captured by the English at the battle of Homildon Hill, 14 Sep. 1402, and d. of the plague shortly thereafter. (SP I 18, 173).

35. ELIZABETH DOUGLAS, m. betw. 6 and 16 Oct. 1423, Sir Alexander Forbes, 1st Lord Forbes, who was b. ca. 1380, d. 1448. (SP IV 47-48; CP V 544).

36. JAMES, 2nd Lord Forbes, d. betw. 20 Sep. 1460 and 30 Jul. 1462; m. Egidia (still living 14 Aug. 1473), dau. of William Keith, 1st Earl Marischal, by his wife, Mary, dau. of Sir James Hamilton. (SP IV 50-51; CP V 544-545).

37. WILLIAM, 3rd Lord Forbes, d. betw. 9 Jul. 1477 and 5 Jul. 1483; m. (charter dated 8 Jul. 1468), Christian Gordon, dau. of Alexander, 1st Earl of Huntly, by his 2nd wife, Elizabeth, dau. of William, Lord Crichton. (SP IV 51-52; CP V 545). (The 3rd Lord Forbes' immediate successors were his sons, Alexander, 4th Lord, and Arthur, 5th Lord, both of whom d. without issue).

38. JOHN, 6th Lord Forbes (succeeding his brother Arthur, 1493); d. 1547; m. (2) bef. 26 Feb. 1509/10, Christian, dau. of Sir John Lundin of Lundin. (SP IV 53-55; CP V 545).

39. WILLIAM, 7th Lord Forbes, d. 1593; m. 19 Dec. 1538, in the Abbey Church of Lindores, Elizabeth (d. bef. 13 Nov. 1604), dau. of Sir William Keith, of Inverugie, co. Banff. (SP IV 55-57; CP V 546).

40. ISABEL FORBES, b. 16 Oct. 1548, bur. at Aberdeen 22 Mar. 1622; m. 1567, Sir John Gordon, 3rd Laird of Pitlurg, co. Banff, who d. 16 Sep. 1600. He was son of John and Janet (Ogilvie) Gordon, and grandson of John Gordon, 1st Laird of Pitlurg, by his 1st wife, Jane, dau. of Sir John Stewart, 1st Earl of Atholl, and granddau. of Sir James Stewart, the Black Knight of Lorn, by Queen **JOAN** (de Beaufort) (252-34), wid. of King James I of Scotland, and great-granddau. of King Edward III of England. (SP IV 57).

41. ROBERT GORDON, 5th Laird of Pitlurg (succeeding his brother, John, the 4th Laird, 1619), and 1st Laird of Straloch (by which title he is generally known), b. at Kinmundy, Aberdeenshire, 14 Sep. 1580, d. 18 Aug. 1661; the distinguished Scottish geographer, mathematician, and antiquary; m. (1) 1608, Katherine (d. 3 Aug. 1662), dau. of Alexander Irvine, Laird of Lynturk. (Dict. Natl. Biog. VIII 226-227; Balbithan Ms., p. 31, written ca. 1730 and published in The House of Gordon, edited by James Malcolm Bulloch, M.A., vol. I, 1903).

42. ROBERT GORDON, 6th Laird of Pitlurg, b. 1609, d. 18 Apr. 1681; m. 1638, Catherine, dau. of Sir Thomas Burnett, 1st Baronet of Leys, by his 1st wife, Margaret, dau. of Sir Robert Douglas of Glenbervie. (George Burnett, LL.D., The Family of Burnett of Leys, 1901, pp. 59, 62; Balbithan Ms., p. 31, in Bulloch, op. cit., vol. I).

43. THOMAS GORDON, b. prob. at Pitlurg, co. Banff, ca. 1652; settled in the Province of East New Jersey 1684, held numerous offices: Deputy Secretary and Register for the East Jersey Proprietors, Clerk of the Court of Common Right, Register of the Court of Chancery, Judge of the Probate Court, Attorney-General of the Province of East New Jersey, Member of the General Assembly of the Province of New Jersey, Speaker of the General Assembly, Chief Justice of New Jersey, Member of the Royal Council of New Jersey, Attorney-General of the Province of East New Jersey, Member of the General Assembly of the Province of New Jersey, Speaker of the General Assembly, Chief Justice of New Jersey, Member of the Royal Council of New Jersey, Attorney-General of New Jersey; d. at Perth Amboy, N.J., 28 Apr. 1722; m. (1) Helen _____, who d. Dec. 1687; m. (2) 1695, Janet, dau. of David Mudie of Perth Amboy. He had issue by both wives, but only his children by Janet seem to have survived childhood and to have left issue. (Testimony by Rev. Alexander Innes, of Monmouth Co., N.J., 12 Mar. 1712/13: "I can certify with a good Conscience that he is descended from an honorable Orthodox, and Loyal Family, being Grand child of the Eldest Son to the memorable Robert Gordon of Pitlurg and Straloch", New Jersey Archives, 1st series, vol. IV, pp. 177-178; Letter from Thomas Gordon, brother of the Laird of Straloch, to George Alexander, advocate in Edinburgh, dated "From the Cedar Brook of East New Jersey", 16 Feb. 1685, quoted in George Scot's The Model of the Government of the Province of East-New-Jersey in America, 1685 (published in Whitehead's East Jersey under the Proprietary Governments, 1848, pp. 326-327); and Milton Rubicam, "The Honorable Thomas Gordon: Attorney General and Chief Justice", Proceedings of the New Jersey Historical Society, vol. 57, Jul. 1939, pp. 148-150, and documentary evidence cited in the footnotes therein).

27. **HENRY FITZ AILWIN,** son of Ailwin, son of Lefstan, son of Ongar, seen 1165, first mayor of the Commune of London 1187-1212. (J.H. Round: The Commune of London, 105; Farrer: Honours and Knight's Fees III 347-350).

28. **PETER FITZ HENRY,** seen temp. Richard I, m. Isabel, dau. of Bartholomew de Chesney (or de Caisneto) and received with her a moiety of the manor of Addington, Surrey, held by "pantry service". (Farrer, cit. (Honor of Warenne); J.H. Round: The King's Sergeants, 246-249).

The reader will be interested in the meaning of "pantry service". The holder of Addington was required as a condition of tenure to provide a special dish to the monarch at coronations. This dish was called "dillegrout" and was provided at the coronation of Richard II in 1377 by **WILLIAM BARDOLF** (257-34). The following is quoted from Round's The King's Sergeants p. 248-249, under the title, "The King's Sauser."

"It has been ingeniously suggested that this mess of potage (as it is subsequently described) may be represented by the recipe for "Bardolf" in an Arundel MS., said to be of early 15th cent. date. It runs thus:

"Take almonde mylk, and draw hit up thik with vernage, and let hit boyle, and braune of capons braied and put therto; and cast therto sugre, claves (cloves), maces, pynes, and ginger, mynced; and take chekyns parboyled and chopped, and pul of the skyn, and boyle al ensemble, and, in the settynge doune from the fire, put thereto a lytel vynegur alaied with pouder of giner, and a lytel water of everose, and make the potage hanginge, and serve hit forth (Household Ordinances (Society of Antiquaries), p. 466).

After the Reign of Richard II this "mess" was presented at coronations, from the reign of Charles II onwards, by the Leigh family, but the "merry monarch," we are told, carefully abstained from eating it. It was still presented by the lord of the manor at the coronation of George III, and even at the last banquet, that of George IV, the right was claimed and obtained by the Archbishop of Canterbury (The Archbishops held Addington from 1807 to 1897). Accordingly, the Deputy appointed by his Grace the Archbishop of Canterbury, as Lord of the Manor of Bardolf, otherwise Addington, presented the mess of Dillegrout, prepared by the King's Master Cook (Sir George Nayler's narrative reprinted by Mr. Legg, p. 358).

29. **JOAN,** the yr. dau. and coheiress, m. (1) Ralph de Parminter; m. (2) 1212, William Aguillon, (perh. son of William who 1200 covenanted to deliver his son William to King John as hostage) obtained Addington with his wife. (Farrer, cit.; Round, cit.) He withdrew from allegiance to King John, but returned, lands restored 17 Sep. 1217. He d. 1244.

30. ROBERT AGUILLON, s. and h. 1244, held lands in Addington, Surrey; Walton, Herts; Greatham, Hants.; seen 1260, 1267; sheriff of Surrey and Sussex, constable of Guilford Castle 1264, lic. to crenellate manor house of Perching and to ditch 1268; d. 15 Feb. 1285/6; m. (1) in or bef. Aug. 1256 Joan, dead Oct. 1267, widow of Sir John de Mohun (dead by 1254), dau. of **WILLIAM FERRERS,** Earl of Derby (127-30) (by his 1st wife Sibyl, one of seven daus. and cohs. of William Marshall, Earl of Pembroke); m. (2) Margaret, "Countess of the Isle", dower assigned in manors of Addington, Surrey; Bures Taney, Essex; Greatham, Hants.; etc. She d. 1292. By his 1st wife, Joan, he left an only dau. and h. (Farrer, cit.; CP I 416; IV 199; IX 21).

31. ISABEL, b. ca. 1258 (ae. 28 in 1286), seen 1292, lady of Perching 1316; m. bef. 1282, Hugh Bardolf (son of William (see Gen. Mag. XV p. 56 & p. 62 note 23), d. Dec. 1289), b. ca. 29 Sep. 1259, d. Sep. 1304, sum. 1298/9 1st Lord Bardolf. (CP I 417-418; IV 196-199; Farrer, cit. 350).

32. THOMAS BARDOLF, 2nd Lord Bardolf, s. and h., b. 4 Oct. 1282, d. 15 Dec. 1328; m. Agnes, d. 11 Dec. 1357, perh. dau. William de Grandison, Seigneur de Grandison on Lake Neufchâtel, Switzerland, by Blanche, dau. Louis de Savoie, Baron Vaud. (CP I 418).

33. JOHN BARDOLF, 3rd Lord Bardolf, s. and h., b. 13 Jan. 1311/12, d. Jul. or Aug. 1363, ae. 51; m. 1326, Elizabeth, only dau. and h. Roger Damory, Lord Damory, d. ca. Mar. 1321/2, by **ELIZABETH** (11-30) ae. 19 or 20 in 1314, 3rd and youngest dau. of Gilbert de Clare, Earl of Gloucester, by Joan, dau. King Edward I. Elizabeth (11-30) had m. (1) 30 Sep. 1308, John de Burgh, Earl of Ulster d.v.p. 18 Jun. 1313; m. (2) 4 Feb. 1315/6, Sir Theobald de Verdun, d. 27 Jul. 1316; m. (3) ca. Apr. 1317, Sir Roger Damory. She d. 4 Nov. 1390. (CP I 418-419; IV 42-46; V 715 note d).

34. WILLIAM BARDOLF, 4th Lord Bardolf, of Wormgay, s. and h., b. 21 Oct. 1349, d. 29 Jan. 1385/6, ae. 36, will dated 12 Sep. 1385; m. Agnes, dau. Michael, Lord Poynings, to whom William Bardolf had been in ward. She m. (2) shortly aft. 10 Apr. 1386, Sir Thomas Mortimer, dead 9 Jan. 1402/3. She d. 12 Jun. 1403, will dated 9 Jan. 1402/3, pr. 13 Jun. 1403. (CP I 419).

35. CECILY, d. 29 Sep. 1432, bur. Ingham Priory; m. Sir Brian Stapleton of Ingham and Bedale, (son of Sir Miles of same and Ela, dau. Sir Edmund Ufford (Topo. et Gen. II 274)), ae. 40+ in 1419, d. 7 Aug. 1438, bur. Ingham Priory, will dated 5 Apr. and 4 May 1438, pr. 6 Aug. 1438. (CP V 397; Norfolk Arch. VIII 222-223).

36. SIR MILES STAPLETON of same, 30+ in 1438, d. 30 Sep. or 1 Oct. 1466, bur. Ingham Priory, will 4 Aug. 1442, pr. 17 Nov. 1466; m. (1) ?; m. (2) Katharine, dau. and in 1430, h. of Sir Thomas de la Pole of Grafton Regis, d. Aug. 1320 (said by Burke, in error, to be youngest son of Sir Michael de la Pole (CP XII pt. 2, 444, note m shows that Thomas can not be son of 2nd Earl Michael (as shown in Burke, DNB, etc.) 1st Earl of Suffolk, by his 1st wife Katharine, dau. and h. Sir John Wingfield of Wingfield, Suff. by Eleanor, dau. of a

Line 257 (cont.)

Glanville. Lady Ann de la Pole (2nd wife, his widow) d. July 1330). (Baker's Northamptonshire II 161-2). She was 14+ in 1430, d. 13 or 14 Oct. 1488, will 7 Jul., 5 Sep. 1488, pro. 23 Jan. 1488/9, bur. Rowley Abbey. She had m. (2) Sir Richard Harcourt of Wytham, d. 1 Oct. 1486. (CP and Norfolk Arch. cit.)

37. ELIZABETH, dau. by (2), d. 1509, dau. and coh., m. (2) Sir J. Fortescue who d. 28 Jul. 1500; m. (3) Sir Edw. Howard, K.G., Lord High Admiral, slain 25 Apr. 1513; m. (1) as second wife, Sir William Calthorpe, b. 1409, Sheriff of Norfolk 1442-58, 1464-76, d. 1494, ae. 85, leaving a will. He had m. (1) Elizabeth, d. 1437, dau. Reginald, Lord Gray of Ruthyn. (Norfolk Arch. IX fac. p. 1).

38. ANN CALTHORPE, will 1494; m. as (1) wife, Sir Robert Drury of Hanstead, M.P. Suffolk, Speaker of the House of Commons 1495, Privy Council 1526, etc., d. 2 Mar. 1535/6, bur. St. Mary's Church, Bury St. Edmunds; m. (2) Anne, dau. Edward Jerningham of Somerley, wid. Edward, Lord Gray, by whom no issue. (DNB; Norfolk Arch. cit.)

39. ANNE DRURY, m. (1) **SIR GEORGE WALDEGRAVE** (200-39), son of William of Smallbridge and m. (2) Sir Thomas Jermyn. (Muskett II 354).

Line 258

The Virginia Genealogist, vol. 11, no. 1 (1967), pages 15-19 shows that the royal and noble lineage previously accepted for Col. Richard Lee of Virginia is false. An article in the same publication, vol. 12, no. 1 (1968, pages 11-14, shows a pedigree for him that can, with the possible exception of the last two generations, be supported with adequate evidences. This correct descent is as below. References for all generations shown appear in cited article.

27. RICHARD, Earl of Cornwall, King of the Romans (24-27), 2nd son of **JOHN** (1-26), King of England and **ISABELLA** (117-27), b. 5 Jan. 1209, d. 2 Apr. 1272, had by Joan, dau. or w. of Sir Reginald de Vautort or Valletort at least one illeg. child.

28. RICHARD DE CORNWALL, d. 1272 at Berkhamstead Castle, bur. Hayles Abbey, m. one Joan, had

29. EDMUND DE CORNWALL of Kynlet, eldest son, d. 22 Mar. 1354, knt. of the shire for London 1324; m. 1313/4, Elizabeth, dau. Sir Brian de Brampton, bapt. 12 Dec. 1295, d. 1354.

30. BRYAN DE CORNWALL of Kynlet, b. ca. 1315 or later, sheriff of Shropshire 1378; m. **MAUD** (259-30), dau. Fulke, 1st Lord Strange of Blackmere, had,

31. ISABELLA DE CORNWALL, dau. and h.; m. as (2) wife, John Blount of Sodington, d. 1424.

32. SIR JOHN BLOUNT of Kynlet, dead 26 Oct. 1443, wid. surviving; m. Alice, dau. Kinard Delabere of co. Hereford, whose d.c. e. 28 Oct. 1445.

Line 258 (cont.)

33. HUMPHREY BLOUNT, sheriff of Shropshire 1460-74, writ. d.c.e. 12 Oct. 1477, proof of age and received father's estate 8 Feb. 1444; m. Elizabeth, dau. Robert Wynnington of Cheshire.

34. JOHN BLOUNT of Yeo, Salop, and Hereford, proof of age of his elder brother 1478; m. Elizabeth, dau. of John Yeo of Yeo.

35. KATHARINE BLOUNT, bur. Alveley 30 Aug. 1591; m. Humphrey Lee of Coton Hall, Nordley Regis, Shropshire, b. 1506, d. 6 Dec. 1588, Inq.p.m. 12 Mar. 1589.

36. JOHN LEE of Coton and Nordley Regis, b. 1530, bur. Chesham, Bucks, 13 Jun. 1605; m. settlement 24 Jun. 1553, m. Joyce, dau. of John Romney, bur. 4 Dec. 1609.

37. RICHARD LEE, b. 1563, bapt. Alveley, 6 Oct. 1563; m. at Alveley, 21 Oct. 1599, Elizabeth, dau. of John Bendy.

38. COL. RICHARD LEE, b. Nordley Regis, ca. 1613, went to Virginia in 1640, will dated 6 Feb. 1663/4, d. Dividing Creek, Va. Mar. 1664; m. Jamestown, Va., 1641, Anne Constable. Note: Evidences for the filiation of generations 36, 37 and 38 are not totally conclusive. Col. Lee was almost certainly of this family but perhaps of other parents.

Line 259

29. ELEANOR GIFFORD (29A-30), dead 1324/5; m. Fulk le Strange, b. ca. 1267, dead 23 Jan. 1324/5, 1st Lord Strange of Blackmere, Seneschal of Aquitaine. (See also 29A-30).

30. MAUD LE STRANGE m. **BRYAN DE CORNWALL** of Kynlet (258-30), b. ca. 1315+.

Line 260 Charles Evans doubts the existence of the persons in Gen. 32, no contemporary evidences; perhaps invented for dynastic reasons. Rest of line sound.

29. JOHN, King of England (1-26), b. 1167, d. 1216; m. 1200, **ISABELLA OF ANGOULÊME** (117-27). (DNB).

30. ELEANOR, b. 1215, d. 13 Apr. 1275; m. (1) 23 Apr. 1224, William Marshall, Earl of Pembroke, d.s.p. 15 Apr. 1231 (son of **WILLIAM MARSHALL**, Earl of Pembroke (66-27)); m. (2) 7 Jan. 1238/9, Simon de Montfort, Earl of Leicester, son of Simon IV de Montfort l'Aumary, b. Normandy ca. 1208, killed at Evesham 4 Aug. 1265. (DNB 38: 284; CP VII 520, 543-547).

31. ELEANOR DE MONTFORT, b. ca. Michaelmas 1252, d. 1282; m. 13 Oct. 1278, Llewellyn ap Griffith (son of Gruffydd ap Llewellyn, d. 1 Mar. 1244 by Senena, perh. of Man, son of **LLEWELLYN AP JORWERTH** (176-6), by his mistress Tangwystl verch Llywarch the Red of Rhos), d. 11 Dec. 1282. (J.E. Lloyd: Hist. of Wales 1954, II pp. 766, 686, 706-707, 716-764; Dict. Welsh Biog. 597-598, which incorrectly states that they had only one dau., Gwenllian, a nun. Dict. Welsh Biog. 317-318 for Gruffydd; Burke: Dormant and Extinct Peerage, p. 377, states "By Llewelyn ap Griffith who was slain 10 (sic) Dec., 8th Edward I, 1282, she had

Line 260 (cont.)

issue two daus., and coheirs, the younger of whom, the Princess Gwenllian, b. Jun. 1281, a nun of Sempringham, d. there 7 Jun. 11th Edward III, 1337. The elder dau., the Princess Catharine, heiress of the monarchs of North Wales, was mother by her husband Philip ap Ivor, Lord of Cardingan, of the Lady Eleanor Goch, who m. Thomas, representative of the sovereigns of South Wales ap Llewelyn ap Owen ap Meredith . . . "; J.E. Lloyd: Hist. of Wales, 768; John Edward Griffith: Pedigrees of Anglesey and Carnarvonshire Families (Leicester, 1914), p. 106).

* * *

32. CATHARINE, b. 1279/80; m. Philip ap Ivor. (Burke, cit.; Griffith, Anglesey, etc., cit.) (See note at start of this lineage.)

* * *

33. ELEANOR GOCH, heiress of Iscoed; m. **THOMAS AP LLEWELLYN** (254-33).

Line 261

30. WILLIAM DE FERRERS, Earl of Derby (127-30), b. ca. 1193, d. Evington, near Leicester 24 or 28 Mar 1254; bur. 31 Mar. 1254; m. (1) bef. 14 May 1219 Sibyl Marshall, d. bef. 1238, 3rd dau. and eventual coh. of Sir William Marshall, Earl of Pembroke, by **ISABEL DE CLARE** (66-27), dau. and sole h. of Richard de Clare, Earl of Pembroke. (NGSQ 59: 254-262; 60: 25-35; CP IV 196-198; Sanders, English Baronies, pp. 62-64, 148-149).

31. MAUD (or **MATILDA**) **DE FERRERS,** Vicomtesse de Rochechouart, b. ca. 1230, d. 12 Mar. 1298/9; m. (1) Simon de Kyme of Kyme, d. sh. bef. 30 July 1248, s.p.; m. (2) ca. 30 July 1248 William de Fortibus (also styled le Fort), d. sh. bef. 22 May 1259, lord of Chewton, Somerset, son of Hugh de Vivonia, Sheriff of Somerset and Dorset, by his wife, Mabel, dau. and coh. of **WILLIAM MALET** (234A-28), Magna Charta surety; m. (3) by 4 Feb. 1267, Sir Emery (or Aimery), Vicomte de Rochechouard in Poitou, living Apr. 1284. (CP IV 199, chart; Sanders: English Baronies, pp. 9, 38-39, 62-64); Knights of Edward I, II 80, IV 156; Cal. Inq.p.m. 1: 298; 3: 400-401; Cal. Pat. Rolls (Henry III, A.D. 1247-1258), p. 23; List of Ancient Correspondence of the Chancery and Exchequer, Lists & Indexes, no. XV, p. 355; NGSQ cit.)

32. JOAN DE VIVONIA, eldest dau. and coh., lady of Chewton, Somerset, through her father, heir (Inq.p.m. on her lands from Wm. Marshall) to a 1/8 interest in the barony of Curry Malet, Somerset, through her mother, inherited an interest in the barony of Long Crendon, co. Buckingham, b. 1251 (ae 8 in 1259), d. 1 Jun. 1314; m. (1) ca. 10 May 1262 Ingram de Percy, d.s.p. sh. bef. 10 Oct. 1262; m. (2) as (2) wife (his 1st named Alice) **SIR REGINALD** (or **REYNOLD) FITZ PIERS,** Knt., (262-30), lord of Blaen Llyfni, co. Brecknock,

Line 261 (cont.)

Sheriff of Hampshire and Constable of Winchester Castle, 1261, d. 4 or 5 May 1285, h. of elder bro. Herbert and son of Peter Fitz Herbert, lord of Blaen Llyfni, co. Brecknock, by his first wife, Alice Fitz Roger of Warkworth. (CP IV 199, chart; V 465, notes c and d; Cal. Inq.p.m., 2: 364-366; 5: 274-275; Sanders, pp. 89, 38-39, 63; Knights of Edward I, II: 52-53, 80; VCH Bedfordshire II 351-352; Sussex IV 158-159; CP V 465 notes c and d; NGSQ cit.)

33. **SIR PETER FITZ REGINALD (or FITZ REYNOLD)**, Knt., eldest surviving son of (2) to whom mother gave Chewton 1299, lord of Chewton, Somerset, conservator of array, Surrey and Sussex, 1321, b. ca. 1274 (ae. 40 in 1314), d. 18 Nov. 1322,; m. Ela Martell, ae. 7 in 1280, living 1306/7, dead by 1322, elder dau. and coh. of Sir Roger Martel, d. 1280, lord of Hinton Martel and Broadmayne, Dorset, Glen Magna, co. Leicester, and Merston, co. Sussex, by his wife, Joan. (Her sister Joan, then ae. 4, m. Reynold fitz Reynold, yr. bro. of Peter). (VCH Sussex IV 158-159; VCH Leicester, V: 77, 104; CP IV cit.; NGSQ cit.; Public record Office, L. & I. 17: 51; Sanders, English Baronies, pp. 38-39; Knights of Edward I, II: 56-57; III: 123; Cal. Inq.p.m., 2: 201; 5: 274-275; 6: 242-243, 459-460; Cal. Pat. Rolls (Edward II, A.D. 1313-1317), p. 403, (Edward II, A.D. 1317-1321), p. 459; E.A. Fry and G.S. Fry, ed., Dorset Records V 240 (being Dorset Feet of Fines from Richard I).

34. **ROGER FITZ PETER** (or Roger Martel), eldest son and h. app., b. say 1295, d.v.p. by 6 Dec. 1322, of Chewton, m. by 30 Nov. 1318 to an unknown wife who was prob. dau. of Sir Henry de Urtiaco (or otherwise del Ortiay or de Lorty), d. 1321, Lord Urtiaco of Curry Rivell, Somerset, by his wife Sibyl, also d. by 1322. (VCH Sussex IV 158-159; VCH Leicester V 104; NSGQ cit.; Sanders, English Baronies, pp. 38-39, 84; CP IV 199, chart; X 183-184).

35. **SIR HENRY FITZ ROGER**, Knt., eldest son and h., b. Curry Rivell, co. Somerset 30 Nov 1318, d. 29 Jan. or 18 Feb. 1352, bur. Chewton Mendip, co. Somerset, held manors of Chewton, Somerset, West Kington, co. Wilts, Sturminster Marshall, co. Dorset, Merston, Sussex (which he held jointly with his wife Elizabeth), Glen Magna, co. Leic., Selling, Kent, Hinton Martel and Broadmayne (Mayne Martell), co. Dorset; m. by 23 May 1340 Elizabeth de Holand, d. 13 July 1387, dau. of Sir Robert de Holand, first Lord Holand of Upholland, co. Lancaster, by his wife, **MAUD LA ZOUCHE** (32-30). (NGSQ cit.; CP VI 528-531; Sanders, English Baronies, pp. 38-39; Cal. Inq.p.m., 6: 242-243; 8: 154; 10: 10-11; 16:209-210; VCH Sussex, IV: 158-159; VCH Leicester V: 77, 104; Cal. Inq.p.m. 11: 272, 14: 73, in which the lady of the manor of Glen Magna, co. Leicester is specifically called Elizabeth de Holand, dau. of Robert de Holand).

36. **JOHN FITZ ROGER**, lord of Chewton, b. betw. 1345-1352, dead by 1372 (when his wid. was m. to (2) husb.), 3rd son, but in issue in 1382, h. to his older bros., 2nd of whom, Thomas, b. betw. 1345-52, was god-son of Thomas de Holand and Maud de Holand; m. as (1) of five husbs. by 26 Apr. 1369 Alice (a minor) parentage uncertain, d. 27 Mar. 1426. She m. (2) 1371/2 as (2) wife, Sir Edmund de Clyvedon, d. 16 Jan. 1375/6; m. (3) as (2) wife Sir Ralph Carminow,

d. aft. Jan. 1387; m. (4) as (2) wife Sir John Rodeney, d. 19 Dec. 1400; m. (5) as (2) wife Sir William Bonville of Shute (father-in-law of her dau.), d. 1408. She had surviving issue only by John Fitz Roger. (VCH Sussex cit.; VCH Leicester cit.; Devon & Cornwall N. & Q. XXIV 56-58; XXV 141; NGSQ cit.; Cal. Pat. Rolls, 14 (A.D. 1362-1370), p. 239; Cal. Inq.p.m. 15: 203, 16: 92-93, 209-210).

    37. ELIZABETH FITZ ROGER, dau. and sole h. in 1382 to Chewton, etc., b. 15 Aug 1370, d. 15 Apr 1414, held the manors of Chewton, co. Somerset, Glen Magna, co. Leicester, Merston, co. Sussex, 1/4 of Sturminster Marshall, co. Dorset, m. (1) by 18 Oct 1377, ae. 8 or 9, Sir John Bonvyle (or Bonville), b. ca. 1371 ("aged 11 and no more" in 1382), d. 21 Oct 1396 (see his Inq.p.m. 20 Rich II no. 11), son and h. app. of Sir William Bonville of Shute, Devon by his first wife, Margaret de Albemarle (or Damarell); m. (2) shortly after 1396 and by 2 Dec 1398 Richard Stucle (or Stukeley), gentleman, living 1425, Merston, Sussex, escheator of co. Somerset & Dorset, 1412-3. They made settlement (1410) of the manors of Great Glen, Leics., and Merston on themselves and heirs. Richard Stucle, of Trent, Somerset d. 1410-1414, his wife dying a widow. By John Bonville she was mother of William, 1st Lord Bonville, b. 30 Aug. 1393 at Shute, d. 18 Feb. 1460/1, and others. (CP II 218; VCH Sussex & VCH Leicester cit.; NGSQ cit.; Feudal Aids, III: 123; Cal. Close Rolls (Henry VI), I: 194, (Richard II), VI; 364, 368; Vivian, Visitations of the County of Devon, pp. 101, 721; Cal. Inq.p.m. 15: 203, 16: 92-93, 209-210); Inq.p.m. for John Bonville year:20 Richard II; List & Index Society, 72: List of Escheators for England and Wales).

    38. HUGH STUKELEY (or Stuckley), a younger son, b. aft. 1398, estate administered 13 Dec 1457, sheriff of Devon 1448-9, held manors of Affeton, East and West Wolrington, Bradford Tracy, Bridgerule, Meshaw and Thelbridge, co. Devon in right of his wife; m. by 1451 as her (1) husb. Katherine de Affeton, d. 26 Mar. 1467, dau. and sole h. of John de Affeton of Affeton, Devon, by his wife, Joan Bratton (or Bracton). She m. (2) 9 Jan 1458/9 Sir William Bourchier (or Bourghchier), b. bef. 12 Dec. 1469, bur. Church of the Austin Friars, London, 3rd Lord FitzWarin of Bampton, Devon, son of Sir William Bourchier, Count of Eu by his wife Anne, Countess of Buckingham, Hereford and Northampton, dau. of Thomas of Woodstock, Duke of Gloucester. (CP V 507-508 and notes e and f; Vivian: Visitations of Devon 721; Vivian, Visitations of the County of Devon, pp. 106, 721; Lists & Indexes no. IX: List of Sheriffs for England and Wales, p. 35; Devon & Cornwall N & Q XXVII: 120).

    39. NICHOLAS STUKELEY (or Stuckley), son and h., b. ca. 1451 (ae. 16 in 1467, d. 27 May 1488, held manors of Affeton, East and West Wolrington, Bradford Tracy, Huntshaw, and Meshaw, co. Devon, Trent and Chilton Cantelowe, co. Somerset, and Preston, Halfhyde, and St. Mary Blanford, co. Dorset, m. (1) Thomasine Cockworthy, d. 29 Nov 1477, widow of Robert Chudleigh, and dau. of John Cockworthy of Yarnscombe, Devon, Escheator od Devon, by his wife, Thomasin, dau. of Sir John Chichester of Raleigh, Devon; m. (2) ca. 1479, as her (2) husb. Anne, widow of Robert Budockshide and dau. of Henry Pomeray of Berry Pomeroy, Devon by his wife, Alice Raleigh. (CP cit., especially note f; Vivian, cit.; Cal. Inq.p.m. (Henry VII) 1: 172-173, 178-179, 181, 558-560; Thomasia Stukeley Inq.p.m. 17 Edward IV (Year: 1477/8), Chancery File 63 (49); Devon and Cornwall N. & Q., April 1959, pp. 60-61).

40. SIR THOMAS STUKELEY (or Stuckley), Knt., son and h., b. Affeton, parish of West Wolrington, co. Devon 24 June 1475 (ae. 4 at mother's Inq.p.m.), d. there 30 Jan 1541/2, held manors of Affeton, East and West Wolrington (both with advowsons), Mewshaw (with advowson), Bridgerule, Drayford, Huntshaw, Thelbridge (with advowson), Studlegh, Bradford Tracy, and Pyllaven, all in co. Devon, Sheriff of Devon 1520-1, m. Anne (misidentified by Colby as Elizabeth), dau. and h. of Sir Thomas Wood (or Wode), Chief Justice of the Common Pleas, of Childrey, Berkshire by his wife, Margaret (de la Mare) Lenham, dau. of Sir Thomas de la Mare, Sheriff of Berkshire, 1473-1490. (Vivian cit.; Cal. Inq.p.m. (Henry VII), 1: 558-560; Devon & Cornwall N. & Q. XXVII 52, 61, 120); Inq.p.m. for Thomas Stucley, Knt. Year: 34 Henry VIII).

41. MARGERY STUCKLEY m. Charles Farrington or Farringdon. (Vivian, cit. 340, 721).

42. ANN FARRINGDON m. Thomas Dowrish of Dowrish House, b. ca. 1532, d. 1590. (Vivian, cit. 290, 292, 339, 340; NEHGR 115: 248-253).

43. GRACE DOWRISH m. Robert Gye or Guy, d. prob. 1604-1608, ae. 5 yrs. at Inq.p.m. of his father John Gye 29-30 Hen. VIII. (NEHGR cit.)

44. MARY GYE, b. ca. 1580, living 1666; m. Islington, 28 Oct. 1600, Rev. John Maverick, bp 27 Oct. 1578 at Awliscombe, Devon, son of Rev. Peter and Dorothy (Tucke) Maverick, to Mass. on the Mary and John, May 1630, lived in Dorchester, Mass., d. Boston, 3 Feb. 1635/6, ae. 60. (NEHGR cit.; Weis: Colonial Clergy of New England p. 137).

Line 262

26. EMMA OF BLOIS, illegitimate dau. of **STEPHEN** (137-23), Count of Blois, a leader of the First Crusade, d. 1101 (and therefore sister to **STEPHEN** (164-25), King of England), m. Herbert of Winchester (also styled Herbert the Chamberlain) of unproven ancestry, d. in or sh. bef. 1130, Chamberlain and Treasurer under William II and Henry I, held lands in Hampshire in 1086, and afterwards held other lands in Bedford, Hampshire, Gloucester and Yorkshire. (Eng. Hist. Rev. XLV 273-81; N. & Q. CLXII (1932) 439-441, 453-455; Eyton: Antiqu. of Shrop. VII 146-147; NSGQ 59: 256-7; 60: 33-35; T.F. Tout, Chapters in the Administrative History of Medieval England, I: 76-77; W. Farrer, Yorkshire Charters, II: 27, 127).

27. HERBERT FITZ HERBERT, s. and h., adult by 1127, succeeded to his father's lands in 1130, dead by 1155, brother of St. William (Fitz Herbert), d. 1154, Archbishop of York; m. Sibyl (or

Adela or Lucia) Corbet, living 1157, dau. and coh. of Robert Corbet, mistress of Henry I, lady of Alcester, Warwick and of Pontesbury and Woodcote, Salop (by Henry I she was mother of **REGINALD FITZ ROY** (121-26), Earl of Cornwall). (Eng. Hist. Rev., cit.; A.E. Corbet: Family of Corbet I 34; Eyton, cit. 149; CP V 465 note d; NGSQ cit.)

28. **HERBERT FITZ HERBERT**, s. and eventual h., adult by 1165, d. sh. bef. June 1204, m. by 1196 **LUCY OF HEREFORD** (237-5), living 1219 or 1220, bur. Chapter House of Lanthony, near Gloucester, lady of Blaen Llyfni and Bwlch y Dinas, co. Brecknock, dau. and coh. of Miles of Gloucester, Earl of Hereford, by Sibyl de Neufmarché. (Eyton, cit.; CP, cit., VI 457 note c; NGSQ cit. Sanders, English Baronies, pp. 8-9).

29. **PIERS FITZ HERBERT** (237-6), s. and event. h., seen 1204, d. sh. bef. 6 June 1235, bur. at Reading, through mother, heir to a 1/3 interest in the barony of Miles of Gloucester, Earl of Hereford, m. (1) settlement dated 28 Nov. 1203, **ALICE DE WARKWORTH** (246D-28), dau. of Robert Fitz Roger, 2nd Baron of Warkworth (father of **JOHN FITZ ROBERT** (186-1)), m. (2) after 1204 and bef. 1225, Sibyl de Dinham (Dinan), widow of Hugh de Plugenay, and dau. and coh. of Josce de Dinham. Sibyl's maritagium was the manor of Stanton Fitz Warren (otherwise known as Stanton Fitz Herbert), co. Wiltshire which manor fell to her son, Reginald, and his later descendants; m. (3) in or bef. 1225, Isabel de Ferrieres, d. sh. bef. 29 Apr. 1252, widow of **ROGER DE MORTIMER** (132C-28), dau. of Walkelin de Ferrières, seigneur of Ferrières-Saint-Hilaire and lord of Oakham, co. Rutland. (Eyton, cit.; CP V 465 note d, 442 note c; Sanders: English Baronies 9; NGSQ cit.; The Notebook of Tristram Risdon, pp. 75-77; The Gen., n.s., 10: 29; Devonshire Association, 50: 433-434).

30. **SIR REGINALD** (or **REYNOLD**) **FITZ PETER**, son by (2), and eventual h., adult by 1248, d. 4 or 5 May 1286, succeeded to his brother Herbert Fitz Peter in 1248, lord of Blaen Llyfni, co. Brecknock, etc., Sheriff of Hampshire and Constable of Winchester Castle, 1261; m. (1) by Sep. 1249 Alice, seen 1263 and 1264; m. (2) by 1274 **JOAN DE VIVONIA** (161-32), b. 1251, d. 1 June 1314, widow of Ingram de Percy, dau. and h. of William de Fortibus (also styled le Fort) by his wife, Maud de Ferrers. Through her father, Joan inherited a 1/8th interest in the barony of Curry Malet, Somerset. (Eyton, cit.; CP cit.; Sanders, cit.; CP XI 324; NGSQ cit.; Cal. Inq.p.m. 2: 364-365, 5: 275; Knights of Edward I, II: 52-53, 80).

31. **ALICE**, dau. by (1) (Alice), living 1305; m. by 29 Jun. 1256, Sir John de St. John of Basing, son and h. of Sir Robert de St. John, 1286, Lord Lieut. of Aquitaine, Seneschal of Aquitaine 1293, d. 20-29 Sep. 1302. (CP XI 323-324).

32. **AGNES DE ST. JOHN**, d. 1345; m. **HUGH DE COURTENAY**, Earl of Devon (51-31). (CP XI 325 note e).

INDEX

All references are to the numbers of

The Ancestral Lines --- not to page numbers

Gallo-Romans 180, 190
Galloway 38, 53, 57, 94, 95, 114A, 121A, 121B, 121C, 224, 236, 252
Gant (see also Ghent and Gaunt) 143
Gardenis 42
Gascoigne 2, 3
Gates 211
Gatinais 118
Gaunt 143, 156
Gaunt, John of 1, 2, 207, 234
Gaveston 9, 16A
Geneva 133
Geneville 27, 39, 71, 120, 135
Gerard 9, 170
German Emperors and Kings, incl. Kings of the Saxons 45, 140, 141
   Conradins 192
   Conrad II 45, 157
   Frederick Barbarossa 45
   Henry I "the Fowler" 50, 53, 101, 141, 142, 147, 148, 157
   Henry III 45
   Henry IV 45
   Otto I 45, 147, 192, 241
   Otto II 147
   Otto "the Illustrious" 141
   Philip II 45
Gernon 246
Ghent (see Gant and Gaunt)
Gibbins 17
Gibbon 2
Gibson 17
Giffard (Gifford) 25, 29A, 42, 43, 52, 69, 122, 184, 234A, 246D, 259
Gill 210
Glane 133
Glanville 187, 257
Gleiberg 143
Glemham 15
Gloucester (see also Clare) 1A, 177
   Humphrey 1A
   Robert 63, 124, 125, 132A
   William 63, 124, 178A
Glover 232
Gobion 42
Godiva 176, 176A

Goldington 41
Goodrick 202
Gordon 252, 256
Gorges 59, 209, 210
Gospatric (see Dunbar)
Gournay 255A
Goushill 15, 20, 23, 57, 233
Graham 252
Grandison 27, 28, 85, 257
Grantmesnil 53
Greasley 170
Greene 14, 61, 210
Grelle 18, 94, 99, 255A
Grenville 57, 187, 209, 234
Greville 84
Grey 1A, 13, 30, 38, 50, 55, 88, 99, 143, 187, 188, 197, 207, 212, 214, 219, 223, 257
Greystoke 13, 41, 62, 88, 202, 226
Griffin 99
Griffith 176, 177, 199, 199A, 202
Grimston 121D
Grisgonelle 118
Grosvenor 31, 32A, 233
Guelders 98A, 100, 163, 252
Guincamp 214
Guise 197, 207
Gunne 98
Gunton 15
Gurdon 3, 4
Gurney 255
Gye 261
Gyse (see Guise)

Hainaut (Hainault) 98A, 101, 102, 103, 106, 140, 143, 144A, 151, 155, 160, 163, 163A, 168, 240
   Isabella 163
   Philippa 1, 4, 5, 103
   William 1, 103, 168
Hales (Halys) 16, 155
Hamilton 256
Hamley 246E
Hammerton 2
Harby 201, 210
Harcourt 4, 30, 38, 50, 56, 79, 84, 93, 219
Harford 230
Harington 34, 35, 36, 40, 46,

57, 170, 247
Harlakenden 229
Harley 29A
Harlyngrugge 246A
Harpersfield 17
Harris 199, 246E
Hart 220
Hasbaye 140
Haselden 85
Hastings 55, 56, 93, 99, 123, 139, 207, 225
Hatch 234, 234A
Haugh 31
Havering 170
Haviland 197
Heckstall 11
Heigham 246A
Helion 52
Herbert (see also Fitz Herbert) 37
Hereford (see also Gloucester and Bohun) 177, 193, 194, 235, 237
Heristal 190
Hertford (see Clare)
Heron 223, 224
Heronville 17
Herring 17
Hext 246E
Higham 200
Hildegard 182
Hingeston 51
Hobrugg 187
Hohenstauffen Emperors 45, 166
Holand (see also Holland and Kent) 1, 18, 32, 34, 46, 47, 77, 78, 85, 100, 101, 103, 168, 207, 215, 225, 236, 252
Holford 33
Holland (see Holand)
Hoo 11, 18, 79
Hopton 56B
Horne 98
Horsey 253
Horton 234A
Howard 4, 16, 22, 120, 200, 248, 257
Howell 202
Hubbard 31
Huddleston 37
Hugelville 177

Humez 143
Humphrey 225, 228
Hungary, Kings of 103, 166, 242, 243, 244
    Andrew I 244
    Andrew II 103, 105, 163A
    Bela I 166, 243, 244A
    Bela III 103, 104, 242
    Bela IV 103
    Geza II 103, 242
    Ladislas I 243, 244, 244A
    Stephen V 103
Hungerford 18, 51
Hunter 98
Huntingdon (Huntington) 38, 89, 93, 94, 96, 97, 100, 119, 131, 148, 170, 193, 252
Huntingfield 187, 188, 238
Huntley 252, 256
Hutchinson (Hutchison) 14
Hyde 230
Hydon 214

Ingoldsby 203
Irby 31, 85, 203
Ireland, Kings of 170, 175, 239
    Brian Boru 175, 239
    Dermot Macmurrough 66, 175
    Eva 66, 175
Inge 212
Irvine 256
Isaac 249
Italy, Kings of
    Berengarius (or Berengar) II 145, 146
    Berenger I 146
    Bernard 50
    Lothair I 140, 145, 147, 240
    Pepin 50
Ivrea 146, 147

James 203
Jermyn 257
Jerningham 257
Jerusalem, Crusader Kings of
    Aumary I 114, 118
    Baldwin I 158
    Baldwin II 103, 103A, 118
    Baldwin III 118
    Fulk 103A, 118
    Godfrey (Advocate of the